八木保の直観力

建築家　安藤 忠雄

一九六〇年代は、日本の青春であった。アメリカから流入した新しい文化が花開きはじめていた。私がジャクソン・ポロックなどの現代美術に出会ったのも、ジャズに出会ったのもこの頃だった。宣伝美術という概念を超えて、グラフィックデザインという領域が確立されたのもこの頃だった。

八木保と大阪で初めて会ったのは一九六六〜七年頃。彼はまだ十代の終わりだった。はにかんだような笑顔が印象的だった。それ以来、付き合いは半世紀に及ぶ。

彼は自身の鋭い感性だけをたよりにモノを見極めてきた。

先天的に身に備えた直観力は、人並みはずれている。

一九八三年、香港のエスプリの新しいショップのデザインに倉俣史朗とともに関わった後、当時エスプリの経営者だったダグラス・トンプキンスに才能を認められ、アメリカへ渡った。アメリカのすぐれた開拓者のような、ダグにはとくにかわいがられたが、石岡瑛子、三宅一生、倉俣史朗など多くのアーティストとの交流からまた彼の感性は磨かれていったといってよい。

そしてビジネス社会の人々にも新しい感覚で新しい価値観を吹き込んだ。

彼が育った神戸、須磨の海に無意識に導かれるように、青い海が近いサンフランシスコ、ロサンゼルスとその生活の拠点は移り変わったが、おおらかで明るい性格は常に変わらず、今も不思議なほどに出会った頃の少年の笑顔を失っていない。心の底から他者に優しい八木保。

これからも何人もの人との出会いを重ねながら、いい仕事をしていくだろう。

The Instinctive Vision of Tamotsu Yagi

Japan was in its adolescence in the 1960s and American culture was blossoming. During this dynamic era, Japanese people began looking abroad for new and unique expressions in the arts.

This was when I first discovered contemporary artists like Jackson Pollock, and I listened to jazz. Art forms were evolving, and graphic design moved beyond commercial art to establish its foundation as a solid discipline.

It was around this time, in 1966 or 1967, when I first met Tamotsu Yagi. He was in his late teens and his shy smile somehow left a strong impression on me. I've now shared a special friendship with Yagi for almost 50 years, as our stature in respective industries has grown.

Yagi has always relied on his keen instincts when making decisions. He possesses phenomenal intuition.

In 1983, Yagi worked with Shiro Kuramata to design Esprit's flagship store in Hong Kong. Doug Tompkins, the founder of Esprit, recognized his talent during this project and moved him to the U.S. Doug was an astute American pioneer. He adored Yagi, and was certainly an influence on his career. However, I believe Yagi's design sense was honed through significant mentors like the artists Eiko Ishioka, Issey Miyake and Shiro Kuramata.

As the design world changed dramatically in Japan and internationally, Yagi was a sounding force in introducing and cultivating new business values. He challenged perceptions and created better practices by applying his own cultural principles and innate sensitivity.

It's evident to me that Yagi needs to live near the ocean. He grew up in Kobe by the sea of Suma, and later moved to San Francisco and Los Angeles near the Pacific. Through these transitions, his big-hearted and free-spirited personality has never changed. His smiles are just as I remember when I first met him as a young boy.

Tamotsu Yagi is truly kind to others. He'll continue to travel to cultivate his eye, make new acquaintances and produce great work.

Architect Tadao Ando

THE GRAPHIC EYE of TAMOTSU YAGI

八木保の選択眼

ADP

THE GRAPHIC EYE OF TAMOTSU YAGI

Author: Tamotsu Yagi

Art Direction: Tamotsu Yagi

Graphic Design: *Tamotsu Yagi Design*:
Shinsuke Ito
Yosei Shibata
Ritsuko Yagi

Contributing Graphic Design:
Masaki Morisaki

Contributing Editor:
Yasuko Seki, *TRI+*

Coordination:
Kazuya Enomoto, *Commercial Arts Institute*
Akira Yagi, *Nineteen Fiftysix*
Koji Yagi, *INDES, Inc.*
Takumi Yagi, *Tamotsu Yagi Design*

Photography:
Stefano Massei, *Studio Massei*
Shuji Yoshida, *Gimmicks Production*

Editor (Japanese):
Yasuko Seki, *TRI+*

Translation:
Natalie P. Klug, *Tamotsu Yagi Design*
Kelly Lasser, *Shelter Design*
Noriko Morisaki, *Volcano Design*
Yosei Shibata, *Tamotsu Yagi Design*
Neil Trama, *Blunt Force Trama*
Ritsuko Yagi, *Tamotsu Yagi Design*
Takumi Yagi, *Tamotsu Yagi Design*
Kulapat Yantrasast, *wHY Architecture*

Printing Direction and Coordination:
Kazuya Enomoto, *Commercial Arts Institute*

Digital Retouching:
Kazuya Enomoto, *Commercial Arts Institute*

Date of Publication: First Printing November 15, 2011

Publisher: Keiko Kubota, *ADP*

Publishing House: *ADP Company (Art Design Publishing Company)*
2-14-12 Matsugaoka, Nakano-ku, Tokyo 165-0024, Japan
Phone: 81-3-5942-6011 / Fax: 81-3-5942-6015
http://www.ad-publish.com
Printing and Binding: *Toppan Printing Co.,LTD.*

© *Tamotsu Yagi Design*
Printed in Japan
ISBN978-4-903348-22-3 C0072   All rights reserved. No part of this book may be reproduced without permission.

THE GRAPHIC EYE *of* TAMOTSU YAGI

ADP

About Tamotsu Yagi
八木 保 とは

ロサンゼルスを拠点として、世界を舞台に活躍する日本人デザイナー、八木保がアメリカに移って27年。アパレルメーカー、エスプリのアートディレクターを経て、独立後もサンフランシスコに留まり、アップル、インテル、パームなどアメリカのIT企業、イタリアのベネトン、日本のワールドなどアパレル企業のブランディング、建築のサイン計画、家具や日用品のデザインを手がける。近年、海外で活躍する日本人デザイナーは多いが、八木はその先駆けであり、現地にしっかり根を下ろしている点で稀有な存在だ。本書は、27年間の仕事の軌跡をたどりながら、彼のデザインの流儀や発想の原点を探るものだ。

日本からアメリカへ――1984年、八木は活動拠点を、東京の浜野商品研究所からサンフランシスコのアパレルメーカー、エスプリに移す。浜野商品研究所、通称、浜研は、1970〜80年代にかけて、六本木のAXISビルをはじめとした文化的商業施設の総合プロデュースを担当し、八木はアートディレクターだった。そんなある日、人生を一変する運命的な出会いを果たす。アジアに店舗展開するにあたり、日本人クリエイターのリサーチのために来日していたエスプリのオーナー、ダグラス・トンプキンス（以下ダグ）だ。彼はAXISビルに感動して浜研と倉俣史朗をパートナーに選び、翌年エスプリ香港店をオープンさせると、そのグラフィックを手がけた八木の才能も高く評価する。しばらくして、「エスプリで仕事をしないか」というオファーが八木の元に届いたのだった。

「『今のような状態で仕事をしていると、君は腐ってしまうよ』とも言われて、すごくショックだった。その頃の私は、やりがいのある仕事に恵まれて朝から夜中まで働きづめだったけれど、生活を犠牲にしているという気持ちはなかった。でも、ダグには異常に映ったのでしょうね」。

八木は迷ったが、1カ月間という期限でサンフランシスコに旅立った。そんな彼を待っていたのは、エスプリのコーポレイトイメージに関わるすべてのデザイン開発だった。ダグはエスプリを世界ブランドに育てるために、ヨーロッパの『ELLE』で活躍していたフォトグラファーのオリビエロ・トスカーニとロベルト・カーラ、グラフィックデザイナーの八木 保という最強のクリエイティブチームをつくり上げた。トスカーニは後に、ベネトンで人種やジェンダーを問う衝撃的な作品を発表し、世界的にセンセーションを巻き起こす。

「仕事は、トスカーニが自由に撮影し、ロベルトが物撮りを担当、それを私がレイアウトした。当時2,000人の社員のなかでたった一人の日本人だった私は、話もできず、単位もインチですごく戸惑いました。その上、私だけでなくトスカーニもロベルトも片言の英語しか話せず、デザイン室はイタリア語、英語が飛び交っていたのだから」。

当時のエスプリは、コミュニケーションデザインに力を注いでいた。同じ頃、日本もC.I.ブームで、社名やロゴマークを一新する企業が相次いでいた。

「C.I.とはコーポレイトアイデンティティを指しますが、ダグはコーポレイトイメージだと言っていました。そして、ダグの『マニュアル化した時点でシステムは古くなる』という方針を受けて、デザインもマニュアル化せずに一つずつ開発しました。柔軟であり新鮮であり続けることが、会社を引っ張っていく原動力です」。

1980年代は、アップルのマッキントッシュをはじめパソコンが普及しはじめた時期で、インターネットの登場まではさらに

10年を待たなければならなかった。そんな時代、200万部単位で発行されるカタログがエスプリのビジネスを担い、コーポレイトイメージの核であり、その制作がデザイン室に託されていた。

デザインは生活から生まれる──エスプリの仕事環境は日本とは比較できないほど恵まれていた。広々とした明るい空間、オーナーの全面的な信頼を得ていたので煩わしい会議もほとんどない。カタログ制作では、デザイン室が判型やページ数、用紙、内容まで決定でき、すべてがイメージ優先で進められた。八木が何より驚いたのはプロジェクトが早めに立ち上げられ、じっくりと取り組めたこと。さらに、エスプリ専属とはいえ、時間があれば競合他社以外の仕事をすることも許されていた。実際、八木は倉俣史朗とともに日本のスポーツメーカーのブランディングを手がけている。このような環境の下で、八木のデザイン観は大きく変化した。それは、「デザインは仕事ではなく、生活である」ということ。

「日本のデザインはビジネスオリエンティッド。売れるデザイン、勝てるデザインが求められます。私も日本ではプロジェクトに追われながら、雑誌や洋書をめくってアイデアをひねり出していました。ところがアメリカでは、ミュージアムやギャラリーをのぞいたり、散歩や食事を楽しめて、オーガニックショップやフリーマーケットもたくさんある。日常生活のすべてがデザインソースです」。

とはいえ90年代に入るとエスプリは大きな局面を迎える。最大の変化はオーナーのダグラス・トンプキンス自身で、彼の興味が企業経営から環境保護へと変わっていた。ダグは元から環境に敏感で、社員食堂の食材はオーガニック、カタログには再生紙や植物性インクを使用していた。しかし彼は経営と環境保護の両立は難しいと判断。会社を売った資金で環境保護団体を設立した。同じ頃、八木も独立を考えていた。帰国という選択もあったが、もはや日本の仕事環境には戻れないと判断してアメリカに留まった。最初の仕事は、ニューヨークのキャラウェイ社が出版する世界的フォトグラファー、アーヴィング・ペンの作品集『PASSAGE』の日本語版。その後はダグをはじめ、彼の友人スティーブ・ジョブズ、同僚だったオリビエロ・トスカーニからも仕事が舞い込んでくるようになった。

No Detail is Small＝ディテールへのこだわり──「No Detail is Small」とは、日本語では「小さいことも見逃さない──目配り、気配り、心配り」という意味で理解できる。元はスローガンとしてエスプリのデザイン室に掲げられていたもので、発案者はダグ、日本の会社の社長室にあった社訓に感動して自社でも実行したらしい。独立を果たした八木にとって、この言葉はそれまで以上に意味をもつようになる。

「No Detail is Smallとは、たとえば、紙幣を折り目がつかないようにフワッと折ってぽち袋に納める、食卓を整えるとき箸先3cmを濡らして箸置きに置く……そんな日本的な気配りにこそデザインの本質があるということ。気付かせてくれたのはダグでした。不思議なことに、スティーブ・ジョブズをはじめ、西海岸の企業トップのなかには日本贔屓が多い」。そんな八木にとって、デザインには「美しさ」「機能」、そして「社会的な視点」が欠かせないという。世の中が環境や反原発を考えているのに、それに反するような仕事は一人の人間としてしたくない。とくにアメリカで仕事を続けるには、思想と行動の一貫性が重要で、八木は環境や人権問題に取り組む団体のグラフィックワークを無償で引き受けている。八木の信条である「No Detail is Small」は、「デザインは頭で考えるのではなく、生活で感じとる」という日常の些細な行為も見逃さない態度、さらに「デザインは仕事ではなく、生活である」という精神につながっている。

「季節や街のうつろいを肌で感じたいから、いろいろな道を歩きます。すると、芽吹き、花が咲いた、紅葉したな、落ち葉だ…と、小さな発見があるのです。ときに、その道端の草花や枝葉を部屋にいけたり、気に入った小石を拾った。このような素材が新しいデザインの発想につながるのです」。

八木にとっては、生活の充実こそが豊かなデザインを生む種となるのだ。

「箱」へのこだわり──「箱」は八木のデザインにとって欠かせない要素だ。旅先で出会った小物、紙や印刷物の切れ端など、自分をインスパイアしてくれるものを箱に納めて保存している。「仕事を受けると、箱に詰まった素材やアイデアをピックアップしながらイメージを固めます。デザインソースは、箱の中にある、というわけです」と語る八木にとって、「箱」はプレゼンテーションの大切な手法でもある。ヨーロッパ、アジア、アフリカの香りをモティーフとしたベネトンの香水「トリヴ」（P50）のボトルとパッケージデザインの依頼を受けたとき、八木は透明アクリルの箱の中に各地域を象徴する植物や素材をコラージュしてプレゼンした。箱に詰められた素材たちは、ボトルのイメージのみならず、人々の姿や文化までを想起させ、トリヴの世界観を創造することに成功した。

「プレゼンは最初の20分が勝負。クライアントは、もはやパソコンを駆使したプレゼンやアウトプットには飽きてしまっている。その点、『箱』には、デジタルでは表現できない温もりや世界観を封じ込めることができる。知性ではなく、直観に訴えるというのかな……」。

最近は、オブジェとして飾りたいので「箱」でプレゼンしてほしいという依頼もあるようだ。たしかに、パソコン登場前のプレゼンにはデザイナーの試行錯誤の痕跡が現れていた。原稿や図面、スケッチには個性や思考のプロセスがにじみ出ていて、デザインを決定する手がかりにもなっていた。大きな「箱」という意味では、仕事場の空間にもこだわっている。建物が古くても、夏は暑く冬が寒くても構わない、日差しがあって空気が流れ、広々とした解放感がある場所。2年前に移ってきたロサンゼルスのアボット・キニー通りのスタジオは、洗濯工場だったというガラーンとした建物だ。八木は、そこにお気に入りのジャン・プルーヴェの家具や世界中で集めたコレクションを配置して、居心地の良い場所につくり替えた。

「私は、デザインの基本は整理整頓だと考えています。季節に合わせて家具やアートを並べ替えて、新鮮な気持ちで仕事ができるように心がけています」。

デザインへのこだわり── 世界中のプロジェクトを手がける八木にとって日本語だけでなくアルファベットを使いこなすことは重要で、最近ようやく自然に扱えるようになったと感じている。レタリングを徹底して仕込まれた世代なので、書体や字詰めに対するこだわりも強い。ボドニーなどセリフ系の書体がお気に入りだそうだが、主張の強い文字よりも環境との調和を優先するからだろう。

「イタリアのパロマでボドニー書体だけの博物館に行ったことがあります。セリフ系の書体の起源は、古代ギリシア・ローマ時代の石板に刻まれた文字。均整のとれた美しさに加えて、線に強弱があって人間的な温もりがあるところが好きです。けれども"S"や"R"は気に入らないので手を加えて使います」。

デジタル時代の現在、書体にも変化が起きている。写植時代、八木は字間を詰め気味で調整できる軽くて読みやすいボドニーや明朝などの書体を使っていた。ところがデジタル時代の今、字間があって空間感のある、たとえばアクシスフォントを使うことが多くなった。

「私たちの頃にはレタリングという授業があって、書体の特徴を身体的に教え込まれたので、行間、字間、歯送りなど、文字にはすごく敏感だった。今は昔と比べて、文字に対して感覚が鈍ってきたのかなあと思います」。

八木のこだわりは用紙などのさまざまな素材にも及ぶ。デザインは最終的には素材に還元される。時代性を映し出すのも素材だからだ。今は環境や資源問題を無視できないから、リサイクルされた素材、リサイクルできる素材を使わないわけにはいかないのだ。八木は20年以上前、エスプリ時代から再生紙やソイビーンのインクを使ってきた。当初は紙質も悪く、印刷を均質に仕上げるためには手間とコストがかかったそうだ。

「そんなとき、『重要なのは同じイメージに見えること。印刷に多少のばらつきがあっても構わない。無駄は省こう』というダグの言葉で気持ちを切り替えることができた」。

これは、先述の「C.I.とはコーポレイトイメージだ」というダグの姿勢を如実に表した言葉といえるだろう。
「私は素材を加工したり、無駄に使うことはしたくないので、魅力的な素材を見つける手間は惜しまない。料理もそうでしょう？ 新鮮な食材があれば手を加えなくてもおいしい。デザインも同じだと思う」。

アメリカを離れられない理由——八木は年に何度か帰国し、日本のいいものを探訪する。話をしていると、私たちよりも、日本の伝統や美への想いの深さに感心してしまう。そんな日本に惹かれながら、なぜアメリカに留まり続けるのだろうか？
「デザインに対する考え方や仕事の進め方かな。欧米では、デザイナーにとってのベストワンの提案を求められる。ディシジョンが明確で決断も速い。ディレクターやマネジャーが予算も決定権も握っているからでしょうね。一方、日本では2、3案求められ、決定はその場の空気が大きく影響するし、ゆっくりしている。中国圏は、際限なくアイデアを求められる」。
そんななかで、もっとも印象的なプロジェクトの一つがアップルストアのコンセプトづくり(P124)だ。スティーブ・ジョブズが直接指揮をとり、依頼を受けて2カ月でまとめ上げるというすさまじいスケジュールだった。ジョブズは、八木がエスプリ時代にまとめた『コンプリヘンシブ・ブック』をデザインマネジメントに欠かせない本として高く評価しており、社運を賭けたこの仕事を託したのだった。最短で最大の効果を上げるために、コンセプトづくりには原寸模型という方法がとられた。ジョブズが現場に来るたびに、原寸模型によってアップルストアの骨格はつくられていった。
「アップルストアは当初から多店舗展開が予定されていたので、不都合が起きたら改善して完成度を高めるという考え方だった。まさに走りながら考えるという感じ。原寸模型という方法は、スティーブが直感で判断するために採用されたもの。彼は、予算や常識では妥協しないし、デザインへの判断力もすごかったが、何より全体の考え方がすばらしく、トレンドになびかない一貫性を強く感じた。彼にとっては、製品もショップも含めて、アップルのイメージやバリューの一貫性こそが重要なのです」。
パームの仕事も印象深い(P158)。携帯電話のパッケージはiPhoneが一つの原型をつくり上げてしまった。後はどうやってもiPhone風に見えてしまう。そこで八木は、パッケージの一面を折って傾斜をつけて、そこにバーコードを印刷することにした。
「このアイデアは、デザインディレクターのピーター・スキルマンの『日本の折り紙の要素を入れてほしい』という一言から思いついたのです。折ることで一手間分のコストがかかるけれど、サイズを極限まで小さくしてクリアしました」。
プレゼンでは、八木がスキルマンの目の前で折り紙を実演し、「師匠！」と感嘆されたそうだ。デザインは即決された。

八木 保の選択眼——八木がアメリカに留まる理由は、人々が自分にとって大切なモノやコトがわかっていて、それを実現するために優先順位をはっきりさせて、必要なことには時間と労力を惜しまない、そんな生活への姿勢に惹かれるからだ。とくに西海岸は、豊かな自然によって人々の気質や文化が育まれ、生活との調和が実感できるのだそうだ。
八木 保のデザインは、「No Detail is Small」という日本的感性と西海岸の恵まれた生活環境の化学反応からもたらされたもの。そして、八木のクリエイションの真骨頂は、その洗練され磨き抜かれた「視覚的な選択眼」にある。

エディター 関 康子

About Tamotsu Yagi

27 years have passed since the multi-talented designer Tamotsu Yagi left Japan and moved to the United States. He first established himself as the art director for the apparel company Esprit, and later set up his own design studio in San Francisco. He has worked on design projects covering a wide array of business categories, from technology companies such as Apple Computer, Intel Corporation and Palm, to branding designs for apparel groups like Benetton of Italy and World of Japan. Yagi has also worked on architectural signage systems, as well as furniture and product designs. While more Japanese designers are venturing outside of Japan today, he was certainly a forerunner of this trend. Now based in Los Angeles, Yagi continues his design work today. He is one of the few Japanese designers who have successfully established their business in the U.S. This book follows Yagi's design career from the time he left Japan, and explores the origins of his ideas and design styles.

From Japan to America—Yagi started his design career as an art director for the Hamano Institute in Tokyo, where he worked from the 1970s into the 1980s. The Hamano Institute was a unique think-tank specializing in concept creation and the design of cultural and commercial facilities. One of Hamano's best-known projects was the AXIS Building in the Roppongi district of Tokyo, which was completed in the early 1980s. This unique design center caught the attention of Douglas R. Tompkins, who was then the owner of Esprit. Tompkins was visiting Japan in search of creative talent who could help with the expansion of the Esprit brand into Asia. Tompkins appointed the Hamano Institute and the prominent Japanese designer Shiro Kuramata as his creative partners in Asia. During this time, Tompkins also noticed another talent—Tamotsu Yagi, who handled all the graphic design work for the flagship store. Tompkins soon offered Yagi a chance to work at Esprit's headquarters in San Francisco. In 1984, Yagi left Japan hoping to build up his experience on a supposedly short-term assignment. Instead, Yagi found a great opportunity to develop a comprehensive design system for Esprit's corporate communications. In order to establish Esprit as a leading worldwide brand, Tompkins handpicked members of his creative team from around the world. Other members of this team included Oliviero Toscani, the fashion photographer of ELLE and Vogue magazine fame, along with Roberto Carra, another well known Italian photographer. Needless to say, the Esprit headquarters quickly became very cosmopolitan. Toscani, Carra and Yagi all communicated with each other in broken English. Toscani was in charge of fashion photography, while Carra handled all still lifes. Yagi was responsible for integrating their images into superb designs. At that time, Esprit's corporate focus was to develop a strong foundation for its design identity. Corporate Identity and the concept of "CI" was gaining wide attention internationally, and numerous corporations were heavily investing in creation of refreshed corporate names and logos. However, Tompkins believed "CI" should stand for "Corporate Image," not "Corporate Identity." Rather than establishing conforming protocols, Tompkins directed his creative team to stay flexible so they could constantly remain current. Esprit's main form of communication was its product catalogues, which acted as the company's core vehicle for both the corporate image and building business.

"No Detail is Small"–This principle was posted on the wall of Esprit's design studio. Tompkins adopted the idea of posting a message in every department at Esprit after visiting a company in Japan. He placed a large sign that read "No Detail is Small" in Yagi's department for each employee to reflect upon and emulate. The phrase became close to Yagi's heart, and later his life and design philosophy. This phrase was based on the notion of "attention to details," a prevalent philosophy in Japanese culture. Tompkins reminded Yagi of this Japanese way, and its relationship to design. Interestingly enough, Yagi later noticed that many of the business leaders he worked with on the West Coast were deeply inspired by this Japanese concept, including Steve Jobs of Apple Computers. "No Detail is Small" continues to be reflected in Yagi's everyday life. He believes that this design principle not only applies to his work, but is a daily practice. He enjoys taking different routes to appreciate how the city takes on various colors and character by each season. He collects items that catch his eye, such as rocks and branches, or any kind of found object, and stores them in his "box." These items which he calls his "lovable junk," later help him in his design process. Yagi finds the origin of good design in his daily mission of living a fulfilling life.

Yagi and his "box"–The "box" that both symbolizes Yagi's method for storing design inspiration and his presentation format, is essential to Yagi's creative process. When and wherever he encounters something intriguing, such as memento from his travels or interesting piece of newsprint, Yagi stores them in his box. The first thing he does when starting a new design project is refer to his box of resources for inspiration. Yagi often uses the box format both literally and symbolically as a method for presenting his designs. The box concept was used successfully when presenting his initial bottle design for the Benetton fragrance "Tribù." This product's concept was to capture fragrances of Europe, Asia and Africa. Yagi used a clear acrylic box to create a collage of materials and plants representing those regions. The unique display effectively created the bottle design image, and succeeded in establishing the product's philosophy by evoking the people and cultures from those regions.

Yagi's design philosophy–Yagi has been an advocate for using recycled paper and soy-based inks since his days at Esprit. During that period, recycled paper was of poor quality as it was fairly new and the techniques to produce it were still undeveloped. Yagi discovered the inconsistencies of printing the same colors on various recycled papers. To reflect Tompkin's belief in maintaining the overall corporate image, Yagi integrated these inconsistencies into his design concepts. Tompkins supported this decision, understanding that some details are less significant than the bigger picture. The financial and extra effort required to enforce reproduction consistency was not the primary concern. Yagi continues to be a strong believer in finding the right materials for each project. He doesn't consider applying an unnecessary process or creating waste. Therefore, he intentionally takes the time to look for the perfect material for each project. He believes the same applies to cooking–There's no need for embellishment if he starts with good, fresh ingredients. Yagi ultimately creates designs that reflect his core values of beauty, function and social responsibility. He feels that the key to conducting business in the U.S. is that his ideology must be consistent with his actions, and regularly offers pro bono contributions to environmental organizations.

Editor Yasuko Seki

CONTENTS

156–176 PALM
手のひら
Design in the palm of the hand

128–147 APPLE
原寸模型
A full scale look at refining the first Apple retail concept

108–123 HIROSHIMA
水の都 ひろしま
Designing the Hiroshima Naka City Incineration Plant

85–100 ROHTO: EPISTEME
触感美
The science of beauty within simplicity

69–84 KENZO ESTATE
藍 紫
Making of a winery and its comprehensive graphic identity

45–63 CONCEPT BOX
箱
Seven projects focusing on 3-D concept presentation boxes

27–44 MATERIALS
素材
Nine projects focusing on the use of materials

16–26 SF to LA
From San Francisco to Los Angeles

12–15 序文
Foreword by Douglas R. Tompkins
ダグラス・トンプキンス

4–9 八木保とは
About Tamotsu Yagi by Yasuko Seki
関 康子

まえがき
Preface by Tadao Ando
安藤 忠雄

目次
Contents

148–155 NICO®
Nigo® / Creative Director

124–127 片山 正通
Masamichi Katayama / Wonderwall Inc.

101–107 緒方 俊郎
Toshiro Ogata / Kyoto Cuisine by Owner Ogata

64–68 矢崎 和彦
Kazuhiko Yazaki / Felissimo

対談
Conversations

ダグについて
Introduction on Douglas R. Tompkins by Tamotsu Yagi
八木 保

エスプリ時代の上司であり親友でもあるダグは、だれよりも先見の明があると思います。彼がどんなチャレンジにも成功している理由は、そのためなのでしょう。2010年にダグが国連主催の生物多様性に関する会議にスピーカーとして招かれて来日した際に、私はダグ夫妻を案内して10日間国内を旅行しました。20年ぶりに訪ねた日本の変わりように、ダグは驚愕していました。とある晩、宿泊先のホテルのロビーで安藤忠雄さんと偶然の再会を果たすこともでき、ダグにとっては特別な日本滞在となりました。お互い忙しい生活を送っている私たちですが、常に連絡を欠かさないようにしています。2011年夏にダグから受け取ったメールで、私たちの新しいコラボレーションがはじまりました。自然環境への意識を高めるための本の制作です。「最高の本にしたい。これで政府を説得することができれば、新しい国立公園の設立につながるかもしれないんだ」。私はダグと出会ったことを幸運に思います。デザインにおいても人生においても、彼からはたくさんのことを学びました。彼はよく言います。「人生はエンターテインメント。生き残ることはゲームだ」。この本の制作を機に、ダグとのさまざまなコラボレーションへと発展することを楽しみにしています。

As my former boss of Esprit and long time friend, I always thought Doug was three steps ahead of everything. That's probably why he's been able to successfully and fearlessly accomplish any endeavor he ventures into. In 2010, Doug was appointed speaker of the United Nations Program on Bio-Diversity which took place in Japan. He asked me to join him so I could guide him and his wife Kris through Japan after his conference. He was amazed by how much Japan had changed since his last visit with me 20 years ago. Although Doug and I have busy lives we make it a point to stay in touch and correspond quite frequently. In 2011, I received an email from Doug requesting a collaboration on another environmental awareness book. Doug wanted this book to be extraordinary. I remember him saying, "This ones needs to be our best work yet as it will represent my portfolio of environmental work to persuade government figures to develop another national park." I am thankful that our paths have intertwined as it has led to many lessons in life and design. Doug often said "life is entertainment, survival is a game." With this I look forward to many more adventures and collaborative efforts with Doug in the future.

Patagonia Fall 1986 Catalog Cover: Douglas R. Tompkins, 78° South, 84° West, Antarctica.
Cover Photo by Yvon Chouinard

177–192 T.Y. COLLECTION

202–245 TIMELINE

タイムライン
コレクション
A timeline of projects from 1984 to 2011

著者紹介│英文
About the Author in English — 246

インデックス
Index — 248–251

メイキング
Making of the Graphic Eye — 252–253

あとがき
Afterword by Tamotsu Yagi — 254

クラパット・ヤントラサー
Kulapat Yantrasast / wHY Architecture — 240–241

クリスティーナ・キム
Christina Kim / Dosa — 224–225

デルラエ・ロス
DelRae Roth / Parfums DelRae — 200–201

高木 彬子　吉田 正子 — 193–199

1984 WHAT A MOMENT
NOT KNOW IT UN
TODAY I LOOK BACK WITH A FO
IT SO AMAZING ONE WOULD N
ONE TENDS TO JUMP TO THE TITLE
REFERENCE, BUT FOR ME IT WAS
WAS THE YEAR IN WHICH I MANAGED
TO CALIFORNIA AND HEAD UP OUR GRA
ESPRIT, THE FASHION APPAREL MAKER. 1984. YE
WHAT THE SIGNIFICANCE TO US AND TO TAMOTSU AS
HIS LIFE AND I BELIEVE A GIANT STEP IN AN AMAZING CAREER. A
JAPAN OFTEN, MEETING THE ELITE OF THE JAPANESE CONTEMPORARY DESIGNERS, AI
TIME, IT WAS CLEAR THAT JAPAN WAS AS MUCH ON THE LEADING EDGE OF THE WO

FOREWORD BY DOUGLAS R. TOMPKINS

Photo by Shuji Yoshida

OUS YEAR, ALTHOUGH I DID
TIL YEARS LATER, AND EVEN
M OF AMAZEMENT. WHY WAS
TURALLY ASK, AND OF COURSE
OF ORWELL'S CLASSIC NOVEL AS THE
R MORE IMPORTANT BECAUSE IT
O CONVINCE TAMOTSU YAGI TO COME
C DESIGN DEPARTMENT AT MY COMPANY
NOW WE ARE DECADES LATER AND WE CAN SEE
CH AS ANYONE MEANT. IT MEANT A HUGE CHANGE IN
LOOK BACK TO THE YEARS BEFORE 1984 WHEN I WAS GOING TO
TECTS, ART DIRECTORS, GRAPHIC DESIGNERS, AND DESIGN CONSULTANTS OF THAT
WIDE CONTEMPORARY DESIGN SCENE AS ANY COUNTRY OR CULTURE. EUROPE, WAS

in some ways then beginning to look at Japan for inspiration despite its rather chauvinist Euro-centric attitudes, America was far behind and the rest of the world looked and watched at what was coming from these great design centers. I was enthralled with Japan, the culture deeply imbued with thousands of years of craft discipline, of an aesthetic that transcended trends and design and fashion was setting quality examples of great work in many fields from set design, print graphics, interiors, architecture, clothing and other industrial design, art and photography. There was no lack of creative and forward thinking. Japan was not copying anyone, but forging new design directions backed by a powerful universe of creative thinkers, designers and innovators. I was fortunate to be introduced to many of the great or soon to be great designers of that time. Shiro Kuramata I would put high on the list, not only as a design genius of immense originality, but also as a great human being. His shy manner, modest attitude but powerful ideas and poetic notions of life made a great impression on me. He taught me a lot and we became good friends working on a number of projects together. I think I may have learned the craft of design more from him than anyone else. Plus, he was a wonderful human being. We found a house in Tokyo in those years, Shiro turned it into one of the most comfortable, delightful places to come to Japan and visit, work and stay. It became the center of all of our activities there and introduced me into the inside of Japanese culture and tradition. Shiro designed stores and fixture systems for us in Hong Kong and Singapore.

コラージュ作品「San Francisco」。1986年、エスプリがAIGA (the American Institute of Graphic Arts) のリーダーシップアワードを受賞。コンファレンスは、サンフランシスコで開催され、当時のAIGAメンバー30人が、この街で自分が好きな場所を一つあげてガイドブックを制作。私は、サンフランシスコをイメージしたロゴを依頼され、市バスのチケットをコラージュして「San Francisco」を表現した。

In 1986, the AIGA conference was held in San Francisco as the SF based company, Esprit won the AIGA's (the American Institute of Graphic Arts) leadership award that year. For the event, 30 AIGA members created a SF city guide featuring their favorite spots in the city. I was asked to design the logo for the book which I collaged from San Francisco's public transportation tickets from my collection.

We met often in diverse places like America, Italy and of course in Tokyo and became life friends. The work was stimulating, high quality and taken note of by the design industry and the press. Tamotsu of course was close to Shiro as well, and we combined projects together with signage and graphics and this led to my offer to Tamotsu to come to America and become the head of our graphic department which was just then working on a total image and design project for the company. As many now know, the Esprit total design concept from the product design to its promotion to its display and sale became a phenomena of the 1980s where the company expanded its reach to nearly 60 countries and a very large commercial success, being imitated by countless companies not just in the clothing field but in many other consumer products.

Once Tamotsu had pulled up stakes in Japan and moved to San Francisco, he became a key member of our small design and image making team at Esprit headquarters where we had established a large and fast moving design studio of product and image making people. The principle players on the image making team were Tamotsu on overall graphic design, Italian Oliviero Toscani as the photographer of models which were usually Esprit's own employees, Roberto Carra, another Italian photographer yet formally trained as a graphic designer who shot still life product photography and myself as the de facto art director. The four of us working very well together set the course and principle image for the company. Within a few years we established a very strong brand image and customer following that had a platoon of imitators trying to copy our ideas. Just what you want if you want to be an industry leader, for it means that the imitators must wait until they see your next designs and concepts before they set about copying them, so they must by definition virtually remain behind you.

At the end of the 80s and an intense decade, Robundo Press approached us to make a book on the Esprit graphic and design concepts. Tamotsu headed up the effort and the result was the now classic book, *ESPRIT: The Comprehensive Design Principle* that documented and explained the process of our design work and philosophy. The book sold to designers and architects in all fields and was a critical success and today is still pulled out of design libraries for students and apprentices in design, marketing and architectural studios. In many ways it was one of Tamotsu's early portfolios that highlighted his work and showed the amazing breadth of his skills as a graphic designer. He had worked on catalogs, ad campaigns, labels, packaging, posters, books, store graphics, signage, even museum shows, that were the true comprehensive elements that made the brand Esprit so strong and well known. With a working relationship that was so intense and with such need for close collaboration, all four of us forged lifelong friendships that has transcended the distances and changes that have occurred in all of our lives. For that, Tamotsu remains a friend for life, and when we are back together and I come up from South America where I have been living for the last twenty years, we are together as if no time has passed. Our eyes match up as they always did for aesthetic and design questions, our sense of humors have hardly changed, and we both think that time stood still these last two decades and that we will live like this forever. He will know of a new restaurant to take me to, knowing that I will appreciate it like he does, he will show me work he has been doing for different clients and still invite my criticisms, and he will generously give his time and talents to designing a book or two for my wife's and my environmental or conservation causes.

When I come back to our projects and our young team of architects and designers that work on our projects in Chile and Argentina, I am reminded of that design discipline and the rigor of Tamotsu's craft and skill as a graphic master and recount the numerous lessons I learned in my own apprenticeship under Tamotsu even as his nominal boss. Then too what he learned perhaps more than at any time in his career during our Esprit years together was that salient rule that we can never forget in good design work: No Detail is Small.

Douglas R. Tompkins

NO DETAIL

1984年は、私の人生においてとても重要な年でした。ジョージ・オーウェルの小説『1984年』も世界的に多大なる影響を与えましたが、私にとっては、日本から八木保をカリフォルニアのエスプリオフィスに迎えた、思い入れ深い年なのです。あれから数十年の時が経った現在でも、私は彼から受けた影響力の大きさを再確認すると同時に、彼にとっても私にとっても、彼がカリフォルニアに移住するという大きな決断がお互いのすばらしい現在につながっているのではないかと考えています。

1984年以前のことを振り返ってみましょう。当時私は、頻繁に日本を訪れ、日本の第一線で活躍している建築家、アートディレクター、インテリアデザイナー、グラフィックデザイナーらと会う機会に恵まれました。そして、彼らと会うたびに、日本という国の文化の高さに驚かされていました。建築デザイン、インテリアデザイン、工業デザイン、グラフィックデザイン、ファッションデザイン、どれをとってもとても細密に考慮され、研ぎ澄まされたデザインばかりでした。日本の精緻かつ知的で美しいデザインスタイルは、ヨーロッパのスタイルともどこか違う何か新しいものをもっていると感じていたのです。その頃のアメリカに至っては、何か新しいものを生み出すようなモチベーションすらなかったように思えます。私は幸運にも、その当時の多くのすぐれたデザイナーや、現在も活躍し続けている有能なクリエイターを紹介していただく機会が多く、倉俣史朗氏に出会ったのもその頃のことでした。彼のオリジナリティあふれる力強いデザイン、そしてそれとは対照的ともいえる彼のシャイで詩的な性格と感性は、私に大きな影響を与えたのです。それ以上に彼のすばらしい人間性にも感銘を受けました。彼にはエスプリの香港、シンガポールのインテリアデザインと、ほかにイタリア、アメリカ、日本オフィスのためのデザインなどを手がけてもらったのです。

また、都内に私が購入した家を居心地の良い「生活+仕事空間」に改装してもらい、彼とは仕事のパートナーとしてだけでなく、尊敬できる友人としてつき合っていました。さらに、彼からは、緻密な手作業によって制作される機能性と美術的な美しさを融合させたデザインスタイルについて、多くのことを学んだと思います。そして、その倉俣史朗氏と交友関係があった八木保と知り合ったのです。私は彼ら二人といくつかのプロジェクトを進行させた後、八木に「渡米してエスプリのチーフグラフィックデザイナーになってくれないか」とオファーしました。世界60カ国に支店を展開し、1980年に大きな商業的成功を収めたエスプリの未来は、彼の参加なしでは考えられませんでした。エスプリブランドが提供したグラフィックスタイルはファッション界だけでなく、さまざまなクリエイティブな分野に影響を与え、そのスタイルは頻繁に模倣されたのです。

八木保をサンフランシスコに迎えた当時、私はビジュアルデザインを集中的に手がけるために、小規模のイメージメイキングチームを創設しました。メンバーは4人。グラフィックデザイナーに日本人の八木 保、ファッションフォトグラファーにイタリア人のオリビエロ・トスカーニ、そして元グラフィックデザイナーであり、すでにエスプリの社員であったイタリア人のロベルト・カーラをスティルライフフォトグラファーに、そして私がクリエイティブディレクターとなり、エスプリのブランドイメージを構築しました。私たちは数年のうちに力強いアイデアをデザインという「形」にして、世の中に送り出したのです。その直後に模範的なデザイングラフィックが出回ったことは、エスプリがいかに斬新で、影響力のある会社だったかを実証しているといえるでしょう。

80年代の終わりには朗文堂出版からのアプローチにより、ブランドの歴史やデザインコンセプト、哲学をさらに明確に打ち出す書籍の出版プロジェクトがスタートしました。そして、八木保のディレクションのもと、『ESPRIT: The Comprehensive Design Principal』が出版されました。この本は、多くのデザイナーや建築家に愛読され、現在も各国の学生やデザイナーを刺激しています。カタログ、レーベル、パッケージ、ポスター、インテリアのグラフィックに展示会のサイン関連デザインなど、多種多様なデザインをエスプリ内でつくり出してきた彼にとって、この書籍は彼のポートフォリオといっても過言ではないはずです。

八木 保は、生涯の大切な親友です。私が20年以上生活している南アメリカに彼が遊びにきたときも、それまでの年月が止まっていたかのように長い間、いろいろなことを話し合ったのを覚えています。彼独特の美的センスは一緒に仕事をしていた頃のままで、デザインを探求する姿勢は、年月を経た今も変わりません。彼は、新しいレストランの情報や、進行中のプロジェクト、さまざまなクライアントの話など、常に新しい情報を提供してくれ、同時に私と私の妻の意見や評論にも、熱心に耳をかたむけてくれる、広い心と好奇心の持ち主です。現在、私はチリとアルゼンチンでいろいろな環境保護対策に取り組んでいます。時折、彼とともに仕事をしていた時代を懐かしく思い出しながら、デザイナーや建築家たちと小規模なチームをつくって活動しているのです。刺激的なエスプリ時代を通して、私は良いデザインを生むための一つの暗黙のルールにたどり着きました。

それは「NO DETAIL IS SMALL＝ディテールへのこだわり」ということ。

八木 保と、当時の彼の上司の立場だった私は、お互いに双方から学び合いました。今でもそれらを常に思い返しては前進している日々です。

ダグラス R. トンプキンス

IS SMALL

エスプリのグラフィックデザイン室にかけられていた、全長3mもあるサイン。
This three meter sign was displayed on the wall of the Esprit graphic design studio.

FROM SAN FRANCISCO TO VENICE

2009年の夏、坂道の多い街サンフランシスコから、浜風がいつも涼しく肌に感じるロサンゼルスのベニスビーチへと引っ越しました。26年間暮らした、居心地の良いサンフランシスコからベニスビーチの個性的なアボット・キニーにオフィスを移すことにした理由は、思いきって環境を変えることで別の扉が開くだろうと考えたから。違った環境での新たな人々や場所、ものとの出会いは、日々の生活や仕事に刺激を与えてくれます。新しいことに挑戦するというモチベーションをもって、ここ、ベニスビーチでも仕事をしています。そして今、1984年にサンフランシスコに移った当時と同様に、新鮮な気持ちに満ちています。

In the summer of 2009, we relocated our studio from San Francisco to Venice, California. To be able to call the Bay Area home for 26 years has brought great joy to me. So many fond memories of family, friends and clients in San Francisco, but like all great things, they must come to an end. I felt it was time for a new setting, a new adventure and new inspiration, and I found that in the eclectic and vibrant Abbot Kinney Street in Venice, California. The transition stirred a similar sense of excitement as when I first relocated to San Francisco from Tokyo in 1984.

サンフランシスコのオフィスで使っていた大きな家具が新オフィスに納まるかどうか、原寸のテンプレートをつくってレイアウトした結果、問題なく納まるとわかったので引っ越しを決めた。写真はオフィス移転の案内状に使用したもの。

We made basic paper templates of the furniture from the San Francisco studio to see if it would fit into the new Venice space. With some creative organizing everything seemed to fit quite well and I decided to move into our current space. This photo was also used for our moving announcement.

893A

893 A FOLSOM ST. はサンフランシスコのダウンタウンのSOMAという地域に位置する。SOMAは"South of Market"の略で、文字通りマーケットストリートの南側一帯をさし、元は倉庫街として知られている新興地域。Tamotsu Yagi Design (TYD) の旧オフィスは、汚れた大きな倉庫をリノベーションしたもの。壁、天井はすべてサンドブラストし、フロアには小学校で使用されていた木板を敷き詰め、新しい空間へと変化させた。スカイライトが一つしかなく、夏は暑く冬は寒かったけれど、吹き抜けのある巨大空間は仕事をするにはとても快適なスペースだった。

893 A FOLSOM ST. South of Market area (SoMa) is located in San Francisco, California and the former neighborhood of Tamotsu Yagi Design (TYD) studio. SoMa is comprised of warehouses, nightspots, art galleries and lofts. This raw warehouse space was completely transformed into our design studio. We sandblasted the walls and ceilings and replaced the flooring with reclaimed wood that was recycled from a local elementary school.

このページの写真は、『ELLE DECOR イタリア』のために撮影されたオフィスの写真。カメラマンは、アムステルダム在住のマーク・シーレン。被写体として彼が見たことのなかった小物や家具が多くあったようで、とてもエキサイティングな撮影となった。カメラマン本人も、撮った写真の膨大な枚数に驚いていたほど。

These images were photographed by an Amsterdam based photographer, Mark Seelen for a story that was featured in *ELLE DECOR ITALIA*. Seelen is passionate about photographing furniture and interiors which made this a successful and memorable photoshoot.

Photo by Mark Seelen

2006年、TYDのオフィスの一部で、ジュエリーショップ「チェリオッツ・オン・ファイアー」と共同で雑貨の店をオープン。ショップの什器にはジャン・プルーヴェの家具を使い、ギャラリーのような空間をコーディネイトした。ショップオリジナルのガラス瓶、撮影で使ったアンティークの小物などを販売。

In 2006, the specialist jewelry shop Chariots on Fire opened a temporary store within the TYD studio. Much of the studio's Jean Prouvé furniture collection was utilized as display, such as the long glass table, creating a unique pairing of design disciplines and merging old and new. The gallery-like shop offered a selection of vintage and contemporary jewelry, objet d'art, and other lifestyle goods.

2100B

2100 B ABBOT KINNEY ST. は、チャールズ・イームズの元オフィスがあった地域に位置する。小さなショップやレストランが建ち並ぶ通りを過ぎると、モダンロフトが多くある住宅地に至る。オフィスに選んだのは、工場を改装した3階建てのロフトスペース。一日中、自然光に包まれ、ベニスビーチの潮風を感じることのできる空間だ。写真はオフィススペースの主役であるジャン・プルーヴェのインダストリアル・テーブル。

2100 B ABBOT KINNEY BLVD. In 2009, TYD moved from San Francisco to our new studio in Los Angeles located on the pedestrian friendly, Abbot Kinney Blvd. in Venice. The neighborhood has a nice creative energy and was once the home of Charles Eames' studio. Now located in a three story modern loft space, the studio enjoys plenty of natural light and the fresh ocean breeze. This photo is of a large Jean Prouvé Industrial Table, located in main space of the studio.

Photo by Kazuya Enomoto

自然の中で自然をモチーフに作品を生み出すアーティストがいる中、それとは対照的な作品を生み出すロバート・ニッケルのアート。町中で拾った紙などでコラージュ。
There are artists who work closely with nature, but artist Robert Nickle's influence is the urban landscape. Pictured here is a collage of materials he found in the city environment.

1988

When I design, I select materials based on its application to accentuate its character. In 1988 at Esprit, I began using recycled paper for select printed materials. This decision involved developing a special printing technique to bring out the best quality of print on recycled paper. This achievement was recognized with an environmental award to Esprit in 1990 as the first major apparel company to use recycled paper and soy based ink. I concluded that the materials we choose during the design process in essence *is* design and it greatly influences our work and message. There are a variety of materials being developed everyday with new possibilities. Interpreting these new materials is essential.

MATERIALS

Nine projects focusing on the use of materials

素材

私は、デザインをする上で、素材の持ち味をいかしたいと常々思っています。一九八八年、エスプリは一部の印刷物に再生紙を使いはじめました。再生紙と植物性インクの特質を考慮して特殊な製版技術も開発され、再生紙独自の良さをいかしたデザインを徹底。その功績が認められ、一九九〇年、はじめて再生紙を使用した企業として「環境アワード」を受賞したのです。素材をいかしきれば、おもしろい効果が期待できるデザインも可能なのだと、認識したのです。日々、さまざまな素材が開発されています。素材がもつ可能性を探り、どのような形に仕上げていくのか、いつの時代でも、デザイナーにとって「素材」を意識することは重要なことだと考えています。

広島市環境局中工場で精製されたスラグの拡大イメージ。建設資材(コンクリートブロックなど)の材料として再利用される。
Slag is a rock-like, vitreous material formed during the smelting or refining process of metals. Pictured here is a piece of slag from the Hiroshima City Naka Incineration Plant.

和泉正敏 STONE WORKS 2 の招待状
Invitation for Izumi Masatoshi Stone Works 2

展覧会の招待状には、どうしても和泉正敏さんの石を送りたいという、JAPONESQUEのオーナー原孝一さんからのアイデアでスタートしたデザイン。リサイクル段ボール紙の中に石を埋め込んで、テープでとめるというデザインを提案しました。そこで、四国の牟礼から、厚み約2cmのハニカム構造のダンボールに入る石を100個送ってもらい、デザイン科に通う学生と一緒にボランティアで、すべて手作業で100人分の招待状をつくりました。

I was asked to design an invitation for the opening of the *Izumi Masatoshi Stone Works 2* exhibition, held at the Japonesque gallery. The owner, Mr. Hara envisioned sending offcuts of Mr. Izumi's stone sculptures as part of the invitation. I decided to embed the stone into a thick, recycled cardboard material called honeycomb board and requested approximately 100 pieces of stone, half inch in thickness. With the help from art school students, we carefully laid each stone by hand into the honeycomb boards. Invitations were sent to 100 guests and each invitation was unique as were the shapes and colors of Mr. Izumi's stones offcuts.

ハニカム構造にある部分的空洞をいかして、表面を石のシルエットにそって小さめに切り取る。その後、石を強く押し込んで埋めることにした。
As the name suggests, this cardboard has a hollow, honeycomb construction throughout.
We hollowed out a silhouette of every stone in the honeycomb board and embedded each stone into the invitation.

石 Stone × 送る Send

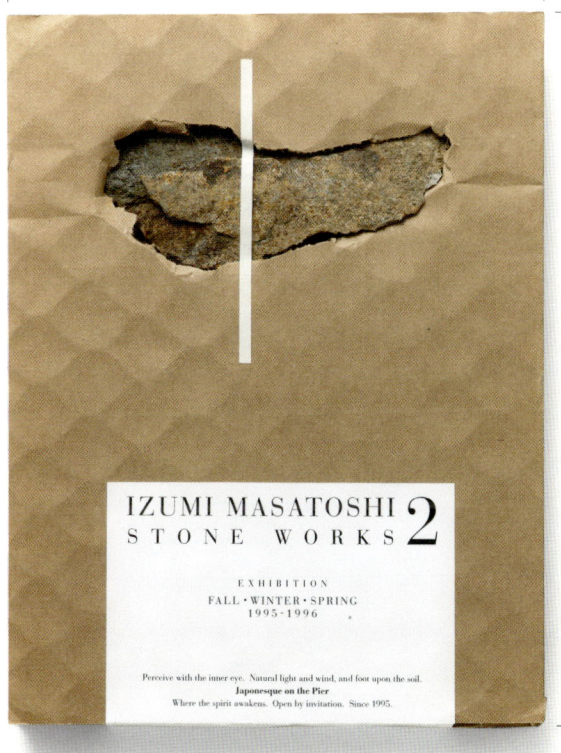

21.5

28

IZUMI MASATOSHI
STONE WORKS 2

EXHIBITION
FALL · WINTER · SPRING
1995 · 1996

Perceive with the inner eye. Natural light and wind, and foot upon the soil.
Japonesque on the Pier
Where the spirit awakens. Open by invitation. Since 1995.

原寸 | Actual Size

牟礼にある和泉さんの石材所の石塀には、彫刻で削り落とされた石の欠片が埋め込まれている。エッジがシャープで、色や形が異なり、紙の素材の中にバランスよく納まった「石の欠片」。紙と石という異質な二つの素材が一つの招待状になった。

Mr. Izumi has a wall made of stacked, offcut pieces of stones at his studio. These fragments were once a part of his stone sculptures before they were chiseled away. Each stone is different in color and shape, as the stories they hold. These precious stone artifacts were sent as part of the invitation for his exhibition.

ネクストマルニの椅子
Nextmaruni Chair Project

「和楽」2005年8月号 掲載

背座を支えるための高度な技術を要する合わせの木の骨組みが特徴。マルニの熟練された木工技術によって実現した。
Maruni's technique and knowledge of wood construction was instrumental in maintaining the visual aesthetic and framework which gave stability to this chair.

Photo by Noboru Morikawa

木 Wood × 躾ける Discipline

デザイナーの黒川雅之さんが「日本の美意識との対話としての小椅子」をテーマに、12人のデザイナーに依頼した『マルニ木工』の木の椅子のプロジェクト。私は、毎日の生活で、靴を履く、朝食をとる、デスクで仕事をするなど、シーンに応じていろいろな椅子に座ります。そのなかには、お気に入りの1940〜50年代の3本脚の椅子もあります。そこで、折り鶴のような端正な和をイメージした3本脚の椅子をデザインしました。両足をしっかりと下ろして5本の脚で姿勢よく座ることによって、木の椅子に「正しい座り方」を躾けられるのです。

The *Nextmaruni* chair design project was produced by Japanese product designer, Masayuki Kurokawa for Maruni. I was among the 12 designers asked to design a chair that conversed with the Japanese spirit and sense of aesthetic. There are different types of chairs designed to suit various situations. The sitter's experience can also be influenced by the design of the chair they sit on and this interaction between an object and the user is something special. I've always admired the elegance of 3 legged chairs from the 1940-50s, so I designed a 3 legged chair with the elegant image of an origami crane. While placing both of your legs firmly on the ground, there is now a harmony of 5 legs equating an experience of discipline and balance.

上／折り鶴からイメージした、紙による椅子の背骨の原寸模型。下／スーツケースから取り出したパーツを机の上ですばやく組み立てた、三本脚の椅子の模型。
Top: Actual size model made of foam core. The chair design was inspired by an origami crane. Bottom: Mock-up of the 3 legged chair. The chair was separated into pieces to fit inside the suitcase then shipped to Maruni. The chair was re-assembled at the meeting.

「グラフィックデザイナーがデザインする木製椅子とはどんなものだろう？」と、素朴な疑問を抱いていましたが、その答えは八木さんが広島に持参した原寸模型を見た瞬間に解消しました。きれいにカットされたスチレンボードをスーツケースから取り出して手際よく組み立てる八木さんの目の前に完成した模型は、平面を美しい立体へと変換させた折り鶴のような椅子でした。安定性の問題から四本脚のみの製品化を考えましたが、最終的に三本脚も加わって二種類を設定しました。
川上敏宏（株式会社マルニ木工 開発部）

I asked myself, what kind of chair would a graphic designer design? The answer was displayed in front of me as Mr.Yagi unpacked pieces of carefully cut foam core boards out of a suitcase he had sent to our Hiroshima office and swiftly assembled the pieces together. The chair was like an origami crane that came to life. For variation, we produced a 4 legged version of the chair but in the end, the original 3 legged version of the design was also produced.
Toshihiro Kawakami (Development Dept. at Maruni Wood Industry)

鏡 Mirror ✕ 切る Cut

2009年、三保谷硝子店101周年記念として、16人のデザイナーとアーティストがガラスと鏡の可能性に挑戦する企画展が計画されました。私はピカピカに磨かれた、曇りのない素材としての鏡が好きです。そこでイメージしたのは、フォンタナの作品『raw canvas』。フォンタナのように、鏡の表面をスパッと一直線に切り割いてみたかったのです。割れやすい鏡を切る、それも一部分を切るという、鏡での表現技術の限界に挑戦する作品を、すばらしい加工技術をもつ三保谷硝子店に提案しました。結果、鏡を切ることはできなかったのですが、切れているように見える作品が完成しました。

In 2009, Mihoya, a Japanese glass specialist observed their 101 year anniversary with a program to celebrate glass. They commissioned 16 designers and artists to design an object made of glass which would continue to challenge Mihoya's ability to work with this fascinating material. I immediately thought of Fontana's "cut canvas" art. The transparent and fragile nature of glass is its distinguishing trait. Combining these two characteristics, I wanted to see if it was possible to cut glass in the way Fontana did with his canvas. In production, we found that it was not possible to cut glass in this way but we were able to simulate the look.

I ESCAPE SYMBOLICALLY, BUT ALSO MATERIALLY FROM THE PRISON OF THE FLAT SURFACE. — LUCIO FONTANA

"私は象徴的かつ物質的に、平面という名のしばりから抜け出している。"
ルーチョ・フォンタナ

フォンタナの作品には、切り口が外側か内側に反っている2つのタイプがある。鏡ではどちらの切り口が効果的なのか…。それを確認するために、ミラーペーパーで原寸のプロトタイプを制作した。
There are two different details of Fontana's cut canvas paintings where the canvas curls inwards and outwards where the incision is made. I made a working model using reflective paper to mimic an actual mirror to see which version would be visually appealing.

Photo by Stefano Massei

三保谷硝子店一〇一年目の試作展

Mihoya Glass 101 Year Anniversary Project

上／AXISギャラリーで開催された展覧会で発表した提案作品。下（右・左）／三保谷硝子店ではじめて見たサンプル。ガラス面の盛り上がりで、思っている以上に一面が切れているように見えた。

Top: The exhibition of the final proposed piece at Axis gallery.
Bottom (left, right): First prototype by Mihoya. The raised line created the illusion that the mirror was cut straight down the center.

硝子は脆い素材です。深い傷や切れ目が一つでもあれば、そこから亀裂が走ります。実際、そうした特性をいかして板硝子は切断されます。しかし一方でガラスにはもう一つ別の顔があります。それは、熱可塑性です。熱を加えると一転して成形の自由度が高まります。この作品は、まるで裂け目をもつ鏡の如く、エッジを立てて加熱曲げしてあります。硝子の特性からは到底ありえないと思われる発想を、いかに硝子ならではの形にもっていくか"腕の見せ所という訳です。
三保谷 昌弘（三保谷 専務取締役）

Since glass is a fragile material, even a small scratch can turn into a crack. Scratching a line on the surface of the glass is a technique we use to cut glass. Alternatively, heat may be applied to make glass more malleable so it can be bent and formed into a desired shape. Understanding the unique properties of glass and its limits as specialists, we continue to challenge ourselves to find new applications for this fascinating material.
Masahiro Mihoya (VP of Mihoya)

Photo by Kazuya Enomoto

紙 Paper ✕ 染み込ませる Infuse

私は海外へ行くとリサーチの一つとして香水のテスター用紙を集めます。それらに知人や友人のイメージに合った香りをふって、メモを添えて封筒に入れて送るのです。このような「香り紙」を商品化できないかと考え、友人に13代目の中川淳さんを紹介してもらいました。中川政七商店の本社は墨の生産地でもある奈良にあります。そこでその土地柄を意識し、墨入れ箱をモティーフとした木箱に和紙のような紙質の8枚の紙香を入れるというデザインをしました。

I often collect fragrance tester papers when I travel and imagine how the fragrances connect with the brands. When I write letters to friends, I often insert a scented tester inside, matching a particular scent to the person. Luckily, I met Mr. Nakagawa (owner of Nakagawa Masashichi Shoten in Nara) when I was thinking about making scented papers. The final product which I named *Kamikou*, contained eight fragranced papers infused with traditional Japanese incense inspired scents. *Kamikou* was packaged in wooden boxes that are commonly used to package Japanese *sumi* ink, a speciality of Nara. These wooden boxes made of Balsa wood were ideal containers for their porous quality and their ability to absorb scent.

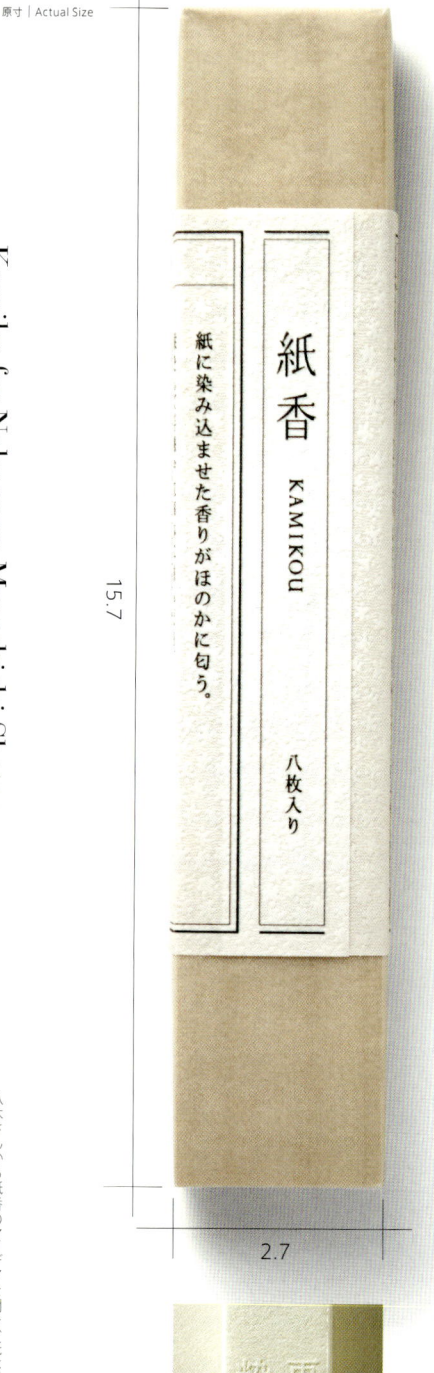

テスター用紙は、ブランドごとに紙質とデザインに特徴をもたせている。ブランドのなかには、香りを身に付けられるように、ブレスレットとして腕に巻けるデザインを提供しているものもある。

Most brands have their own fragrance tester papers. Pictured are a few samples collected from my travels, including one that is shaped like bracelet so that the scent can be worn.

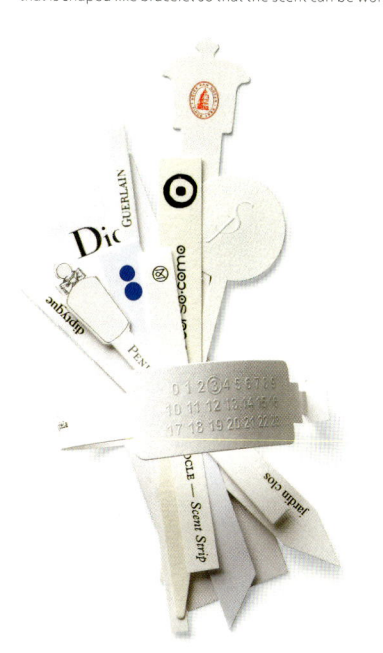

中川政七商店の紙香
Kamiko for Nakagawa Masashichi Shoten

原寸 | Actual Size

15.7

2.7

八木さんから紙香のアイデアを聞き、紙は香りを染み込ませることができる素材ですし、商品化にあたって課題はありましたが実現できるなど思いました。香りとうまく結びついた八木さんのパッケージデザインで完成しました。使用法は人それぞれでいいと思います。たとえば、栞やちょっとしたメモ代わり、あるいはパスポートなどの間に挟んで香りを染み込ませたり。ブランドの新しい世界観を表現できるのでは、と考えています。
中川淳 (代表取締役社長 中川政七商店 十三代)

When I first heard about the idea of *Kamikou* from Mr. Yagi, I wasn't sure how we were going to create this product. I then realized that paper can be saturated with liquid fragrance so we decided to produce this product. *Kamikou* can be used as a bookmark or even placed between pages of a passport, so objects can be scented and fragrance can be carried and enjoyed. I think this product fits nicely with our brand identity.
Jun Nakagawa (CEO of Nakagawa Masashichi Shoten)

土佐の手漉き和紙に"粋更"のロゴをエンボス加工した。
Right: The brand logo is embossed on the paper that is made in Tosa, a city in Kōchi prefecture, Japan.

原寸 | Actual Size

15.6

5.2

香 Scent × 組み立てる Assemble

Tribù for Benetton
ベネトンのトリブ

ベネトン社から、今まで見たこともないような香水のボトルをデザインしてほしいと依頼がありました。そこで思いついたコンセプトは、卵の中に試験管を入れたようなボトル。ガラスとプラスチックという、相対する2種類の素材を組み合わせてデザインすることによって、それぞれの素材がもつテクスチャーを引き出そうと考えたのです。プラスチックは、ベネトンの関連会社であるスポーツブランド、ノルディカのスキーブーツの素材から選びました。

The client requested for me to design a perfume bottle that no one had seen before, something different. For Tribù, I based the shape of the bottle from a glass test tube and an egg, a combination of hard and soft elements. I also introduced materials from a ski boot by Nordica (Benetton's subsidiary company) for the outer shell of the bottle which allowed for customized assembling of colors by scent.

左／2mmのアクリルをボトルの形にレーザーで抜きとり、約30枚のアクリルを重ねて一つのボトルをつくったアクリル製抜き型。右／卵の中に試験管を入れたX-rayのコンセプトのコラージュ。
Left: Laser cut layers of 2mm acrylic sheets. A total of 30 sheets were layered for the study in designing the bottle.
Right: X-ray image of an egg and a test tube overlapping one another.

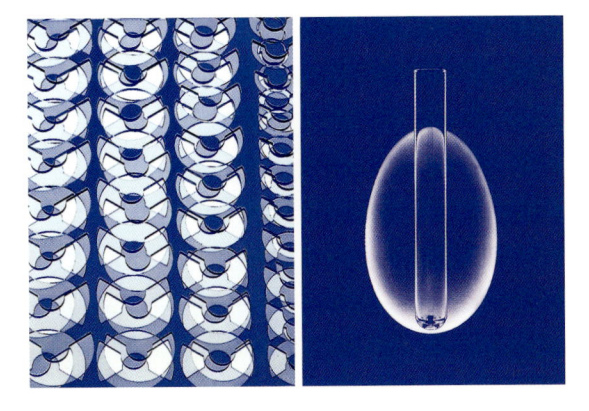

硝子 Glass × 変える Recreate

Glass Bottle for Feliciti
フェリシティのガラスボトル

2003年にスタートした、フェリシモの「フェリシティ」プロジェクト。その一環で、ペットボトルの形をしたガラスのボトルを提案しました。というのも、自宅の還元水をペットボトルに詰めてオフィスへ持参するのが日課でしたが、何度も使っているとボトルの内側が濁ってきて透明感が無くなるのが気になっていたのです。プラスチックのペットボトルの形がシンプルで好きだから、その形をそのままガラスでつくれば、見た目にも美しく、環境にも優しく、リサイクルにも便利だと考えました。コストを抑えるために、中国で一つひとつボトルを手づくりして、6種類のボトルを3,000本ずつ、計18,000本を生産。商品化されたガラスボトルは、フォーシーズンズホテル・丸の内東京のレストラン「ekki」でウォーターボトルとして採用されました。

原寸 | Actual Size

Felissimo's Feliciti project offered a playful selection of practical lifestyle goods and began in 2003. As a part of this project, I proposed this design in the shape of an ordinary plastic bottle. I would bottle filtered water to bring to the studio from home and discovered that over time, plastic bottles became dull and undesirable containers to reuse. Since I liked the shape of ordinary plastic bottles, I designed glass bottles with a similar design which would carry a clean visual aesthetic. These bottles are designed to last and encourage reuse. To make these products affordable, 3,000 bottles in six different shapes were handmade and a total of 18,000 bottles were produced. I was pleased to see these bottles being used in restaurants. In particular, the Ekki restaurant at the Four Seasons Hotel Tokyo at Marunouchi.

「フェリシティ」のブランドカラーは「新鮮な野菜の白のグラデーション」、「健康と感じる空気感」をデザインし、カタログでは「その気配感」を表現しています。八木さんの口から出てくる言葉には正直驚いてばかりで、極めつけは「デザインしないデザインが見立てるデザインが重要」と言う言葉です。どの素材をどう見立てて使うか、そのために中国でいろいろな素材を集めて回ったことを今でも忘れません。時には優しく、時にはスパルタでご指導いただきながら進行した「このプロジェクトは、今でも私の大きな財産となっています。

藤原 眞二（フェリシモ マネージャー）

"The subtle color variances of a white colored vegetable," "creating an atmosphere to inspire a healthy lifestyle" I remember being amazed by the language of design that Mr.Yagi spoke. My most memorable lesson was the idea of 'the undesigned design.' I'll never forget our trip to China for material research for a project we were working on. 'One of the most important process and skill in design is to train the eye for the good materials and then to use it well.' The lessons I learned from Mr. Yagi's kindness and persistence to good design to this day has been most influential.

Shinji Fujiwara (Project Manager at Felissimo)

"硝子はワレルという緊迫感があの美しさをささえているような…" 倉俣 史朗
"The idea that glass can break is what's holding its beauty…" Shiro Kuramata

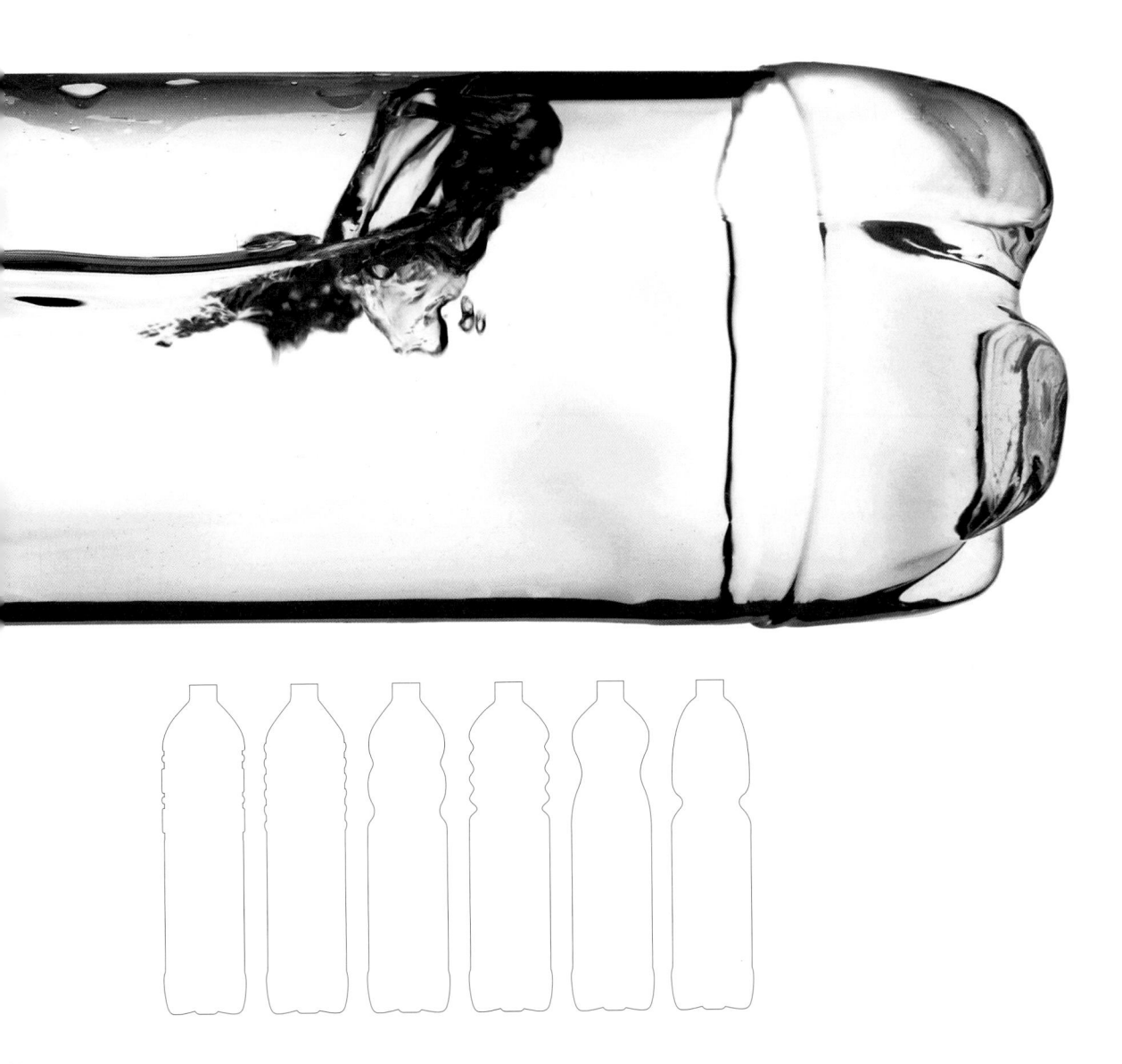

Photo by Stefano Massei

軽銀 Aluminum ✕ 彩色 Dye する

一円玉のリデザイン
Redesigning the One-Yen Coin

クリエイターをゲストに迎え、デザインの再生に挑むフジテレビの番組『NEW DESIGN PARADISE』。私の課題は[一円玉のリデザイン]でした。硬貨のなかでも一円玉は地味な存在。道ばたに落ちていても目立たない色で、拾いにくい厚みが改善点ではないのかと考えました。そんなある日、ロンドンの街の道端でカラフルな色のアルミ缶のプルトップを拾ったのです。アルミはアナダイズという手法で染色が可能なので、一円玉を赤色などに色付けし、拾いにくい薄い形状はプルトップのようにエッジを曲げようと閃きました。さらに、エッジに小さな切れ目を入れれば、一円玉を重ねて、ゴムで束ねられます。このアイデアによって、集めたくなる新たな一円玉ができあがりました。

New Design Paradise is a Japanese TV show by Fuji Television, that challenges designers to redesign everyday objects. When I was asked to redesign the 1 Yen coin, I took inspiration from the simple joy of finding a lucky penny on the ground. With this in mind, during a trip to London, I walked the streets looking for ideas. I came across a colorful anodized soda can tab and decided to anodize the 1 Yen coin, which is also made of aluminum. Being a collector of objects, I enjoy the ritual of displaying and archiving in addition to the excitement of a discovery. I imagined that having multiple color variations would make each find more memorable so besides red, I proposed yellow, blue and green. For function, I slightly bent the edge so the coin would be easier to pick up. Grooves were added on the sides so the coins could be stacked and bound with a rubber band.

フォトエッチングで一円の表面にレリーフを付け、現物に一番近いサイズと重さでつくったテレビ番組用のサンプル。
The samples of the proposed coin were the same weight and size as an actual 1 Yen coin and was made by a photo etching technique.

野菜 Vegetable × 包む Cover

101 Vegetable Faces 一〇一ベジタブルフェイス

フォトグラファー、ロベルト・カーラの娘アンナと、私の娘、理都子が週末よく遊んでいた郊外にあるロベルトの家。裏庭には小さな野菜畑があり、そこで採れる野菜で顔の形をつくって遊んでいたのがはじまりでした。ロベルトのアートディレクションのもと、まるで話しかけてきそうな表情の野菜とフルーツの写真が100枚以上撮影され、出版社の協力で製作されたのがこの本です。子どもたちが自分たちの友だちや知り合いの顔に似せて野菜をレイアウトし、子どもたちの楽しいと感じる遊びのアイデアがこの本のスタートだったのです。

Roberto Carra's daughter Anna and my daughter Ritz as kids, spent many weekends playing at Roberto's country house. There was a small vegetable garden in their backyard and while these vegetables were being prepared for dinner, the two began making faces with them. This spontaneous and playful moment sparked the idea for us fathers to photograph these faces. Under Roberto's art direction, we photographed over 100 of these unique faces made from vegetables and fruits, that looked like their friends and family. This project was purely for fun and with Robundo's support, we were able to publish this book.

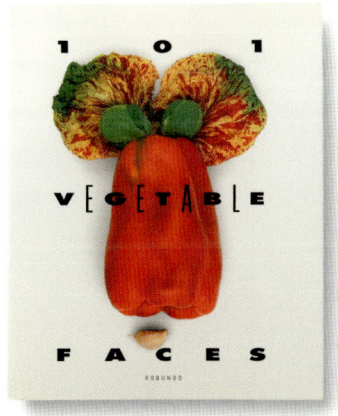

本を見たロンドンのギフトカード専門店「HIP」からの依頼で、ベジタブルフェイスのハガキ、ギフトカード、ラッピングペーパーなどがシリーズ化され、商品として世界に向けて発売された。

Hype, a paper product company based in England saw this book and contacted us to reproduce these images. The vegatable faces were printed onto wrapping paper, post and gift cards and were sold worldwide.

ケールの緑、トマトの赤、そしてピーマンの黄色からイメージされた3色を本の部分に使用し、野菜そのものをイメージにデザインした。
The book's primary colors used for the cover, inside cover and trim were inspired by the colors of kale, tomato and yellow pepper.

Photo by Shuji Yoshida

ナイロン _Nylon_ ✕ 働き _Function_

海外出張では、かならず機内持ち込み可能なサイズのバッグを持っていきます。ウエストコーストから東京までのフライトを快適に過ごすためには、必要な物が完璧に揃っていることが必然であり、同時に、必要なときにそれらを取り出しやすいデザインのバッグを持ち込むことが大切です。ファスナーのサイズやポケットの位置はもちろん、空港のキオスクでペットボトルや雑誌を購入した際に、いかにスマートにモノの取り出しができるか…。このバッグのデザインは、グラフィックデザイナーとしてではなくユーザーの視点を意識したことによって、製品の機能美につなぐことができました。

To make my business travels pleasant, it is helpful to have access to all my essential things. A well designed carry-on bag with the right details and compartments greatly improves the experience of carrying things around during travels. For example, where would one carry a water bottle? Where and how would the bag expand? The design details were focused around functionality and aesthetics from the traveller's perspective and inspired by a helmet bag design.

DESIGN FOR FUTURE

この商品は、フェリシモデザインプロジェクトの対象商品であり、協力デザイナーとともに現地の職人育成や高付加価値商品の開発を進めていくため、バッグ1個あたり1,000円が支援金として社会貢献に活用されます。こういった活動を通し、次世代デザイナーの育成、デザイナー同士の交流促進など、未来をデザインする活動の支援に、フェリシモは取り組みました。

For every bag sold, 1,000 Yen is donated to the _Design for Future_ project, a program designed to share the works of artisans from around the world. This program sustains local, human resources by helping people develop products that raise awareness of a local craft or speciality.

Photo by David Cenciotti

ヘルメットバッグは、空挺部隊がヘルメットを入れて運ぶために使用されているバッグ。ナイロンを使ったシンプルなデザインによって、バッグ全体が軽量化され、水にも強くなった。

The bag shown in this image was designed specifically for pilots to carry their helmets in. Since the design of the bag was simple, we let the texture of the nylon reveal itself.

自他共にバッグ好きと認める八木さんが一番こだわられたことは、"どんなシーンで使っても「品」を感じさせること"。このアッパーケースのカタログでは、製作プロデューサーである浅葉克己さんが、"世界中を飛び回る八木さんにとって、このバッグは「モノを運ぶ」という機能性と持つ人を表現するファッション性を融合した必要不可欠なアイテムであること"、"それはまさに人と人をつなぐコミュニケーションツールなのだ"というコンセプトを見事に表現してくださいました。"二人の想いがつまったアッパーケースは、お客様からも多くのご支持をいただいています。"

山本真純（フェリシモ プロダクト・ディレクター）

Having the reputation of being a bag enthusiast, Mr.Yagi designed this bag with a tasteful design suitable for any occasion. When graphic designer, Katsumi Asaba was commissioned to design the catalog for these UpperCase bags, he revealed the items that Mr.Asaba would normally carry during his travels. By showing the contents, Mr.Asaba showed the versatility of the bag's functional design.

Masumi Yamamoto (Product Director at Felissimo)

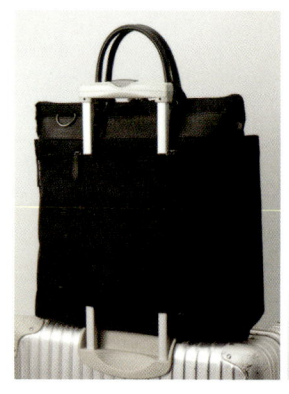

軽量化のため中空糸という糸が使われ、軽くて強く丈夫なのが特徴。撥水加工がされていて汚れにも強い素材。

Special fabric was used to make this bag. The nylon thread of the fabric is lightweight, waterproof and very durable.

Bag for Felissimo
フェリシモのバッグ

Photo by Koichi Tanaka

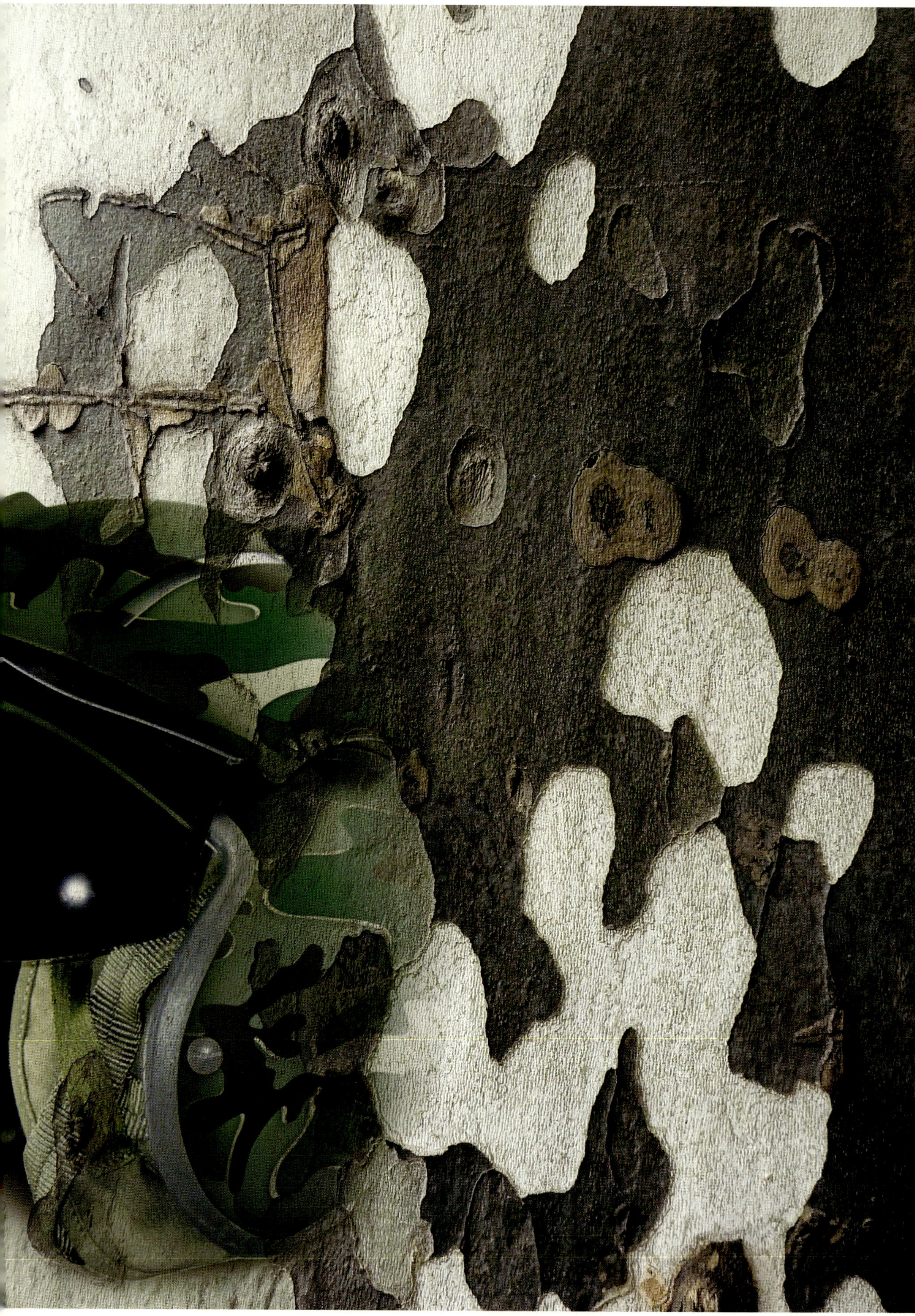

| PANTONE® 341 U | PANTONE® 341 U | PANTONE® 341 U | PANTONE® 341 U | PANTONE® 341 U | PANTONE® 341 U | PANTONE® 341 U | PANTONE® 341 U | PANTONE® 341 U | PANTONE® 341 U | PANTONE® 341 U |

1990

CONCEPT BOX

Seven projects focusing on 3-D concept presentation boxes

In 1990, I worked with Benetton, an Italian apparel company with a unique voice in fashion especially with their controversial advertisements. Oliviero Toscani, a photographer and the creative force behind the brand, asked me to work on a few projects for Benetton, which I remembered being my first major assignment since establishing myself as a freelance designer. One of these projects was to develop the comprehensive brand identity for their Tribù fragrance line, which included package, bottle, display and advertisement design. The concept behind the scent was to capture the essence of cites around the world and I often traveled with Toscani to Treviso, Italy for this project. "Smell box," as Toscani called it, was the first words he used to describe the presentation style that I often used to visually communicate a concept through tangible objects. I assembled various natural materials, colors and objects and created a landscape with a Tribù bottle at the center to present the world of Tribù. To this day, I still use the concept box to present my design ideas to my clients.

箱

一九九〇年当時、ファッション業界に影響を与えたアドバタイジングを発信し、アパレルメーカーとしてもとても有名な、イタリアンブランド、ベネトン社。当時カメラマンでもあり、クリエイティブディレクターだったオリビエロ・トスカーニからの依頼でスタートした仕事は、私がフリーランスになって以降、一番スケールの大きいプロジェクトであり、その一つがフレグランスライン「トリブ（部族）」のパッケージデザインでした。トリブのコンセプトは、世界各地域を香りで表現するというもの。私は何度もイタリアに足を運んで、視覚化できない香りの表現方法を模索しました。そして、トスカーニとの協働から誕生したプレゼンテーションキットが「SMELL BOX」だったのです。以来、「箱」というツールを使って、素材、色、物を組み合わせたビジュアルコミュニケーションを試みています。

カナダから取り寄せた、バーティカル・ガーデンのキット。四十八個の正方形に区切られた五〇×五〇センチのボックスを四箱使用し、一つの大きなパネルに組み立ててプレゼンテーションに臨みました。植物はほとんど水を必要としないサーキュランスを中心に選び、植栽はラフスケッチをしてバランスを考えながら何度もレイアウトを変えて完成させました。

八木 巧（TYDデザイナー）

This vertical garden panel was sourced from a company in Canada. We put together four 20 x 20 inch panels consisting of 48 small compartments to create one large panel. We chose to grow succulents for their vibrant colors and ease of care. The layout was sketched to determine a nice color balance. After experimenting with a few variations, the vertical garden was completed.

Takumi Yagi (TYD Designer)

Photo by Kazuya Enomoto

CONCEPT BOX

Design to me always involves the process of organizing and systematizing elements, the message and the client's objective for the design. Systematizing is as important as the act of adding decorative elements to a design. Essentially, it is the process of editing and defining a clear direction from which to design. At TYD, we continuously process and organize information in order to create effective designs. To do so efficiently, we take the time to comprehend the nature of the projects we are working on and strategize presentation methods to spark meaningful conversations with the client. I continually build a collection of my favorite materials that can be used for presenting ideas for future projects. I store these collections into boxes and they are my design resource. Organizing this collection by category to me is also designing, like one would organize and develop ideas in a sketchbook. Archiving is a practical and enjoyable process for me and my ideal studio is a space that functions like an archive and the studio itself is like a huge archival box.

デザインとは「整理すること」だと思います。辞書で「整理」の意味を調べると「秩序を立てて整えること。無駄を取り除くこと」とあります。たとえば、レイアウトは紙上で整理するようなもの。紙の上でタイプ（文字）と写真をどのように整理（レイアウト）するかです。箱にモノを入れることも、整理の一つ。私は、自分に必要な素材・資料・小物などをすべて、さまざまなサイズの箱に入れて保管します。ですから、頭で覚えきれないものや手に触れてわかる素材など、人から見るとガラクタとも思えるものも箱の中に入っていたりします。私は、「アーカイブ」という言葉の響きが好きです。日本語に訳すと「書庫」を意味するようですが、いろいろなところに棚や引き出しがあって、そこに多種多様な素材がしまってあり、取り出すことができる。そういう、棚と箱でつくられたスペースが理想のオフィスだと思っています。ある意味、オフィスも私にとっては「大きな箱」なのですから。

ジャンクボックス（P66,67）という名をつけた箱は、25年ほど前に気に入ったバインダーがなかったために自分でつくりました。スメルボックス（P49）と名前のついた箱は、ベネトンのトリブのプロジェクトで、当時のクリエイティブディレクターだったトスカーニが「トリブの世界観を箱に詰めたい」と言ったことから、私がアクリルでつくったことがはじまりでした。1995年、SFMOMA（サンフランシスコ現代美術館）のオープニングの際、私の展示コーナーでは4箱のスメルボックスを立体的に展示しました。P50,51はスメルボックスのグリーンです。P52,53は東西南北という商品コンセプトをインスピレーションできるように表現した、アクリル立体のカラーパレットです。

P54,55は同じくSFMOMAで正面に展示したワールドのブランド「UNTITLED（アンタイトル）」のコンセプトフレーム。このネーミングは、ブランドを立ち上げるときに「新しい気持ちで世界をもう一度見直すことからはじめよう」と、ワールドのスタッフと世界一周の旅をしたことがきっかけでした。通常のリサーチはファッションが中心になるのですが、まったく違ったコンセプトからモノを見つめ直そうと、ファッションではなく世界中の代表的な美術館をいくつも巡りました。不思議なことに、私たちが気に入ったコンテンポラリーアートのほとんどのタイトルが「Untitled」であることに気づいたのです。帰国後、ネーミングのリサーチを行ない、「UNTITLED」と決めました。P56-61は、異なる3社のスポーツブランドのプレゼンテーションの際、使用したコンセプトボックスシリーズです。

「箱（box）」は、コンセプトボックス、マテリアルフレーム、カラーマテリアルボックスと、クライアントや時代によって、私のプレゼンテーションの表現も少しずつ変化し続けています。けれど、すべての箱は、大小に関わらず、中に入った素材を通して独特の世界観をイメージできるようにデザインしています。たとえば、手で自由に中の素材に触れることができるように、ふた無しの箱も制作しました。P62,63の子供服ブランド、ファミリアのコンセプトボックスの制作にかかった時間は、約3カ月。ブランドが昔から使用している色違いのチェックパターンの上に、中に入れる卵の色の掛け合わせでオリジナルの色をつくって、レイアウトしていきました。こうして、素材が整理されたコンセプトマテリアルボックスは完成したのです。

P49: Benetton Tribù "smell boxes" and our office motto: Good design is in the nature of things. P51: An actual size Tribù bottle. P52-53: Tribù presentation palette. P54: Framed interior materials for the fashion brand Unititled. P55: The entrance to Tamotsu Yagi's exhibition at the SF MoMA. P56: Framed interior materials and paper samples for the sports-wear brand Fila. P57: Materials for the Fila store fixtures. P58-59: Framed color boxes for the Sports Planet store. P60: Color concept box for Bridgestone's Synergy line. P62-63: The concept presentation and design process for Familiar, a children's clothing brand.

SFMOMAの展覧会では、ディスプレイのためのハードウェアもオリジナルで製作しました。たとえば、壁から突き出たアクリルボックスの留め具、スキー板をアクリルチューブの中に浮かして止める道具など、何度も彼のオフィスに出向いて打ち合わせました。今となっては、とてもいい経験だったと思います。

ゲーリー・イノ（バカ・プロダクション 代表）

For Tamotsu Yagi's exhibition at the SF MoMA, all the hardware was custom made for the display, for example the clasp for the acrylic box placed on the wall and a special fixture to suspend a ski inside an acrylic tube. I made frequent trips to the TYD studio for meetings to discuss the construction details and fabrication of each piece. Looking back, I had a great time being a part of this project.

Gary Ino (Founder of Baka Productions)

Photo by Roberto Carra

THINK OUTSIDE THE BOX
——— 型にはまらない考えをする。

DESIGN IS IN THE NATURE OF THINGS GOOD DESIGN IS IN THE NATURE OF

平面表現の多いグラフィックのマテリアルを、できる限り変化に富んだ展示に表現したい。そのため"good design is in the nature of things"というオフィスのスローガンの周りにスメルボックスを横向きに展示してみた。そうすることによって、もっとも効果的に立体感を演出できた。

Most graphic materials are displayed flat against a surface and for that reason, I wanted my exhibition at the San Francisco Museum of Modern Art to vary in dimensions. "Good design is in the nature of things," TYD's design motto was placed in the center around the concept box while the other four boxes were mounted vertically from the wall. By doing this, I was able to create a dynamic display within the exhibition space.

THOMAS JEFFERSON
UNITED STATES
THOMAS JEFFERSON
UNITED STATES

時間の流れとともに色が変わる素材、時間がたっても変わらない人工的な素材。ボックスの中央にある商品が引き立つようにバランスよく素材を選んだ。

Natural specimens were placed in the concept box to show the change of color overtime. The Tribù bottle by contrast is accentuated at the center of the concept box.

Photo by Shuji Yoshida

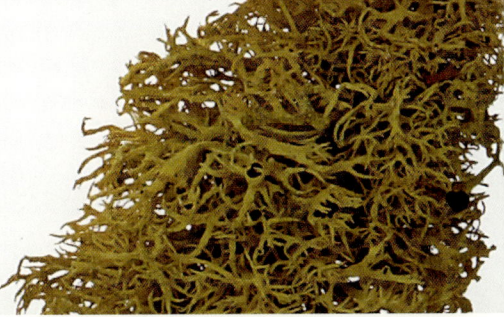

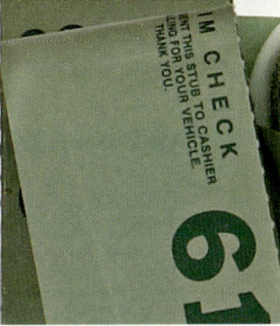

WEST

45

40

SOUTH

CONCEPT BOX

NORTH

EAST

A LANDSCAPE OF DESIGN INSPIRATIONS FROM DIVERSE SOURCES

———さまざまなインスピレーションが重なり合いながら、コラージュというかたちでデザインが生まれる。

パーツを組み合わせることによって、東西南北の香りを表現。小さなアクリルボックスには自然の素材を入れて、実際に香りが伝わってくるようなプレゼンテーションに仕立てた。

These Tribù presentation boxes show variations in color to represent scents inspired from the north, east, south and west. The smaller acrylic boxes within the themes contain materials such as wood and glass to inspire the essence of each fragrance.

Photo by Sharon Risedorph

CONCEPT BOX

ファッションブランド「UNTITLED」のためのマテリアルパレット。上から、温かみのある自然素材を使ったレディースのためのマテリアル。モノトーンを基調としてクールさを表現したメンズのためのマテリアル。タイル、ホーローのサイン、白を基調にハイテックをイメージしたオブジェクトのためのマテリアル。

These three material boxes were created for the store decoration for the Japanese fashion brand, Untitled. Evocative of the art world and of artistic pursuits, these panels were assembled from selected objects representing the lines within the brand: Untitled (ladies), Untitled Men and Untitled Object (homeware).

70

50

すべて手作りのボックス。試作も含め百個以上のボックスを制作。もちろん中のオブジェクトも一つひとつ吟味しオリジナルでつくりました。ガイドラインの各ページも通常の印刷ではなく、小さなプリンターで各ページに二十分かけて印刷しました。その背景が一番ブランドコンセプトに合っていたから。「一つひとつの表現や、細部への気配りの積み重ねがデザインにつながる」と感じたプロジェクトでした。

高東拓司 (T2 Field 代表 元TYD グラフィックデザイナー)

Every concept box for this project was created by hand and assembled in-house. I recall making over one hundred boxes with carefully chosen objects and informational text. We tested print qualities from several laser printers at the TYD studio. The smallest printer gave the lightest and most delicate print quality, which matched Untitled's concept and image. Through this project, I learned how caring for the small details can lead to great design.

Takuji Takato (Principal of T2 Field & Former TYD designer)

Photo by Sharon Risedorph

TAMOTSU YAGI

THE BODY IS YOUR CANVAS

——着る人の感性で好きなように、描くように着る。

> UNTITLED is a new fashion brand and label created by World Co., Ltd. A term commonly used to identify paintings, photographs and other works of art not titled by their authors, UNTITLED is evocative of the art world and artistic pursuits. Inspired and free-spirited, the UNTITLED collection offers the opportunity to mix and match from an eclectic palate of unique clothing and accessories. They are the raw materials from which the wearer creates her own unique composition. Hence the expression, "THE BODY IS YOUR CANVAS." UNTITLED is self expression as an art form, guided by creative intuition and imagination.

Photo by Ben Blackwell

SF MOMAの展示会場入り口に展示されたコンセプトフレームとアクリルボックスに入っているUNTITLEDの企画書。

This is a concept box panel and brand manual (inside the acrylic box) exhibited at the entrance of the *Tamotsu Yagi* exhibit at the San Francisco Museum of Modern Art.

ファッションブランド「フィラ・スポーツ」のプレゼンテーションのためのサンプルボード。使用物はすべてリサイクル素材。上／ペーパーサンプルは植物性インクで印刷された紙や、加工されたクラフト紙をレイアウトし、円形の透かしから素材の組み合わせが見えるようにコラージュした。下／インテリアサンプルボードは、実際に店内で使用したリサイクルの素材で構成。

This is a material concept box for the sportswear brand Fila. The box on top shows the printed qualities of soy-bean based ink and textural samples of recycled paper. The bottom box features recycled material selections for the store interior. The clear circular "windows" within the opaque lid pinpoint key details within the overall presentation.

CONCEPT BOX

店内で利用されるインテリアマテリアルとディスプレイ
を積層させた部分のサンプル。箱の角には商品で使用
された布や糸クズを詰めた。

These are material concept boxes for the Fila
store fixtures. The boxes contain parts of
the actual fixture as well as samples of materials such as recycled wood and textiles used
for actual products sold at retail locations.

Photo by Sharon Risedorph

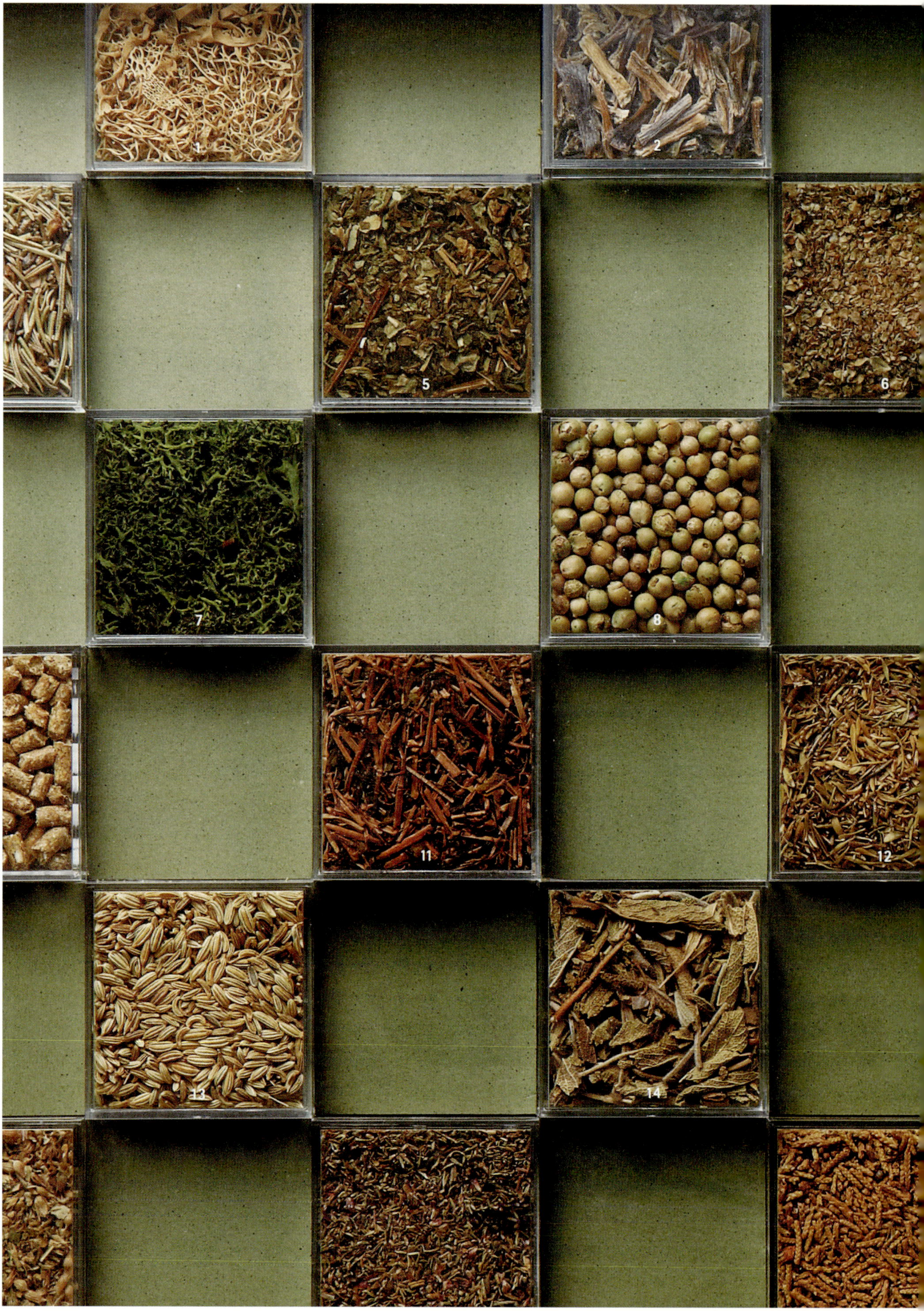

1
2
5
6
7
8
11
12
13
14

CONCEPT BOX

大型スポーツショップ「スポーツプラネット」のブランドカラーボックス。アクリルの小箱にはグリーンとブラウンのカラーチップの代わりに木の実や葉を詰め、18個に絞り込んだ箱をレイアウト。これらの箱にはナンバーをつけてパントーンカラーと合致するように考えた。

This is a color presentation box for the store identity for a Japanese sporting goods company, Sports Planet. Rather than just chosing a green or brown Pantone color for the brand, we designed 18 boxes containing natural specimens in the shades of green and brown. Each box was numbered so the client could later reference colors they liked.

私はこの作品を、二点リビングに飾っています。背景に施されたリサイクルペーパーとのコントラストが美しいこの作品には、小さなアクリルの箱の中に数種類のハーブや種が入っており、季節の移り変わりとともに色彩の変化を感じることができます。本来は「香り」を楽しむハーブですが、植物がもつ造形美を「視覚」で楽しむという表現方法に、強く心を奪われたのです。「サイン(SIGN)」で展開している、植物や木の実など、自然のオブジェクトをガラス瓶に詰めた作品と、これとの出会いがきっかけとなっています。

溝口至亮（サインディレクター）

Mr. Yagi gave me these two concept boxes as a gift and I have them displayed in my living room. I love the balance of the recycled paper, herbs and seeds. Since these natural specimens are contained inside the acrylic box, I've noticed that the colors have changed overtime. Normally you would enjoy the smell of herbs, but this presentation allows me to enjoy them visually. This display has inspired me to collect and archive natural specimens and I have been selling similar objects at my store.
Yoshiyuki Mizoguchi (Director of Sign)

Photo by Shuji Yoshida

CONCEPT BOX

Synergy

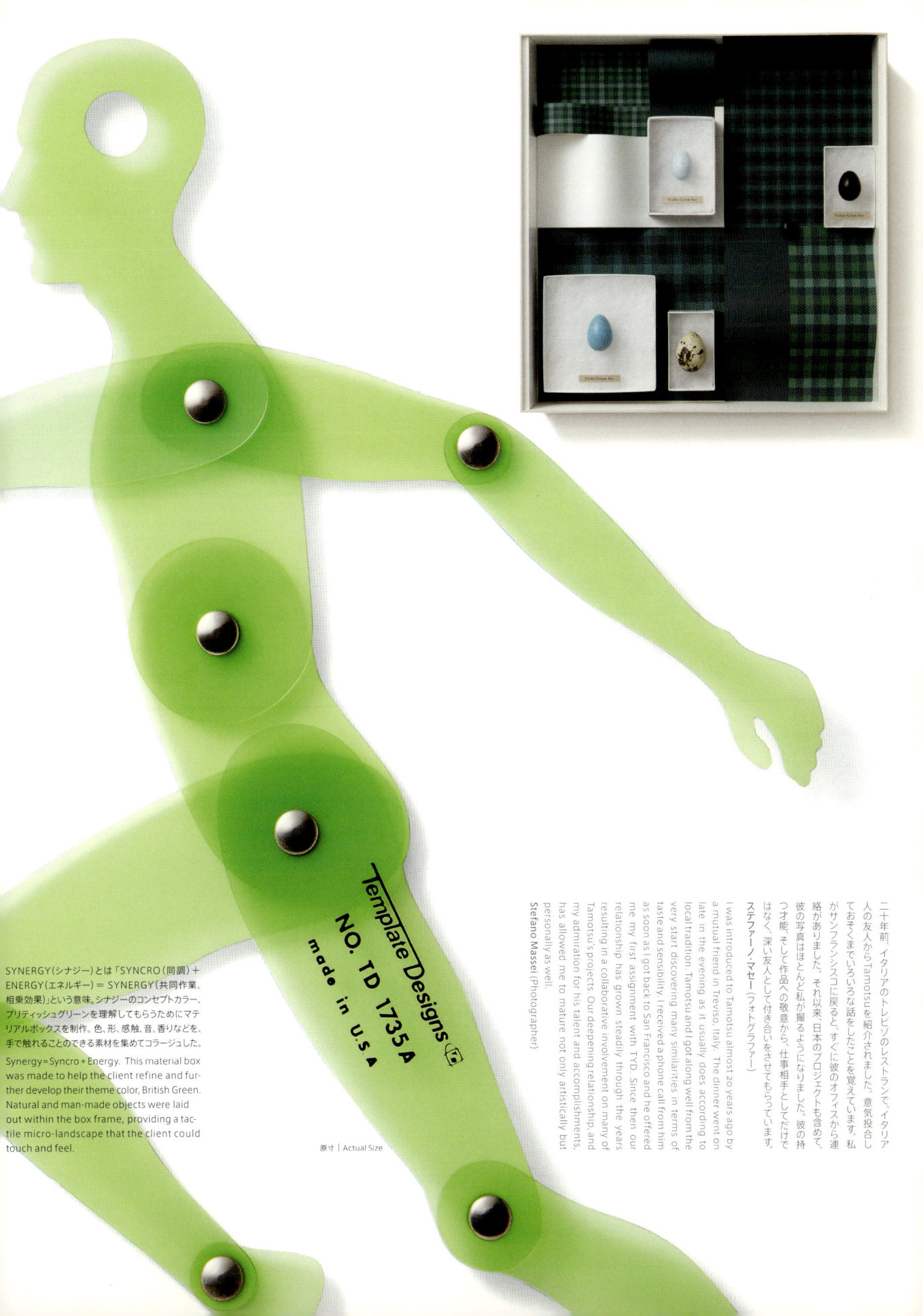

SYNERGY(シナジー)とは「SYNCRO(同調)＋ENERGY(エネルギー) ＝ SYNERGY(共同作業、相乗効果)」という意味。シナジーのコンセプトカラー、ブリティッシュグリーンを理解してもらうためにマテリアルボックスを制作。色、形、感触、音、香りなどを、手で触れることのできる素材を集めてコラージュした。

Synergy=Syncro + Energy. This material box was made to help the client refine and further develop their theme color, British Green. Natural and man-made objects were laid out within the box frame, providing a tactile micro-landscape that the client could touch and feel.

原寸 | Actual Size

I was introduced to Tamotsu almost 20 years ago by a mutual friend in Treviso, Italy. The dinner went on late in the evening as it usually does according to local tradition. Tamotsu and I got along well from the very start discovering many similarities in terms of taste and sensibility I received a phone call from him as soon as I got back to San Francisco and he offered me my first assignment with TYD. Since then our relationship has grown steadily through the years resulting in a collaborative involvement on many of Tamotsu's projects. Our deepening relationship, and my admiration for his talent and accomplishments, has allowed me to mature not only artistically but personally as well.

Stefano Massei (Photographer)

二十年前、イタリアのトレビソのレストランでイタリア人の友人から「Tamotsu」を紹介されました。意気投合しておそくまでいろいろな話をしたことを覚えています。私がサンフランシスコに戻ると、すぐに彼のオフィスから連絡がありました。それ以来、日本のプロジェクトも含めて彼の写真はほとんど私が撮るようになりました。彼の持つ才能、そして作品への敬意から、仕事相手としてだけではなく、深い友人として付き合いをさせてもらっています。

ステファーノ・マセー (フォトグラファー)

CONCEPT BOX

ファミリアのためのコンセプトプレゼンテーションボックス。2010年秋冬のシーズンテーマのプレゼンで使った箱。背景にあるタータンチェックは、ファミリアが1950年に独自開発したファミリアチェックを基本にシーズンごとに色を変えたもの。色の組み合わせで合計16種のボックスをつくった。

Pictured are concept presentation boxes designed for Familiar's 2010 fall/winter season. A Tartan check pattern was used in color variations from the original Familiar check, which was created in 1950. A total of 16 variations of colored patterns were designed.

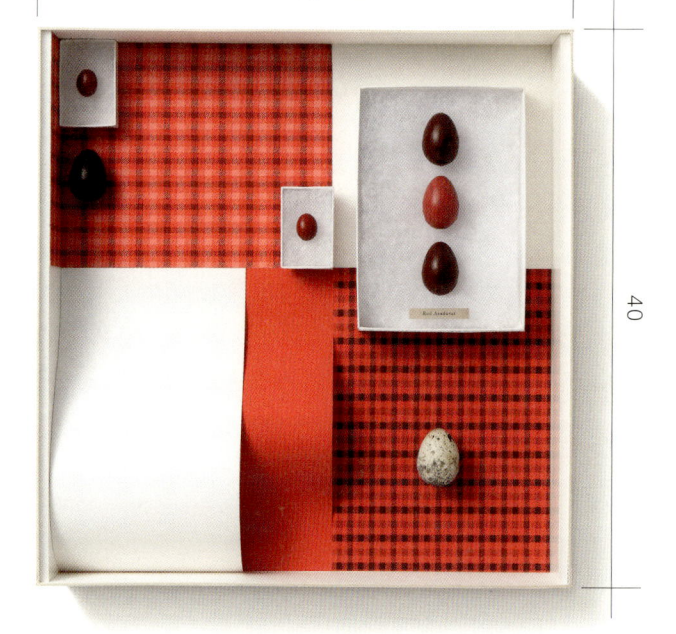

Photo by Shuji Yoshida

DESIGN PROCESS

2000年にスタートした、子供服ブランド、ファミリアへのシーズンコンセプトプレゼンテーション。毎年春夏、秋冬と年2回に分けて、シーズンテーマ、テーマのネーミング、使用するカラーを提案します。パリで開かれるプルミエール・ヴィジョンなどのファッショントレンド情報を参考に作成する独自のシーズンパレットは、ファミリアの展示会場でも反映され、シーズンごとの世界観を演出しています。

TYD began creating seasonal concept presentations for Familiar, a Japanese children's clothing company in 2000. Dividing the seasons in two, spring/summer and fall/winter, every concept explores the naming and color palette for the season. The concept functions as a guide and inspiration for the collection and the exhibition space. As part of our consulting, we also research current trends in fashion, textiles and colors such as the *Première Vision*.

卵の彩色から箱の制作まですべて手作業。百個以上の卵をスタッフの手で一つひとつ丁寧にペイントしていきました。この時期は来客が多く、"TYDってグラフィックデザイン事務所…なんですよね?"と、不思議そうな顔で尋ねられることもあったほど。コンピュータでミリ単位の正確な図面を制作しながらも、同時に手作業でしか表現できない暖かみのあるデザインも大切にする、"コンセプト"を、"カタチ"にするための行程や作業中の会話は、次のプロジェクトのアイデアにつながることも多いのです。こうしてカラフルで暖かみのある十六個のボックスが完成しました。

柴田陽生 (TYD グラフィック・デザイナー)

From the coloring of eggs to the assembling of the presentation boxes, everything was created in-house by hand. For the 2010 season's concept, we painted over 100 eggs in different colors. During this project we had numerous visitors to the office and many asked, "isn't TYD a graphic design studio?" While the computer is precise and convenient, we are made aware of the warmth of handmade presentations which cannot be translated through a screen of a computer. While our hands were busy creating mock-ups, our minds were free to engage in interesting conversations which often lead to new design ideas. A total of 16 colorful boxes were made containing these colored eggs.
Yosei Shibata (Graphic Designer at TYD)

カラーリングされた卵はオフィスの中央のデスクに並べられ、一足早いイースターのような光景だった。
Our long desk was transformed into an egg coloring station. It was as if Easter came a little early to TYD that year.

対談 Conversation

想いを箱に詰めて届ける

フェリシモ　矢崎 和彦

「haco」というネーミングが出発点

八木：1984年、私がアートディレクターとして働くことになった、アメリカのアパレルメーカー「エスプリ」では、当時200万冊ものカタログをつくって通販ビジネスを展開していました。ここでの経験は、私に大きな影響を与えています。「エスプリ」での経験を生かした上で「フェリシモ」と仕事をしてみると、カタログの作成チームにはプロフェッショナルな女性スタッフがたくさんいらっしゃって、内容はもちろんですが、カタログや商品のネーミングの発想にいつも感心しています。

矢崎：ありがとうございます。

八木：1999年に創刊された『ecolor(エコラ)』というカタログがありましたね。「ecology(エコロジー)」と「color(カラー)」を組み合わせた造語ですが、当時から環境問題に着目し、時代を先取りしたネーミングには唸りました。

矢崎：『ecolor』は、復刊して、2、3年前から、順調に売り上げも伸びています。

八木：フェリシモのカタログには、『ecolor』以外にも魅力的なネーミングのカタログがたくさんありますね。商品でもビジネスでもネーミングはとても大切で、受け手はそのネーミングからいろいろなイメージを想像しますから。通販カタログ『haco』も、そういう意味で、すばらしいネーミングだと思います。このネーミングに決めたきっかけは何だったのですか？

矢崎：『haco』のコンセプトを練っている当時は、セレクトショップが一世風靡していました。フェリシモのターゲットは若い人たちなので、彼らが魅力を感じてくれる「セレクトショップ」や、彼らが出かけたくなるような「街」をコンセプトにしようと決めたのです。二次元の平面の紙に商品写真を貼り付けたようなものではなく、三次元の空間的な広がりのある平面を超えたカタログを目指そうということで、『haco』というネーミングにしました。それに『haco』は、シンプルで覚えやすい名前でもありますしね。

八木：覚えやすいことは重要ですね。それに「箱」という言葉には、いろいろな意味があるように思います。

矢崎：以前、『箱』というタイトルの哲学的な内容の本を読んで、すごく印象的だった記憶もあります。一方で「箱物行政」「箱入り娘」とか、わりとネガティブな意味合いで使われることも多いのです。私自身は、入れ物としての「箱」はあまり重要ではなく、そこに何を入れるか、箱の中身が大切だ、と思っています。

八木：たしかに。私も、デザインのプレゼンテーションで、よく「箱」を使います。箱の中には私たちのメッセージやイメージを詰めて、それをクライアントに見ていただきながら、私たちのデザインの世界観を伝えていくんです。『haco』は、通販カタログという形式の箱の中に、どのような情報を詰めていくか、消費者にどんな魅力を感じてもらうかという、「フェリシモ」にとっての実験モデルと受け取っているのですが？

矢崎：そう、『haco』というカタログの中に、一つの「街」が存在する、というイメージなんです。

八木：なるほど、箱が街で、その中にさまざまなショップやブランドが軒を連ねているということですね。

商品の裏にある想い

矢崎：今の若い人たちのショッピングは、単に洋服を買っているのではありません。その背景にある物語やイメージも見ています。2001年9月11日ニューヨークのテロ事件が起きたときに、私たちフェリシモでは、その遺児や孤児たちの支援を目的としたTシャツをつくることにしました。ちょうど『haco』プロジェクトの準備中で、取引先やデザイナーさんたちとコラボレーションしながら進めていきました。つまりこのTシャツは単なる商品ではなく、たくさんの人たちの支援活動への想いが込められているわけです。

八木：そのTシャツはまだありますか？

矢崎：あると思います。Tシャツにはロゴなどは一切入れていませんが、最終的には10何万枚か売れて、基金も4、5000万円になったと聞いています。このプロジェクトはその後もいろいろな方に協力してもらって、どんどん進化しているのです。Tシャツの素材であるコットンも、『haco』の名付け親であるスタッフがインドまで出かけて行って、フェリシモが買い上げを保証するというかたちで、オーガニックコットンをつくってもらっています。

八木：プロジェクトを通して人から人へ、土地から土地へと拡がりを感じますね。ブランドのファンは、こういった商品の背景や物語に共感しているんでしょうね。

矢崎：最初は、単に洋服を詰め込んだ「箱」だったのが、今ではいろいろな人の想いや願いを詰めた『haco』に進化しています。さらに、国内外でフェリシモの理念が広まりつつあって、こうした企画を実践している企業の商品だからこそ、ぜひ買いたいと言ってくださるお客様も増えています。とはいっても、私たちだけがいくら念じていても、周辺に同じ想いを抱いている方々がいないと何もはじまりません。そういう意味で、お客様が私たちの想いに敏感に反応してくださってはじめて、いろいろなことが実現できると思っています。

八木：社会に対する信頼性を示すという点では、アメリカにも同じような動きがあります。たとえば、建築。デザイン、マテリアル、オペレーション、施工業者などが優れていると選定された建物に対してLEED(Leadership in Energy and Environmental Design)から4段階に分けた認証を与えることによって、良い建物の建設を振興するのです。サンフランシスコですと、レンゾ・ピアノが設計した「サイエンス・オブ・アカデミー」が知られています。私のクライアントであるナパバレーのホテル「バーデソノ」や、バークレーにある「デビット・ブラワー・センター」なども認証をもらっています。こう考えてくると、企業活動も建築も、社会的責任に目を配らなくてはならない時代になったと感じますね。カタログなどを通して社会へのメッセージを発信することが、フェリシモという企業のアイデンティティになっていると思います。

矢崎：来年度の新卒採用の募集には、例年の倍、2万人弱の応募がありました。彼らに、なぜ当社で働きたいのかと質問したところ、ほとんどの方がこうした活動に関わりたいことを理由の一つにあげていました。

幸せの箱を届ける

矢崎：話は戻りますが、「箱」はフェリシモにとって絶対的に必要なエレメントの一つです。

八木：お客様がフェリシモから最初に受け取る商品は「箱」に入っていますし、カタログタイトルもそうですからね。

矢崎：実際は通販カタログを最初にお届けするのですが、カタログで注文していただいた商品は、かならず「箱」に入ってお客様のもとに届きます。昨日の面接で、うれしさのあまり泣きそうになった話がありました。九州から来た女子に入社希望の理由を尋ねたのです。その子の母親がフェリシモのお客様だそうで、箱が届くたびにその子のお母様はとても嬉しそうに開けていたとか。その箱の中にはときどき自分や兄弟のものが混ざっていることもあったそうです。子育てで外出もままならない母親とその子どもたちにとって、毎月届く「フェリシモ」の箱が大きな喜びであり、生活の潤いだったと言うのです。そして、その子どもが成長して当社を受けることになったというのですから、たった一つの「箱」にも、いろいろな想いが詰まっているのだなあと、あらためて感じ入りました。

八木：母から子どもへ、まさに「幸せの箱」ですね。社員一人ひとりが、フェリシモに就職する以前から、このブランドに対する思い出や熱い想いを抱いているのですね。商品の送り手として、送られるお客様の立場を経験し、理解しているからこそ、伝えられることも多いのだと思います。

矢崎：同じ買い物でも、店での買い物は代金と引き替えで商品を受け取るので、すぐに手に入る喜びはありますが、それでしかない。ところが通販の場合、注文してから手元に届くまでの時差があるから、ワクワクする気持ちが持続するし、支払いは自分なのだけれど自分への贈り物のような気持ちを持つこともできます。最近は、特別感を高めようと考えて、「クリスマスは赤の箱」といったように、季節やイベントに合わせて箱に色柄をつけたりもしています。

八木：フェリシモさんの箱はまさにビジネスの「かたち」ですね。箱を通してブランドの理念が表現されているように感じます。

矢崎：そう、フェリシモは「箱」に、私たちの想いを託しているのかもしれません。

八木：ストライプの箱を見たときに思いました。どの媒体を介して自分たちのメッセージを発信するのか、企業にとってその部分のデザインが一番重要なポイント。「箱」も何の仕掛けもなければただの箱です。けれども、ストライプの箱にすることで、ある種のメッセージが発せられて、「フェリシモ」だけの箱になる。僕はエスプリ時代に、レシートの裏側をデザインしたことがあります。お客様は買い物の際、かならずレシートを受け取りますよね。こんなすばらしい媒体だから、企業のメッセージをレシートの裏側にも、デザインしようと思い立ったわけです。デザインを通して、ブランドの世界観や想いを隙間なく伝えることに重要性を感じています。

矢崎：「箱」という話題だけで、八木さんのデザイン感を通していろいろな話に、つながっていきましたね。

八木：また機会があったら、ゆっくり「箱談義」をしたいものです。

TO BOX AND DELIVER AN EXPERIENCE
KAZUHIKO YAZAKI / Felissimo

Stories Inside the Box

TY: Kazuhiko Yazaki is the president of Felissimo, a company based in Kobe. Today I would like to discuss your company's products, business model and theory. Let's start with the success of your catalog. What I appreciate about Felissimo's catalog is that it captures the theme of the products with a clever title. When I started working at the American apparel company Esprit in 1984, we printed 2 million catalogues. I was amazed at the volume of sales that mail order could generate. Overseeing the art direction and layout of this catalog had an immense impact on my future design work, including projects for Felissimo. This experience also makes me appreciate how your catalog captures the theme of the products with a clever title.

KY: Thank you.

TY: I remember one catalog named "Ecolor." Ecology + Color = Ecolor...what a great name.

KY: We started the catalog in 2009.

TY: Naming is very important in any type of business. A customer's first impression of a company is formed by the brand name. The name also communicates the brand's identity.

KY: Yes, names and new business models are both important. When we developed the "haco" catalog, most young people shopped in retail environments. Our challenge was to attract the younger generation to a 2-dimensional catalog without losing the real life shopping experience: We wanted to simulate the familiar 3-dimensional shopping excursion within the flat pages of the catalog. The name "haco," meaning box, was both appropriate and easy to remember. We tried to express that there was a story to be discovered within our "haco" catalog, like the story that would normally unfold when you shopped in the city.

TY: So your Haco actually symbolizes a city, full of multiple stores and opportunities.

Stories Behind the Products

KY: Customers today are knowledgeable about a product's story and background. They shop to fulfill their needs, and ideally serve a larger purpose. After the unfortunate terrorist attack on September 11, 2001, we made T-shirts to raise money for charity. We collaborated with multiple designers and different clients to orchestrate this project. Our efforts became more than just T-shirts, they were the realization of many peoples' efforts to support the cause.

TY: That's wonderful, did Felissimo document this good-will project and keep shirts for their archive?

KY: I think so. We ended up selling one hundred thousand T-shirts and raised $500,000 for a good cause. The organic cotton used for the shirts was from India, and was purchased directly through Felissimo.

TY: I can see the link here between people around the world all trying to offer support.

KY: Exactly. This project also introduced our brand to many people overseas. It attracted new customers who identified with our philosophy. The T-shirts, like the catalog, became a "haco" which told a story filled with universal emotions.

TY: Along with supporting those in need, it is also becoming a global priority to design with environmental consciousness

LEED (Leadership in Energy and Environmental Design) is an internationally recognized green design certification system. Corporations are aligning their values to demonstrate both social and environmental awareness.

Stories Send a Message

KY: I heard an interesting story yesterday when I was interviewing a potential employee. I asked this woman why she was applying for a position at Felissimo, and she described the impact of receiving our boxes when she was a child. Her parents worked and did not have time to shop for the family, so they purchased products by mail-order. The family received packages from Felissimo every month, and this exciting experience remained one of the woman's happiest childhood memories. Now as an adult, she wanted to work in the shipping department at Felissimo to share that same joy. It is particularly satisfying to receive something you really desire. Mail-order requires patience as the package has to be shipped, but there is something very special about the expectation. Although there is a cost for that product, there are multiple returns and benefits.

TY: Felissimo's box is shaped by the company's philosophy.
KY: Indeed, we package our personal values and emotions within the box.
TY: Your simple striped package design is very elegant. Although the outer shipping box is primarily just protection for the goods, even the smallest design element helps differentiate this box from others. The box itself can become an extension of the brand's identity. This is true for other parts of the package along with purchase records. At Esprit, I designed a special receipt as another opportunity to apply the brand's image.
KY: Yes, what starts out simple can actually become quite complex...just as our conversation about "boxes" has grown into something more compelling.
TY: Thank you so much, I look forward to discussing these topics further.

TY: Tamotsu Yagi
KY: Kazuhiko Yazaki

Tamotsu Yagi's Design Resource Collection Box

矢崎 和彦　1955年、大阪生まれ。株式会社フェリシモ代表取締役社長。1987年学習院大学経済学部卒業。2005年神戸大学大学院経営学研究科修了。元神戸経済同友会代表幹事、神戸商工会議所二号議員。神戸市デザインアドバイザリーボードメンバー、ソーシャルビジネスネットワーク常任顧問などを歴任。1995年よりユネスコ本部との共催によるデザイン21プロジェクトを運営。事業性、独創性、社会性の融合を目指すコーポレート・スタイル・デザイン経営が関心テーマ。2010年毎日経済人賞受賞。

Kazuhiko Yazaki was born in Osaka, Japan in 1955 and is the Representative Director of Felissimo. After graduating from Gakushuin University Faculty of Economics in 1987 then graduating from the School of Business Administration in Kobe University, he worked at the Kobe Association of Corporate Executives and at the Kobe Chamber of Commerce and Industry. He was also a member of the board of Kobe City's Design Advisory and Executive Adviser of Social Business Networks, and started Design 21 Project in 1995.

DEN
THIS BAG DUE TO TRANSFER AT
DEN
Air Canada
YYC
CALGARY
079855
FLIGHT No VOL N°
ASE
50-04-05
ASPEN, CO
cabin baggage
ASE
American Airlines
DCA
DCA
DCA
DCA
DCA
ON LINE TRANSFER TAG
FS 657 Rev 11/85
Garuda
DONESIAN AIRWAYS
FRAGILE
ABQ
FLY SOUTHWEST
FLIGHT
TO
ABQ
TRANSFER
SFO
SAN FRANCISCO, CALIF.
FLIGHT
TO
SFO
DEN-D
THIS BAG DUE TO TRANSFER AT
CONTINENTAL AIRLINES
16·13 9
SFO
SAN FRANCISCO, C
TRANSFER AT
EN-D

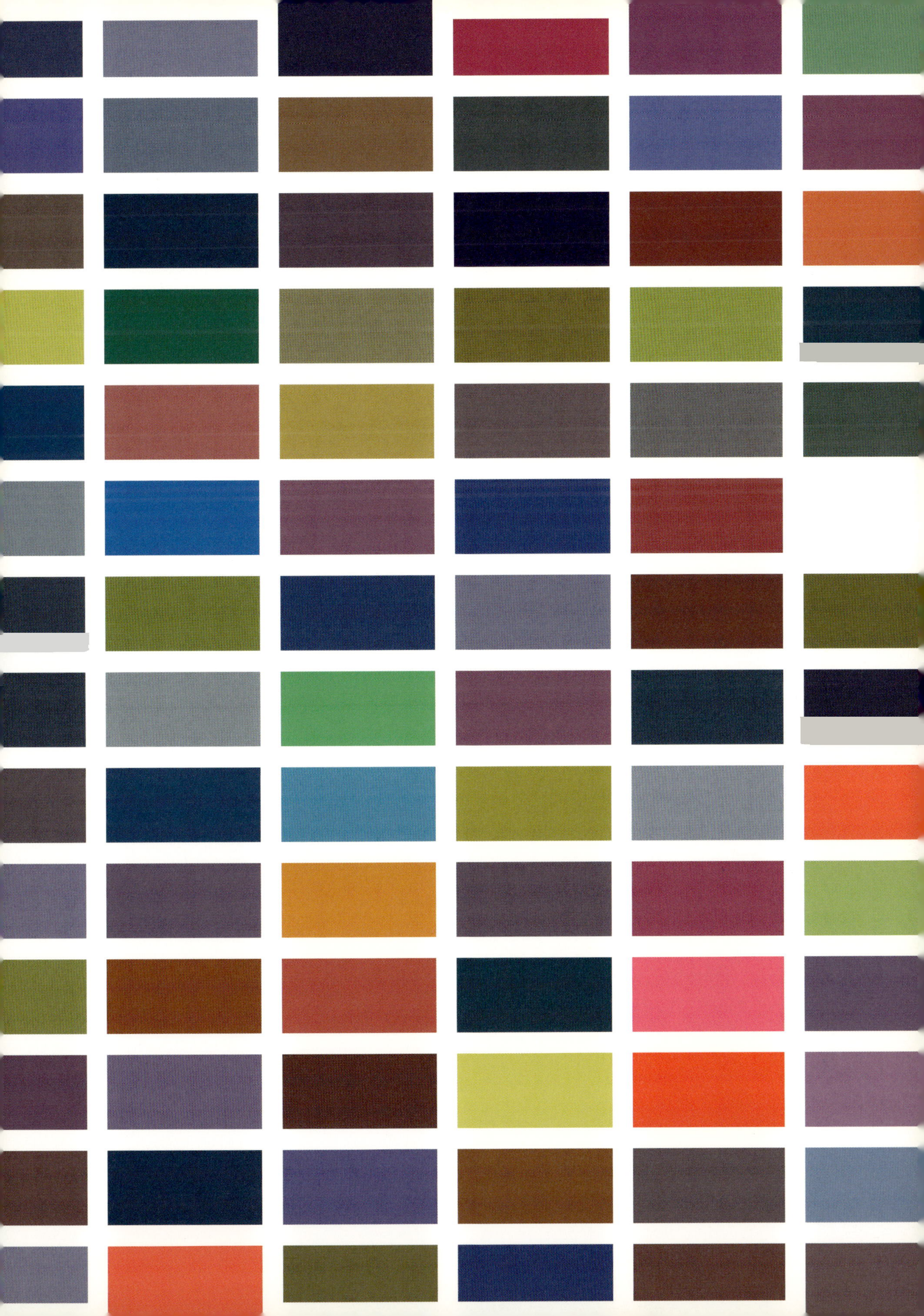

2006

KENZO ESTATE

Package Design and Brand Identity

In 1921, the Spaulding brothers donated 382 pieces of their legendary collection of Utamaro's Japanese *ukiyo-e* prints to the Boston Museum. They requested the prints to be archived inside the wooden box it came in so that the delicate colors would not fade over time. When the prints were revealed to the public in December of 2006, people were awed by Utamaro's art, rich in *ai* (indigo) color that had been so well preserved. For Kenzo Estate, the story of Utamaro's indigo shared qualities with wine making, from the delicacy of these natural ingredients to the wines they inspire. The naming of the wine, "ai" and "murasaki" were given by the owner of Kenzo Estate, Mr. Tsujimoto. This story that influenced the wine naming inspired the brand development for the winery.

藍　紫

Making of a winery and its comprehensive graphic identity

一九二一年にスポルディング兄弟は、喜多川歌磨の浮世絵三八二枚を、ボストン美術館に寄贈。退色を防ぐため、作品を木箱に納め、保管し、一切の展示を禁じました。二〇〇六年十二月、二百年以上の歳月を経て開封された歌磨の浮世絵の鮮明な紫色に、みな驚愕したのです。歌磨の紫とワインの世界には、「ART + SCIENCE」という多くの共通点があることから、誕生したワインは、ケンゾーエステイトのオーナーの辻本憲三氏の考案したネーミング、「藍＝ai」、「紫＝murasaki」に決まりました。
そして、ブランドアイデンティティの展開は、今も進行しています。

THE COLORS BEHIND THE NAMING

"THE MOST BEAUTIFUL EXPERIENCE WE CAN HAVE IS THE MYSTERIOUS - THE FUNDAMENTAL EMOTION WHICH STANDS AT THE CRADLE OF TRUE ART AND TRUE SCIENCE."
— ALBERT EINSTEIN

"私たちが経験するいちばん美しいことは、MYSTERIOUS(神秘的)なことだ。その根本的な感情こそが、真のARTそしてSCIENCEを育てることになる。" アルバート・アインシュタイン

Photo by Stefano Massei

MATERIAL PALETTE

ai

Ai is Japanese for indigo dye or the plant itself. *Ai* has a very distinct, dark blue color and dyes deeply into various materials. The use of *ai* dates back hundreds of years and is deeply embedded in the Japanese culture. The similarity between the historic craft of *ai* dyeing and wine blending is the inspiration behind the naming of ai, Kenzo Estate's red wine. Grapes, like *ai* are natural ingredients therefore their flavors vary due to factors such as the weather, the vineyard, as well as the blending technique.

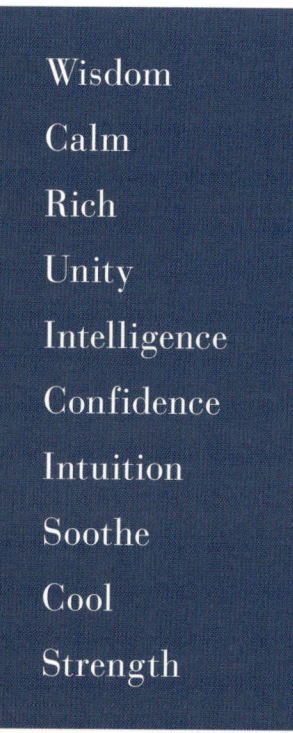

Wisdom
Calm
Rich
Unity
Intelligence
Confidence
Intuition
Soothe
Cool
Strength

Royal
Noble
Dignity
Mystery
Rebirth
Divine
Compassion
Imagination
Inspiration
Vision

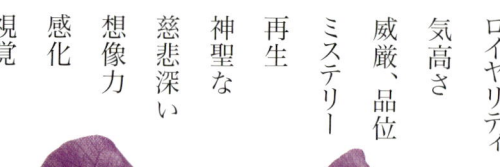

ロイヤリティ
気高さ
威厳、品位
ミステリー
再生
神聖な
慈悲深い
想像力
感化
視覚

murasaki

Scientific analysis of the unique purple color used by the Japanese *ukiyo-e* artist, Utamaro Kitagawa revealed a careful mix of red safflower and blue asian dayflower, both delicate flowers prone to fading. Kenzo Estate's vines are grown with great care to produce the best quality grapes for winemaking. Utamaro's artistic and scientific process of blending and working with these delicate natural ingredients inspired the naming murasaki, (purple in Japanese) for Kenzo Estate's other red wine.

「藍」は藍草の葉で染めた色の総称であり、あるいは染料となる「藍」という植物を指すこともある。また、絹や羊毛などの動物繊維にも、木綿や麻などの植物繊維にもよく染まることから、世界中のあらゆる地域で使用され愛されて行った。気候風土やブレンドによって品質が大きく左右されながらも、世界各地で行なわれているワインづくり。藍染めの工程とワインづくりには多くの共通点があることから、このワインは「藍」と名付けられた。

藍

知恵
静穏
豊富、裕福
単一、調和
知能、知恵
自信
直感
なだめる
冷静
強さ

紫

喜多川歌麿の浮世絵の紫の色を科学的に検証したところ、赤系の紅花と青系の露草を混ぜ合わせた色であることがわかった。歌麿が使った紫が色褪せしやすく、はかない色だからこそ、大切に慈しみながら色を遺していく。大事に育てられた葡萄も一粒一粒はつぶれやすく繊細なもの。その葡萄からつくりだすワインを後世につなげていきたいという想いと、深い赤紫の葡萄色という事実を重ねて「紫」と名付けられた。

Photo by Stefano Massei

COLOR STUDY

藍白

古代紫

日本には美しい色を表わす、名前がある。藍が使われている色名には、藍白、青藍、紺藍、紫が使われている色名は、京紫、古代紫、若紫など、91種類もある。
In the Japanese language, there are a total of 91 *kanji* character combinations paired to capture the color variances within the indigo and purple color group.

ケンゾー エステイトは、カリフォルニア州のナパに位置する。ワイナリーの敷地は東京都の中野区とほぼ同じ大きさで、標高80mの丘陵地は豊かな自然に包まれている。私たちは、その広大な敷地の中で鳥の羽、鳥の巣、落ち葉、枯れ葉、石、土などのさまざまな自然素材を拾い集めて、ブランドイメージをつくる手がかりの一つとした。

Kenzo Estate's 70 acre vineyard is located in Napa, California and is a vast property with incredible wildlife. We collected objects such as bird feathers, bird's nests, leaves, rocks and soil samples from the property as essential research to create the brand identity.

青藍

京紫

紺藍

若紫

Photo by Shuji Yoshida

COLOR STUDY

カラーピクセルで表現した葡萄。そのピクセル（デジタルの画像の1粒）を見ながら、私たちがイメージする藍、紫の色に近いものを選び出し、その色のパントーンカラーにあてはめる。そして、藍はパントーン8781C、紫はパントーン8802Cに決定。

Pictured is a pixilated image of a grape. We examined the pixilated colors that made up the image of the grape and selected two colors to represent Kenzo Estate's ai and murasaki wines. The selections translated to Pantone #8781c for ai and Pantone #8802c for murasaki.

PANTONE 8781 C

PANTONE 8802 C

GRAPHIC IDENTITY

KENZO ESTATE

ai

murasaki

KENZO ESTATE

2.5

4.5

「ai」の「A」と「murasaki」の「M」の洗練されたスクリプトフォントと、漢字の「藍」や「紫」は、同じうっすらと光るパール箔で印刷して、ラベルのレイアウトでの上下のバランスをとった。レストランの卓上で、エレガントな光り方でフォントが浮かび上がように奥ゆかしい和の美を意識した。

Secondary elements, "A" and "M" of ai and murasaki and its *kanji* characters where foil stamped with a pearl color. The pearl finish captured the understated Japanese aesthetic but gave the label a light and elegant shimmer, an effect that could be enjoyed in a restaurant setting.

原寸 | Actual Size

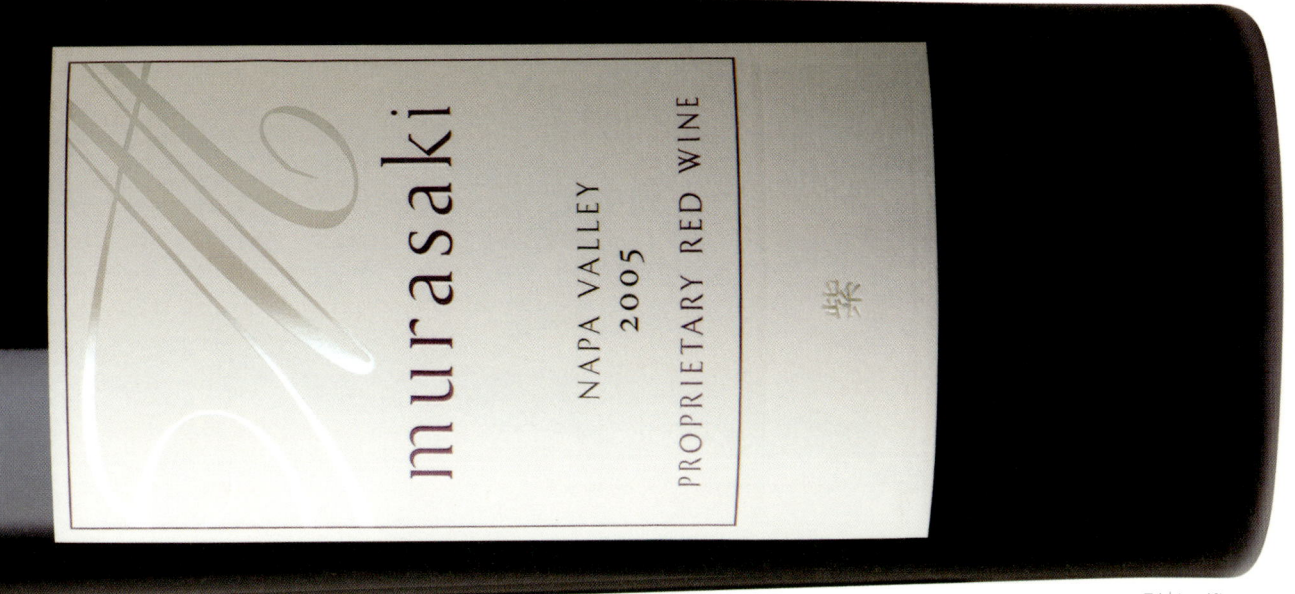

原寸 | Actual Size

2005年はオフセットで印刷、2006年からエングレービングで印刷した。
Labels from the 2005 vintage were printed in a waterless offset and in 2006, the labels were engraved.

Photo by Shuji Yoshida

PACKAGE DESIGN

上／2005年のファースト・リリースは、藍と紫のツインボトルをそれぞれ藍色と紫色の風呂敷に包んで木箱に納めた。和洋折衷でありながら現代的な感覚にマッチした贈り方を意識した。
下／「藍」のハーフケースの木箱。6本のボトルは「藍」色の薄紙で、1本ずつ手作業で包んだ。年号を印字したシールも1本ずつ手で貼ってある。

Top: The 2005 vintage bottles were wrapped in traditional Japanese *furoshiki* cloth in indigo and purple colors. The wrapped bottles were then packaged inside a wooden case, representing a mix of eastern and western sensibilities.
Bottom: A wooden case for six ai bottles. The wines were individually wrapped in indigo colored tissue and secured by hand with a monogramed sticker.

A ai

M murasaki

サンフランシスコ在住のデザイナーのポートフォリオには、ワインラベルのデザインの仕事が多い。そういう意味でも、私にとって、ケンゾー エステイトのプロジェクトに参加できたことは、デザイナーとして価値のあることでした。さらに栽培家デイビット・アブリュー、醸造家ハイジ・バレットという、ワインの世界で一流と評価されている人々と一緒に仕事ができて、未知なるワインの世界の扉が開きました。現在、ケンゾーエステイトの広大な敷地では、ワインだけでなく、上質なオリーブオイルやハチミツの生産体制も整い、それらのプロジェクトも進行中です。

This project was exciting for me as the client was Japanese but the winery was based locally in Napa Valley, an area close to San Francisco. This project opened my eyes to the fascinating culture of wine and I was privileged to work with some of the world's leading artisans, David Abreu, renowned viticulturist and Heidi Barrett, the talented wine maker. In addition, I was also asked to design the complete package for the Moegi olive oil, harvested from the trees that grow on the 3,800 acre property of Kenzo Estate.

「ai」と「murasaki」がセットで入るオリジナルの木箱は、木のささくれがなく、角に滑らかな丸みをもたせることで手に馴染み、持ちやすいものとなった。

The edges of the wooden box set of ai and murasaki were rounded to present a smooth and elegant finish.

VISUAL PRESENTATION

限られた時間でよりわかりやすいプレゼンテーションを行なうために、眼で見て触れることのできるサンプルをつくって、デザインの意図を説明します。ワインは、もともと西洋のものですが、日本語のブランド名を英語と漢字でどのように表現し、ラベルのなかに納めるか、いくつものアプローチからアイデアを導き出しました。普通はメーカー名をフロントラベルに置きますが、私はあえて「KENZO ESTATE」をバックラベルにレイアウトしました。

To effectively present our designs and to best utilize our time during our meeting with the client, we created presentations that simulated real life products. This format helped aid the client in visualizing the finished product, which is often a challenge when working off flat renderings or digital files. The unique heritage of the winery, one that is a blend of western and eastern roots were considered in the overall graphic design.

The presentation for Kenzo Estate was one of the most memorable projects I was involved in during my internship at TYD. The front labels were arced to mimic the curvature of a bottle and different color caps were prepared in a way that could be changed during the presentation. The presentation materials were placed on a large table as if they were exhibited like an art piece. From the meeting's atmosphere, I felt the passion and seriousness of Mr. Tsujimoto. I had a great experience learning the most efficient and productive way to deliver a design concept that integrated all five senses.

Dai Hikita (Graphic Designer at HDO)

TYDでインターンシップをしていた頃、一番印象に残るプロジェクトがケンゾー エステイトのプレゼンテーションでした。デザインの方向性を決定するために用意したものは、デザイン案すべてに「アール」をつけ立体的に表現されたフロントラベル。その場で付け替えられるよう準備されたキャップのカラーバリエーションでした。それらはまるで美術館の展示のように美しく、クライアントの辻本氏が思案されているときも、真剣さのなかに楽しげな空気が流れていたように感じました。常に相手の状況に合わせ、もっとも効率的で、かつ五感で魅せる仕事の進め方に対して、心から凄い！と感心し、勉強になりました。

引田 大（H.D.O. グラフィック・デザイナー）

2011年にリリースされたロゼワイン、「結＝yui」のプレゼンテーション用につくった紙のキャップのデザイン。キャップはこのようにオリジナルのボトルに入るようにつくり、フロントラベルと合うかを検証しました。「yui」は、漢字で書くと「結」。「結納」など「結ぶ」という意味にちなんで、祝い事のときに飲んでほしいロゼワインです。

The yui rosé wine was released in 2011. Pictured is a paper mock-up of the cap design for the presentation. The caps were designed at the same time as the label in order to keep the overall design congruent. Yui's *kanji* character means "to tie" or "to merge" and is the perfect rosé to be enjoyed for a celebratory occasion.

キャップは、スペインでつくるので最初に入稿することになった。特別な色は、ペイントでつくって業者に指定。2カ月で、指定色近いサンプルができあがり、最終決定をした。

The caps were made in Spain therefore, its design was a priority. Various pearl pink colors were specified, matched then approved for the final cap design.

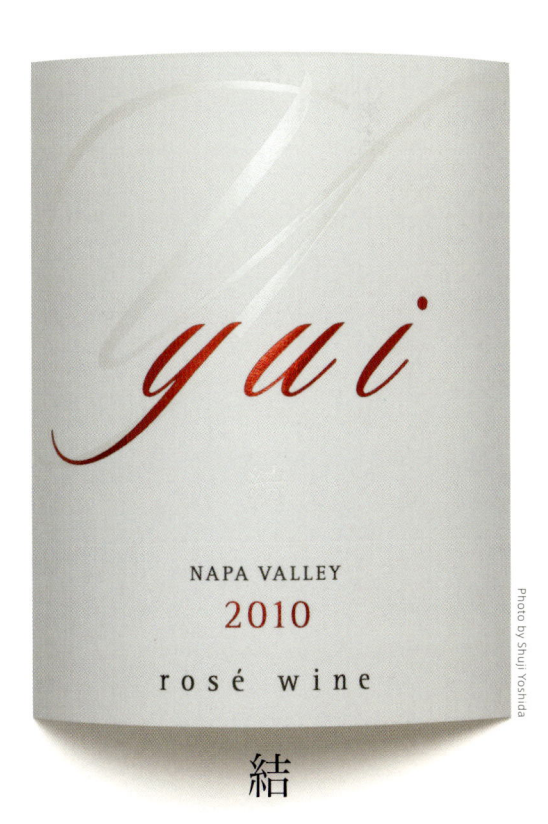

yui

NAPA VALLEY
2010

rosé wine

結

「yui」の750mlのラベルは、ロゴと年号には赤の箔、「yui」のスクリプト「Y」と漢字の「結」は、「藍」や「紫」と同様のパール箔の印刷で、おめでたい紅白のイメージを表現した。
Yui's 750ml label was designed having a similar aesthetic of ai and murasaki by featuring a letter "Y" script on the front label. The red and white pearl foils made the design festive.

84 | Kenzo Estate

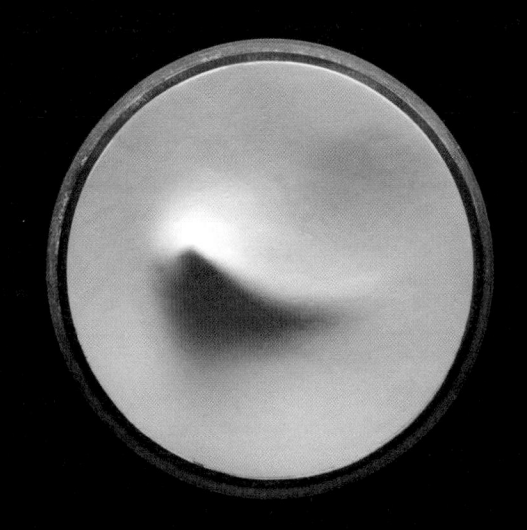

"WHEN I WORK, I WORK VERY FAST, BUT PREPARING TO WORK CAN TAKE ANY LENGTH OF TIME."
—CY TWOMBLY

"私の作業時間はきわめて短い、しかし下準備には永遠と言っても良い程の時間をかける。"
サイ・トゥオンブリー

2009

Established in 1899, Rohto's extensive scientific research helped develop Episteme, their new line of skin care products. Episteme translates to "true knowledge" in Greek and reflects the integrity of Rohto's research as Japan's oldest pharmaceutical company. The brand identity and package design for this project began in the winter of 2007 as a collaboration between Axis and TYD and the project moved at a fast pace through different time zones of Tokyo and San Francisco. With much success, Episteme was launched in the fall of 2009.

ROHTO: EPISTEME
Package Design and Brand Identity

触感美
The science of beauty within simplicity

一八九九年創業のロート製薬が長年にわたる普遍の美への研究と追求、そして科学の視点から開発したスキンケアブランド、エピステーム。エピステームとは、ギリシャの哲学用語で「真の知」を表わし、物事の本質をとらえて探究していく姿勢を意味しています。二〇〇七年冬、アクシス社と私たちのコラボレーションというかたちで、ブランドアイデンティティやデザインのプロジェクトがスタート。東京とサンフランシスコの間であっても時間差のないリアルタイムでスピーディなやりとりで商品化が進み、二〇〇九年秋に、エピステームはデビューしました。

アクシスとのコラボレーションというかたちでスタートしたこのプロジェクト。実は、私とアクシスとの関係は随分と長く、今までにもさまざまなことでお世話になっています。そもそも、1981年にアクシスビルがオープンした際の一連のグラフィックを手がけてからのお付き合い。今でも印象に残っているのが、オープニングイベントであったエットレ・ソットサス展です。私はそのとき初めてソットサス氏と出会い、また、アクシスのスタッフである宮崎光弘さんや関康子さんとも出会ったのです。関さんには、2011年2月の21_21デザインサイト企画展、倉俣史朗とエットレ・ソットサス展の一連のアートディレクションも紹介していただきました。今回のエピステームのプロジェクトはアクシスの宮崎さんからの紹介でした。宮崎さんは『AXIS』誌のアートディレクションを務め、私たちがいくつかのプロジェクトでアクシスフォントを使用できるのも彼のお陰です。アメリカで仕事をしていると、どうしても日本の情報が入ってきづらいので、情報に困ると宮崎さんに連絡することも多く、元アクシスのスタッフの方々ともいまだに懇意にさせてもらっています。宮崎さんやスタッフの方々も、スカイプなどのITを駆使して時間差なく作業を進められ、より深い情報を共通認識し合いながら、ブランドにふさわしいデザイン制作が可能になりました。

This collaborative project with Axis and my relationship with this influential design center began a long time ago. Over the years, we have intersected and supported each other on many special projects. In 1981, the Axis building opened in Tokyo and it was a design hub as it is today. I was very fortunate to work on the graphic identity for Axis and its opening exhibition of Ettore Sottsass, where I met Sottsass for the first time. I also met Yasuko Seki around then, whom in 2010, invited me to work on the graphic design for the Shiro Kuramata and Ettore Sottsass exhibition at the 21_21 Design Sight in Tokyo. This Episteme project was made possible due to Mitsuhiro Miyazaki, whom I also met through previous Axis projects. Today, Mr. Miyazaki is the director of *Axis* magazine and he's kindly let us use their Axis font on various projects, including this very typeface that is used throughout this book. Our ongoing relationship has allowed us to work together on this project with ease.

Photo by Takesue Ezumi

EPISTEME DESIGN PROCESS

11.11.2007 from AXIS

2週間でロゴ、容器、外箱のデザインを提案するというタイトなスケジュールでのコンペ。数日間リサーチを行ない、方向性をスカイプで共有してから、デザインアップまでに1週間。その後は、容器の素材を検討した。素材感は言葉で伝えきれないため、TYDのイメージに近い現物を送ってもらい、日本で似たようなものを探してTYDへ送る、といったやりとりを経て決めていった。外箱については紙を貼り合わせる合紙による一工夫したデザインだったので、どの用紙が一番効果的に見えるか、どのような印刷方法であればデザインがいかせるのか、印刷会社の方と試行錯誤しながら制作を進めた。

A design competition was held for Rohto's new brand Episteme and competitors were asked to design a logo, a bottle and package design in two weeks. We spent a few days Skyping with TYD, with whom we collaborated on this project. We shared our research and ideas and were able to submit a design proposal within a week. Our design submission was chosen for the competition and we immediately started to research materials so the production of the bottles could be coordinated. TYD sent us samples of their material selections, from which we then collected similar samples from sources in Japan. We wanted a distinct paper for the outer package design, therefore we began to gather many paper samples and contacted printers to initiate this process.

11.18.2007 from TYD

デザイン開発にあたっては、医薬品会社であるロート製薬の化粧品であることを常に念頭においた。"肌は肌単独で成り立っているものではなく、体の一部である。体の健康は肌の正常な生育につながり、美肌をつくる。肌の美しさは心を充実させ、体の健康へと還元される"という「循環」という概念からリサーチをスタートした。知的で、厳しい選択眼を持った女性に対する潔さをどうデザインとして表現するか。アクシスとの綿密なスカイプミーティングは時差の関係なく続けられた。実際にクリームを指でなぞったようなキャップデザインのラフ案をアクシスを通してロート製薬へ提案した。

Rohto is a reputable pharmaceutical company with medical and scientific integrity therefore it was important to link this underlining heritage to their new beauty line. The human skin is a living element of the body, and a healthy body promotes the growth of healthy new skin. With this beauty concept in mind, our design objective was to capture the spirit of a woman who is conscious of her potential for physical and inner health. Our design exchange with Axis was very intuitive and effective, a meeting of similar design minds. Our collaboration also utilized both our resources and time very efficiently. For Episteme's cap design, we pitched an idea of somehow capturing traces of a finger stroke, as one would when applying a similiar product.

ロート製薬のプロジェクトリーダーの方とは旧知の間柄で、「宮崎さん、誰か優秀な女性デザイナーを紹介してもらえませんか」と最初に相談を受けました。プロジェクトの内容を聞いて、"私のなかではまずは八木さんの顔が浮かび、「女性ではないですが八木さんを推薦しました」と。すぐにサンフランシスコの八木さんに電話すると、宮崎さんと一緒ならこのプロジェクトに参加してもいいですよ"とうれしい返事をいただき、このプロジェクトがはじまりました。ですから、このコンペに自分がデザインで関わるとは思ってもいなかったのです。

宮崎 光弘（アクシス 取締役）

I've known Rohto's project manager for a while now and when I was asked "do you know of any female designers appropriate for this project?" and although my answer wasn't what I was asked, the first person that immediately came to mind was Mr.Yagi. I recommended him for the project and called Mr.Yagi in San Francisco. He was not keen on entering the competition alone, and proposed that Axis and TYD collaborate. That was how this project began and by chance, we were involved in this memorable project.

Mitsuhiro Miyazaki (Director of Axis)

12.05.2007

from AXIS

プレゼンテーションで提案したデザインに対して、ロート製薬側から、シンプルな美しさにプラスして、「優雅さ」「柔らかさ」「ホッコリする感じ」をプラスしてほしいという要望があった。女性が自宅に帰ってから、就寝前に自分を慈しみ、リラックスする時間に使うための化粧品とはどういったデザインなのか？ まず、色と素材の見直しを行なった。そして、数十人の女性スタッフに"医薬品と女性らしさが組み合わさったデザインはどのようなものか？"とリサーチしながら、試行錯誤を繰り返した。この時期にいくつかの候補の中からブランド名称「エピステーム」が決まり、ロゴの検証をはじめた。

Upon presenting our design ideas to Rohto, the client was keen on emphasizing key points of our design direction, which were to focus on serenity, femininity and to highlight the notion of beauty within simplicity. We asked ourselves, "What kind of skincare would a woman want to use before retiring from a hard day at work?" We collected data from females with a poll on the topic of beauty and skin care which was quite useful. We explored materials and colors at this phase and also selected the brand name, Episteme which allowed us to begin the logo design for this project.

Photo by Shuji Yoshida

キャップの制作はとても印象的でした。所作をキャップのデザインに取り入れるには、実際に指でなぞってみないとその表現ができないのでは？ということで、シンプルな円柱の紙粘土を何十個もつくり、その円柱をキャップに見立てて開け閉めする動作を重ねていきました。また、クリームをすくいとる動きを表現するために、実際にホイップでも試してみましたし、シリコンなども使って試作しました。最適な方法が何であるのかわからないなかで、さまざまな素材を使用しながらその場の手作業によって形づくっていきました。
村山麻衣子（アクシス グラフィック・デザイナー）

The process of designing the cap was very involved. To recreate the trace of a stroke of a finger, it was necessary to test the movement with clay. We made many column-shaped clay figures and also tried to capture the motion of opening and closing the cap. In addition, we used whipped cream and silicone for this test. As this was an experiment in itself, our studies were very hands on and involved the use of many types of materials.
Maiko Murayama (Graphic Designer at Axis)

EPISTEME DESIGN PROCESS

01.09.2008 — from TYD

ブランド名の決定を受け、ロゴタイプのデザインなどもパッケージデザインと同時にスタートした。デザインはできるかぎりシンプルに。容器の質感や光沢などで上質さや効果を。さらに、ロート製薬の肌の本質を捉えようとするまっすぐな研究姿勢を表わすよう、科学的であり、透き通った美しさのイメージを彷彿とさせる「試験管」をインスピレーションの源流として、デザインの検討を重ねた。最終的にはコンピュータデータでの制作だったが、この段階でのビジュアルデザインはすべて手描きののスケッチ。ロゴも含めたビジュアルデザインは、手作業でのデザインにこだわった。

Once Episteme was chosen as the name for the brand, we started on the logo and package design. We kept our designs minimal by not adding more decorative elements than needed and aesthetically intergraded Rohto's scientific heritage and message of "pure beauty from within." Given that the product's selling point was also in its effectiveness, we wanted the design to look solid and reliable. With these points in mind, the initial designs were drafted by hand in the earlier stages and then later translated to designs on the computer.

02.19.2008 — from AXIS

試験管をイメージしてデザインされた二重構造を実現するために、当初は磨りガラスで制作しようとしていたが、ガラスだとかなり制約が多く、重くなりすぎてしまうため、プラスチックに変更。素材を変更しても、二重構造のボトルでは太い径になってしまい、女性の手に持つには大きすぎてしまった。そこで、きちんと片手で持てるサイズにし、高さも含めて持ちやすい容器にするために、何度も試行錯誤を重ねた。プレゼン時から懸案になっていた、「優雅さ」や「柔らかさ」について、具体的にどのように表現すればよいか、色の検証を含めて素材の見直しを行なった。

Episteme's inner and outer approach to skin care was considered in developing an elegant bottle design. To visually express this concept, we took inspiration from a scientific test tube and designed a bottle with double layered glass. Mock-ups were created which resulted in a heavier bottle than desired, therefore we substituted the glass with plastic. However, the double layering also produced a bolder bottle which lacked delicacy and was hard to handle. In the end, we modified the design to achieve a bottle that was bold yet easy to handle.

episteme

古巣ロサンゼルスへの移住を決意し、2010年末をもってアクシスを退職。当時の上司であった宮崎さんの勧めで八木さんのスタジオを訪問しました。進行中の本書の台割を拝見し、是非制作のお手伝いをしたいと申し出たところ、偶然にもTYDとアクシスデザインのコラボレーション/ノロジェクトを記録した、本章のデザイン・レイアウトを担当させていただけることになりました。改めて知るエピステム誕生の舞台裏に興味深く作業に取り組みました。
森崎真紀（グラフィック・デザイナー）

When I decided to move back to Los Angeles in 2011, Mr. Miyazaki, the director at Axis, recommended that I visit TYD. During my visit, Mr. Yagi showed me a craft of this book, and kindly offered me an opportunity to help with the production of the book. Coincidentally, I was assigned to work on this particular chapter, a documentary of the collaborative project between TYD and Axis design. Although I was aware of the project while at Axis, it was fascinating to rediscover the thoughts and effort that went into the launch of the Episteme brand design.
Masaki Morisaki (Graphic Designer)

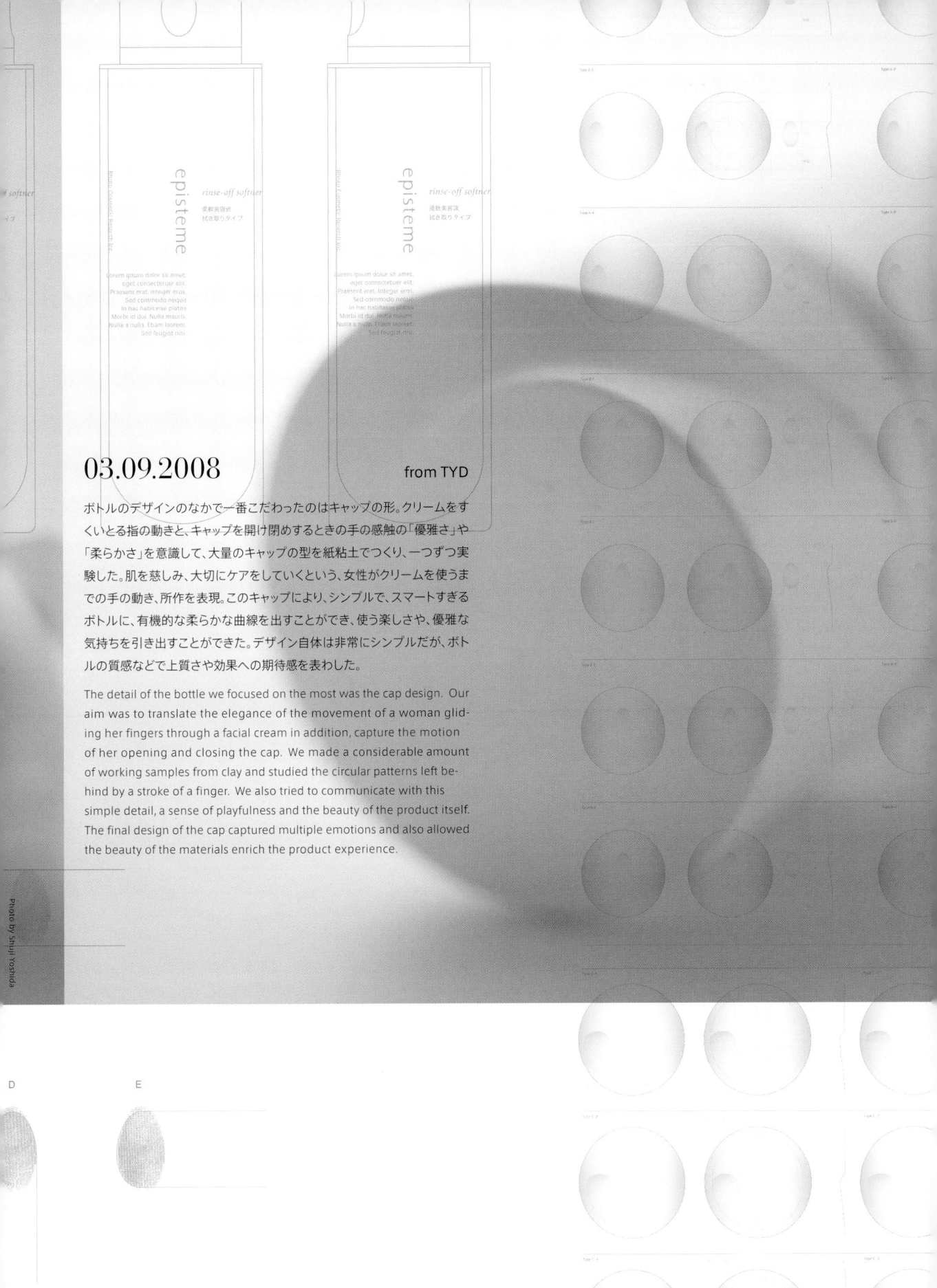

03.09.2008

from TYD

ボトルのデザインのなかで一番こだわったのはキャップの形。クリームをすくいとる指の動きと、キャップを開け閉めするときの手の感触の「優雅さ」や「柔らかさ」を意識して、大量のキャップの型を紙粘土でつくり、一つずつ実験した。肌を慈しみ、大切にケアをしていくという、女性がクリームを使うまでの手の動き、所作を表現。このキャップにより、シンプルで、スマートすぎるボトルに、有機的な柔らかな曲線を出すことができ、使う楽しさや、優雅な気持ちを引き出すことができた。デザイン自体は非常にシンプルだが、ボトルの質感などで上質さや効果への期待感を表わした。

The detail of the bottle we focused on the most was the cap design. Our aim was to translate the elegance of the movement of a woman gliding her fingers through a facial cream in addition, capture the motion of her opening and closing the cap. We made a considerable amount of working samples from clay and studied the circular patterns left behind by a stroke of a finger. We also tried to communicate with this simple detail, a sense of playfulness and the beauty of the product itself. The final design of the cap captured multiple emotions and also allowed the beauty of the materials enrich the product experience.

001003240111   001003240112

101003240111   101003240112

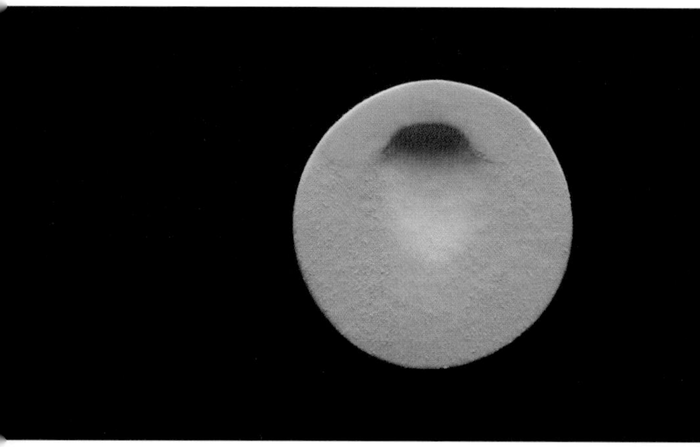

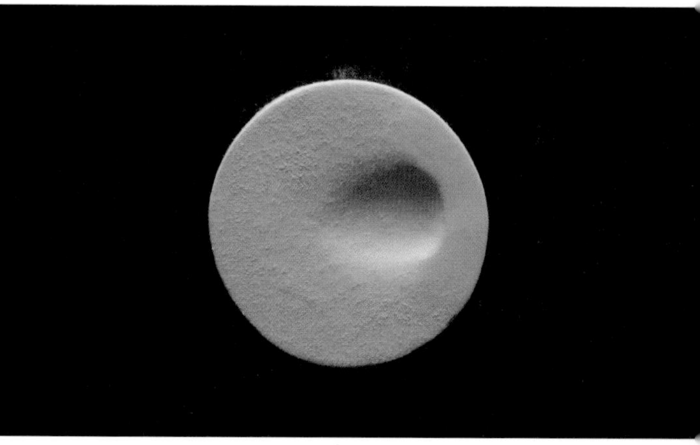

201003240111   201003240112

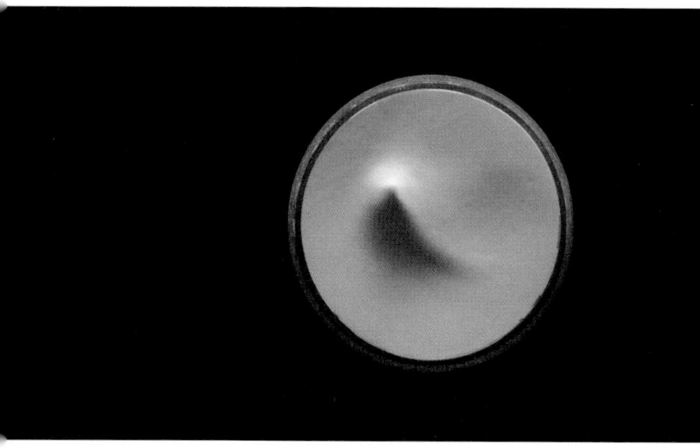

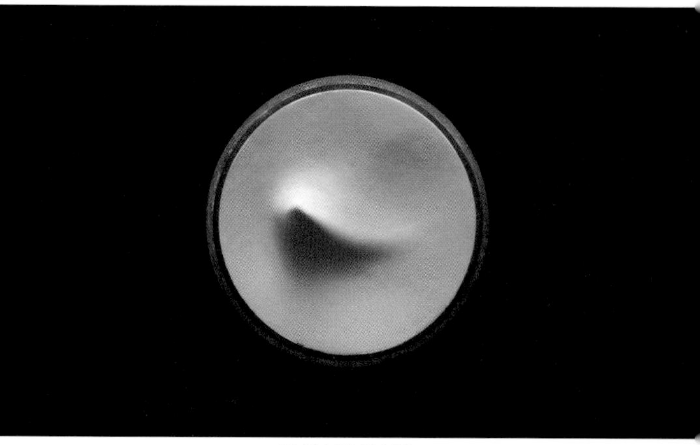

301003240111   301003240112

401003240111   401003240112

001003240113

001003240114

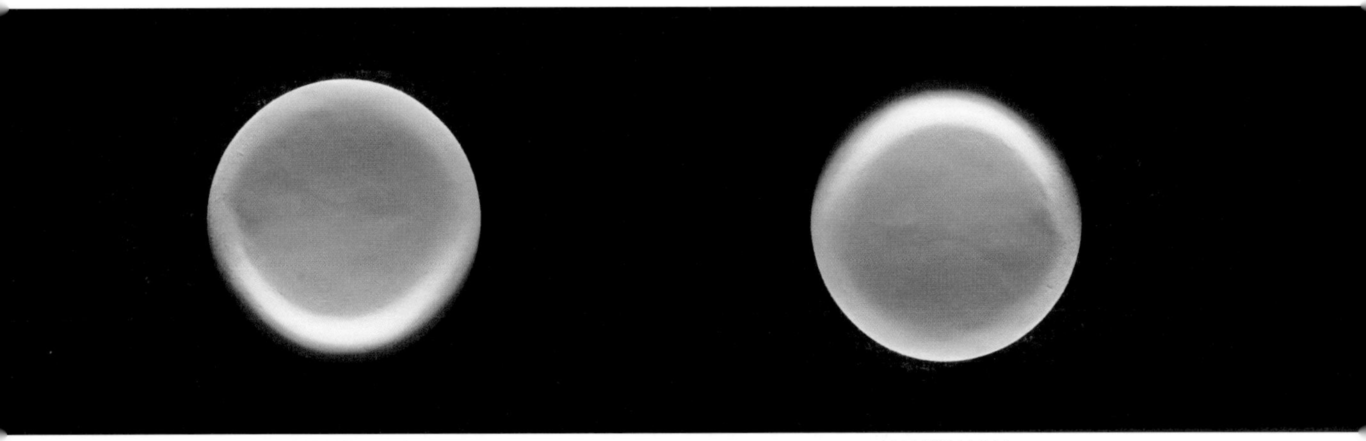

101003240113

101003240114

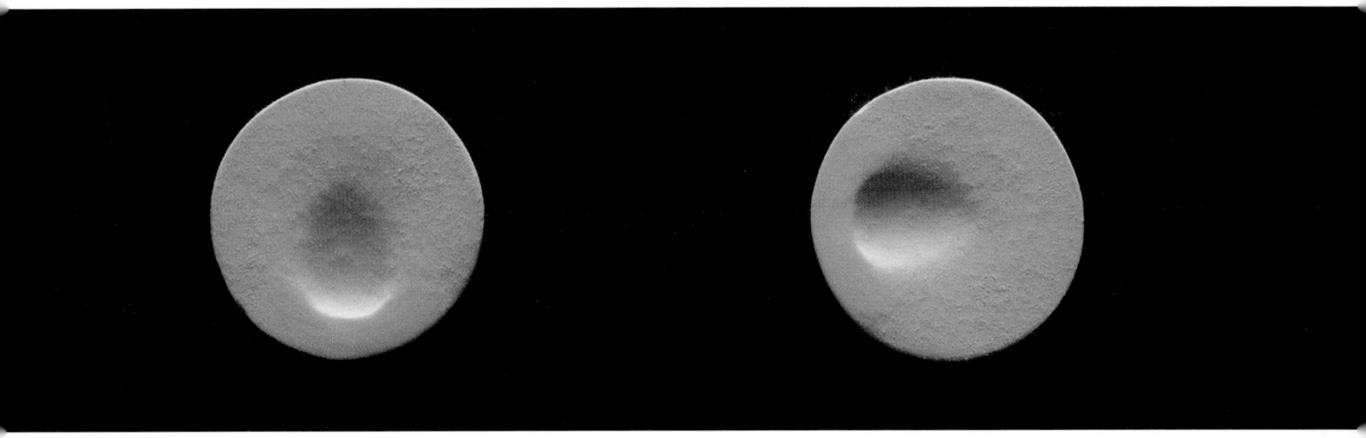

201003240113

201003240114

301003240113

301003240114

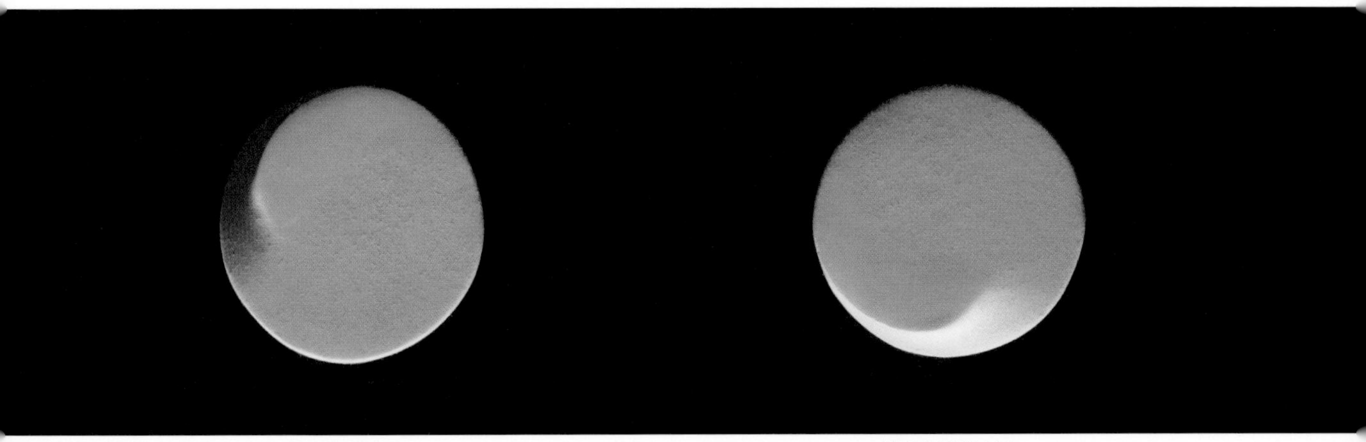

401003240113

401003240114

EPISTEME DESIGN PROCESS

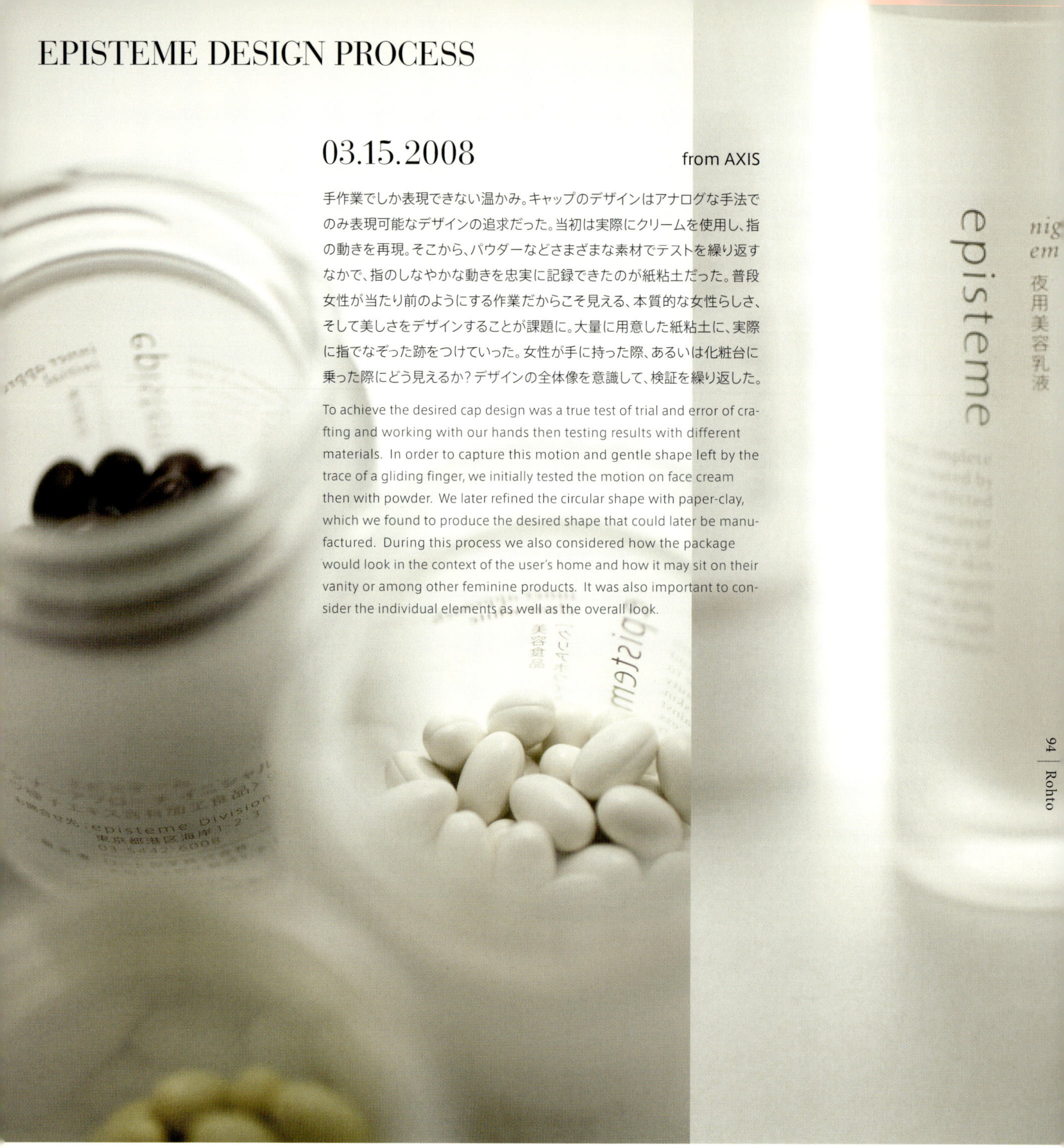

03.15.2008

from AXIS

手作業でしか表現できない温かみ。キャップのデザインはアナログな手法でのみ表現可能なデザインの追求だった。当初は実際にクリームを使用し、指の動きを再現。そこから、パウダーなどさまざまな素材でテストを繰り返すなかで、指のしなやかな動きを忠実に記録できたのが紙粘土だった。普段女性が当たり前のようにする作業だからこそ見える、本質的な女性らしさ、そして美しさをデザインすることが課題に。大量に用意した紙粘土に、実際に指でなぞった跡をつけていった。女性が手に持った際、あるいは化粧台に乗った際にどう見えるか？デザインの全体像を意識して、検証を繰り返した。

To achieve the desired cap design was a true test of trial and error of crafting and working with our hands then testing results with different materials. In order to capture this motion and gentle shape left by the trace of a gliding finger, we initially tested the motion on face cream then with powder. We later refined the circular shape with paper-clay, which we found to produce the desired shape that could later be manufactured. During this process we also considered how the package would look in the context of the user's home and how it may sit on their vanity or among other feminine products. It was also important to consider the individual elements as well as the overall look.

04.17.2008
from TYD

二重構造の中のボトルも、内側からの肌の輝きを演出するためにホワイトパールに色を変更。パールの光沢や光の透過具合については試作ボトルを制作し、上品なパール感を演出した。また、ショップのテスター台のデザインは「砂丘」をイメージ。ボトルの二重構造が効果的に見えるように下面から光を入れるため、そして「砂丘」の造形を具現化するために、白い大理石のようなテクスチャーの素材、コーリアンを選定。どのように制作加工していくのかは未知数だったが、砂丘や雪山の稜線の写真から試作品が完成した。その後、素材特性とデザインとの調整を行ない、テスター台の完成に至った。

We chose to apply a clean, pearl white color to the inner layer of the double layered bottle as it conveyed the feeling of inner brilliance. We constructed numerous samples to achieve the glowing effect from within the bottle. For a similar radiant effect, we chose to use Corian, for the counter design for Episteme's retail stores for its soft, clean and luminous characteristic. Corian also turns opaque when light is shown through the material so we also played with the translucency of this material. We tested this effect which helped complete the counter design.

05.28.2008
from AXIS

ショールームのロゴサインは、壁面材である鋼板を文字状にくり抜き、白アクリルと透明アクリルの2段重ねの文字を乗せた。そうすることで、文字のまわりに中から光がじんわりとにじむ効果を狙った。表面の白アクリルをカマボコ状に加工したかったため、複数の業者にサンプル制作を依頼し、精度と完成度を追求した結果、納得のいくものに仕上げることができた。一方、最後まで検討を重ねていたのがカウンターのディスプレイプラン。商品ラインナップとともに、医薬感を表わすものとしてメスシリンダーを採用。「肌とともに進化し続ける」ブランドを表現するため、試行錯誤が続いた。

For the logo design for the showroom space, we layered white and clear acrylic boards and cut them out into the desired letters which were then mounted onto the wall. By shining light from behind the wall, the letters glowed around the edges. After approaching multiple contractors, we chose the one who best produced the desired effect. For the counter display, we used glass and cylindrical shapes as a reference to science and Rohto's medical background. The clean counter design served as a platform for the Episteme beauty line and radiated their brand vision.

Photo by Shuji Yoshida

コンペのプレゼンは、東京とサンフランシスコをスカイプでつないでスタートしました。TYDとのすばらしいチームワークで乗り切ることができたのです。時差もある限られた時間を、逆に緊張感を持ったスピーディな打合せで進行することができ、このプロジェクトを成功させることができました。

松田一仁（エピステーム上海 有限公司 総経理）

The presentations for this competition occured mostly through Skype between Tokyo and San Francisco. Since it wasn't an actual face to face meeting, we were slightly concerned about being able to communicate the details of how to execute the designs. However, our great communication with TYD led to amazing teamwork regardless of our limited time to complete this project and the time difference between two countries.

Kazuhito Matsuda (General Manager of Episteme Trading, Shanghai)

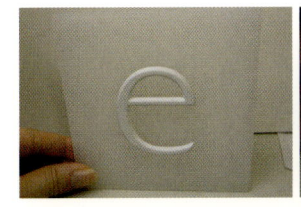

SHOWROOM DESIGN

02.09.2009

from TYD

ロゴやボトルデザインと並行して検討を進めていたショップディスプレイ。化粧品ではあるけれども、ロート製薬の実直な研究姿勢を感じさせるよう、どのような売り場にしたらよいのかを検討した。ボトルのデザイン同様、絶妙な光の重なりからなる美しさに注目し、山積みの幾重にも割った硝子の光の反射によって生まれる透明感のある光をデザイン。商品のパッケージの世界観をテスター台やショールームでも表現した。さまざまな淡い光の融合によって生まれるディスプレイデザイン制作はすべて手作業で進められ、インスタレーションアートの制作に近い作業だった。

We were also developing retail display options alongside designing the products and its identity. Taking inspiration from Rohto's science background and the physical layered makeup of skin, we choose to use glass and mirrors and played with the idea of layering. We found beauty in layers of light, which reflected from mirrors. We tested this by breaking a mirror into pieces then piled them at varying angles to produce reflections of glowing light. This experiment with light inspired the package design, store display, as well as the showroom design. This installation-like study was effective in developing our ideas and it also served as a visual tool to relay our ideas to the client of our design intent.

ショップ用ディスプレイの手法についてはスメルボックスなどいくつかの方向性があがっておりましたが、具体的なイメージとして「商品ラインナップを光とともにディスプレイする」という提案にクライアントからすぐさまOKをいただきました。最終的には白い砂を砂丘のようにセットし、鏡を割り、"反射角度と位置を確認しながらその場の手作業により完成しました"。柔らかく揺らぐような光をどのようにつくり出すか?
鈴木万利子(アクシス(建築士))

We had several different design directions for the showroom displays for one, the use of Mr. Yagi's smell box. The overall feel we wanted to convey in a showroom display was one that had a balanced integration of the product line as well as the lighting. Our challenge was in our treatment of the light so that it was not too bright, rather soft, warm and welcoming. To achieve the ideal lighting, we formed white sand into a miniature sand hill with broken pieces of mirror to allow the light to reflect onto the products. The display design was handmade which nicely captured the essence and beauty of the products.
Mariko Suzuki (Senior Registered Architect of Axis)

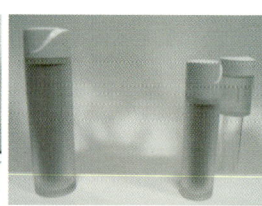

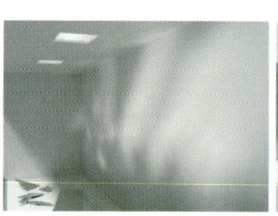

COUNTER DISPLAY DESIGN

Photo by Yoshihito Imaeda

03.25.2009 — from AXIS

エピステームのコンセプト、"肌は肌単独で成り立っているものではなく、体の一部であり、体の健康が肌の正常な生育につながり、美肌をつくる"。それと同様に、パッケージ、ロゴ、ボトル、ショールーム、どのデザインも単独で成り立つものではない。すべてをトータルに考え、キャップで使用した白色を基本に、同じ色調の白のコーリアンという素材をショールームカウンターに使用。コーリアンを透かして見える色味は「色」というより「色味のある"光"」の印象で、女性の内面からの美しさを意識した。色の強さもデータと実際の現場での見た目とは異なるため、何度も検証を繰り返した。

Staying true to Episteme's message in that the skin is an extension of the human body, the showroom design is also the extension and foundation for the entire product line. We utilized the color white as it expressed the qualities of elegance, pure femininity and it sent a clear message of Episteme's innovative products. The white Corian counter was also the perfect material surface for its ability to transmit and capture light which was perfect for reflecting light off the mirrored shards. White was a neutral yet rich, palette that radiated the product concept.

05.19.2009 — from TYD

アクシスとのコラボレーションプロジェクトとして、約1年半後の日本でのプレス発表にまでこぎつけた。350名ほどのプレス関係者を集めて、グランドハイアット東京にて新作発表会を開催。ロート製薬が本格的な百貨店化粧品ブランドを展開し、新しい概念に着目したトータルエイジングを提案したとして、業界でも非常に話題となった。その後、9月2日から、東京の伊勢丹新宿店、大阪高島屋本店にて発売を開始。使用する前から製品の質の高さをパッケージを通して感じてもらえるような、ロート製薬の叡智を集結したこのスキンケアブランドにふさわしいデザインが完成した。

Our collaborative efforts with the Axis team resulted in a successful delivery of Episteme's finished products all the way through to the Japanese press release. Around 350 press members were invited for the press release which was held at the Grand Hyatt Tokyo. There was a lot of anticipation for Episeme as Rohto's new beauty line and the line was met with rave reviews within the beauty industry for the concept of "total aging care." Soon after the release, Episeme made its debut at department stores Isetan, in Tokyo and at Takashimaya in Osaka.

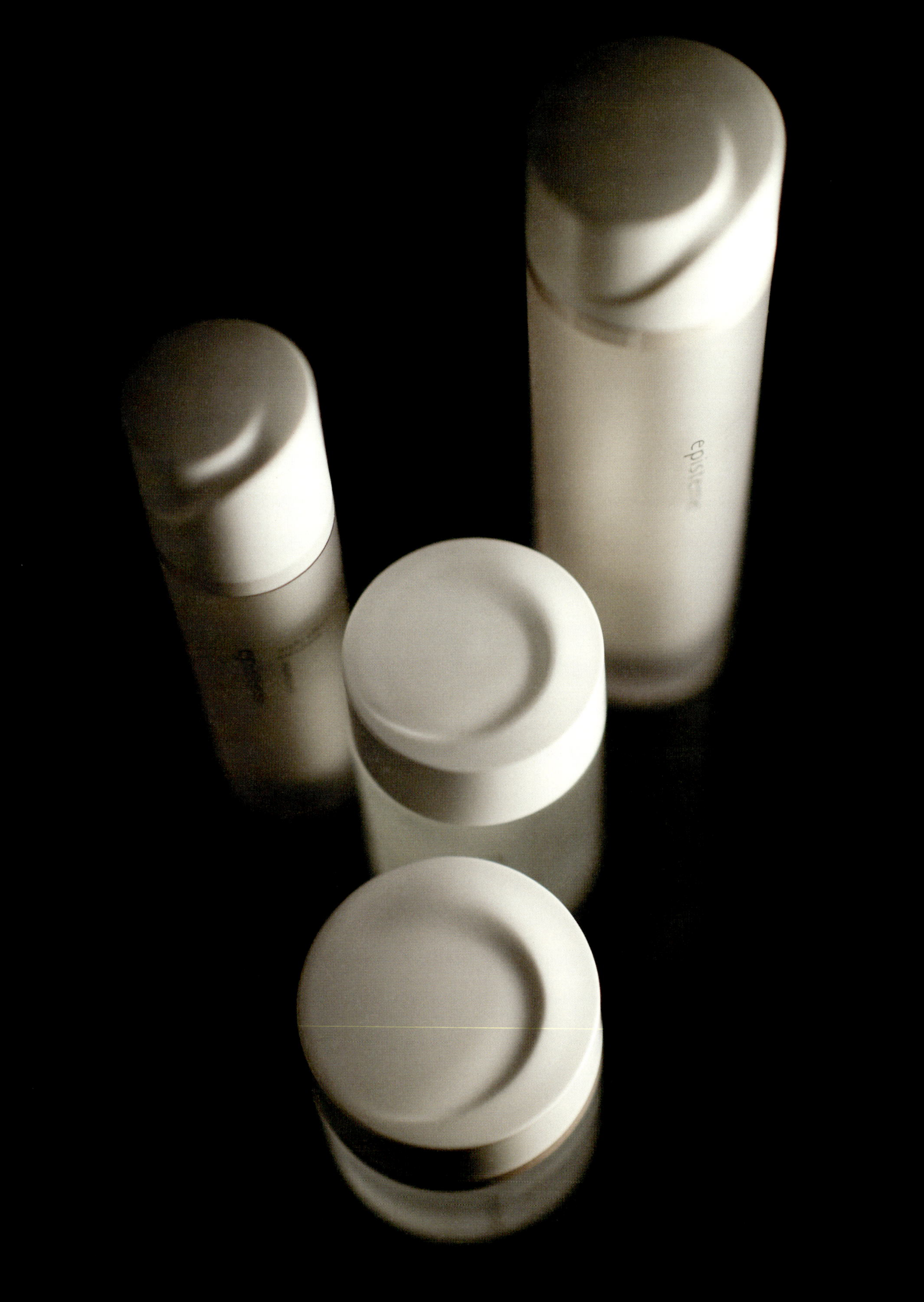

"IF THERE IS SOMETHING THAT CAN SAVE US, THAT HAS TO BE BEAUTY."
— ETTORE SOTTSASS

"われわれを救ってくれるものがあるとしたら、きっとそれは美にちがいない。"
エットレ・ソットサス

Photo by Shuji Yoshida

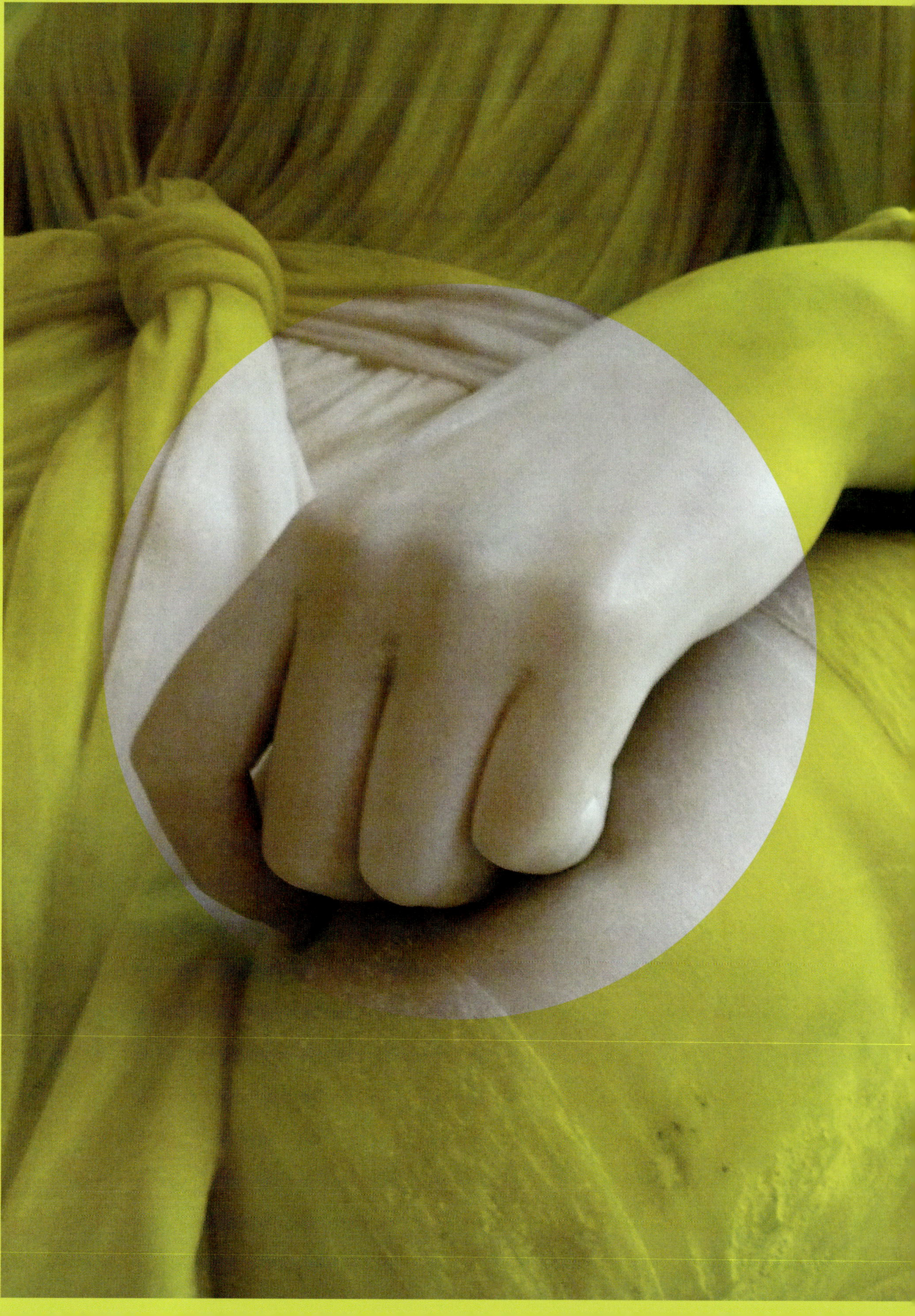

八木明 陶房 / 京都, 2010・晩夏
Yagi Akira Studio / Kyoto, Summer 2010

対談 Conversation

料理は物語

京都料理「緒方」主人　緒方俊郎

料理は引き算で考える

八木：デザイナーには、論理的に思考する人、瞬間の感覚をかたちにする人がいると思うんです。私は後者で、四季の移ろいや日常生活のなかで感じることが、新しいアイデアを生む原動力になっています。だから、日々の食事を大切にしているし、食べることがすごく好きです。

そんな私にとって、「緒方」は、うかがうたびに新鮮な驚きがあって、よい刺激を与えてくれるお店。たとえば、昨年の秋にいただいた松茸ごはん。松茸ごはんは、炊きこむものだと思っていたのに、緒方さんが目の前で生の松茸を手で細く裂いて、炊きたてのごはんに、その松茸をサッと入れて混ぜてできがあり。その一連の流れが実に即興的で、ハッとするサプライズでした。そして、何ともいえず、美味しかった‥‥。

今日はそんな緒方さんの料理の秘密を聞きながら、表現することの意味を探りたいなあと思っています。

緒方：そうですね、秘密はないのですが、料理をつくる上で、いつも考えているのは「物語」をどうつくっていくかということでしょうか。日本料理は、もともと使う食材や料理法がそれほど多くはないので、足し算をして変化をつけやすいのだと思います。でも僕は、プラスするのではなく、食材のもつ魅力をどのように引き出していくかにこだわりたい。

たとえば、先ほど八木さんがおっしゃっていた松茸ごはんですと、松茸の一番の魅力とは何かといえば、僕にとっては「香り」なんです。ひょっとすると、香りを引き出すには油で揚げることが一番かもしれない。でも、フライという方法を僕自身が許せるかどうか。それでさらに考えて、椎茸やマッシュルームは生のままで食べることができるのだから、松茸もできるにちがいないと、先ほどの調理方法を思いつきました。こうした線引きが僕らしさであり、物語の基になるのだと思います。

八木：海老芋を炊いた一皿もすばらしかったなあ。海老芋の姿形が完璧なまでに、美しかったもの。私にとって緒方さんの料理の魅力は、「less is more」です。引き算の美学というのか、「シンプルである豊かさ」。要は、「下ごしらえ」がきっちりされているということだと思います。それがしっかりできていれば、余計なことはしないほうがいい。

デザインも一緒で、グラフィックデザインだと、タイポグラフィ、ビジュアルなどの素材を吟味し工夫を施して、下ごしらえをきちっと整えてから作業します。料理とデザインには大きな共通性を感じますね。それから、座ったまま頭で考えるのではなく、からだを動かしながら発想していくところも似ていませんか？

緒方：デザイン的に表現すると「余白の美学」でしょうか。忘れられつつある日本の良いものを求めているともいえるかもしれません。たとえば「海老芋」は六角形に形を整えるのですが、そこに日本の伝統的な造形美が反映されています。けれども、生の状態ならきれいな六角形ですが、炊きあがるまでその形を保つには技術が必要。一般的には、芋を湯がいてから味を含ませるという方法を習います。でも最近、僕は、料理とは一種のサイエンスであり、マジックなのかなあと感じていて、自分なりの新しい方法や技術を掘り起こしていくことが大切なのではないかと思っているのです。その新しい方法は、意外に簡単で単純なことかもしれない。でも、そこに気づくか気づかないかは、まるでマジックの種のようかもしれません。

「海老芋」の種をあかすと、あれは出汁で煮るのはなくて蒸しています。煮ると、熱が外から伝わるので煮崩れしやすいのですが、蒸すのは、内側から熱が伝導するので崩れにくい。また、芋は空気にあたると酸化して変色するので、出汁につけたままにしておけばよい。ならば、出汁につけたまま蒸しあげればよいわけです。料理はタイミングが大切ですから、お客様のいらっしゃる時間から逆算して料理をすれば、もっとも美味しい状態でお出しすることができます。僕の料理の種を明かすとすごく簡単ですが、そこに辿り着けるかどうかは、科学的で、足し算よりもむしろ引き算的な視点があるのです。

点ではなく面でみる

八木：「緒方」に来ていつも感じることは、主人である緒方さんが、すべての過程をきちんと見ておられるので、心配りが店の隅々にまで行き届いていることです。一周年記念でいただいた一筆箋も、タイポグラフィからレイアウトまできちんとデザインされていました。その一貫性に、感動するんです。このような手抜きのない積み重ねが緒方さんのアイデンティティや、「緒方」らしさをかたちづくっていくのでしょうね。デザインにも通じるものを感じます。

緒方：やはり、いろいろな経験を通して学んだことが基本になっています。たとえば、某店を任されたときには、それまで料理のことだけを考えていればよかったのが、店全体に目配りしなければならない立場になり、物事を「点」ではなく「面」でとらえる訓練になりました。新しい店をつくるに際して、「その店らしさとは何か」ということです。言葉でいうのは簡単ですが、容易にわかるものではありません。結局、日々の行ないのなかで考え続け、行動して積み重ねていくこと以外、「らしさ」はできていかないのではないかと思い至りました。

八木：私は20年ほど前、アメリカのアパレルメーカーで仕事をしていました。その会社は、メンズ、レディース、キッズの三つのブランドをもっていて、僕はそれぞれのブランドに相応しい「らしさ」をデザインしようとしていたのです。すると社長から、「大切なのは、会社として一つのアイデンティティを構築することだ」といわれまして、ハッとしたことがありましたね。これも、「点」で見ていて、「面」で見ることが、抜けていたんだと思います。

緒方：物事を「点」で見ているとそこだけが気になってしまうので、「面」として考える努力が大切なのだと思います。「面」ではじめて見えてくることがあります。

話は戻りますが、はじめて任された店は百貨店の中にあったので、それまで僕がいた老舗料理店とは、お客様やお値段、もちろん料理も変わって当然だと考えました。ならば、今までとはちがった「店」のあり方を開拓しようと、僕なりに点と点をつなぎ合わせてみました。すると「京都駅×百貨店×老舗料理店＝京野菜×乾物」に至りました。京野菜も乾物も京都に欠かせない食材であり、この二つがあれば「らしさ」をい

かしつつ新しい京料理はつくることができる。京野菜を農家に買い付けに行くことは、時代に合っていたのか、いろいろなところから注目されました。

八木：たしかに、緒方さんの野菜料理は絶品ですね。何でもない野菜が思いもよらない料理になって、驚かせてくれます。

緒方：料理に限らず、おもてなし、人様に喜んでいただくということの基本は、手を抜かず、きっちり仕事をすること。そうしていれば、お客様にもわかっていただけるのだと思うんです。はじめて任された店では、こうした自分の気持ちをどうやって店の皆に伝えられるか、点から面へ、まさに経営的な視点も含めて、料理のあり方を学ぶことができました。このようなチャンスをもらえたことに、とても感謝しています。

物語を感じてほしい

八木：独立されたのは、この経験があったからですか？

緒方：僕のなかでは、独立というよりも卒業させていただいたという気持ちですね。13年間、いろいろ学ばせていただいたので、その経験をいかして自分の料理をつくりたいと思うようになったのです。

八木：そして四条通から一筋入った、ここ新釜座通りに店を構えたのですね。街の真ん中に、こんな路地があるなんて、はじめてうかがったときには驚きました。

緒方：この場所に決めたのは、最初にお話したように「物語」をつくりたかったからです。ふつう、料理屋さんは、最初に出店したい街や建物があって、そこから店づくりがはじまります。でも僕は、まず自分がやってみたい料理の物語があって、それを実現するために店の場所、建物、造りなどを選んでいきました。舞台があるから物語が生まれるのではなく、物語のための舞台を探したと言ったらいいかもしれません。

八木：たしかに、四条通でタクシーを降りて、路地を通って「緒方」の暖簾をくぐるまで、これから何がはじまるんだろう、という期待感が膨らみます。「緒方」の物語は何ですか？

緒方：まずは、空間的、時間的な余裕を感じていただきたいなあと思っています。お客様には、四条通の喧騒から一筋入って昔ながらの町屋が並ぶ新釜座通りを散策して、店の暖簾をくぐっていただく。いきなり、「いらっしゃい！」とカウンターに迎えられるのでなく、一旦、「さて、ここからどこにいくのだろうか？」と一息ついていただける小間をつくりました。一見無駄に見える空間がお客様の期待感を高めてくれると考えたからです。店づくりは、中村外二工務店にお願いしました。親方からは、「もっと席数を増やしたほうがいい」とか、貴重な助言や苦言をいただきながら、資金も担保もないなか一緒につくりあげました。

八木：料理もデザインも同じだと思いますが、最後は自分の気持ちをいかに相手に伝えて、理解してもらえるか…そこに行き着きますね。緒方さんの並々ならぬ想いが、資金もない厳しい状況のなかで、親方をはじめ多くの人を動かしたのだと思いますよ。それができたのは、ご自身がしっかりした「物語」を描いていたから。デザインもまったく同じだなあと感心して聞いていました。

緒方：自分の店をつくるに際しては、はじめて「嵐山吉兆」にうかがったときのことを思い出したのです。このとき、どんなお料理が出たかは、うろ覚え。でも、お金をためて、紹介状を書いていただいて、背広を買って、襟を正して出かけたことは今でも はっきり覚えているのです。たぶん、多くのお客様もそうなのだと思います。だったら料理はもちろん大切ですが、路地から店 に入った瞬間から、料理も最初から最後まで、何らかの物語が 必要なのだと考えています。

とはいえ、実際に店を開けて以降、カウンターだけの八人のお客様をお迎えするために朝から晩まで、気がつくと妻と二人で夜中の3時まで仕事をしていることも当たり前。自分ができることの小ささや未熟さに気づいたり、驚いたり…365日働き詰めですけど、ここにいるときが一番落ちつくんですよ。でも、少しずつですが「かたち」になってきている実感があります。

八木：ある雑誌で拝見しましたが、緒方さんは「水」にこだわっているようですね。日本料理は出汁が基本。よくわかります。とくに野菜料理には水は欠かせませんからね。

緒方：八木さんにとっての基本は何ですか？

八木：しいていえば、整理整頓かな。緒方さんもそうだと思いますど、私は汚いところでは仕事ができない。最近、ガラスの机にしたら、汚れていると目立つので、毎朝自分できちんと磨いてから仕事をはじめます。整理整頓は趣味といえるくらい。視覚的なものをデザインするから、その背景となる空間が整理されている必要があるんです。

表現するということ

八木：ところで、緒方さんが料理の道を選んだ理由は何ですか？

緒方：今思えば、父が料理が好きでそういった影響があったかもしれません。僕もモノづくりが好きだったので、何かを表現できる職業につきたいなあと思っていました。僕は広島出身ですが、料理、それも日本料理をやりたいと決めて、それなら京都だろう…と、後先を考えないで来てしまったのです。はじめて京都に行く僕を心配した親戚の叔母さんが「京都に着いたら大きなろうそくのある側に降りるのよ」と、つまり京都タワー側に降りなさいということだった。そんなことすら知らなかったのです。まずタクシーに乗って、飛び込みで二十軒くらいの料理屋を回りました。結局その日は全滅で、泊まったホテルのガイドブックに載っていた老舗旅館の調理場に面接して、入れていただきました。

仕事をはじめて一番困ったのは言葉ですね。先輩の最初の言葉が「チャンバーに行って、むかごを取って来い」だったんですが、まるで外国語のようでした。「チャンバー」というのは大きな冷蔵庫のことなのですが、何度聞いてもわかりませんでした。当初は「おおきに」という言葉も自然と出てこなかったほどです。

八木：僕がアメリカで仕事をはじめたときも同じ。2,000人の社員のなかで日本人は僕一人。言葉には苦労したなあ。寸法は日本ではセンチメートル、アメリカではインチ、これが一番大変でした。でも、デザインの世界は言葉がなくてもどうにかなる。料理も同じだと思うけど、美しい、美味しいという感覚

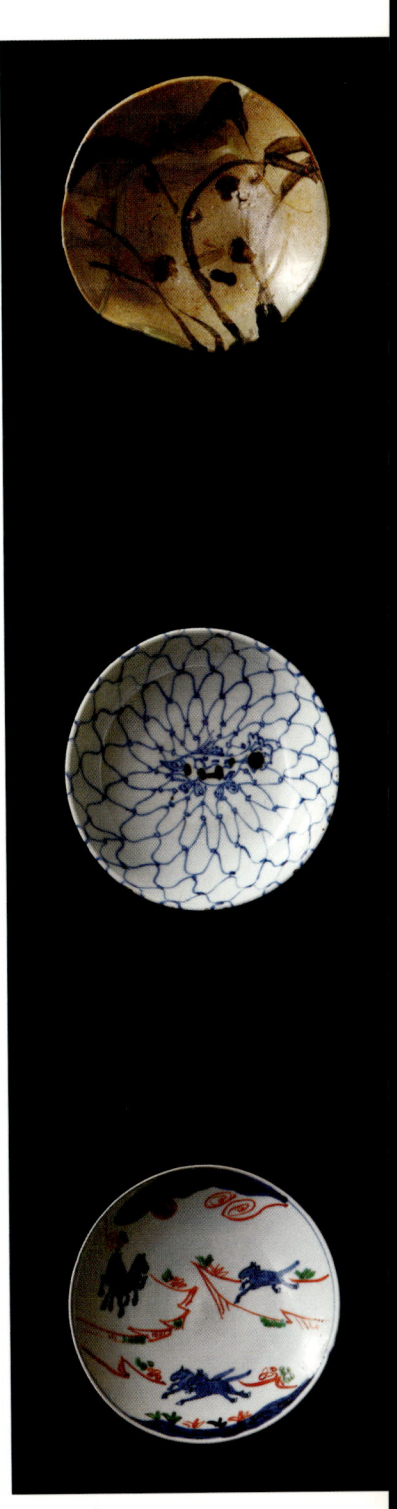

上から 古唐津 桃山時代　古染付 明時代　南京赤絵写し 加藤 静允 作

Kokaratsu from Momoyama period　Kosometsuke from Min period　Nankin Akae Utsushi by Kiyonobu Kato

> "I WANT THE OBJECT THAT WAS BORN, NOT THE ONE THAT WAS MADE." ── SHOJI HAMADA

作ったというより生まれたというような品がほしい。　濱田 庄司

は万国共通だから、言葉の壁をどうにか克服できるのでしょうね。それで、料理の世界に入って一から勉強したのですね。

緒方：現場以外にも、料理本を読んだり、実際に食べに行ったりしていました。そして少しずつわかってきたのは、僕が惹かれる料理は、何のことはない、当たり前なんだけどきちんとした仕事が施されたものだったのです。

八木：料理や棟梁など職人の世界では、親方や先輩の仕事を盗めといいますよね。アートの世界でも偉大なアーティストは先達を盗む、愚かなアーティストはコピーするって…。たしかに、盗むには相手を観察し、感じ、考えることが重要。でもコピーは、何も感じず表面をサラッとなぞればいい、むしろ考えないほうがいい。

緒方：感じることはとても大切ですね。何かを感じて、飲み込んで、消化する…。日本料理はそれほどバリエーションが豊富ではないので、どんな料理でもどこかで見たり食べたりという印象はぬぐえない。けれども、盗んだ技や味には、その人だけの個性や魅力があります。

八木：そんななかで、緒方さんは自分らしさをどうつくっていこうと考えているの？

緒方：僕には、伝統と格式がありませんから、同じ刀をもって闘うことはできません。だから批判されるくらいの大胆な自分らしい料理をしないと、「緒方」の存在さえ、意味がないと思うんです。「僕らしさ」の一つが「物語」だとすると、店の佇まいと同じように、料理でも物語を醸したいのです。

それは、料理や器、そしてお出しする順番です。とくに料理の順番は大切に考えています。ふつうは、酢の物からはじまって椀物、煮物、焼き物などの流れだったり、茶懐石のようにまず四つ椀が出されたりするのですが、いつも試行錯誤しています。でも、自分なりに好きな流れがあって、結局はそれに戻っていきます。一つだけ申しますと、僕は最初に少しだけ温かいご飯をお出しします。それは、お酒を飲む方も飲まない方にも最初にホッコリしていただきたいから。炭水化物を入れることによって脳が活性化し、食欲が増進されるのです。

八木：料理もですが、最後のデザートもすばらしい。日本料理屋さんで、これだけ工夫を凝らしたデザートを出してくれる店は珍しいですよね。海外に長く暮らしていると、最後にデザートを食べないとどうも落ち着きませんから。とくに印象的なのは、純菜と黒蜜の組み合わせ。その発想には驚きました。

ところで、先ほど、物語は料理、器、流れと、おっしゃっていたけれど、新しい料理はどのようにつくっているんですか？思いついたときに、まめにメモをとっておくとか？

緒方：考えてもアイデアは出てこない。たぶんデザインも同じではないですか？僕は、月毎に一つの食材をテーマにしています。たとえば「きゅうり」を、揚げる、焼く、煮る、蒸すなど、いろいろな調理法で料理しつくしてみたり。そうしているうちに意外な発見や発想が浮かびあがってくるから不思議です。頭で考えてつくるものは、どこかで見たり、食べた料理のコピーになってしまい、薄っぺらなんです。

たとえば、お客様に褒めていただいた「醤油酢飯」は、コースの最後のお寿司を探している最中に「醤油をご飯に混ぜてしまってはどうだろうか」と思いつきました。八木さんからご好評の鱧カツも、鱧を湯引き以外でお出ししたいといろいろ試していた途中で、揚げてみようと浮かびました。でも、料理で大切なのはタイミングです。できたてをサッとお出しする。これが何より。料理は感じていただくことが第一ですから…。

八木：物語に欠かせない器についてもお聞きしたいなあ。器は自分で探したり、つくったりされるんですか？

緒方：好みがありますが、出会いですね。料理も意匠が大切ですから…。でも言葉で表わすのは難しいですね。

八木：では、ちょっと質問を変えましょう。たとえば、版画などのアートを額縁に入れて飾りますが、作品をひきたててくれる額縁とそうでない額縁ってあると思うのです。料理も同じで、意匠っておっしゃったけど、自分の料理をひきたててくれる器をわかっているのでしょうね。この料理には、こんな器がいいと直感が働くのですか？

緒方：僕は逆で、器が先ですね。この器に、こんな感じの料理を盛りたいなあ…から発想します。気に入った器に出会った瞬間、沸々といろんな料理のイメージが湧いてくるんです。そんな器に出会うとぞくぞくするし、はたして、自分がこの器に負けない料理をつくれるだろうか…と、力が沸いてきますね。食材と同じように、器からも料理を発想しているんです。もちろん器も料理と同じように、流れとして考えています。古い器ばかりだと重苦しくなりますし、磁器や陶器、漆やガラスなど、多彩な器を使ってどんな物語をつくっていくか。器も流れやバランスが大切です。

八木：緒方さんが大切にしている「物語」にはすごく共感できる。僕もクライアントには、単にデザインをプレゼンテーションするだけではないのです。そのデザインが生まれるまでの背景やその世界観をまず説明します。緒方さん流に表現すれば、デザインの物語を話しているということでしょう。デザインやマーケティングの世界では「物語」ってよく言われるけど、料理の世界で「物語」って聞いたのは、緒方さんがはじめてです。最後に、緒方さんは料理によって何を表現したいのですか？

緒方：最後に辿り着きたいのは、自分なりの「品格」、「品性」でしょうか。僕はこれからも、「緒方」という店で、料理を通していろいろな物語をつくり続けるのだと思いますが、お客様に緒方らしい品格を感じていただけるようになればうれしいです。

八木：次回、また緒方さんの料理をいただくのが、ますます楽しみになりました。

緒方 俊郎　1966年、広島生まれ。京都にて料理人を志す。2008年、独立。新釜座通りに「緒方」を開店。2010年から婦人画報にて、『『緒方』京料理のその先に』を連載中。

TOSHIRO OGATA was born in Hiroshima, Japan in 1966. He aspired to become a chef and moved to Kyoto in 1986. He opened his own restaurant, Ogata, in 2008.

越田 悟全　1957年、東京都出身。日本のみならず、世界中の「食」に関する出会いが生きがい。日本とNewYorkで料理写真集の制作に携わり、『美し乾山四季彩菜・APPETIZING BEAUTY KENZAN AND SEASONAL DISHES』でグルマン世界料理本大賞（Gourmand World Cookbook Awards）の料理本写真部門で最優秀賞受賞。
www.gozenkoshida.com

GOZEN KOSHIDA was born in Tokyo, Japan in 1957. He explored his passion for experiencing global cuisine with an international career in food photography. He recently released "Appetizing Beauty Kenzan and Seasonal Dishes," which won first place in the Gourmand World Cookbook Awards.

COOKING IS STORYTELLING
TOSHIRO OGATA / Kyoto Cuisine by Owner Ogata

Cooking with a Deductive Mind

TY: There are two types of designers, one that thinks theoretically and the other that visualizes directly. I consider myself a visual designer who is inspired by everything around me, from the changing of the seasons to everyday life. This is why I see great value in cooking, and notice the nuances in the way food is prepared and served. For me, the experience of visiting Ogata is a great source of design inspiration. For example, the Matsutake mushroom rice dish I had last Fall. First, this special seasonal ingredient was presented on the counter whole, so that the mushrooms' form and scale could be admired. Then the Matsutake were hand-split in front of me, and the delicate slivers were mixed into cooked rice. Finally, these tender elements were placed in a hand-crafted ceramic bowl, and served directly by the chef. The unconventional spontaneity of preparing the dish before my eyes was very surprising. Today, I'd like to talk with you about the meaning of expression, and the secret of Ogata style.

TO: I am excited to hear your view as well. There is really no "secret" to the way I cook, I simply focus on storytelling. There are only so many natural ingredients and original recipes, so it is easy to alter tastes by adding flavors. However, I am more interested in taking away, or subtracting. I seek to extract the essence, or enhance the charm of an ingredient. I'll use the Matsutake mushroom rice you were talking about as an example. I knew that Matsutake's aroma provides its allure. Although deep frying is the best way to enhance smell and flavor, I questioned whether I could deep fry this valuable ingredient. As Maitake mushrooms or regular mushrooms can be eaten raw, I asked myself why not Matsutake? I used reverse logic rather than responding theoretically to create the Ogata style of Matsutake rice. I realized that developing my own unique cooking philosophy was the first page to my story.

TY: The dish you prepared with *Ebi-imo* (taro) was also amazing. The shape of the *Ebi-imo* was perfectly cut to transform this simple root vegetable into something very beautiful. You demonstrated the idea of "less is more," cuisine with the aesthetics of subtraction or "richness in simplicity."

TY: Your *shitagoshirae* (preparation) is also very well coordinated. This organization is critical in graphic design as well. At TYD, we start projects by researching and assembling typography, visuals, tools and other inspirational sources. As long as those elements are well organized, the rest of the design process can be very simple. I see similarities in cooking and design, both are organic. Rather than sit still and think, we move our bodies and create. Another quality I have found very impressive about Ogata is the attention paid to every detail. Even the letter I received announcing the restaurant's one year anniversary was carefully considered. The typeface, layout and presentation were all very well designed. This finely crafted note effectively communicated your comprehensive discipline, along with respect for your customers. I value the importance of details far beyond my work in graphic design as well.

TO: To focus on just "one point," limits what you will ever be

蒸しアワビ丸（すっぽん）の煮こごり。 Jellied soft-shell turtle.

Photo by Gozen Koshida

TY: Tamotsu Yagi
TO: Toshiro Ogata

able to see. Training yourself to view "the big picture" is important, and requires stepping back to examine the whole. Perspective allows you to apply the same rigor to every aspect of the business, which in turn helps customers understand your message. I learned to view the entire dining experience at the last restaurant I managed, and am especially grateful for the lesson that food needs to be delivered with care.

Wanting Customers to Understand My Story

TY: How did the experience of working at your previous restaurant help you open your own establishment?
TO: Opening my own restaurant was more like graduating. I learned and experienced many things during the 13 years of working for my former employer, and felt I was finally ready to open my own restaurant.
TY: You opened your restaurant in Shin-Kamaza-cho (Kyoto), on a small alley off Shijo-Street. I was very surprised that this type of intimate passage existed.
TO: The reason I selected this location was to introduce customers to the "story" of my restaurant. Restaurant owners usually open their businesses by searching for an area or specific type of building. In my case, I already knew the story of the food I wanted to prepare, so I looked for the location, architecture and interior that best expressed my story. Rather than "telling a story because there is a stage," I began "searching for a stage to tell my story."
TY: I always get the feeling of excitement when I approach Shijo-Street and walk through the alley into Ogata. What exactly is your story?
TO: First, I want people to sense the space and atmosphere. Customers come through the bustle of Shijo-Street into the small, old alley of Shin-Komazawa-Street. I also want customers to walk into Ogata at their own pace. Instead of seeing the counter and hearing "welcome!" right after they enter, diners are given a moment of anticipation. For this reason, I have a small room before the counter where people can sit, relax, and imagine "ok, what is next?" This area may be seen as a waste of space, but I feel that its atmosphere stirs the customers' curiosity and excitement. The interior was designed by Sotoji Nakamura. While many other people offered advice like "you should add more seats," he understood my vision and how to execute my concept with clarity. Nakamura's help was crucial to opening this restaurant, and without him, I would not have been as satisfied. I was especially thankful for his generous efforts when I had no funds other than equity.

My Personality Reflected in My Cooking

TY: How do you reflect your character in your food?
TO: I am the owner a of new restaurant without history or tradition, so I can't compete with other chefs in terms of knife skills. Therefore, I feel it is important to do something bold and humbly risk criticism. As "a story teller," I want each dish to be a part of the journey, just like the space itself. The presentation of each dish, and the order in which they are served is very important. I particularly focus on the meal's progression. Dinner at Ogata usually begins with pickles and soup, then I present a braised dish followed by a broiled dish, similar to the Kaiseki style. I generally serve a total of four courses. I sometimes struggle to break that rule, but always seem to return to the traditional four dish style. However, I do add a small bowl of plain, warm rice as the very first dish. I do this because I don't want my customers beginning the meal on a completely empty stomach, regardless of whether they are drinking alcohol or not. Starting a meal with a carbohydrate revitalizes the brain and increases appetite.
TY: Your desserts are also unique. It's rare for a traditional Japanese restaurant to create such unusual sweets, like your dish combining a root vegetable with black honey. Now that I've been living in America for such a long time, I don't feel like a meal is complete without dessert. Along with focusing on the flow and the order of a meal, do you spend time thinking up new ideas? Do you also document these ideas?
TO: Thinking doesn't automatically lead to new concepts... isn't designing similar? My main theme is to feature seasonal ingredients for each month. With cucumbers for example, I can fry, braise, broil and steam them...I'll try everything to devise an original dish. It's amazing how testing tools and materials leads me to new ideas. The recipes in my head are usually something I've already seen or eaten, so these concepts are unoriginal. Your favorite dish, the fried sea eel, came to me when I was trying to beak away from the traditional boiled preparation. Creativity is important, but even more critical is timing...serving a freshly cooked dish right away is paramount. Cooking is not just about tasting, I actually want customers to feel my food from inside and I want to feel the satisfaction they get from my food.
TY: I also want to hear about your selection of plates. Your serving ware is a special aspect of the Ogata experience, or chapter in your story. Do you usually buy these pieces yourself, or have them made? How do you make selections?
TO: Actually, the plate comes first. I will look at a plate and start to imagine the dish I eventually want to see presented on that plate. The moment I see a new plate, new dishes come to mind. I then wonder if I can create a meal that's more powerful than that plate alone. The total composition and layout with each plate is also carefully considered. I don't just use new or old ceramics, but incorporate porcelain, lacquer and glass. I'm very conscious of the total balance required to compose my own story.
TY: My presentation to a client is also more than just the final product, but to tell a "story." I always explain each stage of how the design evolved. I often hear the term "story" in the design world, as well as in marketing, but this is the first time to hear it from a chef. My last question is what do you want to express through your food and cooking style?
TO: I want to share my "dignity" and my "character" with my customers. I will continue to create more stories at Ogata, and I hope my customers really feel the experience within.
TY: I look forward to a new chapter on my next visit.

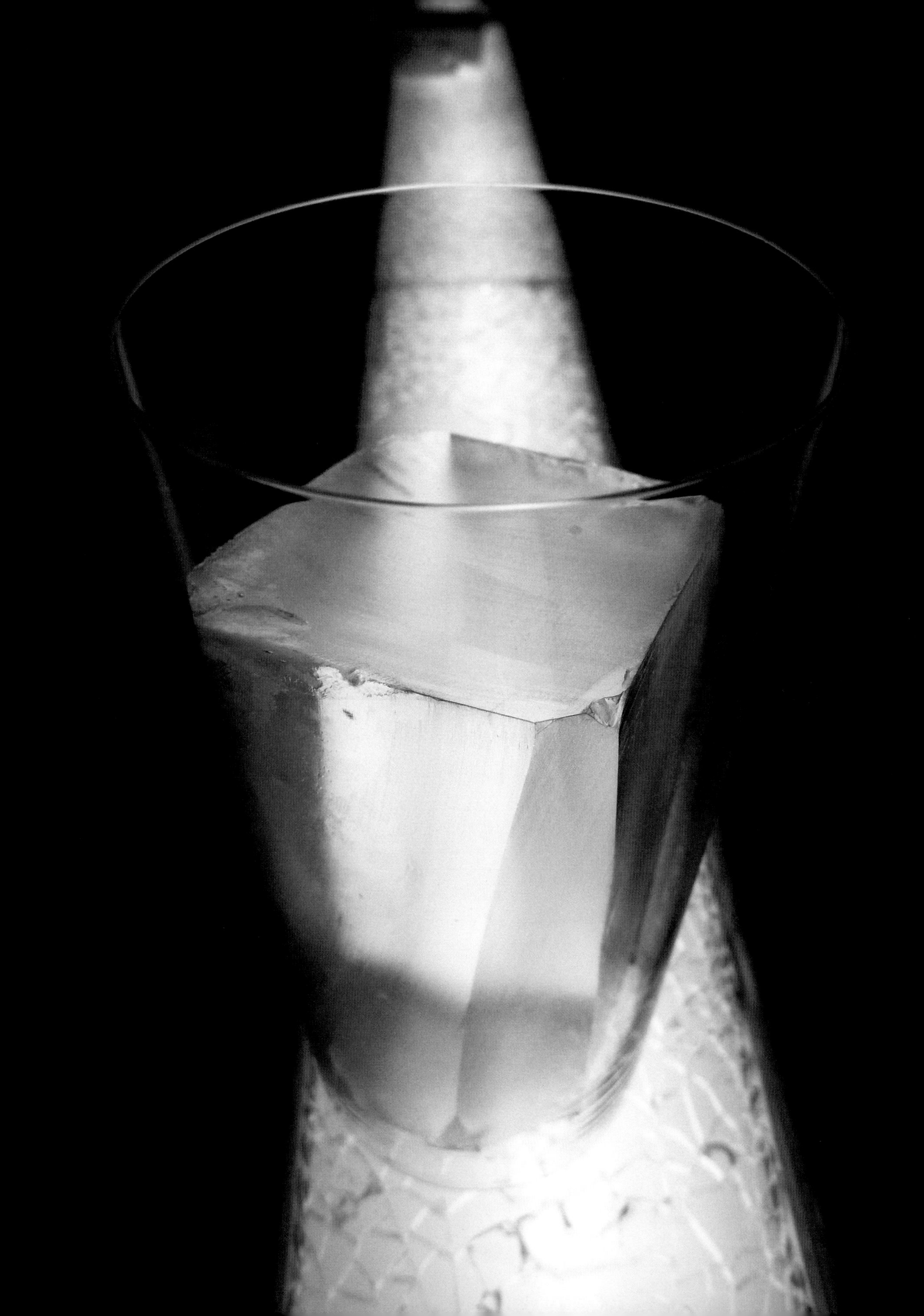

108 | Hiroshima

"WHAT IS BLUE? BLUE IS THE INVISIBLE BECOMING VISIBLE…
BLUE HAS NO DIMENSIONS. IT EXISTS OUTSIDE THE DIMENSIONS
THAT ARE PART OF OTHER COLORS."
YVES KLEIN

"ブルーとは何か？ ブルーとは、視覚化できる透明だ・・・
そう、ブルーは何にも属さない。何色にも属すこと無く存在している。"
イヴ・クライン

Photo by Stefano Massei

2045

The 2045 Hiroshima City of Peace and Creativity Project was initiated in 1995 on the 50th anniversary of the atomic bombing of 1945. The purpose of this project was to create new public infrastructures of integrated design to Hiroshima's urban landscape through the next one hundred years. This project aimed to enrich the cityscape in the field of urban design, architecture, civil engineering and landscaping. The Hiroshima Naka Incineration Plant was one of these proposed projects, completed 8 years after planning and construction by the architect Yoshio Taniguchi. Surrounded by the ocean, sky and water, *Yves Klein Blue* immediately came to mind when I was asked to design the signage and graphic identity for this building. The rich ultramarine color of the *International Klein Blue* inspired the color palette and initiated the design process for this project.

HIROSHIMA CITY NAKA INCINERATION PLANT
Signage and Graphic Design

水の都ひろしま
Designing an incineration plant like a modern museum

A bottle of *Yves Klein Blue* pigment and Le Corbusier's sample color book. Blue and yellow were used as accent colors inside the Hiroshima Naka Incineration Plant.

「ひろしま二〇四五。平和と創造のまち」。

広島市は、被爆百年後の社会へ向けた整備計画の一環として、環境に配慮し、世界に通用する公共施設「広島市環境局中工場」の設計を、一九九五年、建築家、谷口吉生氏に依頼しました。

二〇〇六年一〇月、広島市環境局中工場は着工八年を経て竣工。中工場は、広島市内を南北に走る、吉島通りの南端にあり、正面には広島湾が広がり、まさに「海」「空」「水」に取り囲まれています。

私は「青色」の代名詞、「イヴ・クライン・ブルー」をイメージしました。いつの時代も、深い青色は、人々を惹きつけてやむことはなく、建築の圧倒的な力強さに対峙する力をもっているからです。

中工場のゴミ焼却施設のサイン計画は、カラーパレットを構成することから、スタートしました。

ようこそ
Welcome

受付
Reception

Photo by Shuji Yoshida

エントランスホールでは、アクセントカラーのブルーの壁に大きな矢印と「ようこそ」のステンレスの切り文字が設置された。
A large polished stainless steel arrow was placed on the blue entrance wall along with cutout stainless steel letters "welcome" in Japanese.

SIGNAGE DESIGN

中工場のサイン計画は、建築設計のコンセプトに倣い、シンプルかつ、これまでにない新しい表現を目指しました。サイン計画には、建築のカラーリングと建物のスケールに負けない大きなサインの設置という、2つの領域がありました。中工場には、多くの見学者、なかでも多くの子どもたちが訪れます。見学者は建物の1Fから6Fまで、コンクリート打放しの通路を順に移動しますが、その距離は方向感覚を失ってしまうほどの長さです。そのために、視覚的に強く印象に残る色彩計画と視覚システムのデザインが必須と考えたのです。

To harmonize with the grand architectural concept of the Hiroshima Naka Incineration Plant, we made the signage design minimal yet distinct. We decided to feature two elements of signage designs, one that was informative and the other more iconic and visual, using bold colors of blue & yellow and large scale arrows. Many of these arrows also wrapped around corners creating an inviting and interactive effect. The Hiroshima Naka Incineration Plant is a monumental six stories of uncoated concrete and without directional signage, visitors can easily get lost in its maze. In particular, we felt that children would respond to an iconic and sizable signage during educational tours organized by the Hiroshima Naka Incineration Plant to educate them about waste management.

矢印の先の部分は、45cm角のステンレスの切り抜きで、溶接なしの鏡面仕上げとなった。
The tip of the arrow was cut from the point of a 45cm x 45cm square sheet of stainless steel panel then polished.

サイン設置の際は、すべての図面を原寸サイズにプリントして、実際にコンクリートに貼って確認し、最終の位置を決定。メインエントランスの壁には、ステンレス製の矢印を壁面から浮かせて設置した。鏡面仕上げのステンレスは周辺を映し込み、移動すると車窓の風景のように変化する。

Actual size signage printed on paper was positioned onto the concrete wall to determine the final placement. On the main entrance wall, we placed a large polished stainless steel arrow. The thickness of the stainless steel gave the illusion of a floating signage and the polished surface interacted and reflected as visitors walked by.

計画されたサイン表示は、実際に現場の全フロアで3カ月ほど貼って、問題がないかどうか実験した。その後、問題なく機能したと判断されたので、原寸にプリントされ、テンプレート通りに設置された。

We left the temporary placement signs on the walls for three months to test with the incineration plant's staff for its effectiveness. After three months of testing and adjustments, the temporary signs were replaced with the polished stainless steel arrows.

スケールの大きい矢印は、人の目線に合った高さに設置され、サインそのものに奥行きを与える結果となった。
The large arrows are also an indication of the grand vision of this project.

ECORIUM

ガラスに囲まれた全長100メートルを超えるエコリアムの通路の延長線上には広島湾が広がり、市の中心にある平和公園の主軸と一致する。
The Ecorium is a significant architectural design of the plant which lines up directly at an axis from the Peace Memorial Park. The Ecorium runs through the heart of the plant and out towards the panoramic view of the Hiroshima Bay.

今回、本書のレイアウトのなかで一番印象的だったのがこの広島中工場のページです。私が入社する前のプロジェクトだったため、過去の担当スタッフに連絡をとって、実際に中工場を見学してきました。自分の目で確かめることによって、プロジェクトの全貌や経緯に対する理解を深めることができました。
伊藤心介（TYDグラフィック・デザイナー）

This chapter in particular was one of the most memorable layouts that I've worked on for this book. Since this project was completed before I joined TYD, it gave me the opportunity to contact the team that worked on the project. I also visited the Naka incineration Plant during my recent trip to Japan to experience first hand the significance of this project and the signage design.
Shinsuke Ito (Graphic Designer at TYD)

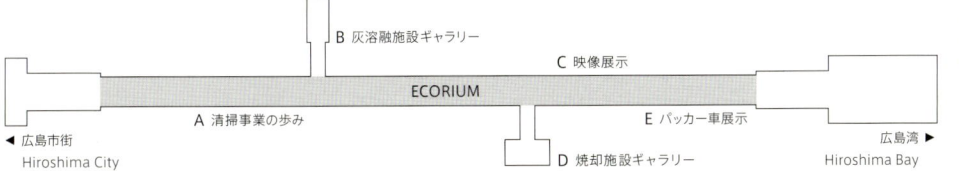

A Clean Project Timeline for Hiroshima City
B Ash Solidification System Gallery
C Plasma Displays
D Incineration Equipment Gallery
E Garbage Truck Installation

B 灰溶融施設ギャラリー
C 映像展示
ECORIUM
A 清掃事業の歩み
E パッカー車展示
D 焼却施設ギャラリー

◀ 広島市街
Hiroshima City

広島湾 ▶
Hiroshima Bay

ECORIUM

市街地から海へと貫く都市軸上に位置するガラスの回廊が、環境展示施設です。このミュージアムともいえる回廊は「エコリアム」と名付けられました。エコリアムは、環境に対する新たな考察を生む場所。環境展示施設は、訪れる人々に清掃工場の公共性を理解、意識を喚起させることがテーマでした。エコリアムのロゴデザインでは、「ガラスの回廊」「無色透明」といった漠然としたイメージを具現化していきました。その結果、ロゴは限りなく透明に近いものになりました。ここから見ることができる焼却と灰溶融固化設備は、ゴミの焼却、発生する有毒ガスの無毒化、灰のスラグへの再生化など、ゴミと公害を限りなくゼロに近づけています。その焼却場の役割を、限りなく透明に近いロゴが象徴しているのです。

We named this long glass atrium leading to the ocean that functions as an exhibition space "Ecorium." This is the heart of the plant where visitors learn about the functions and potential future projects of the plant. The logo and signage design for the Ecorium began from brainstorming key words like "glass corridor" and "invisible." We decided to focus on the material for Ecorium's signage and used acrylic on glass for a non obtrusive effect as if the letters were raised from the existing glass surface. The incineration equipment and ash solidification process can be seen from the Ecorium while ash turns into reusable slag, without producing any poisonous gases. The glass Ecorium symoblizes the cleanliness and ecological philosophy of the plant as one can see what would normally be hidden and the process of clean waste treatment.

ECOLOGY + ATRIUM
エコロジー：生態学　　　　アトリウム：中庭

ネーミングの打ち合わせでは、できるだけ子どもたちが覚えやすく、小学生が読めるレベルの英語の表記にするなど、その方向性について、いくつかの観点から議論が行なわれました。子どもたちにとって、キャラクターになるほどの愛着を抱いてくれるネーミングとは…。私は「エコロジー」と「アトリウム」を組み合わせ、「エコリアム（ECORIUM）」という名を提案しました。
岡崎忠彦（ファミリア代表取締役社長、元TYDデザイナー）
Tadahiko Okazaki (President of Familiar & Former TYD Designer)

When a meeting was held for the naming of the atrium inside the incineration plant, the first priority was to identify our target audience. Since this incineration plant was both a state-of-the-art facility and an educational center, we created a name that children could easily pronounce and remember. The result was Ecorium, the fusion of the two words "ecology" and "atrium."

車のナンバープレートのように、ロゴタイプをガラスとアルミ素材で表現した。
For the Ecorium signage, we drew inspiration from an embossed aluminum license plate. In the place of aluminum we worked with glass.

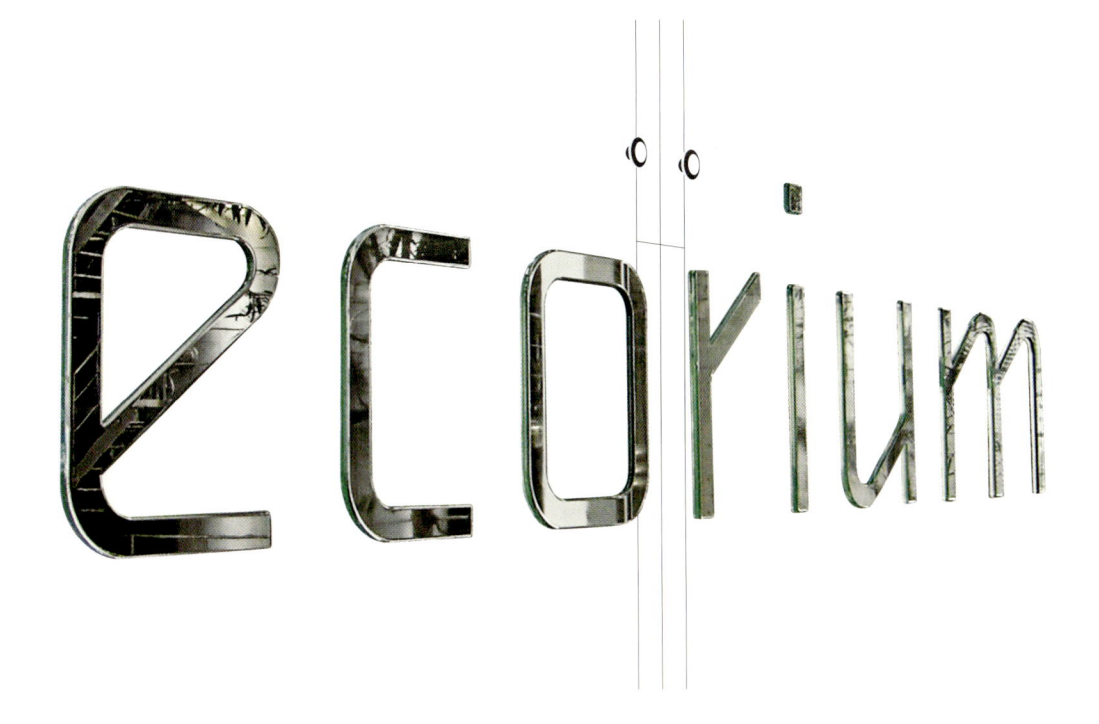

建物を貫くように設けられたガラスのアトリウムは無音、無臭の空間。
The long 100 meter glass Ecorium runs lengthwise through the building. The Ecorium is a quiet and calm space with no odor of waste.

ECORIUM GALLERY

エコリアムでは「焼却施設ギャラリー＋灰溶融施設ギャラリー」という小展示が大回廊の左右に突き出すように併設され、そこで施設情報を得ることができます。小展示部分のガラス面には、二つの施設案内のイラストレーションがシルクスクリーン印刷で表現されています。これらは単なるデフォルメされた二次元のイラストではなく、三次元要素をとり入れた新しい表現となっています。また、ギャラリーの入り口には、大人と子どもの目線の高さに合わせて小さなモニターが付けられており、子どもにもアクセスしやすいタッチパネル式になっています。

The Ecorium features two different exhibition spaces where visitors can learn more about the galleries: *Incineration equipment gallery* and *Ash solidification system gallery*. Two educational illustrations were silkscreened onto a glass wall, easily comprehendible by children. The gallery also featured touch panel screens to allow the visitors to interact and learn about the plant and its functions.

Photo by Kazuo Kirita

焼却施設ギャラリー ｜ Incineration Equipment Gallery

ガラス面にシルクスクリーンで表現された情報イラストレーションの目的は、訪問者に主体性をもって見学してもらうこと。そのために施設内のイラストは、そのスケール感と躍動感とは対照的に、落ち着いた仕上げられています。北澤秀也さんが描いたイラストを白一色でシルクスクリーン印刷するために、オリジナルのイラストを基本にデフォルメしました。それは透明度の高い「エコリアム」で、見学者の目を慣らすためのフォーカルポイントとしても機能しています。

八木章画 (有限会社1956 元TYD グラフィックデザイナー)

Our objective for the silkscreened informational illustration was to stir the interests of the visitors to the functions of the incineration plant. We wanted the illustrations to be inviting as it demonstrated a rather complex subject. The application of the illustrations on the glass wall also functions to alert visitors of the presence of a glass wall.

Akira Yagi (Principal of Nineteen Fiftysix & Former TYD Designer)

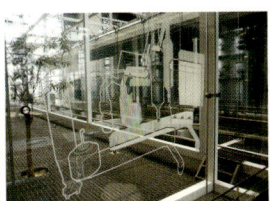

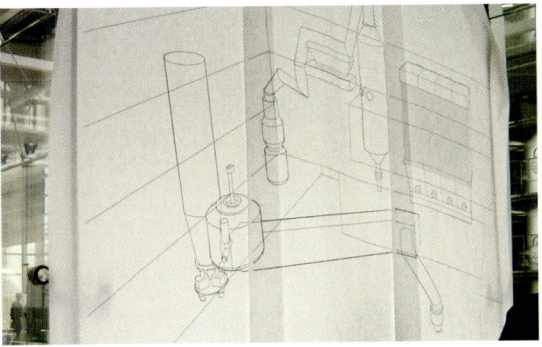

イラストレーションをガラス面のどの位置に印刷するかは、何度も模型で検討。その後、サイン同様、原寸サイズのイラストをプリントして、実際に現場のガラス面に当てて、最終の位置を決定した。

This is a study for the placement of the illustration using an architectural mock-up. A printed version of the illustration was applied to the glass to determine the final placement.

Photo by Kazuo Kirita

B 灰溶融施設ギャラリー｜Ash Solidification System Gallery

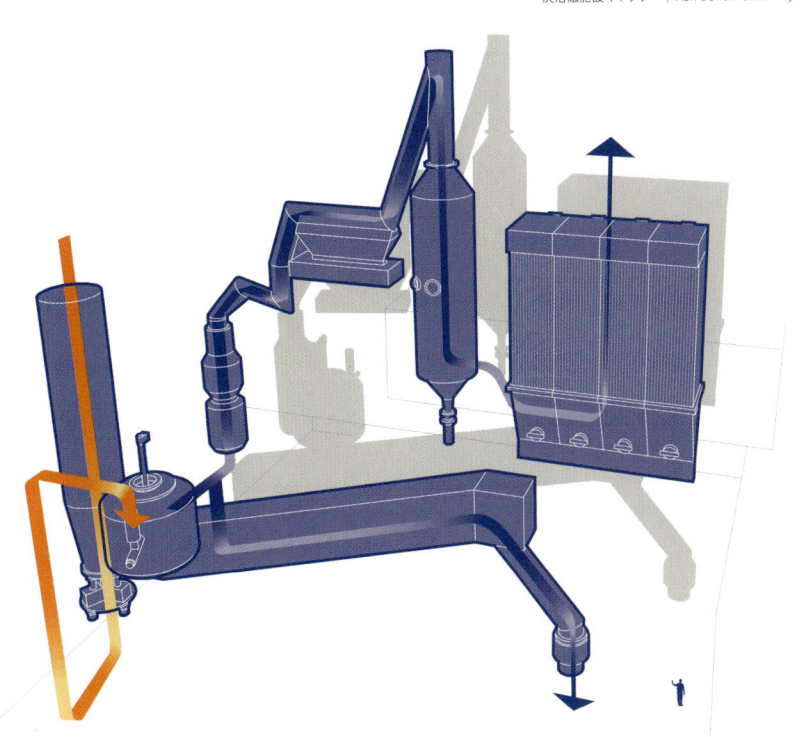

イラストレーションの制作は難題でしたが、プラント設計者との共同作業によって実現できました。「スケール感」と「動き」を、グラフィックとして両立させるために三次元モデルをつくり、何度も最適な視点探しの試行錯誤を繰り返しました。ブルーで描かれたすべての設備のイラストのかたわらには、圧倒的なスケール感を意識できるように縮尺を合わせた小さな人型を配置。さらに、ダイナミックな動きの流れをリボン状の矢印で示し、ブルーの補色であるオレンジでくっきりと描きました。

北澤秀也（イラストレーター）

Drawing this informational illustration was a challenge, but with the help from all the associates, it was made possible. To express the scale and movement of the equipment, I first created a 3D model and studied which angle from which to base the illustration from. To show the scale, I incorporated people in the illustration as a frame of reference. I used ribbon like arrows to show the movement of the equipment's process and applied colors of blue and orange to let the illustration stand out.

Hideya Kitazawa (Illustrator)

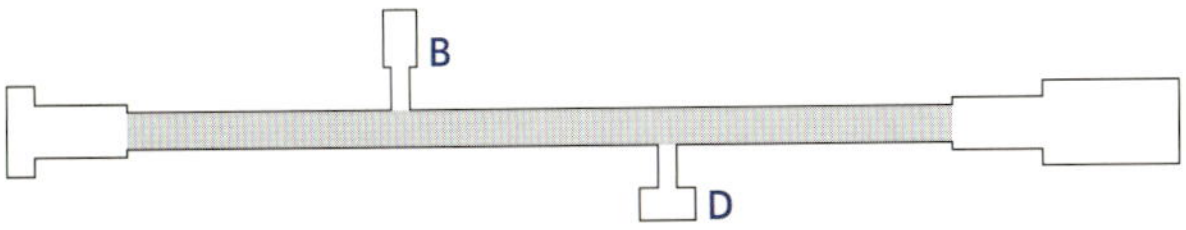

FACILITY GRAPHICS

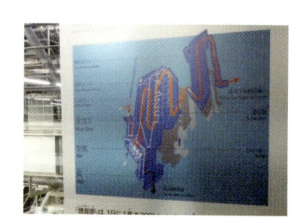

排ガス処理設備
Flue Gas Treatment System

The flue gas treatment system remove harmful gases and dust particles in the flue gases emitted from incinerated refuse. Dusts and DXNs (dioxins and furans) in the flue gas are removed at the filtering reactor. HCl and SOx are removed at the we scrubber. NOx is removed at the De-NOx catalyst reactor.

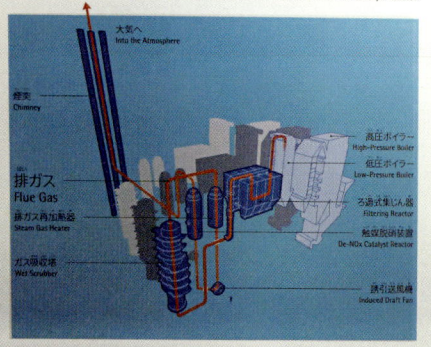

「排ガス処理設備」は、焼却炉でごみを燃やす際に発生する排ガスに含まれる有害な物質を取り除くところです。ばいじん(ちり)やダイオキシン類などを取り除くろ過式集じん器、硫黄酸化物や塩化水素を取り除くガス吸収塔、窒素酸化物を取り除く触媒脱硝装置などが設備され、きれいな排ガスを作る工夫がされています。

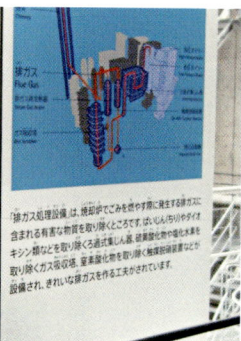

施設内のインフォメーションは、高解像度で美しいグラデーションを再現できる透明なラムダシートによって、施設を見わたすガラス面に直接貼り込む方法をとった。デザイン的には、見学者、とりわけ子どもたちが楽しく、親しみを持てるように、小学4年生以上の漢字にはルビをふり、統一した色使いとタイポグラフィで表現した。さらに、バイリンガルの音声ガイダンスが、焼却設備の理解を深めるよいきっかけとなっている。

Clear Lambda digital film was used to print high resolution graduations of text and adhered onto the glass where one can learn about the overview of the plant. Using unified colors and typography, the information was designed in a way that was also enjoyable to children. The information was displayed in Japanese and English.

ごみピット
Refuse Pit

Refuse collects in the refuse pit temporarily. The pit measures 16 meters by 44 meters and is 15 meters in depth (approximately to the height of a four-story building), and has a storage capacity of 4,200 tons, equivalent to the total volume of refuse combusted in one week. Air from the refuse pit is sucked through ventilation openings in the pit's front wall and transferred to the incinerator, providing it with an air supply. The incinerator's high-temperature combustion eliminates any odors, preventing odor leakage from the refuse pit.

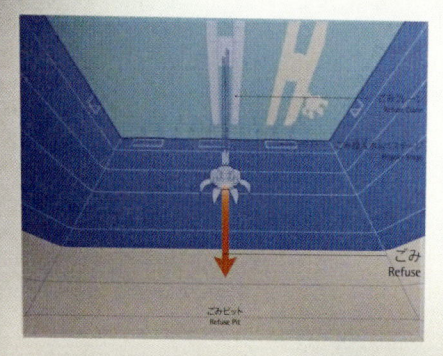

「ごみピット」は、投入ステージから降ろされるごみを溜めておくところです。大きさは、幅44m、奥行き16m、深さ15mで4階建てのビルの高さに相当し、約1週間分のごみ(最大で4,200トン)を溜めることができます。「ごみピット」内部の空気を吸込口から焼却炉へ送り、ごみを燃やすための空気として使用します。ごみを高温で燃やす

当時、ラムダシートをシール加工することは初の試みであったが、出力業者の徹底した品質管理によって実現することができた。見学者は、まるでフィルター越しに見ているかのように、ガラス面に描かれたグラフィックを通して、稼働している巨大クレーンの動きを確かめながら眺めることができる。この新しい設置方法によって、グラフィックの「スケール感」と「動き」は一層高められた。

Printing on the clear Lambda digital film then transferring it to an adhesive had never been done before. By using this clear Lambda digital film, visitors where able to see the large crane in operation while being able to read the information on the glass in front of them. By using this new material, we were able to illustrate the movement of equipment in the Incineration Plant.

下 左/巨大クレーンは4~5tのゴミを一掴みにして焼却炉へ運ぶ。 右/このクレーンにも、アクセントカラーであるブルーがペイントされた。
Bottom Left: This crane can pick up four to five tons of trash and transport it to an incinerator. Right: The crane was also painted in the International Klein Blue.

PLASMA DISPLAYS AND TIMELINE

上／プラズマスクリーン3面の位置は、原寸のモデルを設置しながら何度もテストをして決めた。右／完成したプラズマスクリーンの3面では、社会とゴミの関係の普遍的なイメージが、100枚以上のビジュアルによって構成されたスライドショーで映し出されている。スライドショーの編集はTYDで行なった。

Top: We examined the placement for three plasma screen monitors by making actual scale models. Right: Three plasma screen monitors were used to show over 100 edited images which explained the relationship between our modern society and the amount of waste that is accumulated.

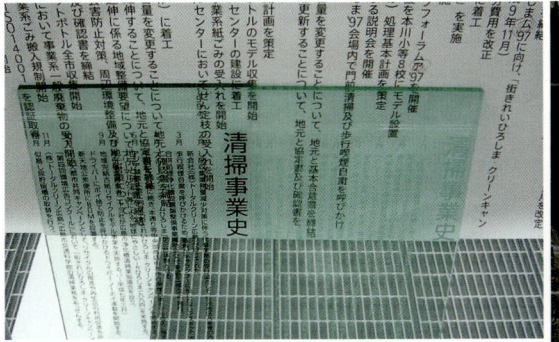

映像展示｜Plasma Displays

上／最終的なガラス素材が決まらなかったので、さまざまなサンプルにプリントして色を決めるためのテストを繰り返した。右／完成された「広島市の清掃事業の歩み」のグラフィック。タイプフェイスの印刷は白か黒か、いろいろなサンプルをつくって検証した結果、黒に。

Right: Information timeline graphics explain the Beautification and Clean Project for the city of Hiroshima. We studied the application of the text in both black and white lettering and chose black for legibility.

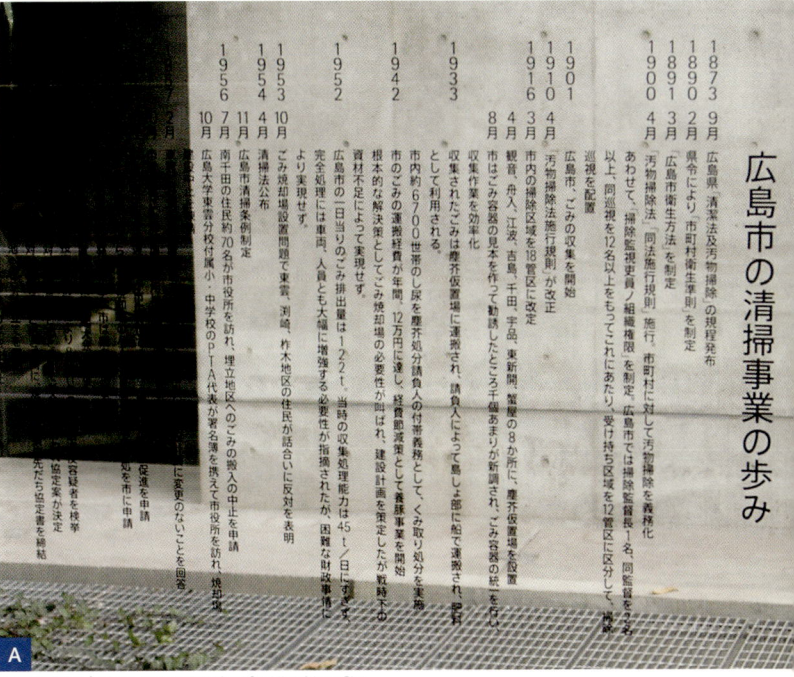

清掃事業の歩み｜Clean Project Timeline for Hiroshima City

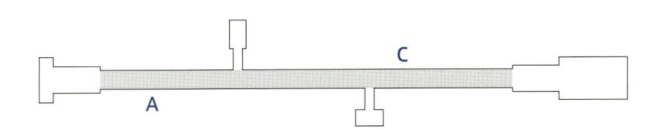

SCALED MODEL

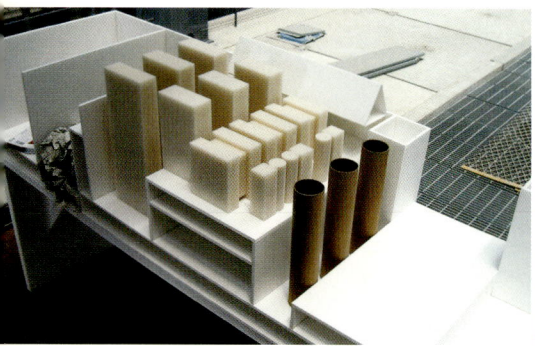

上／模型のスケールとボリューム検証用のスタディ模型。右／広島市環境局中工場の1/100の模型は、エコリアム内の「焼却施設ギャラリー」に展示されている。精密な模型なので、巨大な中工場の全体を把握することができる。

Top: A working model to study the final architecture. This model was made to show the overall scale and volume of the building.
Right: 1/100 ratio model of the Hiroshima Naka Incineration Plant, exhibited inside the Incineration equipment gallery in the Ecorium. Through this detailed architectural model, visitors can view the entire incineration plant.

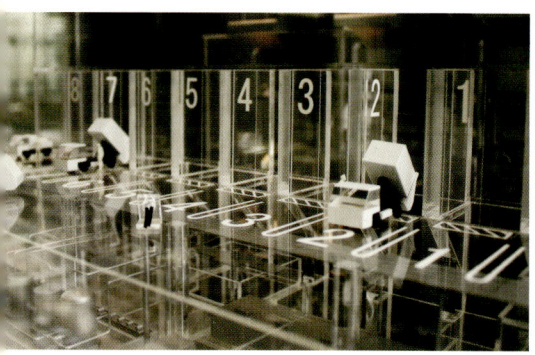

焼却施設ギャラリー | Incineration Equipment Gallery

上／スケールモデルや原寸モデルによって、サイン計画は緻密なシミュレーションが行なわれた。右／見学者が見ることのできないゴミ搬入ステージでは、スケールの大きいゴミ焼却施設にふさわしいインパクトのあるタイプフェイスを選び、アクセントカラーであるブルーを用いた。

Top: A simulation of the signage design was conducted by using scaled models and actual size models.
Right: Choosing a typeface with impact and staying with the International Klein Blue theme color, the garage space was designed to be consistent with the front of the building.

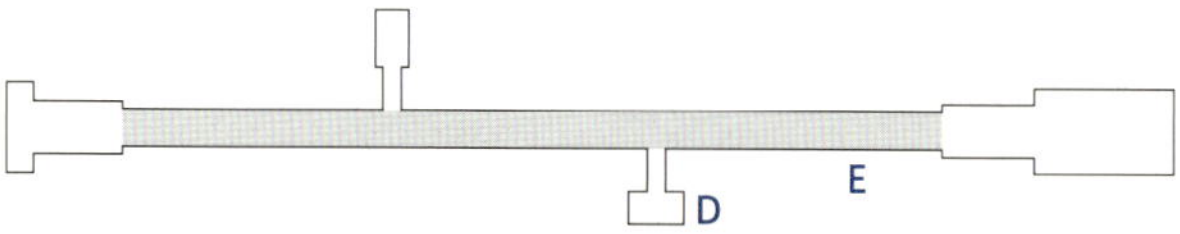

友人から建築家の谷口吉生氏を紹介されて事務所を訪問したとき、進行中のプロジェクトの一つに「広島中工場」がありました。谷口さんから、公共施設のグラフィックに興味があるかどうかの質問を受けて、私は「サンフランシスコに住んでいるので、環境関連プロジェクトを手がけたことがある」と答えました。すると谷口さんは、「このプロジェクトのために、最低でも東京都内と他県のゴミ焼却施設を10カ所以上見学して、私に、このプロジェクトにふさわしいサイン計画とグラフィックデザインをプレゼンテーションして欲しい」と言われました。私はプロジェクトに興味がある意向を伝え、数カ月後、アイデアをまとめて谷口さんのオフィスに送りました。こうして、広島中工場のプロジェクトへの参加が決まったのです。

When I visited Mr. Yoshio Taniguchi's architecture studio, one of the projects he was working on was the Hiroshima City Naka Incineration Plant. He asked if I was interested in designing graphics for a public incineration plant. I showed interest and so we talked about various environmental projects I've worked on in the past. Mr. Taniguchi then briefly explained the project to me and said, "If you are serious about working on this project, you need to visit at least ten different incinerator plants in Japan. If you are still interested after the visits, please contact me and present a signage, graphic design and color scheme." I followed through on my interest by traveling to Japan and visited over 12 incineration plants. A few months later, I presented the design direction and joined the project.

E | パッカー車展示 | Garbage Truck Installation

パッカー車は真っ白に塗装することによって、清掃事業の日常的なイメージから解放される。
All the garbage trucks are painted white, a color that evokes purity and cleanliness to deflect the visitor's usual conception of waste.

対談 Conversation

物語る模型

ワンダーウォール　片山正通

Photo by Kozo Takayama

コミュニケーションを生む模型

八木：片山正通さんのことは、私が「インディヴィ」のプロジェクトを手がけ、片山さんが「インディヴィカフェ」を行なって以来存じ上げていたのですが、お会いするチャンスがなかったです。先日東京へ行ったとき、片山さんの「EXHIBITION OF WONDERWALL ARCHIVES 01 -10 PROJECT MODELS-」展のことを聞いて、さっそく銀座まで見に行きました。そこで、あれほど緻密に、空間の雰囲気まで表現している模型を見て、片山さんの才能に改めて驚きました。

片山：ありがとうございます。

八木：そこで今回は、片山さんと「模型」をテーマにお話ししたいなあと思ったわけです。ちょうど10年前に、私たちはアップルストアのコンセプトデザインをしたのですが、そのときのデザインプロセスが実にユニークでした。
まず私たちチームが1/10のサイズの模型を作成すると、それを基にしてアップルチームが巨大なウエアハウスに原寸模型をつくっていたのです。原寸だと、その場で問題や改善点がわかって、効率よくデザインを決めていくことができました。
以前、片山さんから聞いたCGを駆使したプレゼンテーションの話で、「CGでは、プレゼン側がクライアント側に見せたい見せ場としてのアングルだけが表現されてしまう傾向がある」とおっしゃっていて、「確かにそうかもしれない」と、すごく印象に残っています。
そして今回、片山さんの模型展を拝見してみると、壁や天井を外すことができて、しかも室内のファニチャーを移動することもできるように、細部まで精緻につくり込んだ模型を目の当たりにして、「クライアントが求めている空間がきっちり表現されていて、プロジェクトのポイントが明確に伝わってくる」と感心しました。片山さんは、プレゼンのために常に模型を作成しているそうですが、どんなところにポイントを置いて制作しているんですか？ぜひお聞かせ下さい。

片山：アイデアやイメージを具現化する前段階として、モノレベルで形象化することが重要だと思うんです。…というのも、頭のなかのイメージは、ワーッと思いついた、空間のポジティブな部分ですから、まずそうした部分を模型に落とし込んでいくことが大切です。
けれども不思議なことに、模型にしてみると同時にネガティブなところが浮き上がって見えてきます。実際に空間を構築していく際には、今までの経験から、ネガティブな部分もきちんと拾い上げて全体像を構想していくことが重要なのですが、その点模型はリアリティーがあるんです。先ほど八木さんがおっしゃっていましたが、CGはポジティブな部分だけで、ネガティブなところを隠してしまうという側面があります。良い点、悪い点を含めてアイデアのすべてをさらけ出して検証するためには、「模型」という方法が私には一番わかりやすいんです。

八木：模型で検証するという方法は、片山さん独自のアプローチなのでしょうか？

片山：私が学んだ環境に影響を受けているのかもしれませんが、私の場合、模型をつくってはじめてリアルに理解することができる。私自身がアイデアのポジティブなところもネガティブなところも含めて全体を理解したうえで、クライアントにプレゼンテーションすることがプロとして当然の姿勢だろうと思います。同時に、私たち自身はもちろんですが、クライアント側の理解が不十分な状態でプロジェクトに入ることはとても怖いことですよね。模型だとクライアント側も一目で全体像を汲み取ってくれます。そういう意味では、模型をつくるという野暮ったさも理解したうえで、あえて制作しているんですね。

八木：「模型」といっても、初期のスタディ模型、思考を進める際のスケッチ的な模型、そして完成度の高いプレゼン用の模型と、作業工程のなかでいろいろな種類の模型があり、その意味も違っていると思うのですが…。

片山：その通りですね。私の場合、最初は白い紙を使ってスタディ模型をつくって、空間全体のボリュームをつかんでから、素材や色、仕上げなどのディテールを詰めつつ、さまざまなデザイン的な可能性を検討していきます。
私たちが手がけるプロジェクトの多くは、商品が陳列されるスペース、リテール空間であるという特徴があります。そのために、最初から想像できる範囲内で陳列される商品も表現することを心がけています。たとえば、壁一面に木製の棚をデザインしたとしても、実際に商品が陳列されるとイメージが大きく変わってしまいます。さらに、お客様がたくさんいらっしゃれば、空間の印象はさらに変わってきます。ですから、こうしたすべての要素が入り込んだ段階まで模型を使って、検証を繰り返す必要があります。
八木さんのアップルのプロジェクトのように原寸模型ができれば最高ですが、実際にはそこまでするプロジェクトはごくまれです。私たちが、一見するとジオラマのよう見えるくらいまでで落とし込んだ精密な模型をつくる背景には、こうした私たちなりの事情があるのです。

八木：アップルのプロジェクトでは、私たちが参加する以前に、すでにほかの事務所が8ヵ月ほどかけて準備していた模型が存在していました。最初にその模型を見せてもらいましたが、何て表現すべきか、「ただキレイなだけ」という印象でした。片山さん風に言えば「ジオラマっぽくて、思わず手を伸ばしていじりたくなる」というワクワクした感覚が湧いてこない模型でした。ところが、私たちが新たなデザインを模型でプレゼンしたときには、スティーブ・ジョブズが模型をずっと自分で触って動かしながら考え込んでいた。
たしかに、キレイな模型はたくさんありますが、デザインプロセスの一つとしての模型には、物語を彷彿とさせるような工夫や表現が何より重要なのだと思います。片山さんの模型はまさにそうなのだと思います。

片山：八木さんがおっしゃるように、「キレイな模型」と「物語る模型」には大きな違いありますね。後者にはプロジェクトを達成するという大きな目標があって、それを実現するための一つの手段であるという意識が込められているのでしょう。つまりクライアントや私たちも含めて、プロジェクトに関わるすべての人たちが目標を共有するための「コミュニケーションの手段」と言えると思います。

アップルの場合は、ジョブスさんが模型に手を伸ばした時点で、プロジェクトは良い方向に動いていたのだと思いますよ。模型を囲んで空間を共有することが、議論のはじまる第一歩だと思うんですよ。私たちの提案に対して、クライアントも客観的ではなく主観的に考えてもらう…、模型を使ってそんな環境を誘発したいと考えています。
私たちが模型を出すことによって、クライアントも「ああ、こうなるんだ!」と実感することができ、模型を見ながら「あ、ここはやっぱりこうしたい!」というような積極的な発言も出てくるようになります。

八木:相手を引き込むために、CGでなくて模型で表現する意味があるのですね。

片山:「他人事でない」って思わせるところが模型にはありますね。そこが重要だと思います。

八木:片山さんの模型を見て、あれほどの精度の模型を制作するということのすばらしさを再認識しました。

片山:私も模型をつくるプロセスのなかで、納得できない箇所はどんどん変えていくんですね。ですから、クライアントに対してはもちろんですが、自分自身、社内に対しても、模型のもつ意味は大きいですね。

デザインは世界の共通言語

八木:オフィスに行ったときに、自給自足しているオフィスだなと感じました。必要なモノがいつでも用意されているような。あんな空間のオフィスは東京にはなかなかないと思います。

片山:ありがとうございます。働く環境に関しては、デザイナーとして仕事をしていくうえで、いつでも変化に対応できる環境でなければよくないと思いまして…。事務所のレイアウトもそのように考えています。

八木:模型制作のコストは、どのようにされているんですか?

片山:基本的に模型の制作費は弊社のフィーに含まれています。使用目的の一番は、デザインの検証、そしてその検証した結果を模型としてプレゼンテーションに使用するんです。クライアントにはお見せしないスタディー模型を複数制作するプロジェクトもありますが、それは私たちの責任において納得がいくまで何度も作り直します。クライアントの意向と合わなければ、それはもちろんゼロからつくり直すことになります。ただ、私たちも経験を積んできていて、さまざまな条件に対応できる人材も機材もそろっていますし、このような環境があることが私たちの強みでもあるとも言えます。

八木:片山さんにとって「模型制作」とは?

片山:イメージにリアリティーを与えてくれるツールではないかと思います。模型になると、ポジティブな部分と同時にネガティブな要素も浮き彫りにされる。たとえば、空間の真ん中に大きなカッコいいテーブルを置きたい。けれども、空間的にはインパクトはあるけれど、テーブルの回りが狭くなって動線が一方通行になってしまう恐れがある…というようなケースがあります。

デザインを進めていくうえでは、こうしたリスクを承知で、あえてネガティブ要因に目をつぶってポジティブを前面に押し出すべきか、あるいはほかの解決策はないのか…そんなことをジャッジすることが必要で、このような場合には模型が何より有効です。リアルな模型を通して、客観的に自分のアイデアを見直すことがとても重要なんです。

八木:ITが進化してラフスケッチをすぐにCGに表現できる時代、模型というある種ローテクな方法でデザインをしている片山さんにはとてもオリジナリティを感じます。模型の精度も半端じゃないし…。
アメリカでよくスタンダードという言葉が使われますが、片山さんのスタンダードのレベルは非常に高い。模型を見てもそのレベルの高さを実感できました。

片山:精度へのこだわりは、「デザインは世界共通の言語」だと思っているからなんです。視覚の印象は世界共通ですよね? 模型の精度を上げることは、曖昧な部分をなるべく残さない、私の主張をはっきり表明することとイコールだと考えています。模型で自分のイメージではないものを表現してしまったら、言葉で「ここの木材ですが、実際はもうちょっと薄い色ですよ」と言い訳しても無意味です。素材や色も、可能な限りイメージに忠実に表現して模型を制作していきます。だから、素材のディスカッションがはじまることもよくあります。こういうのは特に海外クライアントが多くなると、有効ですね。
イメージには怖い部分もあって、完成してから「思っていたものと違う!」なんて言われてしまうと大変なことです。そうした事態を回避したいという意味ももちろんありますね。

八木:今までのように模型でのプレゼンテーションは、今後も続けられるんですよね。

片山:そうですね。模型でのプレゼンテーションをベースに、必要に応じてCGを使用していくと思います。

八木:最近、「スーパーAマーケット」のプロジェクトをご一緒しました。社長の佐々木啓之さんが、TYDのオフィスにいらした際に、「どうしても見せたいものがあるんだよ」って見せてくれたのが、片山さんの模型でした。「壁も天井も外すことができて、自由に触れられる模型なんだよ」ととても気に入っておられました。

片山:一緒に壁を外したりして見ながら、たとえば、このテーブル取ったらどうなるんだろうとか、いろいろ動かしながら意見交換できることは、とてもクリエイティブな行為だと思うのです。実際、私たちもプレゼンテーション前の段階でいろいろなケースの検証ができていますから、クライアントの意見に対して誠実に回答することができて、信頼感を深めることにもつながります。

八木:私たちのオフィスでも、手作業でデザイン制作することを大切にしています。また、片山さんの模型とは手法は異なりますが、イメージを具体的なモノで表現する「箱」というプレゼン方法を使ってプロジェクトの世界観を伝えることによって、クライアントとの距離感が縮まっているなぁと実感しています。そういった意味で、今回は片山さんのワンダーウォールさんとTYDのデザイン姿勢や手法に、共通性を感じることができました。今日はありがとうございました。

Photo by Shoichi Kajino

使用する素材と道具。基本的にはつくる人のセンスだと思う。
Pictured here are materials and tools to build models. The work area reflects Wonderwall's sensibilities.

模型の中でたくさんの人がいろいろなポーズをしている。こんなに楽しい模型を見ればクライアントは驚くと思う。
Figures are posed inside the model to simulate the design and stimulate the client's imagination as it would appear in real life.

SUPER A MARKET Miniature Model

片山 正通 1966年生まれ。株式会社ワンダーウォール代表。武蔵野美術大学空間演出デザイン学科教授。クライアントのコンセプトを具現化する自由な発想、また伝統や様式に敬意を払いつつ現代的要素を取り入れるバランス感覚が、国際的に高く評価されている。代表作に、A BATHING APE®／BAPE STORE®各店、ユニクロ グローバル旗艦店（NY、ロンドン、パリ）、NIKE原宿、coletteなど。

MASAMICHI KATAYAMA Born Okayama, Japan 1966. Founded the interior design firm Wonderwall and is a professor at Musashino Art University. His firm elicits an uninhibited sense of energy towards design, where architecture and interior design is known for being one of the most exhilarating in the world. The firm is best known for the interior retail design for A BATHING APE®/BAPE STORE® stores, Uniqlo's global flagship store (NY, London, Paris), NIKE HARAJUKU and Colette.

Photo by Kozo Takayama

STORIES BEHIND THE WORKING MODEL
MASAMICHI KATAYAMA / Wonderwall Inc.

Models Lead to Communication

TY: Katayama, I originally heard about your firm in 1994 when I was working on the INDIVI project, and you were designing the cafe. Although I never met you during that time, I was reintroduced to your work last Fall when a friend recommended I see the show *Exhibition of Wonderwall Archives 01-10 Project Models*. I was very impressed by the atmosphere you created with that installation, and amazed at the detail in the models. Today I would like to talk to you about using models as a design tool.
When I was involved in the Apple store concept and design, we built a 1/10 scale model of the space. Apple later recreated our model actual size inside a warehouse, so we could move through the space and examine the design from every angle. This comprehensive perspective enabled us to make changes very quickly.
You once said when designers give presentations that only use computer graphics, they "tend to only show the parts they want to show the client." Why do you feel models are necessary?

MK: I feel it is important to make a model before even visualizing an image of the future design. My initial idea for a design is usually positive, by expressing that concept as a model I am better able to see the negative aspects. It is critical to anticipate the elements to avoid early in the design process, which can be done most efficiently by seeing the project as a whole.

TY: I assume there are certain steps involved in the process of building a model.

MK: Yes, you're right. We begin by making studies, and mock up the space in white paper to understand the overall volume of the interior. We start thinking about details like materials, color and finishes when we are making the actual model. As many of our projects require display, we must visualize how these interior elements will enhance the appearance of the product. While the actual size representation you built for the Apple store is ideal, this is usually not feasible financially. Therefore, we rely on very detailed models.

TY: When we showed Steve Jobs the model of the Apple project, he was able to be very "hands on" and think through potential changes. Although models can be very refined, I think it is more important for them to tell a story. Your models do this very effectively.

MK: I agree, there is a major difference between a "well refined model," and a model that "tells a story well." Models that tell a story will more likely result in a successful project as they are an interactive tool for communication. More specifically, my firm and our clients use these models as a dynamic means for sharing goals. Your description of the way Steve Jobs utilized the model to engage in refining the design, also represents how models can indicate that the project is moving in a positive direction.

TY: Interactive models definitely draw clients into the design more directly than computer graphics.

Design is a Universal Language

TY: The first time I went to your office, I knew it was set up to do everything in house. You have a full service operation. Anything you need to complete a project is conveniently available, which shows clients how invested you are in overseeing every aspect of their design.

MK: Thank you. As a designer, my work environment must be flexible so that it is able to evolve. The layout was designed so we had the ability to make changes over time based on client or staff needs.

TY: Does your office also function as a full scale environment for interactive modeling?

MK: Yes, touching on what we discussed earlier, the office allows me to test potential furnishings and space planning issues for different projects. For example, I may want to use a cool looking table in the center of a store for impact, but know this piece might limit circulation. By physically installing the table in my office, I can receive my staff's third party perspective, separate from the client's or my own point of view. My staff and I can also work around the table to measure its merits against its risks, and determine whether there is a better solution.

TY: In spite of the resources in your office and the computer's ability to render rough sketches as highly stylized graphics, you choose to display your originality through refreshingly low tech, hand made models. However, the amount of detail your models posses is simply astonishing, and exhibits the level of your standards.

MK: Sight is a universal source of impressions, right? I pay close attention to detail because "design is a universal language." Raising the quality of the models removes ambiguities, and allows the client and myself to be sure all aspects of the design are expressed clearly and honestly. It's pointless to make a model if it is not accurate to what I had imagined, just as it would be meaningless for me to tell a client that "this wood will actually be lighter in reality."

TY: We recently collaborated on Tomorrowland's Super A Market project in Aoyama. The company's President, Mr. Sasaki, was very enthusiastic about showing us your model of the store when he visited my office. He noted that "the walls and ceiling can be detached, it's an interactive model." He was very pleased with the functional aspect of seeing the entire space, as opposed to simply the exterior of a static model.

MK: Mr. Sasaki and I both interacted with the model and shared our thoughts, which was a very creative experience. To help ensure the success of these exchanges, I always prepare by anticipating any question the client may ask so I have solid answers or alternatives suggestions. It builds trust when clients feel that you have carefully considered solutions, and have thoroughly addressed potential alternatives.

TY: I can relate to your design process and strategy very well. At TYD, we feel it is necessary to make models and mock ups with our hands. We often make concept boxes for our projects, and use them in presentations. Although these displays are a little different than your models, they allow us to communicate with our clients in similar ways.

TY: Tamotsu Yagi
MK: Masamichi Katayama

Photo by Shuji Yoshida

"...THE PEOPLE WHO ARE CRAZY ENOUGH TO THINK THEY CAN CHANGE THE WORLD, ARE THE ONES WHO DO."

———"自分が世界を変えられると本気で信じる人たちこそが、本当に、世界を変えているのだ。"
「THINK DIFFERENT」より

二〇一一年一〇月五日の午後、スティーブ・ジョブズ氏が他界されました。ちょうどこの本の入稿を終える前日のことでした。スティーブの訃報を知った瞬間、我々TYDのスタッフ一同は深い悲しみに包まれました。私は幸運にもスティーブと巡り会い、一緒に仕事をする機会を得ました。私にとってスティーブとの友情の意味を言葉で表わすことは容易ではありません。しかし、お互いクリエイターとして決して妥協を許さない姿勢を共有していたことは確かです。スティーブの計り知れない創造力、発明、そして完璧にまで仕上げる根気は、常に私にとってのインスピレーションの源でした。

二〇〇五年のスティーブのスタンフォード大学卒業式での祝賀スピーチにこんな言葉がありました。
「未来に先回りして点と点をつなげて見ることはできない。君たちにできるのは過去を振り返ってつなげることだけだ。」

この本には、私の人生とキャリアを形成する過程で重要であったさまざまな点、出来事、経験、場所、人々が登場します。
私の点がスティーブとつながり、そしてそれが素晴らしいコラボレーションに結びついたことを、ただただ感謝するばかりです。

二〇一一年一〇月五日　八木 保

In the afternoon of October 5, 2011, one day before this book was to go to press, I learned of the passing of Steve Jobs. At that moment, the entire TYD staff stood very still with deep sadness. I've been among the few, fortunate enough to have known and worked with Steve. It is difficult to put into words what our friendship meant to me. But it is clear that we spoke to each other in our approach as creators that "if it's worth doing, it's worth doing it right." His immense imagination for invention and his drive to perfect it has been an inspiration to watch. In Steve's 2005 Stanford University Commencement Address, he spoke about lessons he learned in life. He said, "you can't connect the dots looking forward, you can only connect them looking backwards." The pages in this book contain many dots, marking moments, experiences, people and places that have shaped my life and career. I am thankful that my dots have somehow connected me to Steve and the amazing projects we worked on together. – Tamotsu Yagi 06.10.2011

APPLE

Apple Store Creative Consulting

原寸模型

A full scale look at refining the Apple retail concept and the first store

十一年前の二〇〇〇年のある日のこと、スティーブ・ジョブズ本人からの、一本の電話から、期待高まる仕事がはじまりました。外出していたため、スタッフが代わりに対応したのですが、彼から残されたメッセージは、私が過去にデザインしたエスプリの本の特定されたページを見ておいてほしいという伝言と、大きなプロジェクトの予感のみ。インテリアデザイナーである植木莞爾氏とともにカリフォルニアにある、アップル本社へ飛び、全米における「アップルストア」の一号店のマスタープランと、一連のアートディレクションを手がけるプロジェクトがスタートしたのです。ショップ完成まで六カ月という短期間のスケジュールでしたが、スティーブ・ジョブズの決断の速さに促されるように、原寸で模型をつくり、現場で、プロジェクトチームとデザインのディテールを詰めていくという方法は、そのスケールの大きさといい、まさに未知の体験でした。

2000

In the winter of 2000, I received a call that was the start of an amazing project. I was traveling on business and couldn't be reached, so Steve Jobs left a message referencing specific pages in the *Esprit: The Comprehensive Design Principle* book. I returned the call and quickly sensed that Steve was onto another big project. He asked me to come to his office at 1 Infinite Loop in Cupertino and bring an interior designer. Steve mysteriously did not divulge the reason for this meeting. I convinced Kanji Ueki, an interior designer I had worked with in Japan, to fly to California and attend the meeting. We soon found ourselves in a conference room waiting with anticipation, and anxious to know why we were there. Suddenly, Steve entered and pointed to a model of an interior while asking for input. This was our introduction to Apple's plans for a retail program. Both Kanji and I were hired on the spot to join Apple's creative team. Our assignment was to refine the concept for Apple's retail presence, and the design of the first store that would open six months later. The success of this project was the result of tremendous teamwork, which was facilitated by Steve's decisiveness and his determination to generate the best possible solutions.

1.30.2001 | full scale model

APPLE STORE PROJECT

Steve's initial call mentioned the fixture and display systems from the Esprit Jeans retail shops in the 1980s. I had originally met Steve at the Esprit headquarters back then as well. It was now a new era, and an exciting time for business and retail developments worldwide. I was working on a number of new branding and interior projects for clients in Japan, including collaborations with Kanji on World Co. brands Untitled, INDIVI and Opaque. Kanji was also working with Yoshio Taniguchi on the interior design of the New York Museum of Modern Art, and was eager for another assignment in the United States. Steve approached us for this project recognizing the power of design as a universal language–a way to communicate Apple's complex technology to a larger global audience. He knew the importance of developing the core elements that would define Apple's unique retail experience, and establish the design "DNA" that would transfer to each store. The design process to create the master plan for Apple's retail model was very fast paced, we only had a few months to exchange ideas. The creative team introduced components that were furiously edited until each concept felt right. Steve did not dwell on particular details, he made quick decisions to keep the project moving. Steve also embraced the concept of an evolving design approach, where elements that could be revised or applied later could wait. We knew that products change, technology and services improve, and new lifestyles require regular adaptation.

1989年に日本で出版された『Esprit: The Comprehensive Design Principle』の中でも、スティーブ・ジョブズがとくに興味を示していたのは80年代のエスプリジーンズ・ストアの什器とそのデザインシステムでした。私がスティーブにはじめて会ったのはエスプリで働いていた頃です。彼はビジネスマンとして、複雑難解なテクノロジーを一般消費者に伝える手段としてのデザインの力と重要性を認識していました。そしてこの先、アップル独自のデザインDNAを一貫性をもって一つひとつのリテールストアに展開することが不可欠であると感じていました。

思い返せば、2000年当時は数多くのリテールストアの仕事を手がけていました。とくに、植木莞爾氏とのプロジェクトが多く、当時、谷口吉生氏とニューヨーク近代美術館新館の仕事にあたっていた植木氏は、海外での仕事にも興味があったこともあって、アップルのプロジェクトに対しても非常に前向きに了承してくれました。

プロジェクトは驚くほどの速さで進行し、スティーブによって招かれ、構成された私たちクリエイティブチームは、それぞれが納得いくまで妥協を許さずアイデアを固めていきました。プロジェクト成功の背景には、スティーブ本人の決断の速さに加え、プロジェクトの現在と未来を見据える包容力がありました。時代の流れとともに良いデザインの定義が変化するように、ストアデザインも変化が必要です。その時代の良いデザインに固執せず、アップルならではの美意識の核を残しつつ、進化するストアを目指してプロジェクトは進行したのでした。

The great California architects, Greene and Greene believed that a house wasn't properly designed unless every stick of furniture and every light fixture, sconce and andiron was designed in a comprehensive way which would complement the architecture. We try to follow in this tradition. There are few examples of this today and we are proud to attempt to carry this idea forward. Certainly, there is great logic in this approach because one mentality and style can shine through clearly.

Our first project, 900 Minnesota Street in San Francisco is a good example. Quilts, furniture, carpets, paint schemes and plants are all carefully blended together by one point of view. The results read with a special clarity.

Store fixturing systems have been often designed by the architect himself. Shiro Kuramata, Shigeru Uchida, Antonio Citterio, Joe D Urso, Jon Evans, Norman Foster and the Sottsass Group have all custom designed fixturing systems. The design and refinement of a completely new store fixturing system is a tough and experimental process.

Prototyping takes time: steel, aluminum castings and dies all take painstaking work. In five years we have internationally developed over eight distinctly different component systems for our different stores. Some systems have rolled out to over one hundred and fifteen units and others, although less, may well be used again in the future.

For the most part our vocabulary is an industrial signature that uses aluminum, rubber and various meshes or punched metal surfaces. Colorations are predominantly neutral and finishes tough for wear and tear. Interconnecting parts and components are designed to be highly flexible, not because we want store managers or personnel to move them about easily but because it provides designers the flexibility with which to deal with a multitude of different space configurations. Likewise, we use as little built-in fixtures as possible with an eye towards quick renovation when either the look or the age of the fixtures has reached the end of its effectiveness.

F I X T U

1363

Visitor
Tamotsu Yagi
Representing: Tamotsu Yagi
Contact: Steve Jobs
AC01   Thu, May 16, 2002

原寸 | Actual Size

アップルでのミーティングの際は、一週間前に出席する人の名前を連絡し、当日は本社の受付で本人と確認されてから、このネームタグを貼りミーティングに参加した。

We confirmed our meeting schedule prior to arriving at Apple, and upon confirming our identification at the reception, we were given access along with the pictured name tag.

Fixturing systems designed by Shigeru Uchida are shown here. Starting from top, left and right, junctions and shelving system; below left and right, hanging bars and hanger. This page center, the Jeans shop fully merchandised utilizing the Uchida fixturing system.

内田繁デザインによるフィクスチャリング・システム。上2点はジャンクションと棚のクローズ・アップである。下2点はハンガーと棚柱。中央がこのシステムで全面的に展開された、ESPRIT Jeansのインテリア。

Photo by Shuji Yoshida

APPLE STORE OVERVIEW

The project began by defining how each area within the store would be used, where areas should be placed and the distribution of traffic. Kanji and I knew that a 3D model would be more effective than a flat rendering for this critical dialog. We recreated the space's interior with our design suggestions as a working tool for the first creative team conversation. Using colorful and tactile materials, we made all components of the model moveable. Steve really loved seeing how color brought the model to life. He also appreciated the interactive nature of the model, which further animated the space and let him experiment with different layout options. Once the team established the store's key features and overall flow, we refined the actual designs of the fixtures and graphic elements. Finally, Steve ordered the construction of a life size model made of foam board and the interior materials specified. This practice may be standard in retail design today, but the expense shocked Kanji and me at the time. The actual size model was built in a secret warehouse, and modifications were addressed overnight. Our meetings took place inside the model as we carefully adjusted details like dimensions and finishes. Steve envisioned Apple retail to be an exciting hub. He saw a friendly and inviting place to gather that would serve the general consumer, potential new customers and professionals who were already familiar with Apple's products. We were to stay true to the brand's existing identity—complex technology made approachable and intuitive—and the product design's distinct simplicity. The team carefully applied these guidelines to the functionality, service and overall store structure.

1.23.2001 | miniature model

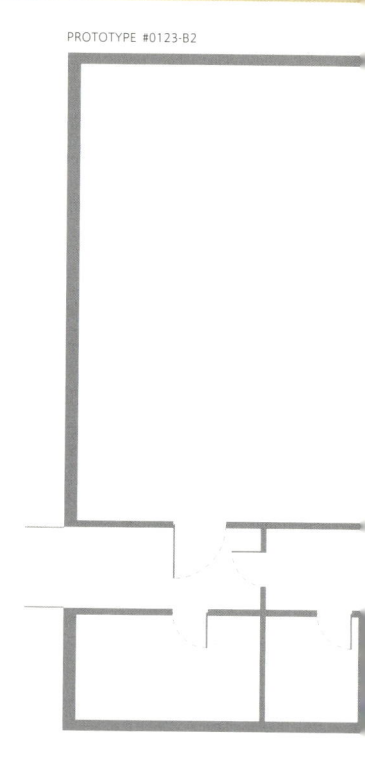

PROTOTYPE #0123-B2

模型をつくった一番の目的は、各商品コーナーの位置とカスタマーの動線を認識するためでした。平面図を見ながらの打ち合わせより、立体的な模型を体験しながらの説明の方がより臨場感があり、実際のショップ環境をシミュレーションしやすいと考えたからです。鮮やかな配色や什器の素材感を意識してつくった模型は、植木氏やスティーブにも非常に好評で、制作したモデルをたたき台にフォームボードや実物の素材を使用して、原寸模型の構成をスティーブの判断を仰ぎながら制作することになりました。

リテール関連の仕事を数多くこなしていた私たちにとっても、原寸モデルで制作することは当たり前のことではなかったのでとても驚きました。アップル本社内の倉庫では、原寸モデルの制作は数週間で完成。その後の打ち合わせは、すべてのエレメントデザインに至るまで倉庫内で行なわれました。アップルの商品デザインがもつシンプルななかからの美しさを基調とし、プロダクトとインテリアが一体となるデザインを実現。

スティーブは、このアップルストアをブランドの核と位置付け、ユーザー同士がともに情報を得る場として機能することを望んでいました。従来のユーザーに加えて、新規ユーザーや、仕事の道具としてアップル製品を使用するプロユーザーが全員一体となって情報を交換できるような場所。それがアップルストアなのです。

I happen to pick up the phone when Steve Jobs of Apple called TYD which lead to the first Apple store project. I was young and a bit nervous talking to Steve Jobs but the way he spoke to me as if he was an old friend helped me relax. Steve inquired about some information regarding some images in the *Esprit: The Comprehensive Design Principle* and that's how it all started.
Matt Dick (Matt Dick of Small Trade Company & Former TYD Designer)

アップルストア1号店のプロジェクトのきっかけになった、スティーブ・ジョブズの電話を受けたのは、偶然にも私でした。あのスティーブ・ジョブズーとのはじめての会話に、私は緊張しました。彼の話し方は、昔からの友だちに話しているような、親近感のある口調でした。スティーブは『エスプリブック (The Comprehensive Design Principle)』からいろいろな質問を私にしてきました。
マット・ディック (マット・ディック・オブ・スモール・トレード・カンパニー 元TYDデザイナー)

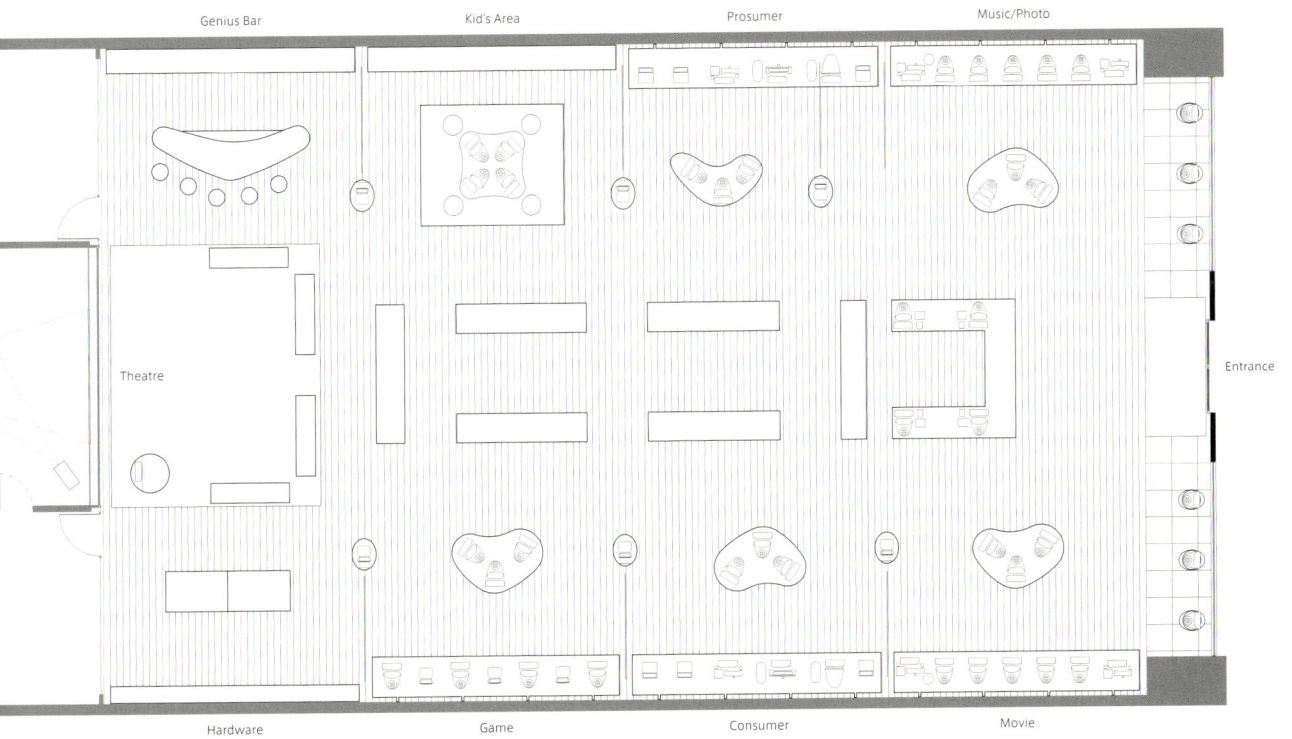

Genius Bar	Kid's Area	Prosumer	Music/Photo

Theatre

Entrance

Hardware	Game	Consumer	Movie

当時のデジタルカメラ(Sony Cyber-shot DSC-P1)で模型を撮影。さまざまな角度から検証した。2000年以降、デジタルカメラをデザインツールの一つとして、使用しはじめた。
The TYD staff took digital photos of the model for discussion using the
Sony Cyber-shot DSC-P1. We began using the burgeoning digital camera technology as a design tool around the year 2000.

APPLE STORE DNA

GENIUS BAR

The Genius Bar was Steve's genius idea. His concept reversed the standard Customer Service approach, by allowing customers to schedule appointments with Apple employees that were extremely knowledgeable about their products. The Genius Bar is about Apple's personalized service and continuing education which was to be a significant aspect of the Apple store experience. Knowing that retail stores have a void area that is often near the back, we strategically placed the Genius Bar in those potentially underutilized spaces. The design of the Genius Bar has evolved, but the concept has remained.

このプロジェクトでスティーブ・ジョブズが終始一貫してこだわったことが、「ジーニアスバー」。ストアの一番奥までカスタマーを引き込むためには、他のショップにはない魅力的なコーナーづくりが欠かせませんでした。多くのショップのサービスセンターが、ショップの陰や隠れた場所に設置されているのに対し、動線を意識して縦長のショップの最奥に配置されたジーニアスバーは、商品に関する質問やトラブルに即座に応えてくれる、言葉通り「コンピュータの天才(専門知識が豊富なスタッフ)」が応対してくれるカウンターです。アップルストアがオープンした頃は、ジーニアスバーでも対応できないことがあったため、アップル本社にダイレクトにつながる赤電話が設置されていました。

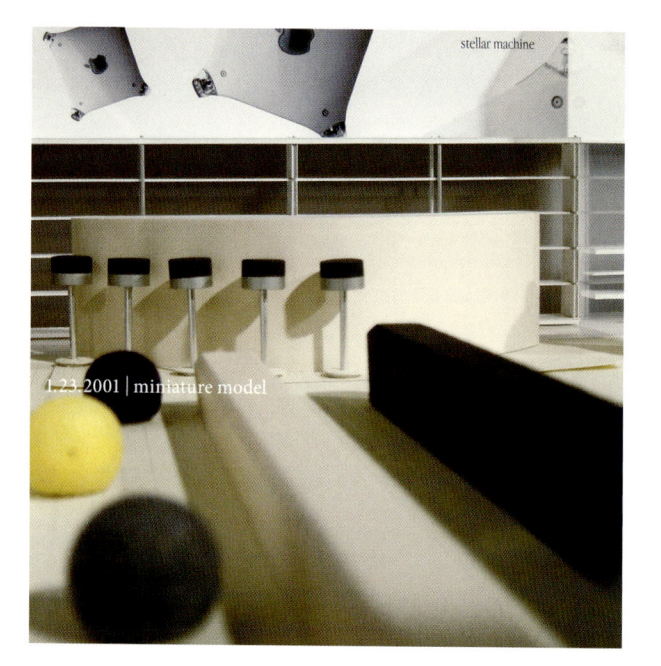

5.17.2001 | actual store

1.23.2001 | miniature model

It's a little known secret, but we created the Genius Bar logo. I recall researching many elements for this project and when the atom symbol came up, it was like, "THAT'S IT!" We cleaned and reworked the details of the icon so it wouldn't look too cluttered. Everything about the icon worked as if we found the last piece of a puzzle and it still brings a smile to my face every time I see it.
Shay Lam (Senior Associate at Perkins Eastman & Former TYD Graphic Designer)

あまり知られていないことですが、ジーニアスバーのロゴデザインをしたのも私たちでした。プロジェクトのために新しいフォントを購入した際、フォントの一つとしてさまざまなアイコンがあったなかで、この原子のアイコンが目に入りました。私たちが頭の中で探し求めていたパズルの最後のピースが見つかったような気持ちだったことを覚えています。洗練され、知的なイメージにぴったりなこのアイコンをリデザインして、ジーニアスバーのロゴとして提案したのです。
シェイ・ラム (パーキンス・イーストマン 元TYD グラフィック・デザイナー)

Photo by Rick English / Tim Hursley

1.30.2001 | full scale model

1.29.2001 | full scale model

「コンピュータの天才たち」から発せられるメッセージの軌道。それは世界中にアイデアの粒子となって拡張し、新しい価値へと結合する原子の放物線を思い起こさせます。私たちはこのアイデアにこだわりました。現在も使用されているジーニアスバーのアイコンはとくに思い入れが強いです。
長谷川 信一郎（グラフィック・デザイナー 元TYD グラフィック・デザイナー）

Apple's technology opened doors to new possibilities. This was the philosophy of the Genius Bar. We wanted to communicate this through the Genius Bar logo where the electrons represented the message orbiting the world. My contribution to the development of this iconic logo is one of the proudest moments of my career.
Shinichiro Hasegawa (Graphic Designer & Former TYD Graphic Designer)

原寸模型のなかでも一番迫力のあったジーニアスバーのコーナー。紙でつくられたカウンターチェアも用意された。
The Genius Bar had the most impact of all the actual size models. The counter height stools were also constructed out of paper.

1.23.2001 | miniature model

Creative consulting team: Steve Jobs, Tim Kobe, IDSA, and Wilhelm Oehl, IDSA, of Eight Inc.; Charlie Kridler of Gensler; Kanji Ueki of Casappo & Associates; Peter Bohlin of Bohlin Cywinski Jackson;

ショップ中央に黒の商品棚を設置。壁面右手より奥へ順に、ミュージック/フォト、プロフェッショナル、キッズ、ジーニアスバー。
High volume accessories were conveniently displayed on black shelves in the center of the Apple store.

1.30.2001 | full scale model

1.29.2001 | full scale model

Apple's technology opened doors to new possibilities. This was the philosophy of the Genius Bar. We wanted to communicate this through the Genius Bar logo where the electrons represented the message orbiting the world. My contribution to the development of this iconic logo is one of the proudest moments of my career.
Shinichiro Hasegawa (Graphic Designer & Former TYD Graphic Designer)

「コンピュータの天才たち」から発せられるメッセージの軌道、それは世界中にアイデアの粒子となって拡張し、新しい価値へと結合する原子の放物線を思い起こさせます。私たちはこのアイデアにこだわりました。現在も使用されているジーニアスバーのアイコンはとくに思い入れが強いです。
長谷川 信一郎（グラフィックデザイナー 元TYD グラフィック・デザイナー）

原寸模型のなかでも一番迫力のあったジーニアスバーのコーナー。紙でつくられたカウンターチェアも用意された。
The Genius Bar had the most impact of all the actual size models. The counter height stools were also constructed out of paper.

APPLE STORE DNA

KID'S AREA

The Apple store needed to offer something for everyone. The Kid's Area allowed children and families to casually play with Apple products. Select Apple stores, especially in residential locations, would cater to their clientele with an organic shaped area where furnishings were made low to the ground and fluid. We sourced colorful, gumball-like seats for the kid's corner, which created a fun and playful habitat for young people to learn.

キッズエリアは、子どもたちが自由にコンピュータに触れることができる環境づくりを目指しました。キドニーシェイプ(腎臓の形)のテーブルの高さはほかのコーナーよりも低めに設定され、丸みを帯びたカーペットの上に置かれました。イスは子どもの姿勢に合わせて自由に変形するヨガボールのような球形のタティーノが選ばれました。親の買い物を待つ子どものなかには、イスの上で寝そべりながらキーボードをタイプしたり、アップロードされたゲームを楽しむ子どももいました。自由な姿勢でコンピュータと遊ぶという発想は、当時子どもが小さかったスティーブの父親としての視点からのアイデアでした。また「年齢の枠を超えて楽しめる製品開発」という、ブランドの理念がカタチに現れています。

5.17.2001 | actual store

1.29.2001 | full scale model

Minature models were functional in aiding our design dialogues, and their appearance was just as important. Every element we used to build the Apple store model was sourced from everyday materials to spark a reaction and capture human connection. I particularly remember sourcing colored stretch leggings to replicate Denis Santacharia's Tato seating for the kid's area. I also found that wood stir sticks from Peet's Coffee made excellent flooring. There is so much design that can be expressed by repurposing ordinary objects and transforming them into something new.

Ritz Yagi (Graphic Designer at TYD)

八木理都子 (TYD グラフィック・デザイナー)

完成したミニチュアサイズモデルは視覚的にデザインを考える上で大切なエレメントでしたが、私たちにとってはそれ以上にモデルを制作したプロセスこそが重要なものでした。モデル制作のために使用した多くの素材は、日常で当たり前のように使用されるもの、例えば、デニス・サンタキアラがデザインしたキッズエリア向けの椅子"タト"のミニチュアモデルをつくった際には女性レギンスを、ウッドフロアを再現するためにはピーツコーヒー店の使い捨てマドラーを使用したりと、身近にあるものを別用途で使うことによって、新たな感覚的意識を高められるようなモデルづくりを目指したのです。

KIDNEY TABLE

Display tables needed to compliment and harmonize with Apple's products. We designed white, kidney shaped tables without hard edges to echo the rounded forms of Apple's then current models like the iMac. The tables' soft, curved lines allowed customers to freely approach and engage the products. This display format encouraged customers to test drive products without obstructions, as if they were in the comfort of their own homes. Steve commented on the balance between the highly technological computer resting on the organic shaped base, which reminded him of Isamu Noguchi's iconic coffee table.

当時のアップルコンピュータのヒット商品「iMac シリーズ」など、有機的な曲線が用いられていたデザインの流れとリンクするように、白のキドニーシェイプのテーブルを考案しました。角がない美しい曲線のテーブルは、周囲のどこからも商品を手に取りやすい形です。これはアップルストアのコンセプト「全商品体験型ストア」のエレメントの一つであり、「実際にカスタマーが自宅でコンピュータに触れているような体験」を可能にします。最新コンピュータのハイテク感に対して、有機的でどこか温かみを感じさせるデザインを、スティーブは「イサム・ノグチがデザインしたガラステーブルにも通じる」と話していました。

5.17.2001 | actual store

Photo by Rick English / Tim Hursley

Sketches by Kanji Ueki

二〇〇〇年代初頭、私たちのサンフランシスコのオフィスとカザッポ＆アソシエイツの植木莞爾氏とのイメージの共有は、すべてFAXで行なわれていました。毎日送られてくる数十枚のFAXをもとに、TYDのオフィスで模型制作を進めました。植木さんからの什器のデザイン画をFAXで受け取って、すぐにスケールダウンしてミニチュア模型をつくって、プレゼンテーションに間に合わせるといったことが日常茶飯事でした。

八木宏嗣（INDES 代表・元TYD グラフィック・デザイナー）

In 2000, the TYD office in San Francisco and Kanji Ueki's office in Tokyo communicated by fax. TYD made models of the Apple store and its fixtures that we scaled down from Ueki's drawings. Time was limited due to the project's aggressive deadline, so we were making mock-ups on a daily basis.

Koji Yagi (Founder of Indes & Former TYD Graphic Designer)

APPLE STORE DNA

THEATRE

5.17.2001 | actual store

1.25.2001 | miniature model

The Theatre was another distinct element of the Apple store concept. Like the kitchen or "heart" of the home, this area was a gathering place where the community could feed their minds and share experiences. The Theatre was also to be a forum were strangers became friends and discussed new ideas. Again, we located this dynamic feature in the potentially void area at the back of the store.

毎年1月に数回開催される新商品の説明会でのデモンストレーションやイベントは、シアターの重要性を引き出しています。大きなスクリーンにはコンピュータ初心者にもわかりやすい解説映像が流れ、マンツーマンのセッションもしばしば開催されます。家の中のキッチンのように、人が集う場所としてショップの一番奥に置かれたことで、ジーニアスバー同様、来店客の誘導効果もあります。

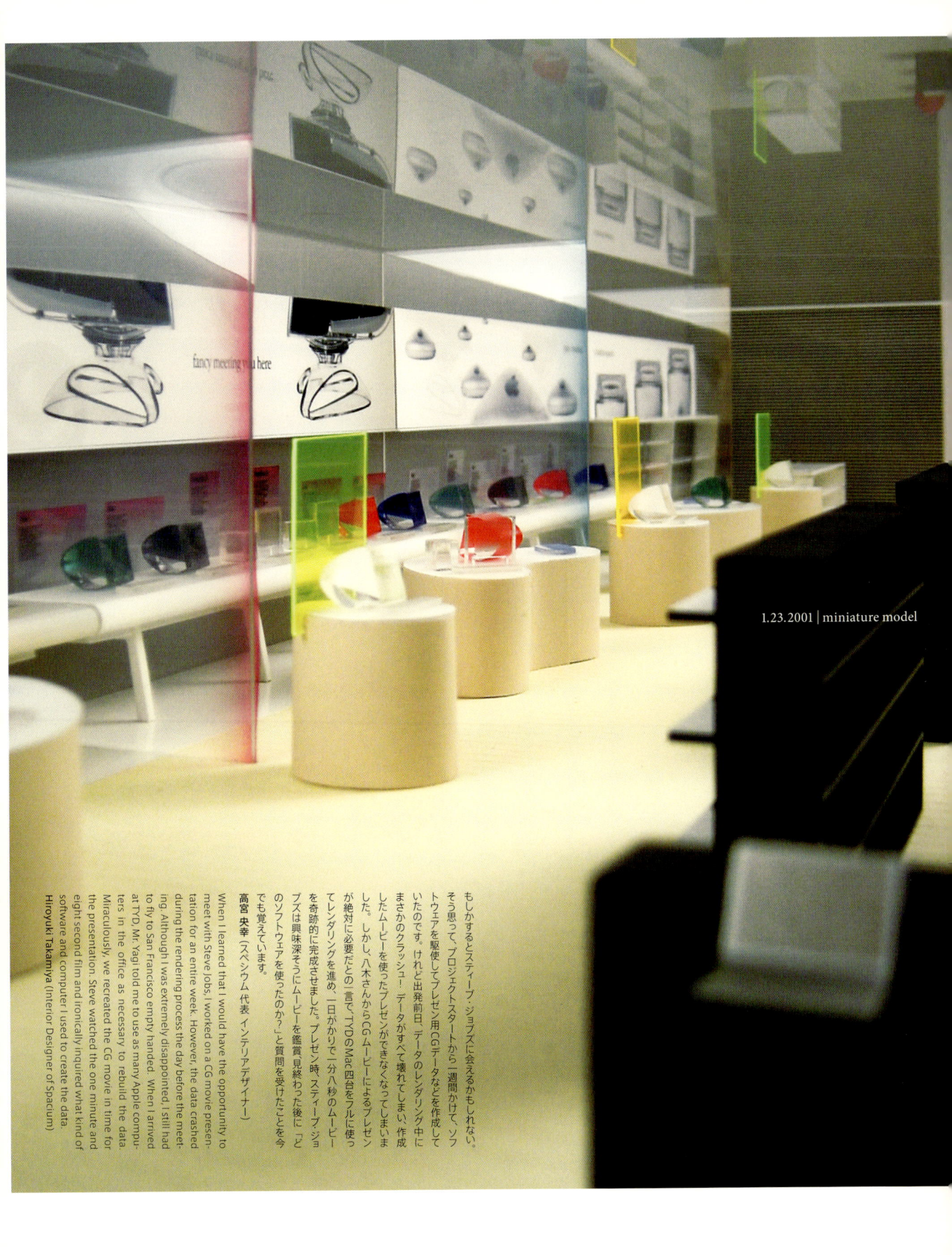

1.23.2001 | miniature model

もしかするとスティーブ・ジョブズに会えるかもしれない。そう思って、プロジェクトスタートから一週間かけて、ソフトウェアを駆使してプレゼン用CGデータなどを作成していたのです。けれど出発前日、データのレンダリング中にまさかのクラッシュ！ データがすべて壊れてしまい、作成したムービーを使ったプレゼンができなくなってしまいました。しかし、八木さんからCGムービーによるプレゼンが絶対に必要だとの一言で、TYDのMac四台をフルに使ってレンダリングを進め、一日がかりで一分八秒のムービーを奇跡的に完成させました。プレゼン時、スティーブ・ジョブズは興味深そうにムービーを鑑賞見終わった後に「どのソフトウェアを使ったのか？」と質問を受けたことを今でも覚えています。

高宮 央幸（スペシウム 代表 インテリアデザイナー）

When I learned that I would have the opportunity to meet with Steve Jobs, I worked on a CG movie presentation for an entire week. However, the data crashed during the rendering process the day before the meeting. Although I was extremely disappointed, I still had to fly to San Francisco empty handed. When I arrived at TYD, Mr. Yagi told me to use as many Apple computers in the office as necessary to rebuild the data. Miraculously, we recreated the one minute and eight second film and computer I used to create the data. Steve watched the CG movie in time for the presentation. Steve watched the one minute and ironically inquired what kind of software and computer I used to create the data.
Hiroyuki Takamiya (Interior Designer of Spacium)

2枚のガラス板の間に薄いカラーグラデーションシートを挟み込み、ストアのセクションごとのデバイダーとして使用。
Partitions of the actual Apple stores were constructed with two layers of laminated glass that contained gradation film.

1.23.2001 | miniature model

Creative consulting team: Steve Jobs, Tim Kobe, IDSA, and Wilhelm Oehl, IDSA, of Eight Inc.; Charlie Kridler of Gensler; Kanji Ueki of Casappo & Associates; Peter Bohlin of Bohlin Cywinski Jackson;

ショップ中央に黒の商品棚を設置。壁面右手より奥へ順に、ミュージック/フォト、プロフェッショナル、キッズ、ジーニアスバー。
High volume accessories were conveniently displayed on black shelves in the center of the Apple store.

Tamotsu Yagi Design; Sylvia Bistrong of ISP Design; Andy Dreyfus of Apple Computer, Inc.; Tommaso Latini of Fisher Development.

コーナーの正面にあるグラフィックパネル。すべてのプリントが社内で出力されて、3Mの特殊糊で何度も外せるようにした。
All the graphic materails for the panels were printed in house at Apple, and used 3M adhesive paper for easy installation.

1.23.2001 | miniature model

模型
Miniature model

144 | Apple

黒くペイントされたファサードには、シンプルかつ印象的なアップル社のロゴマークのみが配置された。
The iconic apple logomark was the only signage used on the flat black facade of the Apple store.

1.29.2001 | full scale model

原寸
Full scale model

1.30.2001 | full scale model

What will Apple stores look like in the future? Today, I still see the original DNA within the updated store designs, and recognize how each store is also unique to its location and time. It will be interesting to watch how our initial blueprint evolves to embrace the company's ever-changing technology, and to reflect our culture.

ショップデザインで重要なことは、進化を遂げ続けるアップル製品やその文化性が反映されていることなのではないか？ そう考えると、アップルストアのあるべき姿とはどのようなものなのでしょうか？ まさに現在から未来へ、変化し続けるということこそが、もっとも大切なことなのです。

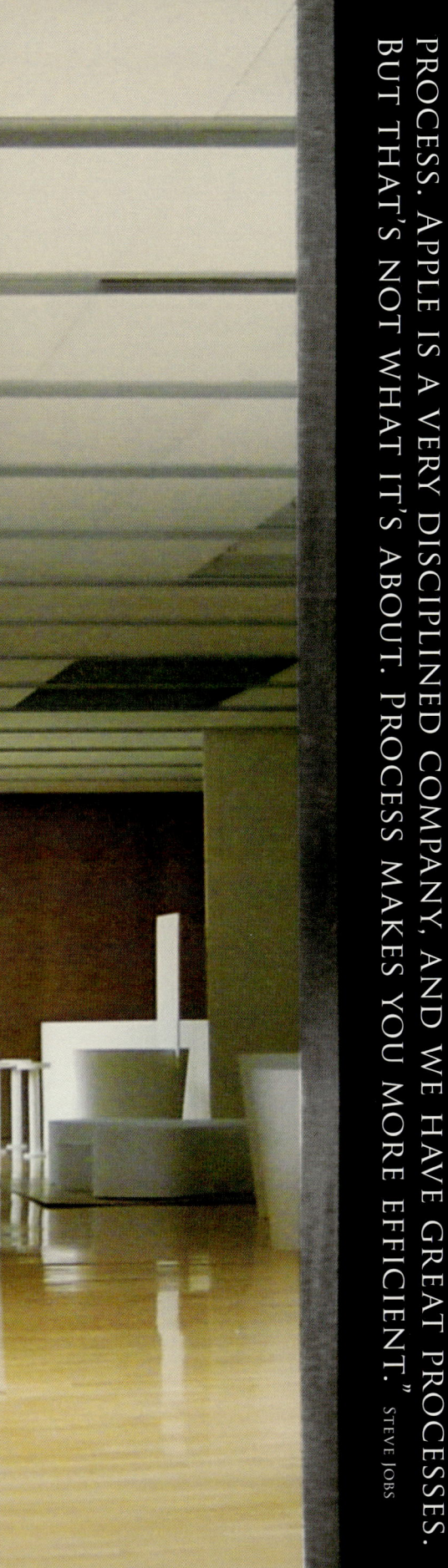

"THE SYSTEM IS THAT THERE IS NO SYSTEM. THAT DOESN'T MEAN WE DON'T HAVE PROCESS. APPLE IS A VERY DISCIPLINED COMPANY, AND WE HAVE GREAT PROCESSES. BUT THAT'S NOT WHAT IT'S ABOUT. PROCESS MAKES YOU MORE EFFICIENT."
STEVE JOBS

——"マニュアル化されたシステムは存在しない。
しかし、システムがまったくないわけではない。
アップルは非常に強靭な企業であり、
物事に常に対応できるシステムを、
経験というプロセスを通して提案し続けている。
それだけでなく、プロセスを深く理解することは、
能率の向上にもつながるのである。"
スティーブ・ジョブズ

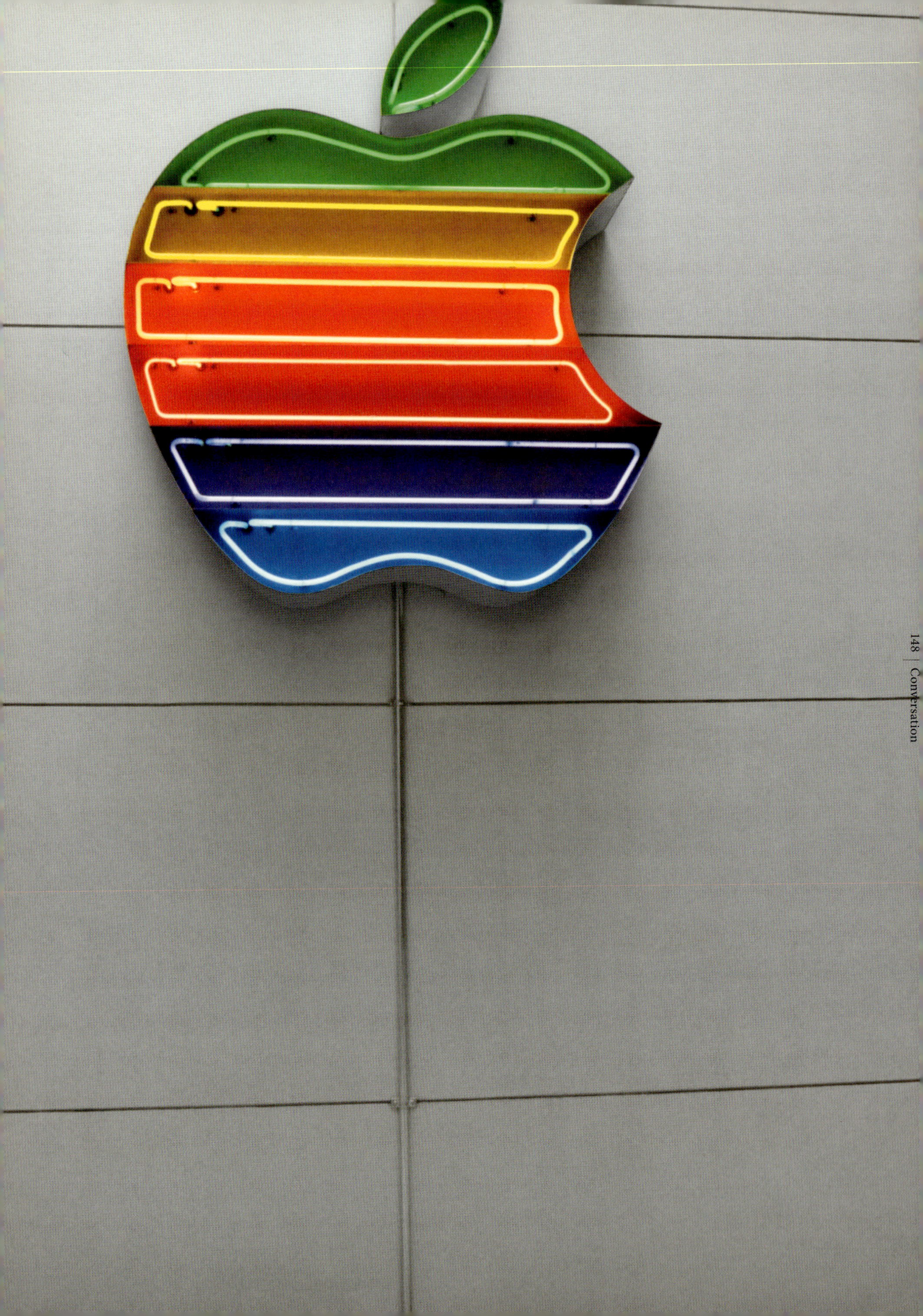

"Realizing the future is in its past."
— "「未来は過去にある」と気づいた。"
NIGO®

対談 Conversation

過去に未来を見出すこと──クリエイティブ・ディレクター NIGO®

エネルギーは「モノ」から得ている

八木：私は身近なものからデザインのアイデアが生まれることが多いんですね。だから、気に入ったもの、好きなものを身の回りに置いていたい。散歩しながら、木の枝とか石ころを拾ってきたり、さまざまな卵を集めたり…。大きなものでは、NIGOさんとの出会いのきっかけにもなったジャン・プルーヴェの家具や現代アートにも興味があります。そんな私にとって、NIGOさんのコレクションはすごく魅力的です。
モノを収集するということは、モノに対する眼力や視座が核となります。今日は、「見る・見立て」といったテーマでお話ができればと思っています。まずNIGOさんがコレクションをはじめるきっかけは、何だったのですか？

NIGO：おもちゃ、フィギュアでした。子どもの頃からおもちゃが好きで、今でも当時、買ったモノをとってあるくらいです。たまたま気に入ったモノがあったので買って、フッとその裏側を見たら製造元や年月日などが書かれていました。そのときはじめて「おもちゃにも背景があるんだなあ」と、興味が膨らんだのです。今では、じつにいろんなモノを集めていますが、結論をいってしまうと、僕は何かをするためのエネルギーを「モノ」から得ているのだと思います。収集し続けることでエネルギーを保っているし、モノという物差しで何でも計っているし、アイデアの源泉でもあるんです。

八木：だから値段は関係ないんでしょ？

NIGO：そうですね。僕にとって値段はまったく関係ないですね。ガラクタから高価なジュエリーデザインを思いついたりするから不思議でしょ。それに、コレクションはすべて自分でメンテナンスをして、ディスプレイしていますが、その時間こそが僕のクリエイションに欠かせない。Tシャツ一着、レコード一枚まで、全部自分で管理しています。

八木：私も同じ。年がら年中、整理整頓しています。

NIGO：必要なときに、すぐに手元にほしいじゃないですか。自分で把握していないと瞬間的に出てきませんよね。出てこないとすごくイライラしてしまう、かえってストレスになるんです。だから、自分で管理するしかない。

八木：モノを収集するようになってよかったなあ、と思うことの一つが、人との出会い。なかでも、プルーヴェの家具を集めるようになって、本当に素敵な人たちとたくさん出会いました。近代美術館のキュレーターとか、普段はなかなか接点をもてない人たちと親しくなれたしね。モノが人を呼び、つなげてくれるということがありますね。NIGOさんとの出会いも、「日本のプルーヴェ・コレクターですごい人がいますよ」と紹介されたのがきっかけでした。お会いしてはじめて、すごく有名なクリエイターであることを知りました。

NIGO：たしかにそうですね。僕もコレクションを集めたこの場所をつくって以降、たくさんのゲストをお迎えしています。とくに海外で、僕のコレクションが知られているようで、東京の観光スポットになっているとか。モノが、まったく違った世界の人たちを呼び寄せてくれているようです。

八木：ところで、プルーヴェを集め出したきっかけは、何だったのですか？

NIGO：もともとファッション系の人間なのでライフスタイルにはこだわっていて、最初はチャールズ・イームズに惹かれて収集していました。そこを入口にして少しずつ間口を広げていったところ、プルーヴェに行き着いたのです。実物を見ると、こちらのほうが独創的でデザインにも大きな影響を与えているように感じたし、今でも現役家具として使うことができるタフさもすごいなあと思いました。

八木：私が家具に興味をもったきっかけは、アールデコ様式のクローム製の家具でした。ところがクロームって指紋や汚れが目立つので、いつもピカピカに磨かないといけないから、「なんでこんなに疲れるんだ」って内心感じていたんです。そんなときにプルーヴェに出会って、「普段着の感覚」っていうのかな、ペンキが剥げかかっていたり、スチールがちょっと歪んでいたり…、それが逆に作品の魅力を押し上げていることがすごいと思った。それから一気に集めましたね。

NIGO：八木さんのオフィスをお訪ねして、その良さをあらためて実感しました。僕が最初に買ったのはデスクと椅子です。…で、僕も八木さんのように実際に使ってみたんですね。そしたら今でも十分使用に耐えられるし、歳月を経てきた表情がいい味になっている。プルーヴェのそんなところに惹かれますね。あの時代のモノは、素材や加工技術がそのまま表面に現れているので「手の温もり感」があるのです。

八木：NIGOさんのコレクションはジャンルも広いけど、感心するのは、集めたモノをただ棚に飾ったり、ファイルに収めたりするだけでなく、実際の生活や仕事に生かしている、活動の原動力になっているということでしょね。きっちり自分のものにしているところがすばらしいと思います。
ところで、コレクションするに際しては、特定のテーマやストーリーがあるんですか？

NIGO：基本はPOPです。でもそれ以外にプルーヴェとか、ソットサスとかいろいろあります。アイテムもおもちゃからファッション、書籍やレコード、オブジェや家具、じつにさまざまです。でも、不思議なことに自分のなかではぶれていないのです。それなりに一本筋があります。たとえば、ある時期不必要だったなと思ったモノでも、しばらくするとすごく大切になっていたり…。いったん倉庫に仕舞い込んでも、5年後に再び自分のトレンドになってディスプレイするなんてことがあります。

「未来は過去にある」と気づいた

八木：収集や整理、陳列という行為を通して、モノと対話されているのでしょうね。コレクションを三次元である「空間」にきれいにディスプレイするだけでなく、そこに四次元である「時間」という軸も加わっている点で、NIGOさんの世界観が表現されている。モノがつくる時空を自由に往き来しながら、最先端のデザインを発想し創造しているのでしょうね。アーカイブとしての価値も相当だと思います。

NIGO：たしかに、コレクションは1800年代から現代まで、おもちゃから家具やクルマまであらゆるジャンルに及んでいますね。この場所も、40年代のプルーヴェの家具から、50年代のアメリカ製のテレビやジュークボックス、60年代のPOPアート、70年代のアップルコンピュータのネオンサイン、KAWSのアートまでディスプレイしています。
最近、モノに囲まれていて、気づいたのは「未来は過去なんじゃないか」ということなんです。たとえば、40年代のジーンズをリメイクする場合、現在すでに失われてしまった技術、たとえば現存しないミシンで縫製されているので、昔のミシンをつくり直すことからはじめなければならない。それって、「未来は過去にある」、あるいは「無意識に昔から何かを引っ張り出して、未来をつくっている」ということなのではないでしょうか。
昔の雑誌などで1930年代のワールドフェアの写真をみると、まさに未来がそこにあるって感じで、ワクワクします。でもそれらを再現しようとしても現代ではできない。当時の素材や技術がすでに失われているからです。クルマのシェイプなども同じですね。僕にとって、昔のモノはすごく不思議で魅力的なのです。

八木：あの1950年代アメリカのプレディクタのテレビもきちんとメンテナンスして、動く状態にしているのだけど、今のお話を聞いて納得できました。NIGOさんのなかでは、過去のモノも、現在から未来に一直線状につながっているんですね。だから、アンティークとして飾るだけでなく、実際に使い、機械が動く状態であることが重要なんだ。

NIGO：テレビをつけてみましょうか。この時代のテレビはまだステレオでなくてモノラルです。でも逆に当時の音楽はモノラルな音質だからこそ成立しているし、魅力的なのだと実感できます。その時代の表現は、その時代の技術を背景に成り立っているんだなあと…。当たり前といえば当たり前のことですが、これは実際に使ったり、動かしてみないとわかりませんよね。

八木：私も同じ時代の、マルコ・ザヌーゾがデザインした、イタリアのブリオンベガ社製のテレビを持っています。NIGOさんのテレビとは対照的に真っ黒で、いかにもイタリアモダンって感じで現代でも通用するデザインです。だから「過去にこそ未来がある」という言葉には共感するなあ。

NIGO：国によってデザインの個性があるって面白いですね。近頃はデザインもグローバルであまり差がなくなってきていますから…

八木：最近ワインのブランドデザインをしています。ビンテージワインのグラフィックだからそれなりにこだわりたいなあと考えて、NIGOさんの名刺みたいに端っこが漉きっぱなしという紙を探したんだけど、もう現存しない。グラフィックの世界では、ほしいなと思う紙はほとんど廃盤だし印刷機もなくなってしまっている。量が出ない、効率的でないという理由で昔のすぐれたモノや技術がどんどん失われているんですね。だから、何でも自分で収集しておかないと、次の世代に伝えられない。プルーヴェの家具を収集した理由も、本当は自分で家具をデザインしたかったんだけど、プルーヴェには敵わないなあと感じたから。自分がよいと思うモノを収集して次代に引き継ぐということは、自分でデザインをすることと同じくらいか、それ以上の意味がある…。私のコレクションには、そんな想いもあるんです。

NIGO：そうなんですか。

八木：それに、日本には「見立て」という言葉があります。あるモノを、場所を移動させたり、使い方を変えることで、新しい価値を与えるということもできますよね。だから、ここに来ると、モノがすばらしいだけでなく、NIGOさん的な見立てとか組み合わせにすごく刺激を受けます。最近の若い人はモノを知らないから、こんな場所で勉強できればいいかもしれない。

NIGO：たしかに、そうですね。それに加えて、若者は、他者から影響を受けないというか、みんなパソコンの画面の中で完結してしまって、わかったつもり、触れたつもりになってしまっているというのかな…。

八木：環境が大切なんですね。モノに限らず、体験からしか得ることのできない知識や知恵のある人だと、「あんな感じの紙」だとか、「…のような色味」とかいうと直感的に理解できるんだけど、実体験のない子はいくら言ってもピンとこない。

モノは生きもの

八木：ところでNIGOさんは、モノの出会いの場やチャンスを意識的につくっているのですか？

NIGO：インターネットがこれほど普及していない頃は、アメリカの大規模なアンティークショーに年に4,5回、リストアップして出かけていって、足が棒になるくらい会場を回って、実際にこの目で見て、手にとって吟味していましたね。最近はインターネットで検索すればある程度の情報は得られるようになっています。でも危うさはありますね。慎重に見極めないと

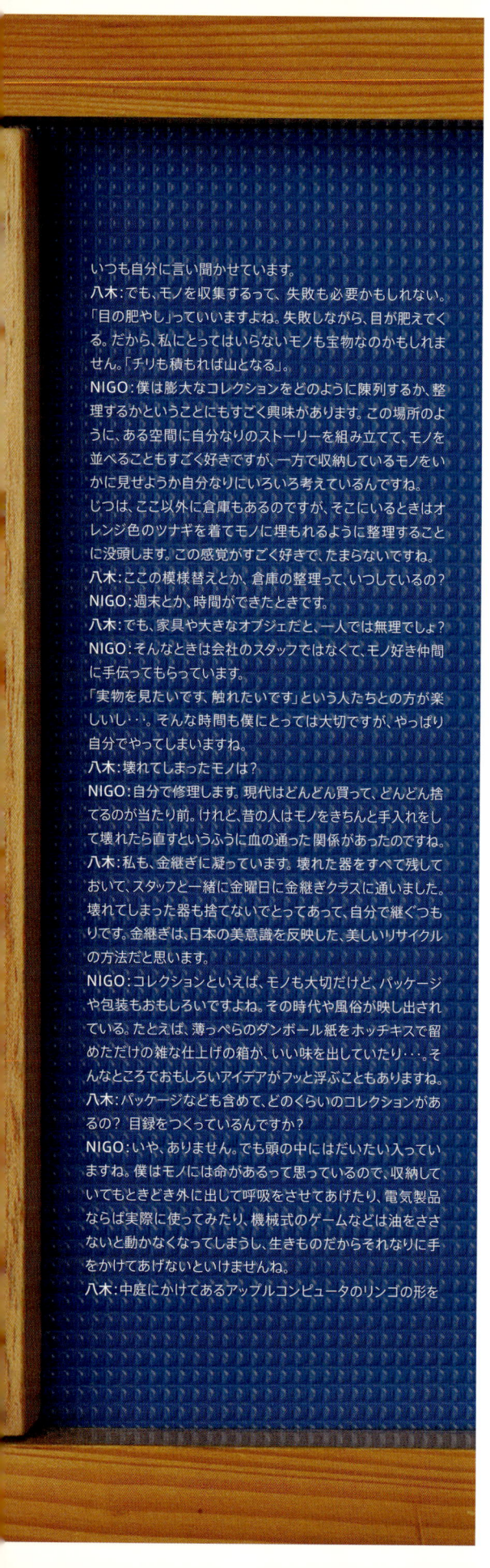

いつも自分に言い聞かせています。
八木：でも、モノを収集するって、失敗も必要かもしれない。「目の肥やし」っていいますよね。失敗しながら、目が肥えてくる。だから、私にとってはいらないモノも宝物なのかもしれません。「チリも積もれば山となる」。
NIGO：僕は膨大なコレクションをどのように陳列するか、整理するかということにもすごく興味があります。この場所のように、ある空間に自分なりのストーリーを組み立てて、モノを並べることもすごく好きですが、一方で収納しているモノをいかに見せようか自分なりにいろいろ考えているんですね。じつは、ここ以外に倉庫もあるのですが、そこにいるときはオレンジ色のツナギを着てモノに埋もれるように整理することに没頭します。この感覚がすごく好きで、たまらないですね。
八木：ここの模様替えとか、倉庫の整理って、いつしているの？
NIGO：週末とか、時間ができたときです。
八木：でも、家具や大きなオブジェだと、一人では無理でしょ？
NIGO：そんなときは会社のスタッフではなくて、モノ好き仲間に手伝ってもらっています。「実物を見たいです、触れたいです」という人たちとの方が楽しいし･･･。そんな時間も僕にとっては大切ですが、やっぱり自分でやってしまいますね。
八木：壊れてしまったモノは？
NIGO：自分で修理します。現代はどんどん買って、どんどん捨てるのが当たり前。けれど、昔の人はモノをきちんと手入れをして壊れたら直すというふうに血の通った関係があったのですね。
八木：私も、金継ぎに凝っています。壊れた器をすべて残しておいて、スタッフと一緒に金曜日に金継ぎクラスに通いました。壊れてしまった器も捨てないでとってあって、自分で継ぐつもりです。金継ぎは、日本の美意識を反映した、美しいリサイクルの方法だと思います。
NIGO：コレクションといえば、モノも大切だけど、パッケージや包装もおもしろいですよね。その時代や風俗が映し出されている。たとえば、薄っぺらのダンボール紙をホッチキスで留めただけの雑な仕上げの箱が、いい味を出していたり･･･。そんなところでおもしろいアイデアがフッと浮かぶこともありますね。
八木：パッケージなども含めて、どのくらいのコレクションがあるの？ 目録をつくっているんですか？
NIGO：いや、ありません。でも頭の中にはだいたい入っていますね。僕はモノには命があるって思っているので、収納していてもときどき外に出して呼吸をさせてあげたり、電気製品ならば実際に使ってみたり、機械式のゲームなどは油をささないと動かなくなってしまうし、生きものだからそれなりに手をかけてあげないといけませんね。
八木：中庭にかけてあるアップルコンピュータのリンゴの形を

メキシカン・ブックシェルフは表裏の両面から使用可能。上記写真は、左右ページに分けて両面を見せている。NIGOさんと私が色違いでコレクションしている作品の一つ。
The *Mexique* bookcase was a collaborative piece by Charlotte Perriand and Ateliers Jean Prouvé. It was designed to function from both sides and was used at the *Maison du Mexique, Cité Universitaire* (campus) in Paris, France. The image is spilt in two to display both sides. Nigo and I have this same bookcase in our collection.

したネオンサインも、ちゃんと点灯している。あれって、たしか70年代のものでしょ？スティーブ・ジョブズが見たら感動するだろうなあ。
NIGO：あれはシカゴで買いました。
八木：NIGOさんは「モノの魂」に惹かれるんですか？単にそのモノがほしいのであれば、壊れてしまったら捨ててしまうだろうし、飾ることはあっても、油をさしたり、風を通したり‥‥そんな手のかかることは自分でしないでしょう。
さっき「モノも生きている」という言葉は、まさにNIGOさんのモノの見方なのだと思うんですよ。
NIGO：現代のモノは大量生産品でどれも均質で、できた瞬間に一番価値があって、古くなると価値がどんどん薄まってしまう。ところが、さっきのホッチキスでとめられたパッケージは、錆びてきているホッチキスの針がすごくいい味を出していて、愛着をもたせてくれるのです。僕にとってモノは、単なるモノではなく「生きもの」なんですね。
八木：話はつきないけれど、NIGOさんのモノの見方とモノを愛する心に、すごく共鳴しました。また、コレクション談義をしましょうね。

NIGO® クリエイティブ メーカー、『A BATHING APE®』『HUMAN MADE®』『Mr. BATHING APE® UNITED ARROWS』『BAPE KIDS®』『A FISHING APE®』『BABY MILO® BY SANRIO』のブランドディレクションほか、現在は6つ以上のブランドを手がける。『HUMAN MADE®』を扱うショップ『COLDCOFFEE』が青山キラー通りにオープン。
NIGO® is the brand director for multiple creative brands: A BATHING APE®; HUMAN MADE®; Mr. BATHING APE® UNITED ARROWS; BAPE KIDS®; A FISHING APE® and BABY MILO® BY SANRIO. He is also responsible for the creation of over six different brands such as COLD COFFEE, a shop located on the popular Aoyama Killer Street, which carries HUMAN MADE®.

Photo by Shuji Yoshida

REALIZING THE FUTURE IS IN ITS PAST
NIGO® / Creative Director

Gaining Energy From Objects

TY: I tend to gather design ideas from my surroundings, so I always keep things I like around me. When I am walking, I pick up branches and rocks. I even collect different types of egg shells. I also collect larger objects like furniture, and I love modern art. These passions are what brought us together. I see similarities in our collecting habits, and find your collection very appealing. The act of collecting is done with a purpose and aesthetic sensibility. Let's talk about this "aesthetic sense and eye for collection." First, what made you start collecting?

N®: It was toys and plastic figures. I have loved toys since I was young, and still keep many of them from my childhood. A while back, I picked up one of my toys and noticed the factory name and manufacture dates listed on the back. I suddenly realized that everything has a history and a story to tell, and my curiosity and appreciation increased. Now I gain creative energy from these objects. The act of collecting fuels my desire to continue and is inspiration for many of my ideas.

TY: So, is price a factor?

N®: No. Even a piece of junk has inspired me to design a line of fine jewelry. For me, the price of an object does not determine its real value. What's important is the quality of the time I spend. I also archive and organize all my finds, and the time I spend doing this is a significant part of my creative process.

TY: The same is true for me. I feel like I'm organizing and revisiting things all year round.

N®: When I need something from my collection, I need it right away. Otherwise, it will stress me out. This means that I need to know where everything is, and have to be the one that oversees the organization.

TY: I am grateful to have met so many interesting people since I began collecting, especially when I focused on the work of Jean Prouvé. For example, I met a modern art museum curator through collecting, and was even introduced to you as a fellow Japanese Prouvé enthusiast.

N®: I agree. I invite many guests to see my collection. Surprisingly, my atelier is famous with people overseas and is known to be one of Tokyo's design destinations. Objects draw different people from all over the world.

TY: What made you start collecting Prouvé's work?

N®: Being in the fashion industry, I am particular about lifestyle in general. I began collecting furniture with pieces by Charles Eames, and eventually found Prouvé. Looking back, I am actually more drawn to Prouvé. I appreciate that his furniture can still be used because of its durability and engineering –It's tough and solid.

TY: My interest in Prouvé stemmed from collecting chrome Art Deco furniture. Chrome was a very difficult material to keep clean, fingerprints and stains stood out unless I polished them often. The maintenance was very tiring. Then I discovered Prouvé, and found his furniture to have an appealing sense of casualness. The paint was peeling off, there were dents in the steel. These features added more character to each piece and increased my desire to collect and use his work.

N®: When I visited your studio and saw your Prouvé collection, I realized the appeal of the imperfect and casual qualities you just described. You can almost trace the warmth of the fabricators' hands when the pieces were created.

The Past Presents the Future

TY: The act of collecting, organizing and displaying is like having a dialogue with your collection. What I admire about your historical presentation is the way you've created your own space, a kind of fourth dimension where different times meet. Your curatorial approach and impressive archive reflect a selective collection that is very new and modern.

N®: I collect things from the 1800s to the present, from toys and furniture to cars. My collection definitely covers a wide genre. We are now surrounded by design from many eras: Prouvé furniture from the '40s; an American TV and jukebox from the '50s; POP art from the '60s, a neon Apple Computer sign from the '70s and current art work by KAWS. Standing among these objects, I recently realized that the "future is in its past." For example, to remake jeans from the '40s requires recreating old sewing machines. Some sewing techniques have been lost, and if the sewing machines from earlier eras doesn't exist, we need to go back one step. We essentially need to pull something out from the past unconsciously to build the future. When I see images of the 1930s World's Fair from old magazines, I feel like these are scenes from the future. Unfortunately, it is impossible to completely reproduce history in the modern context because so many of the original materials and techniques have already been forgotten or modified. This is true for the shapes of cars. Ultimately, I find old objects to be mysterious and alluring.

TY: That 1950s Pedicta American TV is well maintained and it actually works. I can see that objects from the past operate in the future for you. I appreciate that you recognize their value as antiques, but also make them functional. I have a TV designed by Marco Zanuso for Brionvega in Italy, which is from the same time period. This piece is all black and has features of early Italian Modern, but it still looks very contemprary. I can understand what you mean by the "future is in its past."

N®: It's also interesting to consider how design differs from country to country. Design is becoming so globalized that you can't recognize cultural differences anymore. Back to collecting, although objects are intriguing, packaging and wrapping papers can be fascinating as well. Their materials and stylistic character can channel earlier eras. For instance, this thin cardboard package with a simple staple closure has a nice feel…looking at it gives me new ideas. Modern objects are mostly mass produced and homogeneous. They have the most value when they are released, and then they depreciate. However, older objects actually become more valuable to me because they are inhabited and their stories are unique.

Objects are Living Things

TY: Do you actively seek out objects or find them randomly?
N®: Before the internet became popular, I went to America's antique shows about four or five times a year. I would make a list of where to go and what to buy, then I would walk around the venue until my legs got stiff. I had to touch and carefully select each object myself. Now, while the internet makes it easy to obtain things, there are also many risks. It is critical to research any potential purchase.
TY: It is also important to train your eye to become a smarter collector, which takes time and involves making mistakes. When you make a mistake, your eye becomes sharper. At the same time, objects you weren't that fond of initially could later become treasures because your eye has developed.
TY: How vast is your collection including the packaging? Do you have some type of inventory?
N®: No, I don't. My inventory is mostly in my head. I am very mindful of my collection and respect the attention it requires. I believe that objects are alive, and if they are stored in a box, they still need to be taken out to breathe. Electronics and mechanical toys need to be oiled to stay mobile. I believe objects are living things and they require good care.
TY: It's great that your Apple Computer neon sign is still working. It's from the 70s right? If Steve Jobs were to see it, I'm sure he would be impressed.
N®: I bought that in Chicago.
TY: Are you drawn to an object's "spirit?" Let's say one of your objects were to break, would you just throw it away? You can purely appreciate an object's aesthetic beauty, or relate to its "soul" and have a desire to learn about its life and use.
N®: In today's society, it is very common to buy things and throw them away when they break. Many years ago, people had more appreciation for the things they owned. If something broke, they fixed it. I try to do the same.
TY: Nigo, I really enjoyed our conversation and learning more about your collection. Thank you so much.

TY: Tamotsu Yagi
N®: Nigo

156 | Palm

"WHEN I DRAW SOMETHING, THE BRAIN AND THE HANDS WORK TOGETHER." —TADAO ANDO

——"絵を描く時、私の手と脳は共に働く。"
安藤 忠雄

原寸 | Actual Size

Photo by Stefano Massei

1950年代に目の不自由な人のためにつくられた、視覚トレーニング用の道具。両手を使い、触感を研ぎ澄ますこのオブジェには、制作者の名前は残っていない。
This wooden object from the 1950s was designed as a training tool for the visually impaired to exercise their sense of touch. The craftsman's name is unknown.

2008

The Palm project began quickly after one email from the client in 2008. Soon after, we were working with the design team lead by the VP of Design, Peter Skillman on an original package design for their new product. We met often and the team insisted meeting at our studio to be inspired by a different work environment. Our design meetings were very hands on and engaging. We all enjoyed examining objects from within our studio to engage in our design discussions. Our goal was to create a distinct and compact package for Palm, separate from the large standard boxes assigned by phone providers. Our initial idea was to attach the smartphone on the back of the box lid. When the customer lifts the lid off, the smartphone sits on their palm. Skillman's determination to address the best possible solutions for Palm's first original package resulted in the redesign of the Palm logo and the refinement of other key elements of the brand.

PALM

Package Design and Identity Redesign

Design in the palm of the hand

手のひら

二〇〇八年のある日、一通のeメールが届きました。シリコンバレーの大手通信機器メーカー「パーム」からの新商品のパッケージデザインの依頼でした。それは「パーム」にとってはじめての自社オリジナルパッケージであり、社運をかけたプロジェクトだったのです。

当初、ミーティングはパーム本社とTYDで交互に行なう予定でしたが、新商品のデザイン担当副社長のピーター・スキルマンが率いるパームチームは、アートや珍しいコレクションがディスプレイされたTYDの環境が気に入って、白熱したミーティングの舞台は、なぜかTYDのオフィスになりました。

そこで私は、手のひらに乗るような、極小パッケージのデザインを提案しました。

社名である「パーム」とは、日本語で「手のひら」の意味。同時に、コーポレイトロゴやカラーもリデザインして、「一新」を目標にしたプロジェクトがスタートしたのです。

Pictured here is a visual exercise containing photos, words and icons in groups of three to provoke the team in an objective discussion. This exercise stimulated conversation which helped define goals and set a clear design objective.

プロジェクトがはじまる前に、TYDでは、写真、言葉、アイコンなどを1、2、3で表したリストを50枚ほど作成。これを使うことによって、パーム社と競合他社2社のイメージがどれにあてはまるか、ゲーム感覚で自社と他社のイメージに対する認識を共有することができた。

Photo by Kazuya Enomoto

7

原寸 | Actual Size

15

プロダクトデザイナーとしての理想は本体の造形だけに留まらずヘッドフォンや充電台などの「周辺機器=ユーザーが触るものすべて」をデザインすること。でも各々の商品寿命やコストが異なるので、すべてを同時に一新できるという機会は稀です。けれども私は社長交代にともなって、パーム在職中にこの稀有なチャンスに巡り合えました。やるからにはパッケージまで一新したいと感じ、以前「自分の仕事をつくる」という本で知ったTYDにコンタクトをしたのです。最初はパッケージだけの予定だったのが、いつの間にかブランディングまでを依頼していました、それだけすてきなチームでした。

松岡 良倫（グーグル プロダクト・デザイナー・元パームデザイン部 プロダクト・デザイナー）

The ideal scenario for a product designer is to design the entire line of a mobile device, including its headphones, charging station and other components to develop a cohesive user experience. As obvious as this may sound, obstacles such as difference in production cycles or manufacturing costs become barriers. When the brave new CEO came to Palm, we were granted the permission to change all that. Naturally, we were thrilled about this transition and chance to create our own packaging system to match the quality of our product designs. Without hesitation we contacted TYD and when we visited their studio for the first time, we knew we had to work with them. What began as a package design assignment turned into an ambitious creative partnership which also resulted in Palm's identity rebranding.

Yomi Matsuoka (Product Designer at Google & Former Product Designer at Palm)

Photo by Shuji Yoshida

原寸 | Actual Size

私たちはお互いの考えや意見を、スケッチなどを通して視覚的に意見交換をすることで、表面上だけの理解ではなく、深く意見を認識し、アイデアを形にしていきました。建築物のようにエレガントな形のパッケージ構造から、詩的にブランドの意志を伝えるためのすべての印刷物に至るまで、最終的にプロジェクトの成功に至ったのもこのような意見交換のプロセスがあったからこそだと言えます。
ジェファーソン・チャング（グーグル グラフィック・デザイナー 元TYD グラフィック・デザイナー）

Our process involved a unique visual exchange with the client, allowing us to having a deep understanding of each other rather than a superficial one. This resulted in an architectural package and an elegant, informational printed matter that generated a poetic relationship with the consumer, without sacrificing function.
Jefferson Cheng (Graphic Designer at Google & Former TYD Designer)

Photo by Shuji Yoshida

DESIGN BRIEF FROM PALM

Create a simple, iconic graphic identity and language that:
シンプルで、かつアイコンのように際立ったデザインを通し、下記項目を意識した上で
ブランドの世界感を表現してほしいという依頼。

1. Carries through a cohesive accessory and packaging ecosystem.
   携帯本体とアクセサリーのパッケージの統一。

2. Is consistent through the end to end customer experience.
   購入者が商品パッケージや商品使用後の経験を通して、
   一貫した「パームらしさ」を感じてもらえるようにする。

3. Unifies the software and hardware experience.
   ソフトウェアとハードウェアの両方を通して、ブランドアイデンティティを保つ。

More emotion is better than less. Nuance and subjective beauty in graphic design and motion graphics matters because packaging, color, user experience and industrial design in phones is aesthetics as it relates to self esteem. This is the one piece of technology you carry with you all the time. The brand and packaging experience needed to be consistent with the complete design ethos.

Peter Skillman (VP of Smart Devices Ux Design at Nokia and Former VP of Design at Palm)

日々、当たり前のように持ち歩く携帯電話だからこそ、ユーザーと機械の距離を狭めることを意識する必要があります。最新の科学技術を組み込んだ精密機械だが、デザインの力でより人に近く、より当たり前な存在になるように、ブランド力やパッケージデザインすべてが一体となり、生活のなかにとけ込むプロダクトとなりました。
ピーター・スキルマン（ノキア スマートデバイスUx×デザイン部 バイスプレジデント 元パーム デザイン部 バイスプレジデント）

LOGO REDESIGN

プロジェクトのはじめに、パッケージと商品に使用されているロゴタイプを見直しました。ロゴはすでにあるデザインを必要以上に変えるのではなく、時代に即してスリム化する方向で進めました。現行のロゴタイプまわりの円をとって開放感を与えることで、会社名「パーム」が読みやすくなった。そこで、すべてのケースでこのロゴを使用することになり、ロゴのアウトラインを少しずつ5段階でスリム化したものを提案。ロゴまわりがすっきり、スマートになって親しみやすいビジュアルへと変貌しました。最終的には「バージョン3」に決定。

The project began with the examination and redesign of the existing Palm logo. Our objective was to maintain iconic elements of the logo and make minor adjustments to update the design. The approach was not to drastically change the design but to simplify and clarify the details of the logo. We first released the logotype from the circle which improved the legibility of the logotype at all sizes. We then placed the logotype on a "diet" by slimming the letters then brought the characters closer together which resulted in a more current version of the existing logo.

original Palm logo

original and slim logos

original and slim logos at H: 7mm

original weight

slim version 1

slim version 2

slim version 3 | final logo

slim version 4

slim version 5

COLOR REFINEMENT

ロゴに使われていたオレンジを今一度見直すことに。カリフォルニアに本社のあるパーム社。そこで、コーポレイトカラーである、カリフォルニアの太陽のような明るく元気なイメージの特色オレンジは、カリフォルニア州花であるカリフォルニアポピーからインスピレーションを受けて「パントーン152C」で統一し、ブランドカラーに確定しました。

We reviewed the existing Palm colors for the package system and refined the iconic Palm orange by selecting an energetic shade of orange. We were inspired by the California state flower, the poppy. Its rich orange, bathed in sunlight embodied the spirit and origin of the brand. We chose Pantone 152c, a color similar to the poppy.

PANTONE®
152 C

原寸 | Actual Size

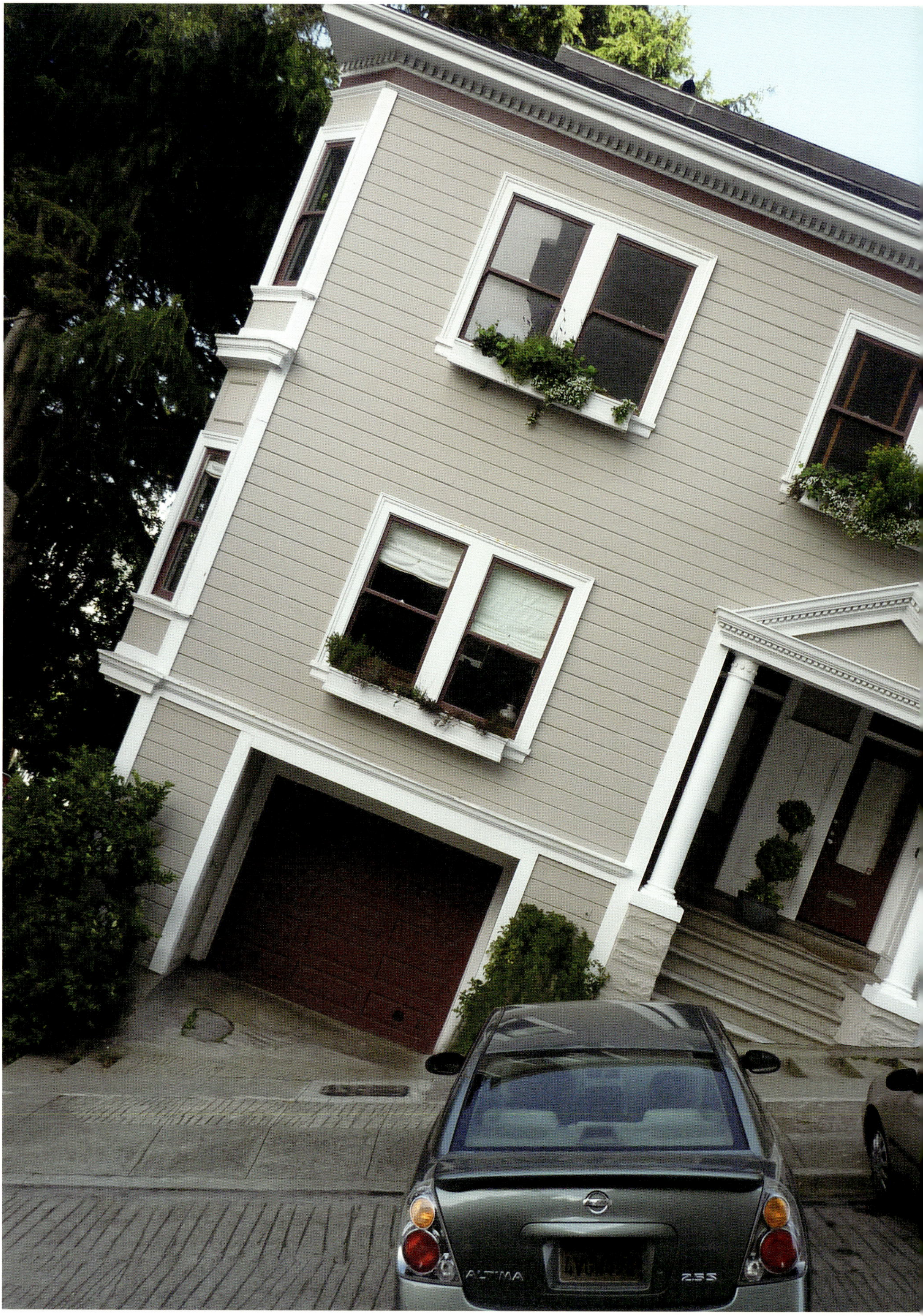
ALTIMA
2.5S

PACKAGE DESIGN

原寸 | Actual Size

Photo by Shuji Yoshida

パッケージとその中に入る製品との関係性は、家と住人との関係性と同じである。パッケージという家の中に、製品とアクセサリーが共存するのである。
Packaging is architecture. The inhabitant of this house is your phone and accessory family.

ANGLE OF CONVERSATION

アメリカやヨーロッパの携帯電話市場では、通信回線のプロバイダーがパッケージを統一支配しています。その結果、必要以上に大きなサイズの紙箱が使われ、携帯本体、ケーブルや取扱説明書、マニュアルブックやCDなどが乱雑に詰め込まれることに。そのためパッケージは、プロバイダーが一方的に決めたただの箱であり、「パーム」のアイデンティティが表現できない状態だった。パッケージをデザインするうえで命題となったことは、パームらしさの表現、パームだけのオリジナルボックスをデザインすることでした。

The primary objective of the phone packaging design was to create an original concept for the Palm brand. In the American and European phone markets, the smartphone service providers usually set the packaging and design formats for phone makers like Palm. The result is an oversized box with designated areas allocated for co-branding. Inside, one will find a loosely packed box containing the new phone, manual and various accessories packed in plastic bags secured with twist ties. Palm wanted to break away from this generic industry standard and create a package that engaged the customer in a intimate experience of unpacking their new Palm phone.

パームがパッケージデザインに求めた最重要課題は、視覚的なシンプルさと清潔感。パッケージに記載が義務づけられているプロバイダーのロゴや情報をいかにすっきりと表現しながら、同時にパーム独自の世界観をデザインできるかだった。解決案としてTYDが提示したのは、プラスチックの透明なスリーブをパッケージにかぶせること。プロバイダーによって記入内容の異なる情報を取り外し可能なスリーブに印刷することによって、パッケージ本体にはパーム以外のインフォメーションが入らない、ミニマルなデザインに仕上げることができた。

Palm needed a creative solution for co-branding their brand information alongside the provider's. Our solution was to introduce a clear sleeve which added a layer of surface area for us to design on. All of the provider's information was designed on the outer sleeve and all of Palm's information was designed on the box. The combined information appeared to be on one surface but in fact they were separated. This proved to be a simple and effective solution that pleased all parties involved.

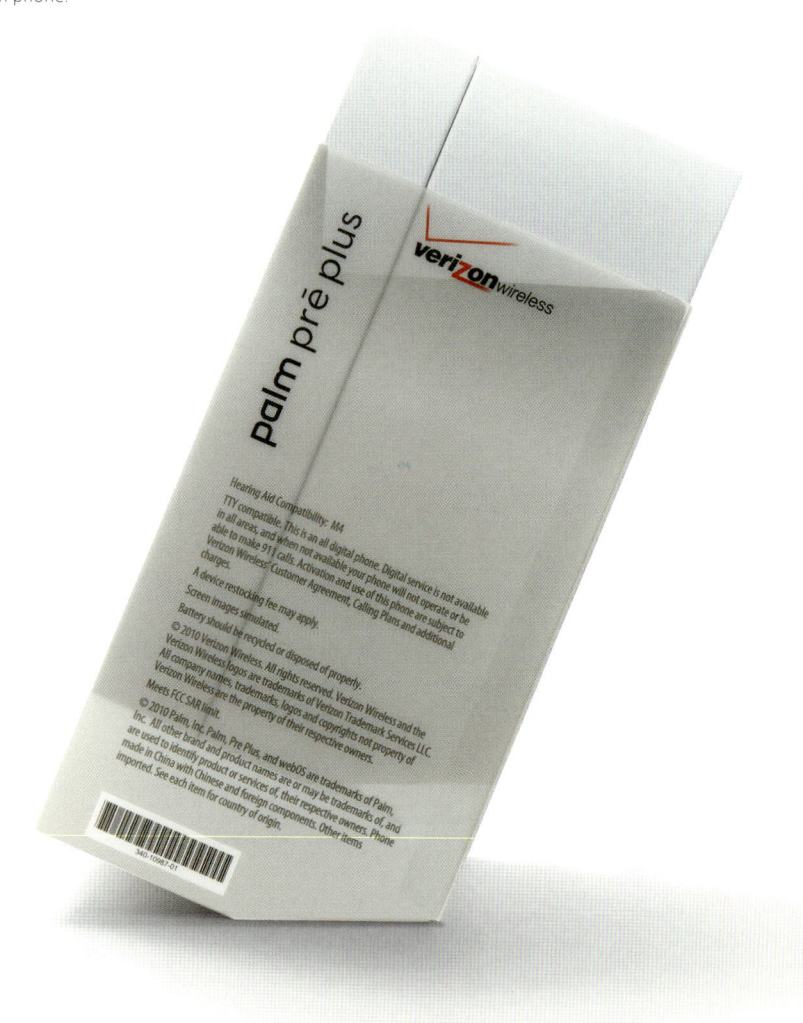

パッケージは一般的な長方形の箱ではなく、角をカットして箱自体が直立するし、傾きもするという絶妙なバランスをもつユニークな形にした。実際、店頭でお辞儀をするように、少し斜めに傾いたパッケージが並んでいると、お客様と製品が対話をしているようで、手に取ってもらいやすい。こうして、角度のついたパッケージは、パームが目指す「携帯電話と人との距離を縮める」親近感のあるデザインとなった。

The box was designed and engineered to rest at a 65° angle, therefore the contents within the box were strategically positioned for optimal weight distribution. This angle gave the product a subtle edge and personality, as if the product was trying to engage in a conversation. The box was also designed to sit upright, offering two display options. We liked this friendly feature of the box.

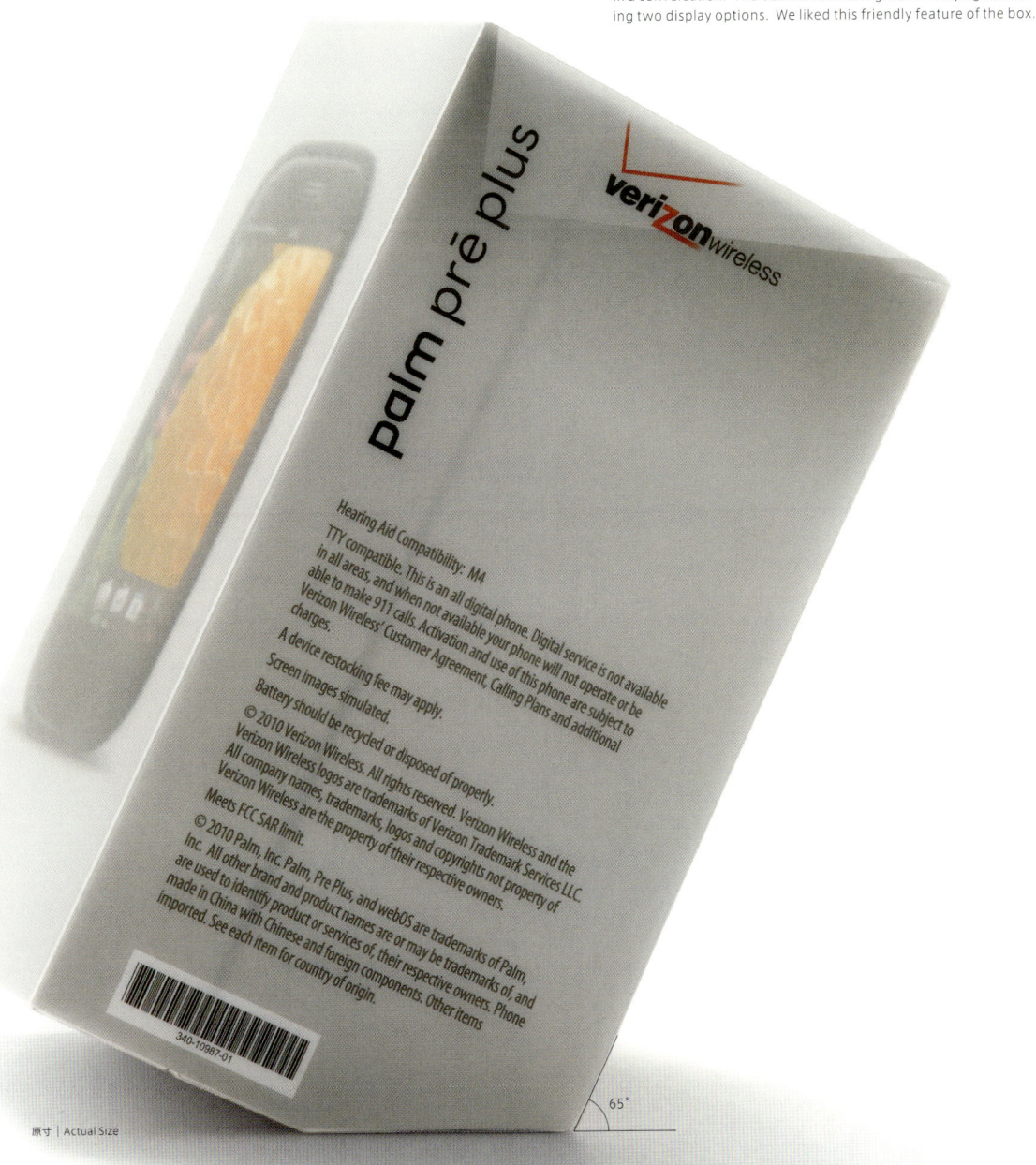

原寸 | Actual Size

ECO FRIENDLY MATERIALS

パッケージの上蓋の裏面に、携帯を守るクッション素材としてチョコレートの保護に使われるワックス紙を使用することにしました。通常、このようなクッションに用いられるのは、リネンなどを使用した再利用不可能な素材が多いのですが、ブランドの環境への配慮、一貫してエコロジカルであるという意志をカスタマーに対して強く表現するため、細かいディテールにも配慮しました。
八木理都子（TYD グラフィック・デザイナー）

We replaced the foam lining on the back of the lid with an environmentally friendly, cushion paper, the kind you would normally find inside a box of chocolates. This idea was a natural progression of design, as we were already working with paper to establish a functional and distinct package system for the inner box. A small detail with a big message. If one noticed, the message has the potential to connect with the customer on a deeper level, a memorable one that leads to more respect and love for the Palm brand.
Ritz Yagi (Graphic Designer at TYD)

原寸 | Actual Size

携帯電話本体が収まる箱の内側のクッション材をオレンジ色にした。白い箱をあけると、パームのブランドカラーである鮮やかなオレンジが目に飛び込んでくるという遊び心をこめた。

We wanted a "wow" effect when the user opened the box and we used color to achieve this. The new Palm orange worked well in contrast with the outer white box for a surprising effect. The use of the brand color was consistent throughout the inner design of the package, an understated yet memorable reference to the brand color.

原寸 | Actual Size

アクセサリーのプラグ、コード、チャージャーなどの収納を工夫した。植物のツタのように、一枚のコルゲート段ボール紙で仕切りをつくることによって、箱の中にきれいに納めることができた。ここでも、ブランドカラーであるオレンジを採用し、段ボール紙の裏面に一カ所「NO DETAIL IS SMALL」とプリントした。

We were inspired by nature to create a simple system to hold the accessories neatly inside the box. Like a free forming tendril of a plant, we designed an interlocking system from one piece of corrugated cardboard which sectioned off and protected the accessories inside the package. Again, the Palm brand orange was used. We successfully replaced plastic wraps with a recyclable material. The slogan "No detail is small" was printed on the back of the corrugated cardboard.

直感的なアイデアや思わぬ発見が、計算して出された答えより良い結果を生むことも多い。たまたま手にした、普通紙を波面にするおもちゃのような機械からヒントを得て、パッケージ内の仕切りに使用し、機能的なパッケージとした。

Serendipity and intuition can be just as important as any rational planning. Playing with the corrugated cardboard inserts resulted in a flexible system to allow every language variant to use the same parts. Enlightened trial and error wins out over flawless planning and intellect.

Photo by Shuji Yoshida

HIERARCHY OF CONTENTS

The way the contents are organized within the package tells a distinct story. As subtle as it may be, the impression that these small details leave is very important when a person opens the package for the first time. We supplied Palm with this playful visual of a hamburger so they could present this analogy to the providers. We took photographs of each ingredient to show the importance of the placement of each item as it would apply to the package.
Takumi Yagi (TYD Designer)

どこににどのように商品を納めるかで、箱を開けたときの印象が変わってきます。ハンバーガーの味は素材の重ね方が変われば、同じ素材であっても誰でも味やおいしさが違ってきます。私たちはアメリカ人なら誰でも食べたことがあるハンバーガーを使ってストーリーをつくりました。実際の素材を使って一つずつ同じアングルで写真を撮り、一番おいしい重ね方のイメージを作成してプレゼンテーションしました。
八木 巧（TYD デザイナー）

パッケージの中の納め方も提案した。従来は、箱の蓋を開けると最初にCDや取扱説明書、箱の底に携帯本体が入っていた。けれど、パームでは、主役は携帯だから、箱を開けるとまず携帯本体があってすぐに手に取ることができるようにと考えた。その結果、上から順に、携帯本体、取扱説明書、プラグ、保証書の順に。取扱説明書は取り出しやすいように最初のページの角を折り曲げ、バーコードは外箱の目立たない位置にレイアウトした。

The organization of contents and its ordering was also considered. Unlike the previous phone package where the CD and manual obstructed the view of the phone, we placed the Palm phone at the very top. Next came the simplified manual, accessories (as shown on P.169) and then legal documents. The simplified manual was also folded on the corner for ease of removal from the box. The barcode was printed on the bottom of the outer box where it was least visible.

Photo by Shuji Yoshida

LESS IS MORE

The partnership with TYD was extraordinary because we sat together and asked the question, "What more can we remove?" This constraint drove purpose into the effort as we sat down together and explored the relationship between the legacy of the brand and how Palm could regain its footing. This was pure creation and play... The epiphany of good design is that the experience became so much better, the brand elements so much more clear and the outcome was a savings of over 52 per package because the weight, volume and palletization of the shipped package was so much smaller. Good design improves the experience. Great design does this and generates financial returns.

Peter Skillman (VP of Smart Devices Ux Design at Nokia & Former VP of Design at Palm)

TYDをデザインパートナーとして動員し、まず掲げた大きな課題はいかにさらにシンプルにするか?でした。ともにテーブルを囲み、パームの過去のレガシーを残しつつ、さらなる進化をどのように実現するか、会話は豊かな想像力からなる遊びの延長のようでした。コラボレーションによって生まれたデザインはとても満足のいくものでした。ブランドが持つ特色が明確になり、同時にパッケージの軽量化を図れたことで、送料や制作費を含め、単価を2ドルほど削減できました。良いデザインはその上に、コスト的な面でも改善することができるのです。

ピーター・スキルマン（ノキア スマートデバイス Ux デザイン部 バイスプレジデント 元パーム デザイン部 バイスプレジデント）

THE NEW PACKAGE IS 50% SMALLER THAN THE PREVIOUS

直径12cmの製品説明のCDをなくすことで、箱のサイズを半分に縮小できた。その結果、新しいパッケージは、従来の半分の大きさになった。
By eliminating the 12cm CD manual, we were able to reduce the size of the package by half.

ACCESSORY PACKAGE

パームのモックアップをつくるときに5種類の道具を使用した。①3M社のスコッチテープ13mm ②両面テープ6mm幅 ③エルマーズグルー ④オルファのカッターナイフ ⑤フィスカース ペーパークリンパー

To create the design mockups for the Palm package, we used these above materials and tools the most: ①3M Scotch tape, 13mm ②Double-sided tape, 6mm ③Elmer's Glue ④Olfa cutter knife ⑤Fiskars paper crimper.

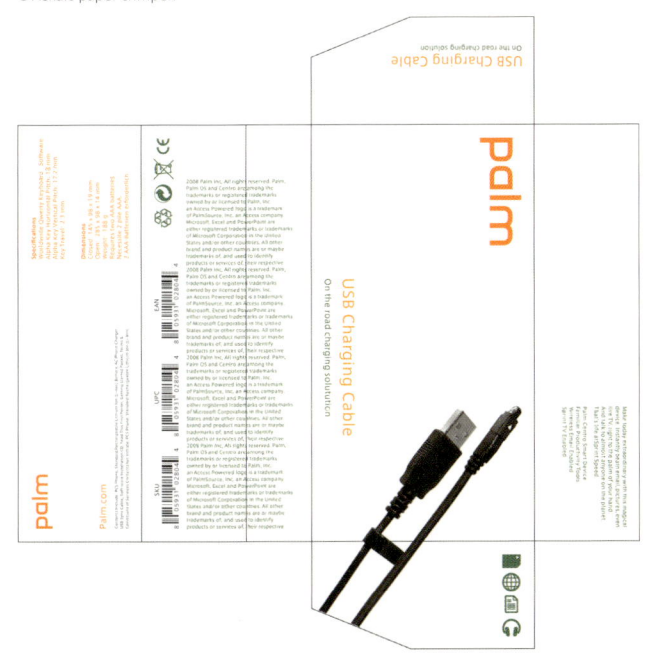

アクセサリー用のパッケージデザイン。外箱は本体の箱と同様、角を切り取って傾けて置けるように。一見、単なる横長のパッケージだが、後ろ側には壁掛や什器に吊り下げられるフックを取り付けました。箱の中のコルゲート段ボール紙は左右2カ所に折り線を入れて立体に、さらに部分的に切り目を入れてアクセサリーのコードを引っ掛けられるようにして、糊しろのないパッケージ内部の土台が完成。パッケージのアイデンティティはコルゲート段ボール紙を中心に形成されました。

The accessory package design was driven from the primary phone box design for a cohesive package system. The outer box was made from a single piece of dye cut paper for easy assembly with a tab added for hanging. The inside corrugated board was scored into various shapes to bend a flat sheet of board into a three dimensional shape, designed to hug and hold the accessories in place.

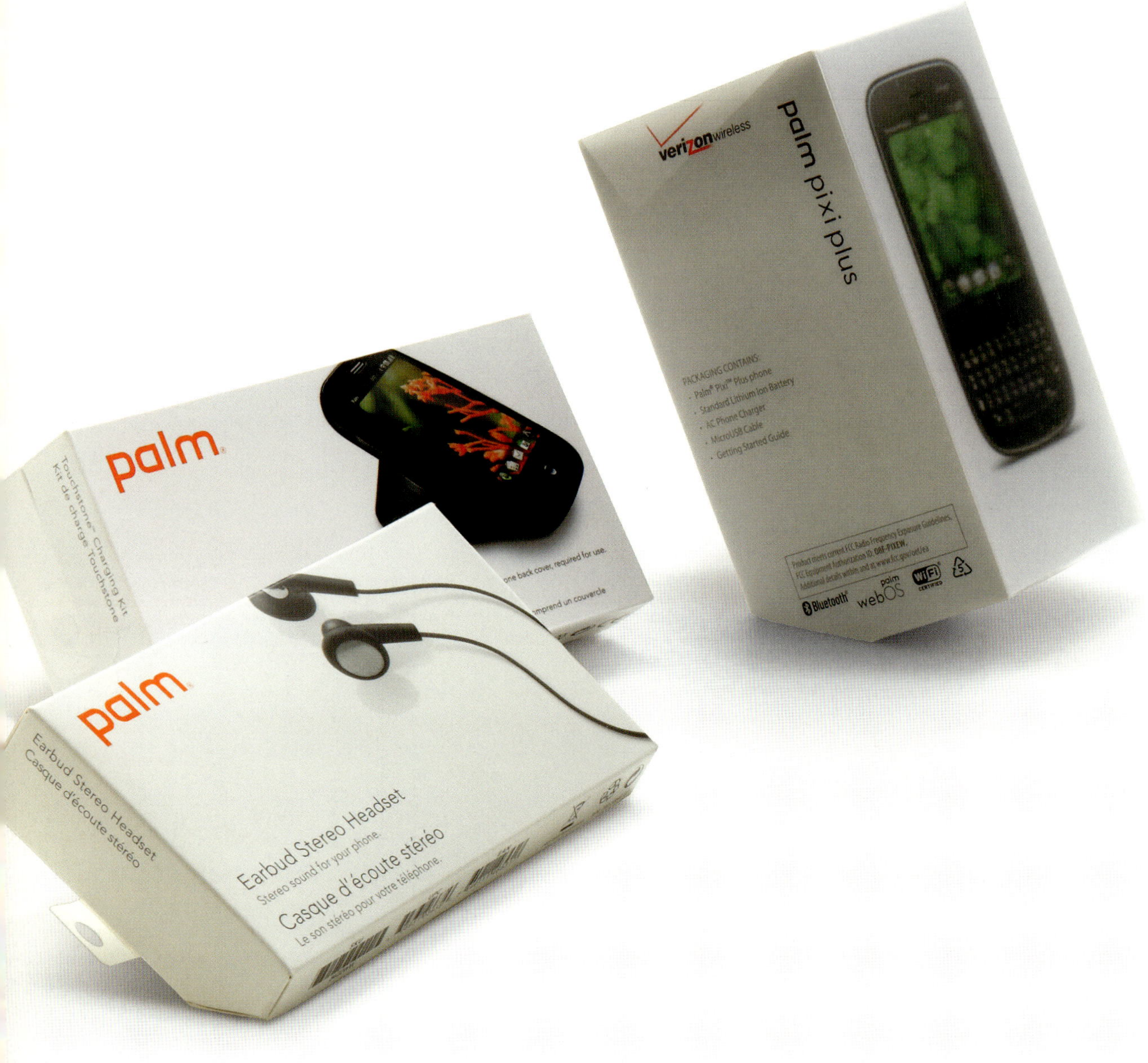
palm
Touchstone™ Charging Kit
Kit de charge Touchstone
palm
Earbud Stereo Headset
Casque d'écoute stéréo
Earbud Stereo Headset
Stereo sound for your phone.
Casque d'écoute stéréo
Le son stéréo pour votre téléphone.
verizonwireless
palm pixi plus
PACKAGING CONTAINS:
· Palm® Pixi™ Plus phone
· Standard Lithium Ion Battery
· AC Phone Charger
· MicroUSB Cable
· Getting Started Guide
Bluetooth
palm webOS

Photo by Shuji Yoshida

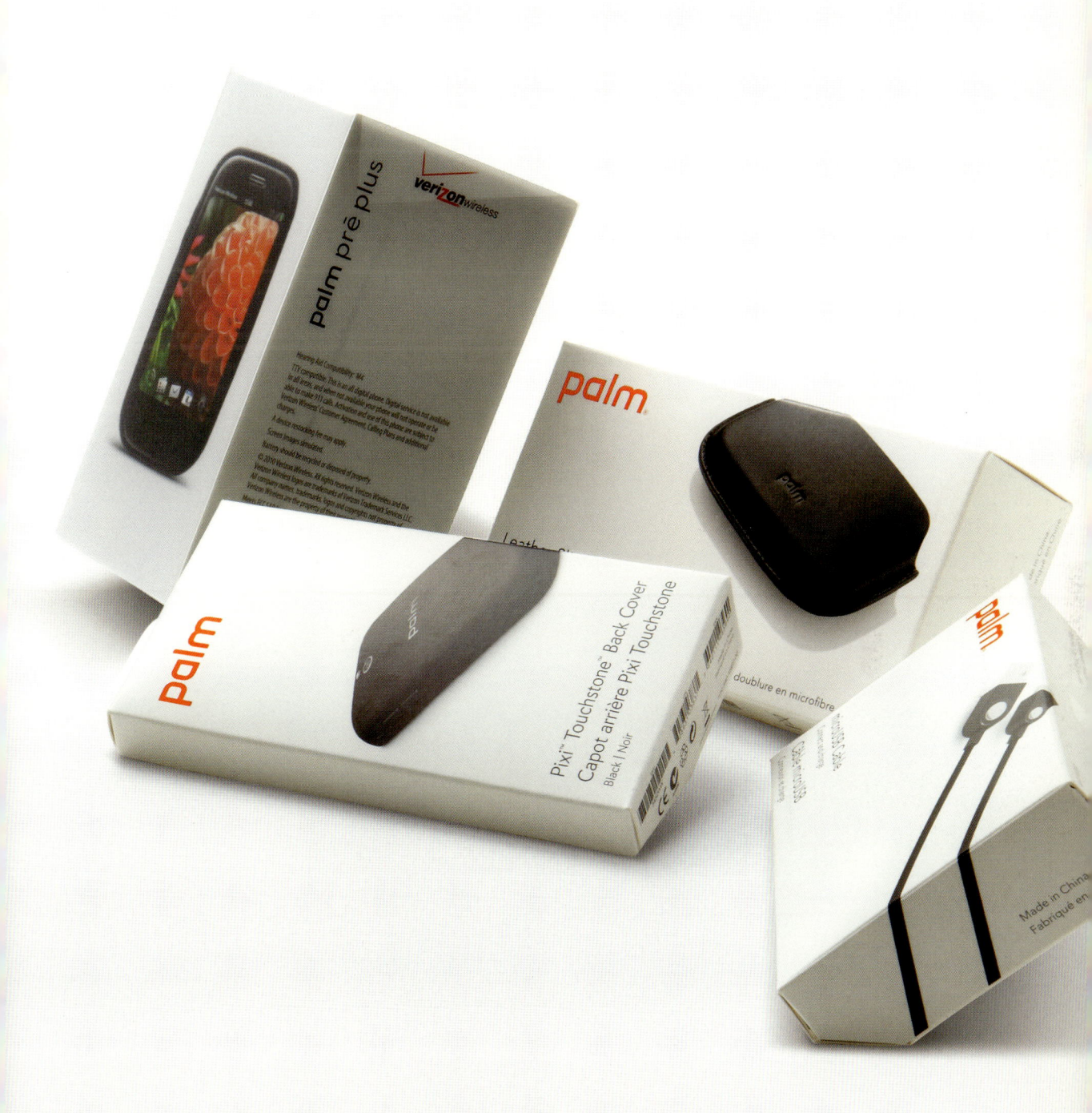

palm

Wireless Keyboard
with Bluetooth wireless technology

palm

Stylus 3-Pack
with Bluetooth wireless

Photo by Shuji Yoshida

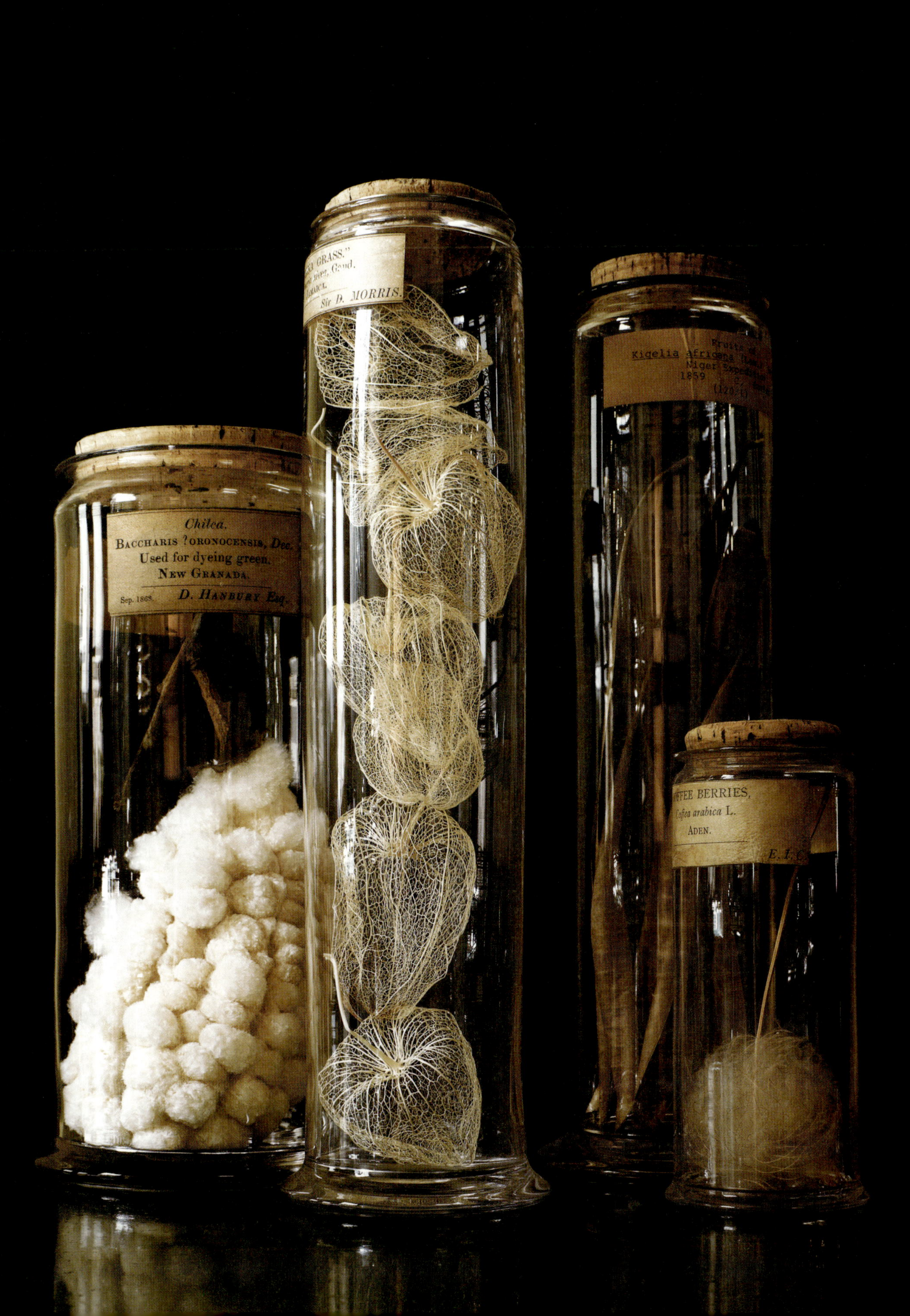

Photo by Stefano Massei

T.Y. COLLECTION

コレクション

Tamotsu Yagi's private collection

倉俣史朗の2種類のテーブルの脚。アクリルは、福岡の「ホテル・イル・パラッツオ」内にあったバー「オブローモフ」のカウンターテーブルの脚。エキスパンドメタルはテーブル「45° North Latitude」の脚。

Table legs designed by Shiro Kuramata. The pink and yellow acrylic leg was once a part of a table of the Oblomov bar inside the Hotel Il Palazzo in Fukuoka, Japan. The mesh leg is from a prototype of the *45° North Latitude* table.

1950

Collections of objects tell a story of a person's lifestyle. Collecting is an important part of my creative process and the objects I collect are a source of my design inspirations. I like to collect found objects from nature to printed materials, 50s furniture and art. I also keep a file of interesting things I come across in magazines and auction catalogs. I often buy directly from sources because I like to examine an object with my own eyes. My collections are an important part of my environment so no matter how valuable the piece, I like to use everything and this also adds character to a piece. I also enjoy decorating my environment by rearranging objects. The entire process is an extension of my creative expression.

コレクションを見ると、その人のライフタイルが想像できるように、集めたものは、自分にとってのデザインソースであり、インスピレーションの源。だから、人から見たら、ガラクタとも思えるような木の実や石、印刷物など、あらゆるものがコレクションの対象です。そのなかでも、一九五〇年代の家具には、思い入れがあります。いいな、と思うものは、オークションカタログ、雑誌を切り抜き、アートと家具のファイリングをして、イメージを膨らませます。現物を自分の眼で見て、購入。そう、選択するのです。私にとって、アートも家具も暮らしのなかで必要なもの。だから、たとえ高価な家具であっても使います。きちんとメインテナンスを施し、長い時間、使いこむことによって、家具も味わい深くなるから…。

Photo by Stefano Massei

海中で採集された「ヴィーナス・フラワー・バスケット」。日本では「偕老同穴(かいろうどうけつ)」と呼ばれる海綿生物。この中に小さな雄と雌のエビが生息している。
Pictured above is a venus' flower basket. Male and female shrimp are known to live in the basket symbiotically.

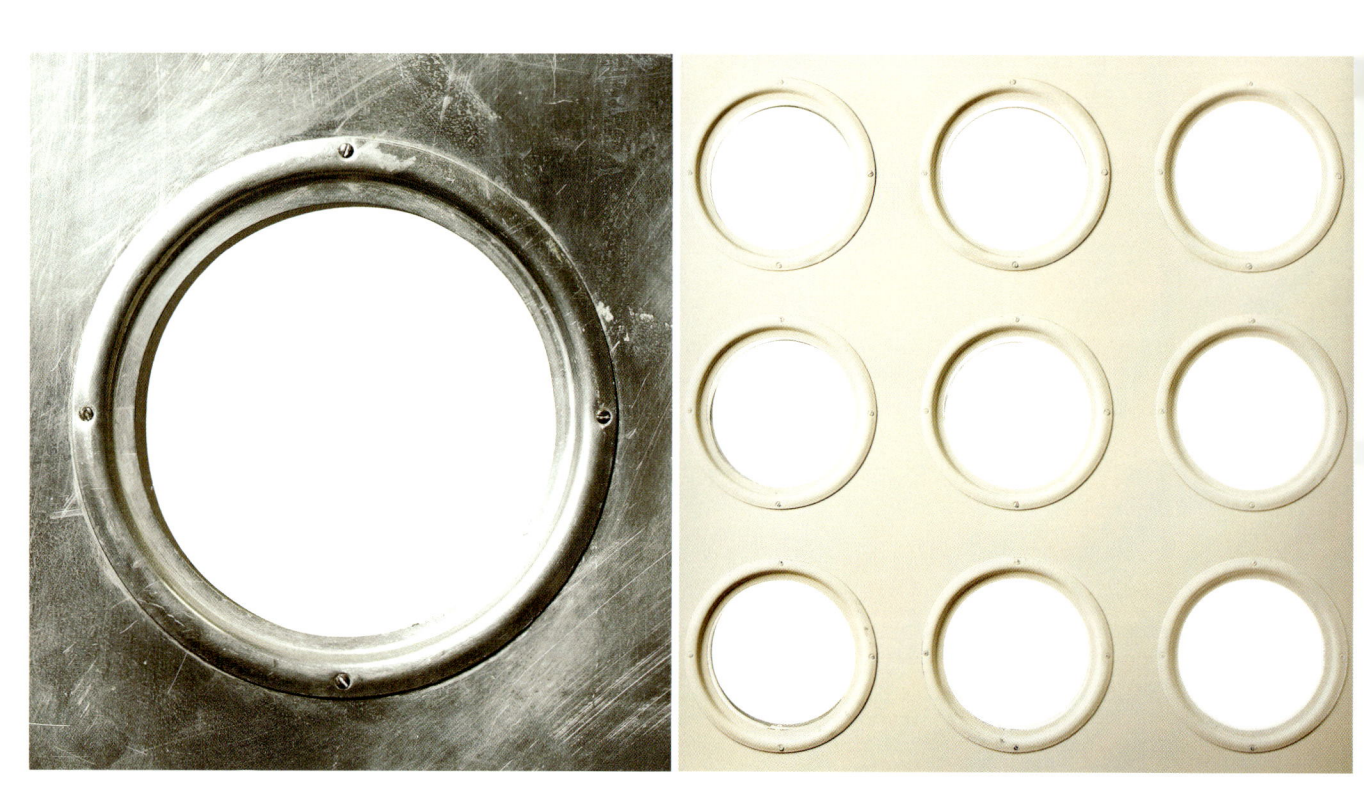

ジャン・プルーヴェが1950年につくったプレハブ建築のパネル「Façade panel」。高さ約3mの両面パネルで、内側がアルミ、外側が白のペイント。

Pictured is a detail of the front and back of the windows of a 1950s *Porthole Panel* by Jean Prouvé. This double sided architectural panel is about three meters high. One side is painted off-white and the other side is raw aluminum with horizontal wooden panels that come up about one meter in length from the ground.

Photo by Stefano Massei

"There is no difference between building furniture and building a house."

———"家具の製作も建築も違いはない。"
ジャン・プルーヴェ

JEAN PROUVÉ

額装は、ピーター・ビヤードのイェール大学時代（1960年代）の作品「Art Homework 1960」。手前にある巨大な蜂の模型（幅50cm）は、パリの博物館から手に入れたもの。
The framed artwork is a painting by Peter Beard titled *Art Homework 1960*, which he created as a student at Yale University.
In the foreground is an anatomy of a bee (50cm long) that was once exhibited in a science museum in Paris.

すぐれた作品とはよい時によい所によい物があってはじめて成り立つ。つまり、いくつもの要素が交わる場なのだ。リチャード・ロング

「リチャード・ロング　山行水行」展図録より抜粋　一九九六年

壁には、ドナルド・ジャッドの作品のようなジャン・プルーヴェのシェルフ。床には、リチャード・ロングの作品「River Avon Driftwood Circle 1978」。68個の流木が、直径 約4mの円になるアート。
The piece that resembles a work by Donald Judd is a wall mounted cabinet by Jean Prouvé. The installation art on the floor is by Richard Long titled, *River Avon Driftwood Circle 1978*. This installation consists of 68 pieces of driftwood, creating a circle four meters wide.

U.S. Geological Survey
SEGMENT 2
SECTOR 8   SECTOR 7

DAY 327, SURVEY CC
SECTORS 7 AND 8

左の額装は、スペースシャトルが撮影した、月の表面のモノクロのコンタクトシート。球体のオブジェは、月をイメージしてコーディネイトした。ジョニー・スペンサーの鉄板のアートの上に陳列している。
右ページ：ジョニー・スペンサーの鉄板のアートをバックに、ジョージ・リッキーの作品「One Line Down Hommage to Giacometti」と、1950年製のマオ(毛沢東)のセラミックの置物。

Left: This monochrome contact sheet of the moon's surface was photographed from a space shuttle and is resting on top of a metal panel artwork by Johnny Spencer. The two round objects stacked on top of each other are miniature moons. Right: Another piece by Johnny Spencer is placed in the background of George Rickey's pendulum titled *One Line Down Hommage to Giacometti*. Next to the pendulum is a ceramic, 1950s Mao Zedong figure.

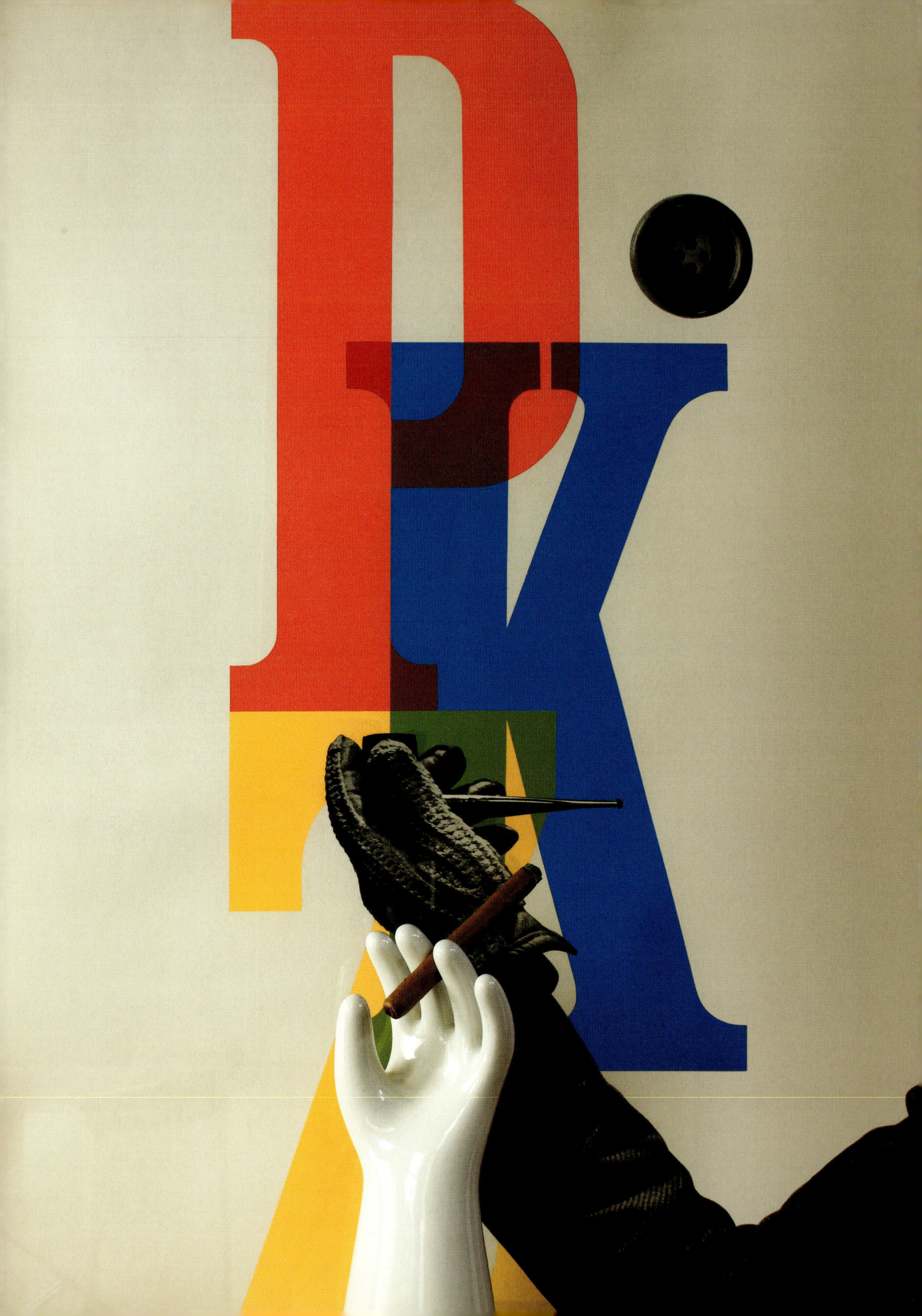
P
K

PKZのポスターのブルーと同じ色のジャン・プルーヴェとシャルロット・ペリアンの共同作品「Tunisie」の部分。
Blue sliding cabinet doors from Charlotte Perriand and Ateliers Jean Prouvé's *Tunisia* shelf and a similar blue color of a vintage *PKZ* poster.

シャルロット・ペリアンのシェルフ。後方の壁面に飾っているのは、マウロ・ジアコーニの作品「Anatomy (2008) Wired Fence Series」。
右／古い医学書の1ページに鉛筆で描かれたチェーンリングフェイスのパターンの部分。
A bookshelf designed by Charlotte Perriand stands in front of a piece by Mauro Giaconi, titled *Anatomy (2008) Wired Fence Series*.
A chain link fence is drawn with graphite over overlapping pages of an antique medical book.

que explican el motivo por
peligrosa ar, la extremidad posterior
c. Prolongacio de la submaxilar. — De l
prenden dos prolongacio una posterior,

A

8
C

o resecada a nivel de la unión de su
r.
accesorio, con 2', su orificio en la pa-
niendo la ampolla de Vater. — 4, con-
— 8, vasos mesentéricos superiores. —

ertos puntos, es retrovis-

a cara anterior de la
regiones que están super-
odenopancreática, la *región*
líaca. La ón celíaca
stá limitada la derecha,
ómago, el ría y la pri-
do por el lóbulo de Spiegel
la aorta excava en el. El
y por la primera lumbar

54

mes de la vida intra
na corresponde a
del sacro; a cer mes
últim ocupa toda l
long del conducto sacro
y de e así hasta la ba
se de ix.

mensiones. —
a medula pinal mide
por término me de 43
44 centímetros de itud.
Su circunferencia es d
milímetros a nivel del e
grosamiento cervical, de 3
milímetros a nivel del e
grosamiento lumbar y d
27 milímetros en la porció
comprendida entre est
dos engrosamientos.

4.º Dir ción. —
sde el n to de vista d
s ón, la medula si
gue tamente las infle
xio la columna ver
tebr nos presenta, por
co 2, dos curvatu
s: una atura cervi-
cal, de conca d poste-
rior, y una *cur a dor-*
sal, de concavidad a a
hacia delante. El ori
superior de la curvatu
dorsal está claramen
marcado, en el plano ante
rior de la medula, por una
especie de *promontorio*, sa
liente hacia adelante
corresponde al ori n del
séptimo o del avo nervio
rvical.

Relaciones. —
La ula espinal como
se laramente en los

La medula vista en su sitio.
mpila ventana en los músculos espinales, y luego post stuche dural par
nas) ha sido resecada. Después se ha incindi uego abierto d anterior del
o: un segmento de la medula ha sido r o para mostrar l

duramadre. — 3, ligamento do. — 4, raíz poster or del s or cerv
4'', raíz posterior del par dorsal. — 5, venas intrarraquídea iga
avo p iza la cara poste de los cuerpos vertebrales. — 7, músculos
terior q

menio vertecora
— 8, ligamentos amarillos.

10
11

54

Los pila
diversos, si
edentes, tan

12
12'
C.

5

8

A, secci
1, aorta
5, 5, pilar ante
7, 7, valva
coronaria derech
Se ve qu l
transparenta l
Una banda med
clásico d
es an
mientos
los pilares

河原温の「I GOT UP」シリーズと宮島達夫の「Changing Time with Changing Self No.27-W」。
A series by On Kawara titled *I GOT UP* and a reflection of *Changing Time with Changing Self No.27-W* by Tatsuo Miyajima.

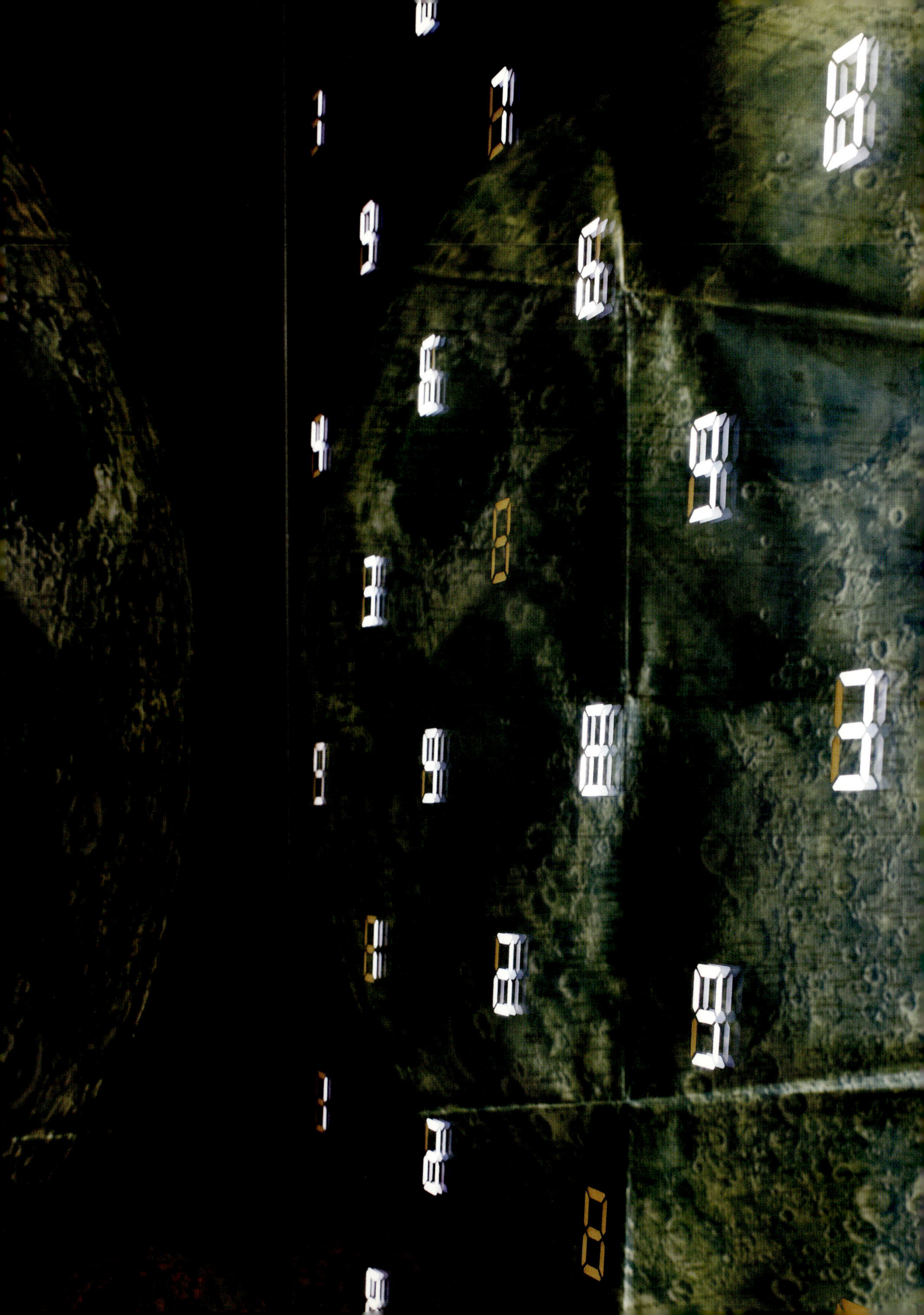

グラスファイバー製の波板に、車の塗装を数十回ペイントしたジョージ・アーンストンの作品「Yellow Pearl 38」。
This is a piece by George Ernston titled *Yellow Pearl 38*. The wavy fiberglass sheet is painted over many times with a thick coating of automotive paint.

Photo by Kazuya Enomoto

Photo by Stefano Massei

対談 Conversation

感じる力、対話する力

アンデルセン 髙木 彬子　吉田 正子

常に鮮度を保てるように努力する

八木：仕事のうえでは、クライアントから教えられることがとても多いです。「アンデルセン」とは長いお付き合いで、その信頼をベースに、お互い刺激し合いながら今日に至っています。私は食べることが大好きなので、「アンデルセン」の仕事はとても楽しいです。
あらためて、「アンデルセン」が企業経営とデザインについてどのようにお考えなのかをうかがえればと思います。

吉田：私たちは食の企業ですから、一緒にお仕事をするうえで、食べることに興味がない方だと、正直なところ困ってしまうんです。その点、八木さんは食に敏感でこだわりをおもちなので新しい食情報や店舗情報についても教えていただけて、お会いする楽しみの一つになっています。
デザインについては、八木さんとのお仕事のなかで、デザインが重要なコミュニケーションツールだということがわかってきました。企業が事業を継続し、発展させていくときに、お客様とのコミュニケーションは要と言っていいぐらいです。私たちアンデルセンが、何を考え、どうやってお客様のお役に立とうとしているのかをお伝えし、また逆にお客様のご意見、ご要望をきちんと理解し受けとめることで、ブランドやお店を育てていくことができると考えています。デザインはそのなかで大きな役割を担ってくれていますね。

八木：最近は、ブランディングなどといわれています。

髙木：私はデザインについてはわかりませんが、はじめてのお店をつくったときには、おそらくデザイナーの方と同じような考えや視点があったのだと思います。せっかく自分たちがつくったのだから、少しでも長く、多くのお客様にご愛顧いただきたい、そのためには日々の努力、創意工夫を怠ってはいけません。よく虎屋さんがおっしゃいますが「伝統とは革新の連続である‥‥」と。
まさにそうなのだと思います。しいて言えば、「常に鮮度を失わないように努力を続ける」ことが重要で、デザインもその一つだと思います。一本筋を通して守るべきは守り、変えるべきは大胆に変える‥‥その連続なのではないでしょうか。八木さんには、私たちのデザインをより魅力的にする「磨き」を助けていただいているのだと思います。

八木：たしかに。その理解と信頼のうえで仕事をさせていただいているのですね。私自身は、「アンデルセン」はすでに確固たる歴史と信頼を築いているので、そのイメージを崩さずに、新しい時代の空気を取り込んだデザインが基本だと考えています。

吉田：以前は、「ビジュアルコミュニケーション」という概念はもっていませんでしたが、漠然と「すてきでありたい」とは、思っていました。それが八木さんとご一緒にお仕事をさせていただくようになって、ああ、こういうことだったんだ、と視野が広がったのです。
それまでは、自分たちの理念や商品のことを正しくお伝えする「言葉」を、とても大切に考えていました。商品情報のみならず、お客様の生活のクオリティを上げることのお役に立つメッセージを発信しようと努めていましたが、ビジュアルについて

は明確な方向性をもっていなかったんですね。
そこに八木さんから、ビジュアルというのはグラフィックだけではなく、店舗、ディスプレイ、スタッフの制服、商品の形など、あらゆる要素があり、それらをコミュニケーションツールとして総合的にプロデュースしていくことが大切だ、と教えていただきました。八木さんが手がけて下さったロゴや紙袋はもちろんのこと、それ以外の部分でも、いろいろと良い影響を受けていると感じています。

八木：デザインがこれだけ認知された現在でも、その本質を理解している企業は意外に多くはありません。たとえば、「もっとデザインしてください」とか「デザインを10個見せてください」とか、デザインを装飾やモノのように考えている企業も少なくないのです。
そんななか、「アンデルセン」はデザイナーの能力をどう生かしていくかをきちんと理解されています。これが一番というデザイン案を一つにしぼって提案しても、私たちの意図や狙いをきちんと了解していただき、的確な意見が返ってきます。言葉で説明しなくても、お互いに、何となくわかり合っているという感覚がもてるのです。

吉田：私たちも、基本的に八木さんにお願いすれば大丈夫、という感覚をもっていますから。私たち以上にお客様にアンデルセンらしさをどう表現すれば伝わるのか、よくわかっていらっしゃるなあと感心することも‥‥。

高木：最初の頃は、素人が手探りのような状態で店やロゴをつくっていたので、創業40年のときにアンデルセングループのアイデンティティを見直すことにして、八木さんにお願いしました。社内では、一時的にロゴができればすべておしまいといった誤解が生まれたのですが、とんでもないことです。ロゴはアイデンティティ確立のための一歩にすぎません。

八木：「アンデルセン」はデザインに対しても意思決定が速くて、会社としてのきちんとした理念がおありなのだと思いました。

お客様目線でいること

高木：夫も私も、パンづくりのプロではないのですが、すばらしい職人さんを得て品質には自信をもってきました。しかし、良い商品をつくっているだけでは不十分です。パンのある食卓や生活のすばらしさをお伝えすることによってはじめて、お客様は私たちのパンに共感してくださる。
私たちが素人だったからこそ、「お客様あっての商売である」という確信がもてました。それがアンデルセンの基礎なのです。
私たちの気持ちをきちんとお伝えするために「デザイン」はとても大切ですね。

八木：人は「美味しい」を五感のすべてで感じるのだと思います。どんなに美味しいものでも散らかった場所で食べたら堪能できないだろうし、逆にそこそこの料理でも友人や家族との寛いだ食卓ならば美味しく感じる。そういう意味では、パンの品質はもちろんですが、食卓や生活全体に対する視線やメッセージが大切ですね。

高木：私は、お客様の喜んで下さっている笑顔がいつも頭にあるんですね。販売員はお客様と対面できますが、つくっている人間はそうはいきません。でも、誰のためにパンをつくっているのか？という想いを忘れては、美味しいパンは生まれません。たとえ自分の家族であっても、あの人に喜んでもらいたいという強い気持ちがなければ、美味しいものなんてつくれないと思うんですこんなふうに考えられるのも、私たちが素人だからなのでしょう。

八木：おっしゃる通り、とくに「食」に関しては、身近な人を喜ばすこともできないで、顔も知らないお客様に喜んでいただくことはできないかもしれません。デザインも同じですね。

高木：けれども、私の考えがすべてではなく、考え方の一つであるということです。会社は一つのチームですから、いろんな人が集まって知恵を出し合いながら仕事をしていくもの。
私のような考え方の人間もいれば、まったく違った発想の社員もいる。その多様さとバランスが大切なのですね。

吉田：パンはデイリーな商品ですから、お客様目線でいることは欠かせません。従業員には私たちの商品はパンであっても、販売しているのは、朝食を大切にするとか、家族と心豊かな夕食を楽しむなどのライフスタイルであるといつも言っています。
八木さんはプレゼンテーションときに、デザインだけでなくそのデザインの背景にある世界観も含めて提案して下さるのでとても参考になります。

八木：言葉では上手く表わせないのですが、私なりに「アンデルセン」にこうあってほしいなあというこだわりがあって、そのイメージをデザインという方法で提案させてもらっています。たとえば、品性、感性ですね。

吉田：ありがとうございます。以前から八木さんによくお話ししていることは「昔からそこにあったかのようなデザインにしたい」ということ。店舗にしても、「ピカピカの新しい店ができました！」ではなく「前からあったような気がする」という自然になじむ店、素直に受け入れられるデザインということです。
私たちとしては、デザインももちろん褒められたいのですけど、「パンが美味しく見える」「ここに来るとホッとする」と言っていただくことのほうがうれしいわけです。主役はあくまでも商品であり、お客様なのだと思っています。

八木：デザイナーとしても「八木さんのデザインをまとうとパンが一層美味しそうに見える」と言われることが何より嬉しいです。「アンデルセン」が何よりもお客様を第一に考えていることは改めて確認できましたが、社会がこれだけ多様化すると、お客様もいろいろでしょう？

高木：ええ。なかには私たち以上にパンの知識や楽しみ方をご存知の方もいらっしゃる。だから、お客様とのコミュニケーションといっても、その内容の深さや広さも違うのだと思います。ワンパターンな会話では、お客様の多様な期待にお答えすることはできません。やはり、社員一人ひとりが日々実践から学ぶしかないんです。

八木：たとえば、広島と東京ではお客様の嗜好は違いますか？

吉田：もはや東京だ、広島だという地域性ではありませんね。一店舗、一店舗でかなり異なります。
東京でも路面店と百貨店では違いますし、百貨店でも新宿と銀座ではまた違います。ですから、「アンデルセン」という会社

高木 彬子 1925年、中国・大連生まれ。株式会社アンデルセン・パン生活文化研究所 相談役。1948年、夫・高木俊介とともに「タカキのパン」を4名で創業。1967年には旧帝国銀行の被爆建物を買い取り「広島アンデルセン」をオープン。1995年より相談役。社外では、1997年に広島商工会議所女性会の副会長に就任、2009年には同・会長に就任している。

Akiko Takaki was born in Dalian, China while her father was working abroad. She and her family returned to Japan after WWII. She founded Takaki Bakery in 1948 with four others including her husband, Shunsuke Takaki. They purchased a bombed bank building and opened the Andersen Hiroshima store in 1967. She became the vice president of The Hiroshima Female Chamber of Commerce in 1997, and later became president of the organization in 2009.

吉田 正子 1954年、広島市生まれ。株式会社アンデルセン代表取締役社長執行役員。1983年、広島アンデルセンのワイン＆ギフトコーナー販売スタッフとして入社。2001年㈱アンデルセン取締役、2006年より現職。ベーカリー「アンデルセン」では、デンマークのライフスタイルをお手本に本格のパンを提供するだけでなく、パンのある暮らしを多彩に提案。さらに、ショコラブティック「ジャン＝ポール・エヴァン」などの展開も手がけるなど、本格的な食文化を追求している。

Masako Yoshida was born in Hiroshima city in 1954. She joined the sales staff of the Andersen Group in 1983. She became director of the company in 2001, and has served as president of Andersen Co., Ltd. since 2006. Andersen Bakery provides authentic European bread and promotes the concept of "life with bread" in versatile ways. The company also operates high quality chocolate shops in Japan through a collaboration with famed French chocolatier Jean-Paul Hévin.

全体を見ながら、同時に店ごとの個性をもたせることがどんどん重要になってきました。

ヒュッゲなひとときを

八木：ところで、「アンデルセン」というと「北欧」というイメージがありますが、やはり北欧的な生活や文化を広めたいというお気持ちが根底にあるのでしょうか？
吉田：私たちがお手本にしているデンマークには『HYGGE＝ヒュッゲ』という言葉があります。「人と人とのふれあいから生まれる、温かな居心地のよい雰囲気」という意味で、他の国の言語には置き換えることのできないデンマーク人独特の共通感覚です。
ただヒュッゲといっても、単に楽しいとかではなく、自分らしくいられる、ということが大切で、自分がヒュッゲなひとときをもつ、あるいは相手にヒュッゲを感じてもらうには、まずは自分自身がしっかりとした考えをもち、何が自分にとって大切なのかがわかっている。突き詰めていくと、一人ひとりが自立していることがヒュッゲの前提のようです。ずいぶん難しい話になりますけど‥‥

八木：今のお話を、企業とデザイナーの関係に当てはめてみると、しっかり自立している企業は、商品だけでなく包材や社員の対応に至るまで、その理念や行動に一貫性があるように思うのです。
デザイナーとしては、そうした企業と長くお付き合いできることはとても光栄なことで、その企業と仕事をしているという事実がデザイナーとしての信頼にもつながります。
髙木：お客様の立場になれば、美味しいパンを買えたり、スタッフとちょっとした会話が楽しめれば、それだけでハッピーな気持ちになって、きっとまたお店に足を運んでくださるにちがいない。
さらに八木さんのようなデザイナーや仕入業者の方など、アンデルセンを支えて下さる皆さんが、このハッピーを共有してくださることが何よりうれしいです。皆がもっと良い生活ができるように‥‥という気持ちが大切なのだと思います。
八木：「アンデルセン」という社名に、創業者である髙木俊介、彬子ご夫妻のお気持ちがこめられているのでしょうね。
髙木：「アンデルセン」というと童話が有名ですが、必ずしもハッピーな話だけではありません。悲しいお話も多いのだけど、人生の幸も不幸も受け入れるという姿勢がすばらしいと思うのです。それにアンデルセンはデンマークの誇りであり、国全体がとても大切にしています。私たちも、そうありたいと願って社名にしました。
吉田：アンデルセングループには長文の企業理念があります。そのなかに「同一市場内でのパイの分け合いではなく、従来なかった新しい市場をつくりあげてきて、結果的にそれが業界の共存共栄の精神につながり、真の利益もここから生まれ、企業の永続的発展の基盤になった」という一文があります。昔の日本ではこのような考え方は当り前のようでしたけど、今となってはデンマーク的な理念といえるかもしれません。

八木：ところで、フランスのショコラティエのジャン＝ポール・エヴァンが日本のパートナーとしてアンデルセンを選んだ理由を聞いて納得してしまいました。
彼は店舗や工場見学をすませた後、従業員駐車場の車が整然と並んでいる様を見て決めたそうです。
吉田：それも一つの理由ですが、広島アンデルセンを訪れたときに、この場所に自分の商品が並んでいるイメージが頭にフッと浮かんだのだそうです。
他社では飛行機はファーストクラスだとか、契約条件の話が多くて、彼にとっては一番大切な、自分のチョコレートをいかに日本のお客様に喜んでいただくかの議論がなかったのだとか。
八木：エヴァンさんと「アンデルセン」は現場第一で共通していたのですね。私も「アンデルセン」の徹底した現場主義には驚きました。数年前、伊勢丹新宿店に出店する際に、地下でパンを買ってから、婦人服フロアにもっていっても恥ずかしくない紙袋を‥‥」とデザインを依頼されました。
紙袋はその後一年ほど伊勢丹で実験してから全国の店舗で使われるようになりました。デザインができたからすぐに使うのではなく、それが良いかどうかじっくり検証して採用するという姿勢がすごいなと思いました。
髙木：そうですね。私たちにとっては、スピードや規模拡大がかならずしも良いことではないんです。急ぐあまり、社員一人ひとりがきちんと理解してないことのほうが問題です。言っていることとやっていることが、会社の隅々にまで浸透していることが大切なのだと思います。
八木：店舗の家具なども大切に使い込んでいらっしゃいますね。
髙木：ええ。多少高価なものでも、長く使えれば決して高くはありません。戦後、日本は安いモノを買ってどんどん捨てるという文化になってしまいましたが、昔の日本のようにデンマークではまだ良いモノを大切に使っています。
吉田：広島アンデルセンでは、1978年以来、デンマーク製の椅子を400脚以上、手入れしながら使い続けています。北欧の国々は、寒くて暗い冬が長く家の中の生活を強いられますから、その制約のなかでいかに快適に暮らすかの知恵がすばらしいインテリアや家具を生みだしたのでしょうね。

食は生きることの基本

八木：「アンデルセン芸北100年農場」の構想にも感銘しました。
吉田：広島の県北に「アンデルセン芸北100年農場」があります。広さはざっと東京ドーム40個分ほど。
もともとは、パン職人養成のためのパン学校をつくろうというところからスタートしたのですが、プランを進めるうちに、私たちが育てたいのは、優れた製パン技術をもつ職人もさることながら、パンを大切にする心をもったパン職人であることに気づき、その想いが広がって、土を耕すところからパンを楽しむ食卓づくりまでを学べる農場になりました。
ここでは、毎年若手社員から5名ほど希望者を募って、2年間のプログラムで土地を開墾し、麦を育て、収穫して粉に挽き、パンを焼いて料理をつくって、最後に食卓でプレゼンテーション、

という研修を実施しています。
高木：目先のことだけでなく、長い目で食文化やパンづくりを広めてくれる若者の育成が重要だと思うのです。ここを出た人たちがパン職人としての生き方を次世代に引き継いでくれることを願っています。
八木：食育なども話題になっていますが・・・。
高木：農場では、近くの子どもや大人の方々も遊びに来てくれたり、ご近所の小学校にも給食のパンを提供させていただいています。パン食は一般的ではない地域なのですが、子どもだけでなく地域の人たちがパンを好きになってくれてとてもうれしいです。
朝食をとらない子どもたちも増えていると聞きますので、このような活動を通して、食の大切さや楽しさへの理解が深められればと思います。最近は、当り前のことが当り前でなくなってきていますが、食は生きることの基本ですから、大切にしてほしいですね。
吉田：食育といえば、デンマークが本家本元なのです。現地の幼稚園や保育園に行くと、読み書きの前にまず「自分でよい食べ物を選ぶこと」を教えています。
たとえば、「食べ物のかけっこ」を題材にしたポスターがあって、「元気よく先頭を走っているのはライ麦パンやミルク、後ろのほうで息も絶え絶えになっているのはフライドポテトやケーキ」といったふうに、視覚的にからだに良い食べ物が理解できるようになっています。
また三歳児から「キッズ・イン・ザ・キッチン」というプログラムがあって、自分で野菜を切ってオープンサンドなどをつくって食べたりもします。三歳児ですよ。日本ではナイフを持たせるなんて危ないと、大人が制止してしまうけれど、生きることは食べることですから、こうした取り組みもデンマークの自立教育の一環なのです。
誰もが自分の人生に責任をもつために、男性が料理をするのは当り前、だからこそ女性の社会進出だってスムース。デンマークは「国民幸福度」も世界ナンバーワンですし・・・私たちが学ぶことはたくさんあります。
八木：日本の国民総生産は世界第三位ですが、幸福度は驚くほど低いですから。
高木：自立し、生活を楽しめる。一人ひとりが自分の幸福を探求する自由が認められている。私たちは、デンマークをお手本に、一人でも多くのお客様に喜んでいただくことを通して、社会のお役に立てればと思います。
八木：美味しいパンを食べることで、笑顔の輪が広がるといいですね。

セリフ体で組んだ"ANDERSEN"のそれぞれの文字の間で、バランスのよい所の文字のセリフの部分を取り除き、一つのスタイルのロゴタイプをデザインした。
The Andersen logotype started from a serif logotype. Then I removed specific serifs from each letter, considering the balance between letters to create this new logo for Andersen.

A SHARED SPIRIT IN COMMUNICATION

AKIKO TAKAKI, MASAKO YOSHIDA / Andersen

ヒュッゲ ―
人と人とのふれあいから生まれる、
温かな居心地のよい雰囲気。

HYGGE – HEART WARMING MOMENT

Design as a Communication Tool

TY: My work as a graphic designer often allows me to learn more about design through my clients. I've been very fortunate to have a long relationship with Andersen, a bakery company based in Hiroshima, Japan. We complement each other in many ways, and I particulary enjoy working with Andersen because I like the culinary arts. Today, I'd like to discuss your thoughts on management and design.

MY: As a baking company, we feel it is important to work with a designer who is interested in food culture. Mr. Yagi, you are very passionate about culinary arts, and the amount of knowledge you share with us is always inspiring. After working with you for many years, I realized how important design is as a communication tool. Communicating with customers is the most important aspect of managing the company. Understanding who we are, what we think, and how to deliver our brand to our customers is critical. At the same time, hearing and understanding our customers' suggestions helps the company improve and mature. Design plays a very important role in this dialogue.

TY: What I do for Andersen is categorized as brand design.

AT: Although I don't have a design background, I did have a vision for our business from the start. We have pride in what we make and want to maintain our customers. It's important to perform our service faithfully and diligently every day. There is a famous quote by the confection company Toraya, "tradition is repeated innovation…" I firmly believe in the benefit of putting more effort into the original vision. This relates to design as well. We don't change something unnecessarily, but we drastically address what really needs to be improved. This is an on going process, and you help us rework and refresh our design.

TY: I agree, and appreciate that we work together with the same trust and understanding. Andersen has a history and a loyal customer base, so our challenge is to not take away from this original vision, but to preserve the trend.

MY: Originally, we didn't have a concept for our visual communication, only the general sense of "being a great brand." While working with you, we started to realize the vision of what we really desired. We initially shared our brand's main focus of improving customers' quality of life through verbal messaging, without graphic elements. You demonstrated how visual identity can be represented through graphics, along with store displays, staff uniforms and even the shape of our products. You showed us there are many different elements we can utilize to communicate a graphic image, and advised us to consider the bigger picture. While the logo and paper bag design you created for us is great, the overall inspiration we received from working with you is invaluable.

AT: When we started the company, our logo and stores were created by inexperienced designers. After 40 years, we decided to revisit our brand identity and asked you for a new design. We initially thought that the logo alone would suffice, but we soon began to understand that this element is just the first step in establishing an identity.

TY: Although design is much more recognized and valued today, few companies truly understand its substance. I often receive requests from clients like "try a different color," or "show us 10 designs." These directions are examples of design as a decorative element, or "object." Andersen, on the other hand, has a broader understanding of graphic design's content. Even when we present just one design, Andersen will approach it with an open mind, absorb the concept and give us precise feedback. We understand each other so well, our verbal communication is almost unnecessary.

MY: We have great confidence in you and trust your work. I admire the fact that you sometimes know more about Andersen than we do.

TY: Thank you. I recognize your prompt decision making regarding design matters, and can see how you have a good understanding of what makes a strong brand.

To See Through the Eyes of the Customer

AT: My husband and I are not trained pastry professionals, so we improved the quality of our bread by working with artisan bakers. However, just making good products is not enough. We value the integrity of our brand, and knew that it was important for our potential customers to sense this honesty and belief in their well-being. We had a clear understanding that "without customers that love our bread, there is no business." This is our philosophy, which design helps communicate.

TY: People experience food using all their five senses. No matter how good something tastes, one may not enjoy what they are eating if they are in the wrong environment. The opposite is also true, people often enjoy food that is merely ok if they are with good friends or family. You know that the bread will taste better in the right setting, where the product's quality and the brand's message are consistent.

AT: I see the faces of customers enjoying our products in my mind. We feel it is impossible to make good bread without asking ourselves, "who am I baking for?" Good products cannot be made without a strong desire and passion for them to be enjoyed.

TY: Exactly. Honoring relationships must start with family and friends if you intend to please customers, especially with food. The same can be said for design.

AT: A company is actually a team or family, and we all try to "think as one" by sharing different ideas at work. I may have similar thoughts as some of our staff, while others have opinions of their own. This variety and balance is important.

MY: Bread is a product that's baked fresh daily, and we as a company need to be just as reliable. It is important to be on the same level as our customers so they feel this respect and equality. I tell our employees that although we are selling bread, we are really sharing a lifestyle. We want our customers to envision enjoying breakfast or dinner with their families. This "story" stems from one of your presentations, Mr. Yagi. You not only offer a design, but an inspiring overview.

TY: It's hard to describe, but I have a strong and very personal sense of how I want Andersen to be perceived. I present these internal images through design, such as a brand's character or integrity.

MY: Thank you. We originally requested that our branding and stores look as if they were created long ago. Instead of a "grand opening," we wanted to appear as though we had been here for a long time. We wanted the design to feel familiar, and therefore likeable. We knew the overall design should both make our breads look good and make our customers feel comfortable shopping in our stores. However, our main focus was always the product, rather than flashy surroundings.

TY: Yes, while I appreciate comments like "the bread looks delicious wrapped in your design," I know that the quality of the product inside is the true measure of taste. I also understand that Andersen's customers are their priority. I assume you have different types of customers, especially having so many different stores in various areas?

AT: Most definitely. Some of our customers really understand baking, and the many ways our products can be enjoyed. When I describe "communicating" with our customers, this level of engagement differs from person to person. Repeating the same conversation like a parrot will not make customers happy. The best way to gain knowledge about the company is through the daily practice of open exchange.

TY: Are the customers different from Hiroshima to Tokyo?

MY: There is no significant difference between customers in each city, but more so from store to store. In Tokyo, retail stores and stores inside shopping centers and department stores really differ. For example, the stores in Shinjuku are different from those in Ginza. Therefore, it is more important to give each store unique character while observing Andersen as a whole.

TY: The name Andersen sounds Scandinavian. Do you have a desire to broaden your customers' global awareness and cultural benefit through your brand?

MY: In Denmark, they use the word *HYGGE*, which we relate to at Andersen. This means "a warm, friendly environment that is made through close relationships." It conveys the importance of being yourself to have honest connections and lasting happiness, rather than short term pleasure. It also implies the need to truly know yourself to offer *HYGGE* to others. There is no similar word in other languages. With a small part of Denmark's culture as our guide, we hope customers will continue to enjoy our products and that we will be a positive addition to society.

TY: Thank you so much. Now I'm hungry for one of your freshly baked Danish pastries.

TY: Tamotsu Yagi
AT: Akiko Takaki
MY: Masako Yoshida

ESPRIT, THE EARLY YEARS
BY DELRAE ROTH

In early January 1984 I decided to return home to San Francisco after living in Paris for a year. I had done graphic design for Esprit in the past, enjoyed it, and hoped I might find some freelance work there. A week later I found myself in Doug's office listening to his plans to create an in-house design studio where he could work more directly on the branding of the company. Doug offered me the position of assistant to a new Japanese art director he had hired by the name of Tamotsu Yagi. I was surprised and pleased, but my first concern and initial question, was "Mr. Yagi, he speaks English, right?" Without missing a beat Doug replied, "Of course, perfectly."

A few weeks later Tamotsu arrived at the Esprit offices and as the staff gathered round to meet him, I realized the extent to which Doug's optimism and excitement had exaggerated Tamotsu's English language skills. My heart sank. He obviously spoke no English, except for the phrase "no problem." I remember having dinner with friends that night, fearfully wondering how long Tamotsu and I would survive amidst an incredible workload, high expectations and the mulitude of personalities within the company, not to mention the impending arrival of the Italian photographers, Oliviero Toscani and Roberto Carra. All of this without any English? How would we communicate? Not possible, I was sure. I thought soon Tamotsu would be sitting in coach class on the plane back to Japan, and I would be looking for another job.

How wrong I was. I look back on this time and I do remember the hard work and long hours, of course. And we worked then, in what now seems like an incredibly antiquated way, without the use of computers. But mostly I remember the award winning projects we designed and the genuine fun we all had. For example, unbeknowst to those around us, we gave many of our colleagues nicknames such as, "Pony genius, 7-up, Bell Pepper, Picolo Picolo, Yosemite." We developed our own code to communicate and it often amused me that many people in the company thought I spoke Japanese! But communicate we did. In fact, the studio and Tamotsu's working relationship with everyone thrived, myself included. With incredible focus, humor and a sincere love for design in its many manifestations, we succeeded beyond anyone's expectations. Tamotsu understood and visually translated in quite a masterful way, the energy, humor and vitality that literally made Esprit a household word and a recognized brand around the world. I feel fortunate and privileged to have been a part of it all.

DelRae Roth

DELRAE ROTH began her creative career as a graphic designer working for numerous clients on image design and development. Most notably, DelRae worked for the international clothing company, Esprit during the company's heyday from 1984-1991. In 1991 DelRae opened her design studio Atelier Graphique. By the year 2000, DelRae had focused her many talents and interests in founding Parfums DelRae.

エスプリのはじめの頃

長年住んだパリからサンフランシスコへの引っ越しを決意したのは、1984年の1月のことです。以前、エスプリでグラフィックデザイナーとして働いていた経験もあり、サンフランシスコでフリーランスの仕事でもあればよいなぁ、といった軽い気持ちでの帰国でした。1週間後、久しぶりにエスプリのオーナーであるダグと再会して、彼からエスプリ内にインハウスのデザインオフィスを設立すること、アートディレクターとして日本から八木 保というデザイナーを招聘していること、そしてブランドに対する新たなプランについて聞きました。最後に、エスプリでもう一度働かないか？というオファーを受けました。「もちろん、Mr.八木は英語が話せるのよね？」という私の質問に対して、ダグが「それはもう、完璧だよ。まったく問題ない」と即答したことを覚えています。

何週間か後、八木はスタッフに歓迎されながらエスプリオフィスに現れました。そのときはじめて、私のアートディレクターが「no problem」というフレーズ以外、まったく英語が話せないという事実を知ったのです。正直、心が沈みました。その日の夜、友人との夕食の際に、不安な気持ちを打ち明けたことを覚えています。当時の仕事の量は、今考えても大変なものでした。コミュニケーションのとれない彼と、一体どうやって仕事を進めていけばよいのか？ 悩める私に追い打ちをかけるように、八木に続いて、少ししか英語の話せないイタリア人フォトグラファーのオリビエロ・トスカーニと、ロベルト・カーラもやってきたのです。同じ言語を共有しない4人で仕事をするなんて不可能ではないか？ 八木がこの国での仕事をあきらめて、帰国していく姿が目に見えました。ところが、それは私の勝手な想像であり、間違いでした。今でこそ、その頃を振り返る余裕がありますが、当時は膨大な仕事量をこなすのに必死な毎日。それも現代とは違い、コンピュータなどまったく使わない、すべて手作業でのデザイン工程。にもかかわらず、本当に楽しい時間を共有した私たち。実は皆が日本語を話せるのでは？と疑われたほどでした。私たちは言葉でのコミュニケーションでなく、デザインという言語でわかり合えたのです。八木がスタジオに持ち込んだユーモラスな笑い、物事に真剣に取り組む姿勢、デザインに対する愛が、私たちの間にあった国境という枠を超えさせたのです。私たちの仕事はその後、数々の世界的なデザイン賞を受賞しました。八木は会社や私たちのことを理解し、言葉では到底言い尽くせない、圧倒的なエネルギーをもって私たちを引っ張ったのです。これこそがエスプリを世界中で認められる会社に押し上げた原動力でした。彼と仕事をし、時間を共有できたことは、私にとって本当に幸せなことでした。

デルラエ・ロス

デルラエ・ロス　1984から1991年までエスプリのグラフィックデザイナー兼ディベロプメントマネージャーとして活躍後、自身のデザイン事務所、Atelier Graphiqueを立ち上げる。その後、2000年からは自身の深い興味から香水ブランドParfums DelRaeをスタートさせる。

シンプルなデザインを意識して制作された名刺。表、裏はロゴタイプを使用せず、裏面は肩書きはとり、名前だけがスミー色に印刷された。エスプリのコーポレートデザインマテリアルはできるだけモノクロでデザインされた。

The design of the Esprit business card was intentionally simple. The logotype does not appear on the front or the back. The employee's name appears on the front without title distinction as Esprit does not use titles on their business cards. The back contained the company name and contact information. For most of the corporate stationery, very little color was used to offset the colorful branding design.

タイムリスト

TIMELINE
A timeline of projects from 1984 to 2011

1984

Business Card - Front

Corrugated Plastic Shoebox

In 1984, I decided to accept a position at Esprit and relocate my family to San Francisco. Seven years later, after what was initially a one year trial, I ventured on my own and founded Tamotsu Yagi Design. My time at Esprit helped expand my knowledge of design as a business and subsequently my client base grew quickly. A valuable lesson I learned at Esprit was to define then follow my own "tradition" through distinct design and strict business practices. This approach in essence brought me work from like-minded businesses with similar visions. I am sincerely grateful and proud that for the last 30 years, I was able to harmoniously work with clients I respected and admired.

一九八四年に、東京を離れて、サンフランシスコにあるエスプリで七年。退社後も、日本へは戻らずに、Tamotsu Yagi Designを立ち上げることにしました。人とのつながりから多種多様なプロジェクトに関わることができたのです。とくに、アメリカで仕事をするうえでは、クライアントとプロジェクトの関係がとても大切だと思う。エコロジカルなプロジェクトをやっていると、エコロジカルでないプロジェクトは引き受けることができません。そういう意味でも、三十年近く、バランス良くいろいろな仕事が経験できたことに、感謝しています。

1984年。プラスティック素材でつくられた最初のシリーズのもの。ロサンゼルス店のディスプレイにおいてもっとも効果的に使用されました。

This is one of the first series of shoeboxes we designed using corrugated plastic for the Los Angeles store. We experimented with the use of bright, playful colors to leave a lasting impression for this new location.

Timeline | 202

原寸 | Actual Size

1983年、エスプリ入社前にサンフランシスコ本社からの依頼で、香港店のためにデザインしたキャッシャーレジスターレシートのデザイン。

This is a cash register receipt designed for the Hong Kong store in 1983. Before I officially began working for Esprit, Doug asked me to work on some small projects for the H.K. store which lead to a full time art director position at Esprit

Photo by Kano Tadanori

"Today in consumer product marketing, the role of graphic design is paramount. In fact everywhere we turn we find a graphic message. The streets and roads, the media, architecture, signage, clothing, stereo components, the dashboards of our cars; everything contains formats, colorations, shapes and forms, typography and just about anything imaginable that man puts his hand to. Consequently, the public is receiving a sort of sensory overload of graphically beamed messages from advertising to public service messages. In order to cut through this clutter and to send out a clear and unique communication to our target audience, a strong and evident style must be established. Gratefully we accepted the AIGA (American Institute of Graphic Arts) Leadership award in 1986. Perhaps we did not receive the award because we developed a totally new and progressive graphic design, but because we had and still have a consistency and dedication to keep our message clear and to articulate this to our target audience. Hence, among the competition we established strong style and identity."
Douglas R. Tompkins (1995) *Esprit: The Comprehensive Design Principal*

エスプリ・デザインシステム

現代の消費社会のなかで、デザインの価値とグラフィックデザイナーの必要性が見直されはじめているように感じています。毎日通るあのドアからの情報、建築、看板、衣服、家電から車のダッシュボードに至るまで、普段当たり前のように接するすべてのオブジェはすべてデザイナーによってデザインされたものであり、使われているタイポグラフィや配色に至るまでデザインが人間によって生み出された作品なのです。人口の増加とともにデザインが増えることも当然であり、その結果、良いものも悪いものも含めてデザインは増えたのです。必要以上にものが増えたために、デザインの良し悪しの判別がつきにくくなっているのも事実です。デザインが溢れた社会で、良いデザインを際立たせるためには、ブランドを確立してリーダーシップアワードをウエストコーストではじめて、しかもファッションの企業にお初受賞をはたしました。これは時代性に流されることなくブランド固有の世界観をアピールすることが必要です。幸運にも私たちは、1986年 AIGA いて初受賞をはたしました。これは時代性に流されることなくブランドの世界観に対してぶれのないデザインシステムを生み出した結果として与えられたものだったのです。

Corrugated Plastic Kid's Shoebox

Corrugated Plastic Kid's Shoebox - Flat

キッズシューズのパッケージは、4つのパーツにはめ込み式にすることによって組み立て遊びを楽しめ、ひもを付けることでバッグとしても使用できるパッケージとなった。

The kid's shoeboxes were designed like a puzzle for fun and made from four separate parts so that they could be disassembled and put back together. We added straps so it can be reused as a bag.

Eyewear Packaging

リサイクル可能なパッケージを、1984年、すでにリサイクルできるように新しいマテリアルを使ってパッケージのデザインを行った。サングラスケースのパッケージは、小物入れとしても人気があった。とくにプラスチック素材でつくられたシリーズパッケージの評判はよく、シリーズ化されてプラスチックを紙の組み合わせなどもつくられた。

Esprit began sourcing recycled materials in the mid 80s and we found ways to integrate it into the package designs. We also considered lasting qualities and functionalities into designs to encourage reuse.

Designed for Reuse

AIGA CORPORATE LEADERSHIP AWARD "The AIGA Corporate Leadership Award was established in the 80s to recognize forward-thinking organizations that have been instrumental in the advancement of design by applying the highest standards, as a matter of policy.

The recipients of this award demonstrate respect for the millions whose lives they touch, a rare commitment to consistency and quality, and a model for the successful interaction between aesthetics and pragmatics." – AIGA (American Institute of Graphic Arts)

AIGA LEADERSHIP AWARD: ESPRIT 1986 Esprit was the first west coast-based recipient of this award. In 1986, we were very excited to receive this award, as it also recognized the west coast as an emerging design center.

1989 Adobe Systems
1989 Apple
1988 The New York Times
1987 Walker Arts Center
1986 Esprit
1985 WGBH Educational Foundation Inc.
1984 Herman Miller, Inc.
1983 Cummins Engine Company, Inc.
1982 Container Corporation of America
1981 Massachusetts Institute of Technology
1980 IBM Corporation

The proprietary hang tag system was developed for the ease of recognition. The triangle represented size, the circle represented color and the square represented the type of product.

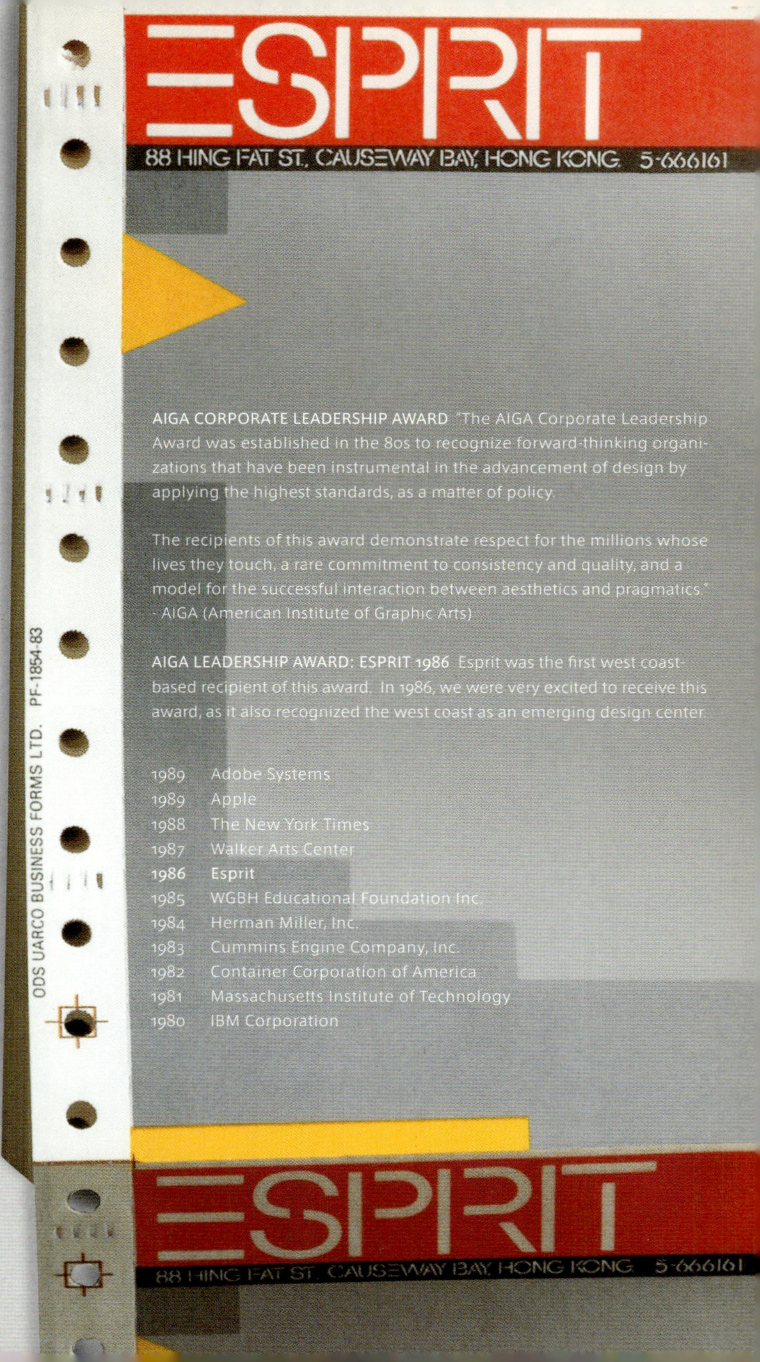

原寸 | Actual Size

Eye-Catching Design

Hang Tags

Cash Register Receipts

Cash register receipts were printed with the same four color process as the shopping bags and designed to leave a lasting impression even after the shopping experience. The graphics were designed to match the different store interiors.

Hang Tags for Esprit Sports

AIGA Leadership Award

Shopping Bags

The Esprit shopping totes were designed in multiple colors for excitement and to match the existing color scheme used in the packaging system. These durable bags were printed in Japan to maintain quality

Timeline | 204

19 8/4

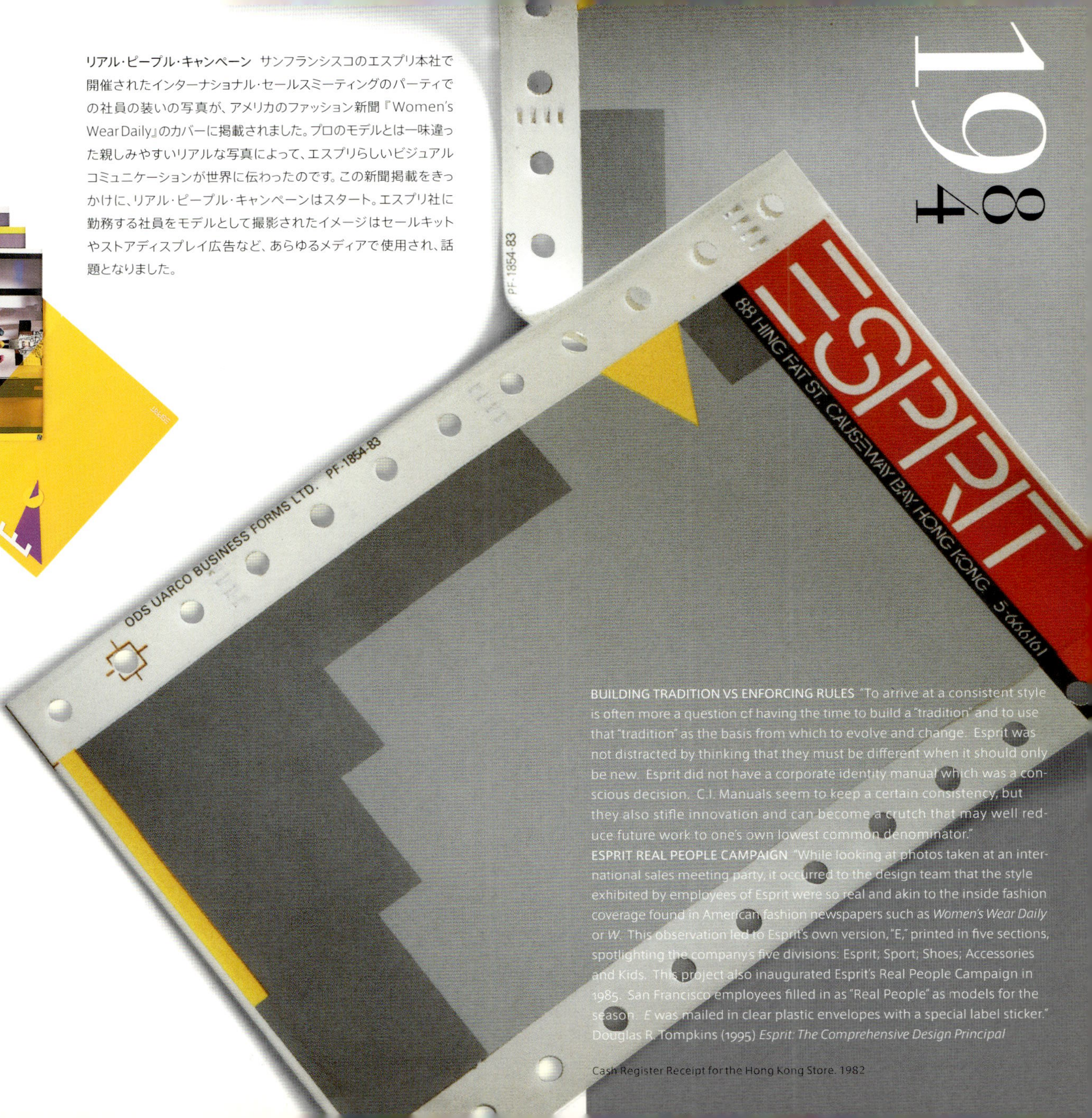

BUILDING TRADITION VS ENFORCING RULES "To arrive at a consistent style is often more a question of having the time to build a 'tradition' and to use that 'tradition' as the basis from which to evolve and change. Esprit was not distracted by thinking that they must be different when it should only be new. Esprit did not have a corporate identity manual, which was a conscious decision. C.I. Manuals seem to keep a certain consistency, but they also stifle innovation and can become a truth that may well reduce future work to one's own lowest common denominator."

ESPRIT REAL PEOPLE CAMPAIGN "While looking at photos taken at an international sales meeting party, it occurred to the design team that the style exhibited by employees of Esprit were so real and akin to the inside fashion coverage found in American fashion newspapers such as *Women's Wear Daily* or *W*. This observation led to Esprit's own version, 'E,' printed in five sections, spotlighting the company's five divisions: Esprit; Sport; Shoes; Accessories and Kids. The project also inaugurated Esprit's Real People Campaign in 1985, San Francisco employees filled in as 'Real People' as models for the season. *E* was mailed in clear plastic envelopes with a special label sticker."

Douglas R. Tompkins (1995) *Esprit: The Comprehensive Design Principal*

Cash Register Receipt for the Hong Kong Store. 1982

Real People Campaign
Wholesale Promotion Catalog

Wholesale Promotion Catalog

リアル・ピープル・キャンペーン　サンフランシスコのエスプリ本社で開催されたインターナショナル・セールスミーティングのパーティでの社員の装いの写真が、アメリカのファッション新聞『Women's Wear Daily』のカバーに掲載されました。プロのモデルとは一味違った親しみやすいリアルな写真によって、エスプリらしいビジュアルコミュニケーションが世界に伝わったのです。リアル・ピープル・キャンペーンはスタートしました。エスプリ社に勤務する社員をモデルとして撮影されたイメージはセールスやストアディスプレイ広告など、あらゆるメディアで使用され、話題となりました。

全長2メートル以上にもなるカタログは、世界各国のエスプリ社員がモデルとして起用されていて、リアル・ピープル・キャンペーン期間中には筒状のパッケージに入れて配布された。

This ten foot long catalog was designed during the *Real People Campaign*, which involved worldwide Esprit employees as models. The catalog was rolled and sent out in tubular packaging. The Esprit collection was on one side and the sports collecion on the flip side

CAFFE ESPRIT

CAFFE ESPRIT "As a service to the San Francisco outlet store customers, a comfortable, indoor/outdoor cafe was designed. It was to provide gourmet pizzas, ice cream and salads. Designer Bruce Slesinger, working with Kalle Tavela, technical architect, installed roll-up glass and firehouse doors to enliven the interior, which consisted of a terrazzo floor, sectioned off by an aluminum grid. An open steel, curved stairway connected the main dining floor with a newly added mezzanine overlooking the bay. An aluminum-clad curvilinear bar, snaking out from under the mezzanine, separates the kitchen prep area from the dining room."

Douglas R. Tompkins (1995) *Esprit: The Comprehensive Design Principal*

Photo by Sharon Risedorph

Caffe Esprit Interior

カフェ・エスプリ サンフランシスコのアウトレットストアの元ガレージを改装し、カフェとしてオープン。「ファッションは健康な体から」と、サンフランシスコの近郊で採れた食材でつくられたピザ、サラダ、アイスクリームなど、カリフォルニア料理を基本としたメニューが、海を一望できるカフェで提供されました。インテリアデザインはブルース・スレシンジャーが担当。テラゾーを使用したフロアやアルミグリッドで仕切られた空間では、カプチーノを飲んだりティラミスを味わったり、オールドファションなブラウン・カウをちびちび飲んだり……、陽気な日差しのトテラスでは自分に合ったスタイルで個々がそれぞれの楽しみを発見できる快適なスペースでした。

Caffe Esprit Design Elements

ESPRIT Graphic Work 1984-1986

Photo by Shuji Yoshida

この2冊を見ればエスプリの世界観がよくわかる。
上が1984年〜1986年にかけて手がけたグラフィックデザインをまとめたもの。プロモーションとして使用された。左/1989年、日本で出版されたエスプリブック。当時15,000円という価格で販売された。

The ESPRIT Graphic Work 1984-1986 and ESPRIT: The Comprehensive Design Principle (sold in Japan for ¥15,000) were initially created as promotional material.

Caffe Napkin Ties

原寸 | Actual Size

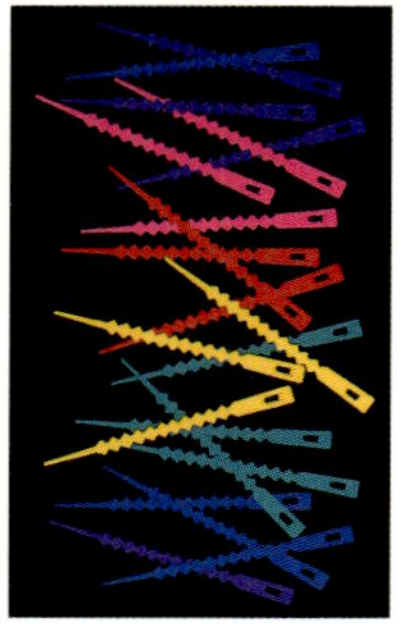

カフェ・エスプリのすべてのパッケージやデザインは、鮮やかな色を基調に統一された。カフェで使用された色鮮やかなナプキンタイは、ゴミ袋を閉じると小さな具をヒントにオリジナルのマテリアルでデザインされた。このようになじみなエレメントに至るまでエスプリの世界観が表現された。

Standard clear plastic cups for take-out were paired with custom made snap-on lids in six vibrant colors. Color was used as an accent to the architecture and the food preparations. The custom colored napkin ties became very popular.

Caffe Napkin Ties

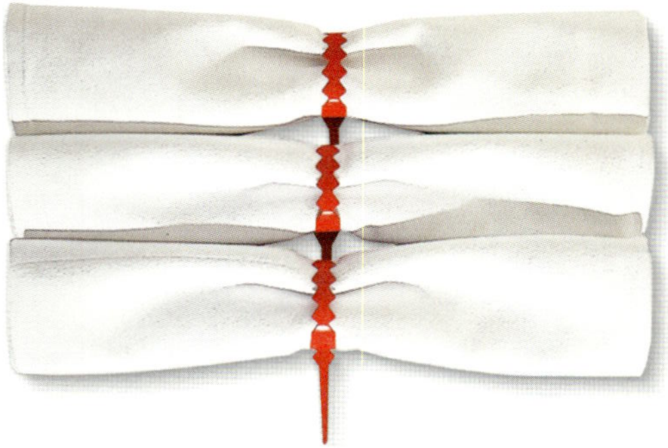

カフェ・エスプリでは、カフェ内で使用されるパッケージなどのグラフィックも人気のーつだった。鮮やかな6色をカフェのアイテムに合わせて使い分け、持ち帰り用のカップやふたなどにも、すべてオリジナルでデザインされた。

Standard clear plastic cups for take-out were paired with custom made snap-on lids in six vibrant colors. Color was used as an accent to the architecture and the food preparations. The custom colored napkin ties proved to be very popular.

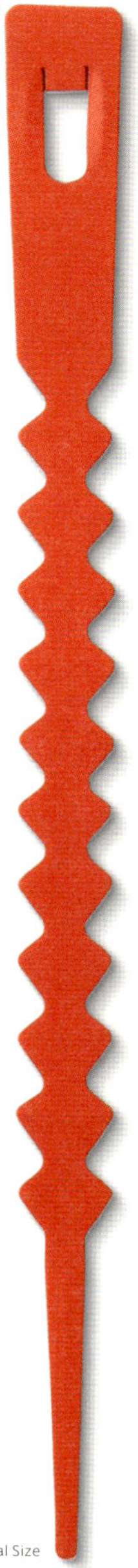

Caffe Cup and Lids

Esprit Eyewear and Jeans

Eyewear Designed by Ettore Sottsass and Associates

ESPRIT EYEWEAR "In 1985 the Austrian-German firm Optyl was licensed to manufacture and distribute eyewear under the Esprit trademark. Sottsass Associates adds a Memphis flare to the design of the products, display elements, catalogs and packaging. The second year, Martine Bedin and Emelot Brakema took over the art direction and design. The eyewear line was a part of Esprit's "total shop concept" allowing customers to choose outfits and style them as well."
Douglas R. Tompkins (1995) *Esprit: The Comprehensive Design Principal*

ESPRIT JEANS "The Jeans clothing concept stressed the industrial nature of the clothing. This industrial concept was repeated in the labelling for the clothing. Garment labels were printed in a neutral color range to correspond to the clothes and pre-washed to a desired finished. Metal buttons were simple and industrial in character. Industrial cement bags inspired the shopping bags using similar paper and construction."
Douglas R. Tompkins (1995) *Esprit: The Comprehensive Design Principal*

エスプリ・アイウェア ドイツで開発がはじまったアイウェア。エットレ・ソットサス率いるデザインチームと共同開発。パッケージ・ディスプレイ・カタログなど、ガラフルな素材によるそれまでにはなかった新感覚のアイウェアラインとなりました。何よりもソットサスならではのカラフルな色の組み合わせがポイント。ソットサスのシリーズ後、マーティン・ベディンとエモレット・ブレークマによってデザインは引き継がれたのです。

エスプリ・ジーンズ 多くの製品のなかでも、エスプリがとくに力を入れたのがジーンズの開発。ジーンズ製造に必要なパーツをすべて別注でオーダーデザインしました。もともと労働用の衣服としてデザインされていたジーンズはルーツであるラフ感を意識しつつ、エスプリがもっと繊細さを意識していねいに製造されました。同時に、工業用セメントバッグを意識したショッピングバッグもつくられ、一貫したイメージのもとでエスプリジーンズは製作されたのです。

オリビエロ・トスカーニのインパクトのあるジーンズのクローズアップ写真が印象的なエスプリジーンズの広告シリーズの1点。
An advertisement from Esprit Jeans photographed by Oliviero Toscani, highlights his distinctive style. He is a master of capturing the active and playful visual image associated with the California lifestyle.

Photo by Oliviero Toscani

ESPRIT EYEWEAR
ESPRIT JEANS
Esprit Jeans Advertisement

Jeans Rivet
原寸 / Actual Size

Eye Exam Chart Poster

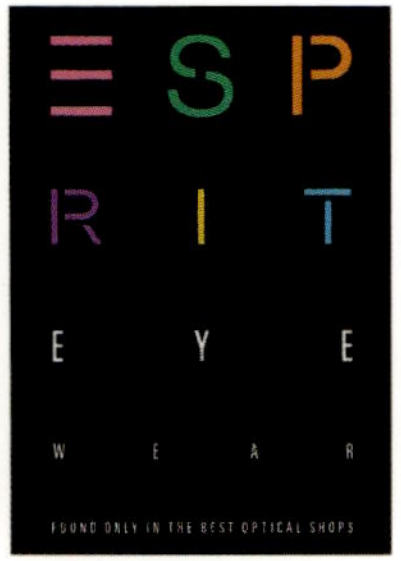

だれもが一度は知っている「視力検査表」をモチーフにしたユーモラスな表現で、ポスター、POP、Tシャツなどに展開した。
This is a poster for the Esprit Eyewear line, designed as a playful spin on an eye exam chart. This popular graphic was re-created into T-shirts and other promotional items.

Ecological Corporate Designs

Catalog Made of Recycled Paper

Photo by Shuji Yoshida

1989年からすべての商品カタログはリサイクルペーパーと植物性インクで印刷され、製版はすべて日本で、印刷はアメリカ国内で行われた。

In 1989, Esprit became the first major fashion company to publish catalogs on recycled paper with soy-based inks. The color separation was created in Japan and catalogs were printed in the U.S.

NEW CORPORATE IDENTITY "As a result of Esprit's evolving values and commitment to corporate responsibility, we began to incorporate ecological and humanitarian concerns into business decisions and everyday operations. We switched to environmentally friendly applications in design and by 1990, almost every product made of paper including Esprit's stationery was made of recycled paper and printed with soy based ink. Using elements from the interior of the flagship store in Paris, we redesigned the corporate stationery." - Douglas R. Tompkins

Recycled Paper Stationery System

リサイクルグラフィック 1990年には、ほぼすべてのエスプリのステーショナリーがリサイクルペーパーと植物性インクで印刷されるようになり、環境問題に対するブランドの姿勢を提示しました。ヨーロッパにおいても同様で、パリの1号店でも「エスプリらしさ」を踏襲。世界に向けて、一貫したブランドアイデンティティを感じてもらえるよう、デザインだけでなく素材にもフォーカスをあてました。基本的にはグリーンを基調色に、さまざまなリサイクルペーパーに印刷をしました。

Gift Boxes Made of Recycled Paper

Shopping Bag Made of Recycled Paper

鮮やかな色を基調としていたエスプリのブランドカラーをむずかしいアーシーな新しいグリーンシステムに沿ってデザインすることはグリーンシステムに沿ってデザインを制作することによって、一つの世界観の作り上げれ、新たなエスプリらしさを確立させることができた。

The Esprit package was completely redesigned and took on earthly green tones. Regardless of this color change from the previous bright and bold use of colors, the Esprit identity was still strong and apparent. To achieve uniform colors on recycled paper was a challenge in the 80s. Rather than enforcing consistency of printed colors on this rather new material, we experimented variances of tones into the design.

Timeline | 208

1990

Contributing to Non-Profit Organizations Through Design

THE ELMWOOD INSTITUTE

IRA-HITI san francisco, california
Graphic identity design

THE ELMWOOD INSTITUTE berkeley, california
Identity and graphic design

イラヤーヒティ

IRA-HITI is a conservation organization founded by Douglas R. Tompkins with offices in South America and in San Francisco. Ira-Hiti is a Native American (Karuk tribe) word for "making the world over." The content for *Clearcut*, a book on industrial deforestation, was organized by Ira-Hiti. After leaving Esprit, I continued to contribute to this organization.

THE ELMWOOD INSTITUTE was founded in Berkeley, California in 1984 by Fritjof Capra, an Austrian born physicist and best selling author of *Tao of Physics*. The Institute functions primarily as an ecological think tank, applying systems thinking to the understanding and solution of current social, economic, and environmental problems. From the introduction of Doug Tompkins, we developed the graphic identity for The Elmwood Institute with the inspiration from an Elmwood tree that grew in front of the center.

The Ira-Hiti logo was created from an original typeface I designed for Ira-Hiti. The body of this typeface was inspired from branches, leaves and pods.

The stationery for The Elmwood Institute was designed with simple elements. Color was used only on the logomark allowing for two color printing, on recycled paper using soy bean based ink.

「イラヒティ」のロゴは、自然あふれる木の実と、異なるからインスピレーションを得てデザインされたアルファベットから制作された。

ザ・エルムウッド・インスティテュート 1984年にブリチョフ・カプラが米国カリフォルニア州バークレーに設立。カプラは、オーストリア出身の物理学者。現代物理学と東洋思想におけるベストセラーとなり、広く知られる著書「タオ」の紹介で彼の研究所のグラフィックアイデンティティを手がけることになり、ボランティアで彼の研究所の前に植えられていたエルムウッドの葉をビジュアル化しました。

イラヒティ ダグラス・トンプキンスが主宰する南米のチリとサンフランシスコにオフィスがある自然保護団体。「イラヒティ」とは、ネイティブアメリカンのカルク族の言葉で「元に戻す(再生)」という意味。世界的な森林伐採の実態を記録した本『CLEARCUT』は、この団体が企画出版したもの。私はエスプリを離れた後も、引き続きこのプロジェクトにボランティアで参加しました。

エルムウッド・インスティテュートの印刷物はシンプルなコレクションと色とデザインで、すべてがリサイクルペーパーと植物性インクで印刷された。

Photo by Shuji Yoshida

原寸 | Actual Size

The Elmwood Institute Letterhead

90

AMISH - THE ART OF THE QUILT In March of 1990, I began to design an exhibition of Esprit owned quilts to be held at the De Young Museum in Golden Gate Park. Doug Tompkins began his quilt collection in the early 1970s. The collection is regarded as one of the premier quilt collections in the world. After much deliberation, 60 quilts, all Amish from Lancaster County, Pennsylvania were selected for the exhibition. These quilts were Doug's favorites and are stunning in color and design. To further emphasize these unique works of art we decided to paint the walls dark grey with dramatic spot lighting. Adjacent rooms were given to display the austere but beautiful Amish clothing and artifacts, along with large black and white photographs of the people and the county. This somewhat monochromatic handling of the entry and spaces were very effective in emphasizing the quilters' sensitivity to color and design. The total exhibition space covered 10,000 square feet. Quilts were hung along the peripheral walls and on four-sided and three-sided freestanding fixtures. The quilts were not covered to show the intricate workmanship and textures of the quilts.

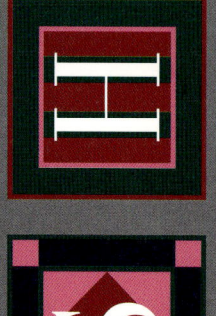

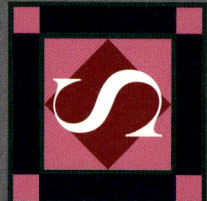

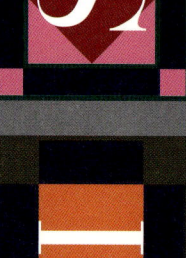

Photo by Sharon Risedorph

AMISH-The Art of the Quilt Exhibition

AMISH - THE ART OF THE QUILT san francisco, california
Graphic identity design | Exhibition design | Book design
Curator: Julie Silber June - September, 1990

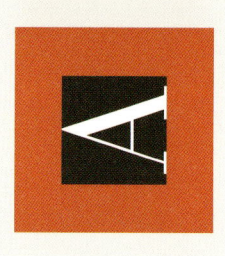

「アーミッシュ・キルト展」デ・ヤング美術館で開催されたエスプリ所蔵のキルトのコレクション展。1970年以降のコレクションのなかから、厳選された60点のみを展示。それらのキルトはすべてペンシルバニア州のランカスター郡に住むアーミッシュの人々が作成したもの。

AGI Letterhead

Alliance Graphique Internationale
International President James Cross
3465 West Si[...]
Los Angeles
California 90020
Tel: 213 389 1010
Tel: 213 389 9002
Fax: 213 389 0064

4 October 1990

Mr. Tamotsu Yagi
Esprit de Corp
900 Minnesota Street
San Francisco, CA 94107

Dear Tamotsu,

I am delighted to inform you that you have been selected by the International Executive Committee for membership in Alliance Graphique Internationale. At the next Congress your slides will be presented to the General Assembly, after which your membership will be official.

Best personal regards,

James A. Cross
James A. Cross
President

cc: Tomoko Miho

AGI

ジェームス・クロス氏から受け取った一通の手紙。1990年、日本人のグラフィックデザイナーとしては、初のAGIメンバーになった。

This is a letter I received in 1990 from James A. Cross, president of Alliance Graphique Internationale, informing me of my induction as an official AGI member.

Nara Sports Growhill Kids Design

Nara Sports Headquarter Model. Architecture by Shiro Kuramata

NARA SPORTS manufactures skis, boots, poles and gloves. I worked directly with Nara Sports to implement a graphic system for these products. Like fashion, the product image was changed seasonally along with yearly implementation of technical advancements to improve the performance of their products. In the 1990s, the Japanese consumers' sensitivity to ski design was becoming more sophisticated. Design, as a determining factor influencing the consumer's choice of a sporting product was apparent.
(continued on the next page)

Nara Sports: Shiro Kuramata × TYD

NARA SPORTS nara, japan
Graphic identity design | Graphic design: skis, boots, poles, gloves

奈良スポーツ株式会社 スキーブーツをメインとするスキーグッズのリーディングメーカー。同社から直接依頼を受け、製品のためのグラフィックデザインをはじまりました。製品と市場状況に関するオリエンテーションが行われ、スキーブーツやグッズもファッションと同じように品質向上はもちろん、シーズンごとにイメージを一新する必要があることを知りました。それは各シーズンに新たなグラフィックデザインを開発し、競合他社との差別化を図っていかなければならない、ということです。私たちは、基本カラーとシーズンカラーを組み合わせていくという大胆な提案を行ないました。このカラーリングシステムは奈良スポーツ製品の特徴として受け入れられました。私は、4ブランドのアイデンティティを倉俣史朗両氏のディスプレイ、フォトグラファーにロベルト・カーラ、インテリアデザイナーに倉俣史朗氏のディスプレイのプロジェクトに迎え、店舗内のスキーボードとスキーブーツのディスプレイのための什器を制作しました。洗練されたアイデンティティによって、知名度はさらに高まりました。

Display System by Shiro Kuramata

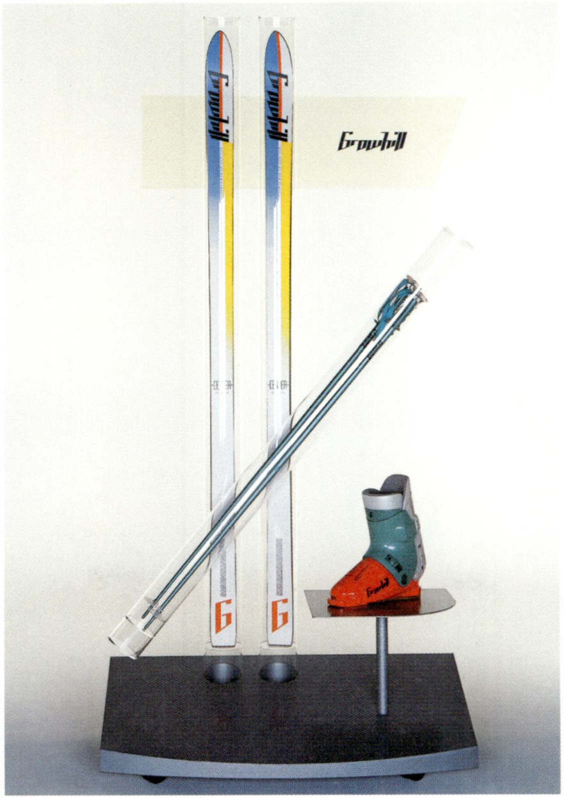

サンフランシスコ近代美術館(SF MoMA)の展覧会では、クリアなアクリルのチューブにスキーボートを入れてディスプレイするという倉俣史朗氏のアイデアをデザインして展示した。

A ski boot display designed by Shiro Kuramata for the Nara Sports exhibition. The silicone captures the ski boot as if transfixed in mid air.

Catalog Tray Design by Shiro Kuramata

Exhibition Display Design by Shiro Kuramata

Photo by Shuji Yoshida

90

(continued from page 211) Understanding this growing expectation, Nara Sports aimed for excellence through the theme "New Art and Design," which aimed for exemplary quality in design as their new company goal. In order to establish a fresh image for each of their brands, new logotypes were created from original typefaces designed, which were also applied to various graphic applications creating an iconic branding. The use of bold colors and its large selection became the Nara Sports' signature. Nara Sports' products came under four different categories specific to the skiers' level, age and sex. These were Gen, Navi, Growhill and Growhill Junior. Gen was designed for the advanced to semi-professional skier and the products were designed to appeal to these customers.

SF MoMA TAMOTSU YAGI EXHIBITION: Nara Sports

Photo by Ben Blackwell

Photo by Roberto Carra

Nara Sports In Store Bench Design by Shiro Kuramata

スキーブーツを履くためのベンチは、展覧会後、各店舗で使用された。
A bench designed for the Nara Sports store for customers to sit on during a ski boot fitting.

『パッセージ』アーヴィング・ペン氏は世界的なスティルライフフォトグラファー。本書は3カ国国語(英、仏、日本語)で発売されるにあたり、アーヴィング・ペン氏が1カ国につき1人のアートディレクターを指名。日本語版は私が担当した。Irving Penn's *Passage* was published in three different languages, French, English and Japanese and all were printed in the U.S. to maintain consistency. I was selected as the art director for the Japanese edition.

Book Design

NEON CLOCK
Book design | Publisher: Hollywood Ranch Market

ハリウッドランチマーケットのオーナー、ゲン垂水さんのネオンクロックのコレクション約250点を1冊の本にまとめた。撮影はロベルトカーラ。本の収益は難病対策研究に寄付された。
Neon Clock: A collection of neon clocks by Gen Tarumi, owner of Hollywood Ranch Market. Photographs by Roberto Carra.

Photo by Shuji Yoshida

PASSAGE - Irving Penn
Book design: Japanese edition
Publisher: Libro Port

Photo by Shuji Yoshida

1991

In early 2000, Tamotsu Yagi Design established its studio on Bryant St. in San Francisco's SoMa district. The two-level industrial loft housed a garage and a meeting room on the first floor. The second floor consisted of the main design area, kitchen and the library. Around this time, we were slowly beginning to integrate design methods using Apple computers, marking a time of adaptation and shift in the design process. This new tool allowed for different design expressions as well as reorganization of the design area at TYD.

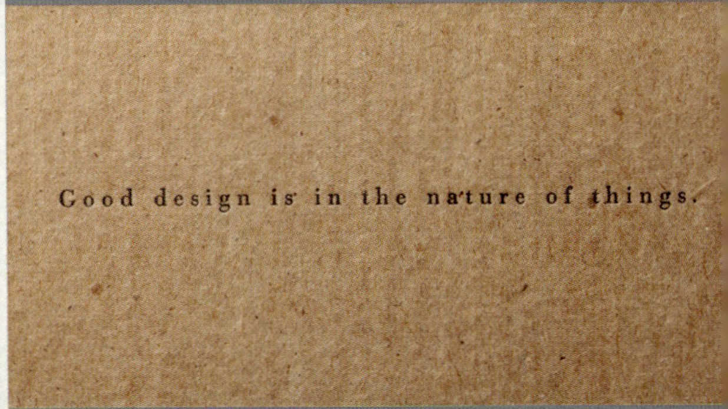

Tamotsu Yagi Design Business Card - Back

Tamotsu Yagi Design Bryant Street Studio

TYD 917 Bryant Street Studio Opens

タモツ・ヤギ・デザイン(TYD) 2000年、スタジオをサンフランシスコのブライアント・ストリートにオープンしました。2階建てのロフトは、1階をパーキングとミーティングルーム、2階をデザインスタジオとライブラリーとして使用。この頃は、コンピュータのあるデザインオフィスははずらしかったが、アップルの仕事をしていたので数台のマッキントッシュを使っていました。すでにジャンブルーヴのコレクションをはじめており、代表作をコレクトしてオフィスで使用していました。

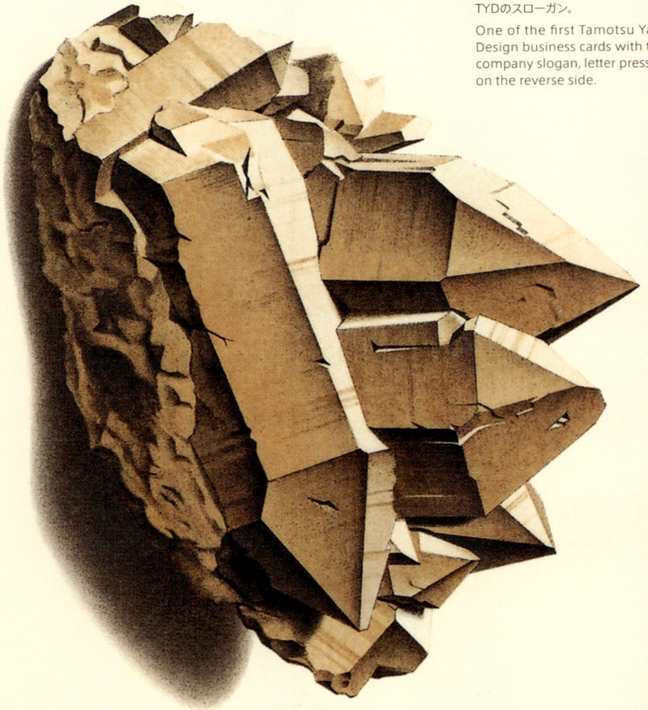

スタジオをスタートしたときに、名刺の裏面にレタープレスでプリントしたTYDのスローガン。
One of the first Tamotsu Yagi Design business cards with the company slogan, letter pressed on the reverse side.

原寸 | Actual Size

Good design is in the nature of things.

Tamotsu Yagi Design Letterhead

Photo by Yoshiaki Nishimura

Tamotsu Yagi Design Bryant Street Studio

Graphic Explorations

LECIEN kyoto, japan
Corporate identity design

AKEBONO tokyo, japan
Corporate identity design | Brand identity design
Package design

LECIEN The new logomark was designed to unify this Japanese fashion company that consisted of many departments. We decided to use Rotis, a fairly unused typeface at the time, created in 1988, for its fashionable and fresh look. The logo was made from a combination of regular and italic letters.

Photo by Sharon Risedorph

AKEBONO The corporate identity design for Akebono, a popular Japanese rice cracker and sweets manufacturer, began in early 1990. To involve the key members of this company, Akebono's president, Mr. Mikio Uekusa hand wrote the Japanese *kanji* character, which was later refined and used as the company logo. The *hiragana*, (the Japanese phonetic alphabet of 50 characters) was written by his daughter, Tomoko, who was born with Down's syndrome. From the several hundred sheets of *hiragana* she hand-wrote, four to five different styles emerged. Within each style, individual characters were selected to complete a full set of the alphabet. Appropriate styles from Tomoko's "typeface" were chosen to create logos for various products like *arare*, rice crackers and *yokan*, a sweet bean dessert. Tomoko's expressive characters translated the warmth of handmade products and of "love" as a source and inspiration to create things with care and to also share it with others. Mr. Uekusa has long been engaged in charitable giving and he continues his philanthropy by donating a portion of his company's profit to the Hunger Project of Japan.

Corporate Identity Design

株式会社ルシアン 新しいロゴマークは、ルシアンの企業グループとしてのアイデンティティを明瞭に発信するコミュニケーションツールであり、異質で多様な事業分野からなるユニークな企業グループの個性を表現するビジュアルメッセージでもあります。ロゴタイプは、1988年に制作されたロティスという新しく洗練された書体をベースに、正体と斜体を交互に組み合わせてデザインしました。

株式会社あけぼの 「あけぼの」のロゴタイプの文字は、社長である植草三喜男氏の娘さんによるもの。半紙数百枚分のひらがなのなかから、4、5種のキャラクターに絞って「あけぼの」から「ん」までのひらがな文字を書いてもらい、縦組と横組のロゴタイプを商品ごとに個性に合った文字組を選んで文字組をし、「あられ」ようかんなど、商品ごとに書道家の文字よりも自然な印象で、個性のある生きさとしてロゴができあがりました。文字を文字としてとらえるのでなく、一つの形として組み合わせる事で、読ませるのでなく、見せるロゴタイプとしての意味を持たせる事ができました。障害者である娘さんをもつ植草社長は熱心なボランティア活動家でもあり、2000年以降、世界の飢えに苦しむ子どもたちを救うハンガープロジェクトのリーダーの一人として、商品の売上の一部を運動のために寄付し続けています。

1992年、あけぼのの工場に集まった子どもたちが、あかい、あおい、それぞれやお菓子などで「おいしい顔」を表現、それを写真家のルトー・カーラが撮影し、1年分のカレンダーとしてデザインしました。

In 1992, we were asked to design a calendar titled *Yummy Faces* for Akebono. We invited kids to the factory to make 12 different faces out of rice crackers and candies. Roberto Carra photographed the finished artwork.

AKEBONO Original Typeface

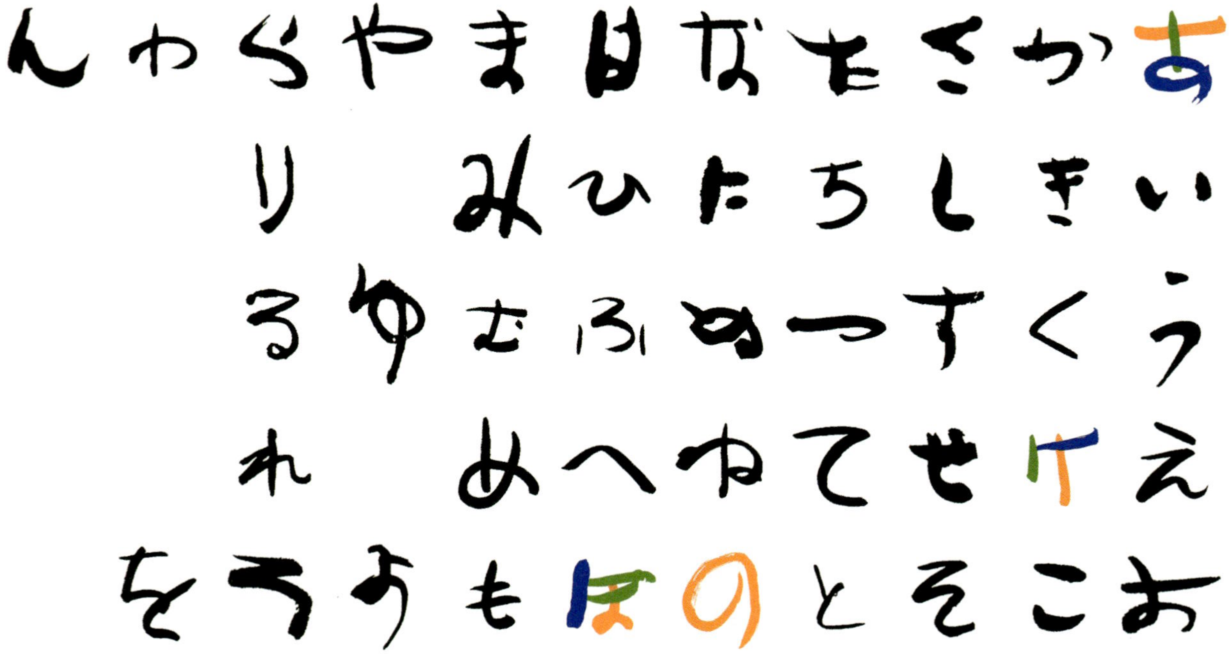

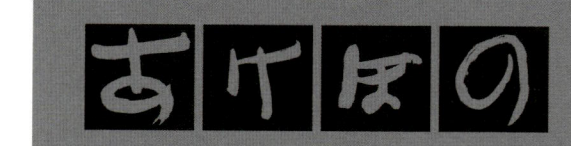

Graphic Shapes and Forms

DANSKIN This package design system was developed for the grand reopening of the remodeled New York Danskin store. We used recycled plastic, a translucent material to reveal a faint silhouette of the product. White graphics were chosen in order to subtly integrate with the color of the material without obstructing the view of the product inside.

Danskin Package Design

Photo by Sharon Risedorph

HAMANO INSTITUTE I was 20 years old when I took my first design position at the Hamano Institute, a multi-disciplinary design studio in Tokyo, Japan. 20 years later, my former boss, Mr. Yasuhiro Hamano, asked me to design the logomarks for four of his new companies. From a single piece of round plastic tubing cut into the letter H, I was able to create a three dimensional monogram. Depending on which way the monogram was positioned and viewed, I was able to create four different logomarks from the letter H representing these new companies.

Team Hamano
Pacific Art & Design Consultant Inc.
Hamano Concept Inc.
Hamano Institute Inc.

ボディウェアメーカー・ダンスキンの新し いショップのためのパッケージデザイン。 半透明のリサイクルプラスチックを使用 し、パッケージの上下の部分を外して折り畳める構造になっている。ニューヨーク店のためにつくられたワイヤーマネキンは伸縮ワイヤー型で、ウェアの素材に直接触れることができる。

We created mannequins for Danskin's bodywear line by free-forming wire into human forms.

私が20代にはじめて勤めたデザインオフィスの恩師、浜野安弘さんの関連会社のロゴマーク。1本のパイプをHの形にカットしてマークにした。TPCHのイニシャルにして見えるように、異なる角度から撮影した。

Photo by Sharon Risedorph

DANSKIN new york, new york
Product design: mannequin design
Package design

101 VEGETABLE FACES
Book design | Publisher: Robundo

写真集『101の野菜の顔』は、写真家のルドー・カーラの娘アナと私の娘、理都子が、野菜を組み合わせて顔に見立てて遊び出したのがきっかけとなった。本の装丁は、ケールの緑、トマトの赤、そしてピーマンの黄色をイメージしてデザインした。

My daughter Ritz and my friend Roberto's daughter, Anna, created faces that looked like their friends and family from vegetables that grew in Roberto's backyard. This book was published from the spontaneous and fun character of the two girls. The colors used in the book was inspired by the colors of kale, tomato and yellow pepper.

HAMANO INSTITUTE tokyo, japan
Logo design

3-D Design

92

NARA SPORTS The theme for Nara Sports in 1991 was 'Ecology and Ergonomics." In "Ecology," the harmony between the designing of ski equipment and the environment was sought through colorations. Taking skiers as part of the natural elements of a snow scene, playful colors were used in contrast for their equipment. Ergonomic considerations such as the interior and the exterior form of the boots; the curve of the levers, all were engineered to fit and work with the human form. The result of this harmony was visually refined yet superbly functional creations. Nara Sports' advertising and sales promotion was developed along the product design theme. Centering around the ecology theme, natural materials like rocks, leaves, and drift woods became the backdrop motifs for the advertising. A dependence and respect for the natural environment was the main theme.

Photo by Sharon Risedorph

NARA SPORTS A prototype of a Nara Sports ski boot. The concept was to use transparent materials to show the inside lining. A clear epoxy was then injected between the shell and lining to form a mold of the user's foot to ensure a perfect fit. Bold colors were used as accents.

TRIBU Perfume Bottle

透明な特殊素材でつくったスキーブーツのプロトタイプ。二つのパイプから液体要素を注入すると、インナーが目分の足型に形成されます。液体は着色されていて、液体が透けて見えます。このブーツはSF MOMAのパーマネントコレクションに選ばれました。

BENETTON Tribù Cosmetic Line

BENETTON TRIBÙ Italian for tribe, Tribù is a line of cosmetics created by the United Colors of Benetton, formulated from natural essences from around the world to create a scent that celebrates the diversity of all cultures. It is a natural formulation free of synthetic ingredients, chemicals and animal by-products. I was assigned to create a trademark bottle design and innovative packaging as distinct as the fragrance. Drawing inspiration from diverse sources, I combined the natural shape of an egg with that of a test tube to create the Tribù bottle.

TRIBÙ

Photo by Stephen Rahn

BENETTON PETA Logomark for the Tribù Cosmetic Line

...ON DE MAIS, FARINE D'AVOINE, PARFUM, POUDRE DE BOIS DE SAN... EXTRAIT DE FLEUR DE PASSION, EXTRAIT DE CAMOMILLE EXTRAI... DTA TRISODIQUE, PARAHYDROXYBENZOATE DE METHYL... FLOUR, FRAGRANCE, SANDALWOOD POWDER, RICE BRAN WAX... E EXTRACT, CONEFLOWER EXTRACT, SILICA, TRISODIUM EDTA, ME... ©BENETTON COSMETICS CORP. DIST., NEW YORK, NY 10022 ...D ON 50% RECYCLED PAPER. ETUI IMPRIME SUR PAPIER RECYCLE A 50%

原寸 | Actual Size

Photo by Shuji Yoshida

Travel Size

Photo by Sharon Risedorph

TRIBÙ by BENETTON new york, new york
Brand identity design | Product design: perfume bottle and display system | Package design

TRIBÙ Stationery

SF MOMAのパーマネントコレクション、建築デザイン部門のキュレーター、パオラ・ポリドリ氏は「トリブ」は、ライフスタイルの提案には無関係のように見えますが、実はそうではありません。このデザインはすべてを表現するのではなく、使用者の創造力や知力を引き出すために、多少の余白を残しているのです」と評した。

PETA People for the Ethical Treatment of Animals
new york, new york
Mark design

トリブは動物生体実験の反対活動にも参加。発売と同時にそのパッケージに「PETA」のロゴマークをプリントし活動実現を行ない、私たちもボランティアとして活動に参加。

As a cruelty free company, Benetton placed the PETA logo on the Tribù packaging to raise awareness of animal cruelty. We provided the logo pro bono to support the organization.

モノを使うときに触感は大切なポイントとなる。このボトルには、ガラスとプラスティックという昔からある素材とモダンな素材、硬いものと柔らかいものトリブという言いものと柔らかいものという、相反する素材がモダナチャーを引き出し、複数のパーツを組み合わせる形をデザインした。

ステーショナリーは、自然のエレメントをコラージュして「森の中」を表現。エレメントがばらばらになっても、一つのアイデンティティーを保つようにデザインし、当時開発されたばかりのサイクルペーパーを使用して、くすんだ紙の色でさらにナチュラルな雰囲気を演出することができた。

The Tribù stationery design was inspired by a forest. Natural elements such as leaves were collaged throughout various components of the stationery and when seen as a whole, the elements connected.

原寸 | Actual Size

Designs for Conscious Life and Style

UNTITLED

UNTITLED is a fashion label created by World Co., Ltd. and a term commonly used to identify paintings, photographs and other works of art where the title was omitted by the artist. The Untitled brand is evocative of the art world and artistic pursuits. Inspired and free-spirited, the Untitled collection allows customers to assemble an outfit from Untitled's vast collection of clothing and accessories. Hence, the expression "the body is your canvas" was created for the brand slogan.

株式会社ワールド 40ブランド以上のアイデンティティ開発プロジェクトに参加。なかでも「アンタイトル」と「インディヴィ」は総合的に取り組みました。アンタイトルはワールドのレディースブランドの一つで、そのコンセプトは「UNTITLED＝無題」というブランド名が示すように、消費者が感じるままに自由にタイトルをつけて、そのらしい着こなしを楽しんでもらうというもの。これは、メーカーからの一方的な押しつけではなく、ファッションは消費者から発信されるという、逆転の発想から生まれたものです。このプロジェクトは、ブランドアイデンティティの確立から関わり、とくにセールスキットにアイデンティティを反映させました。次にショップデザインディスプレイなどを取り組みながら、ブランドイメージを明快に視覚化するように心がけました。ブランドコンセプトは「何かを発見することで、広がりを感じってもらうこと。ディスプレイを創造することなど、広がりを感じってもらうこと。

UNTITLED by World, tokyo, japan.
Brand identity design | Package design | Creative consulting, shop direction, display system | Naming

Photo by Sharon Risedorph

アンタイトルのショップのインテリアに使用するマテリアルパレット。プレゼンテーションで選ばれたのもサインに使用する文字はすべてアンティーク・レターから型を取って作成。ポスターは時中に貼ってあるものを剥がして、同じフロトを仕上げた。

This is a material palette for the Untitled store signage. Each letter was recreated from vintage metal letters that were casted and made as originals.

INDIVI Sales Kit

アンタイトルという名を得るインスピレーションは、よりアーティスティックにデザイン、企画展のインターダーシートンボックスと同じものを使用し、中にスペっている印刷物はすべてインダボで印刷された。

This brand manual was inspired by the brand name, Untitled, alluding to the art world. This tactile and artful binder was handmade and the contents were assembled at our studio similar to my junbox binders.

INDIVI

INDIVI. The naming for the Indivi brand was derived from shortening the word "individual." To keep congruent with the brand's name, the design of the logotype was distinct and sophisticated.

インディヴィ 「インディヴィデュアル」という言葉を短縮したインディヴィというネーミングでロゴをデザイン。独創的なアイデアに基づくコンセプト、大胆かつ洗練されたデザインは、インディヴィ独自の世界を築き上げました。

INDIVI Fragrance Bottle

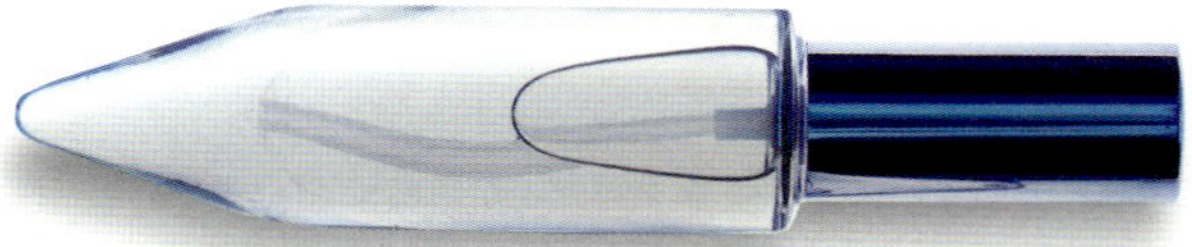

INDIVI by World, tokyo, japan.
Brand identity design | Package design | Fragrance design | Naming

プロモーション用にデザインされたフューム付ボトル。今までになかったボビスタイルを表現。

This promotional fragrance bottle by Indivi was designed with fresh and feminine aesthetics in mind.

Photo by Sharon Risedorph

Timeline | 218

obrero

OBRERO Restaurant
Photo by Nacasa & Partners

OBRERO specialized in clothing for men and women inspired by workwear from the past. The store was built from the ground up and the space was assembled with salvaged materials. Fixtures and incorporated antique furnitures were sourced in the U.S. to create a new, yet warm "lived-in" space.

オブレロ 当時「オブレロ」はブランドのなかでもっとも個性的なイメージがありました。オブレロとはスペイン語で「労働者」という意味で、独特の視点からビジュアルを表現しました。とくにショップに力を入れ、インテリアデザインは植木莞爾氏が担当しました。原宿一号店のショップとレストランのインテリアのポイントとなった鉄枠やガラス素材は、バークレーのリサイクルショップで入手したもの。ブランドのメインイメージはステデァー・ノ・マヤーが撮影しました。

OBRERO Store 
Photo by Nacasa & Partners

OBRERO Calendar
Photo by Shuji Yoshida

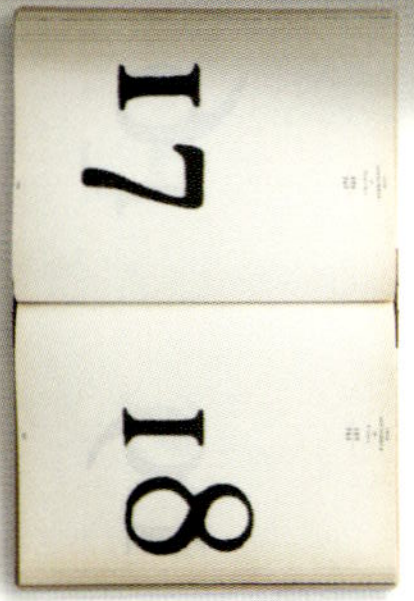

OBRERO by World tokyo, japan
Brand identity design | Package design
Creative consulting: shop & restaurant direction,
Restaurant Interior designer: Kanji Ueki

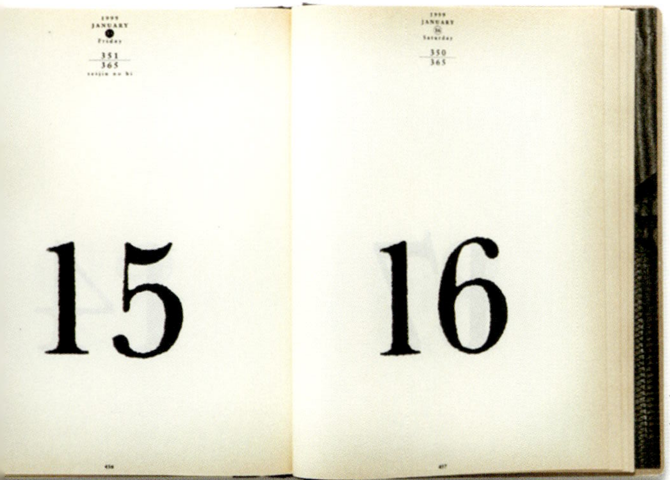

CLEARCUT
THE TRAGEDY OF INDUSTRIAL FORESTRY

CLEARCUT Title Page
Photo by Shuji Yoshida

CLEARCUT: THE TRAGEDY OF INDUSTRIAL FORESTRY is a joint publication of Sierra Club Books and Earth Island Press in 1995. This 291 page book was published with the help of 15 leading ecologists and 33 nature photographers showcasing 15 essays and over 176 stunning photographs and maps. Clearcut reveals the devastation of clear-cut forestry but offers solutions to what can be done to help stop this tragic practice. I was honored to contribute to this project as the book designer.

クリアーカット 34名の写真家、15名のライターをはじめ、多くの人々がボランティアで参加。私たちはグラフィックデザインとブックデザインを担当。この本は伐採をテーマにした内容であったため、リサイクルペーパーを使用して20倍もことも環境に優しい制作プロセスを採用し、バージン紙の使用を最小限に抑えることを前提としました。伐採に関わっているほとんどの製紙メーカー名を紙面で公表し、たまに、製紙メーカーは揃って紙の提供にストップをかけました。そこで私たちは、世界中の大手製紙メーカーに用紙提供をどうするかを呼びかけましたが、いろいろな意味で本の内容が複雑すぎてどうすることもできませんでした。しかし皮肉なことに、世界中から伐採した木を輸入している日本の印刷会社が、この本の出版すべてに協力してくれることとなり、印刷から製本まですべて日本で行なわれました。発行部数は20,000部を超え、現在、第3版が印刷されて世界中で販売されています。

Photo by Shuji Yoshida

INDEX by World tokyo, japan
Brand identity design | Package design
Creative consulting: shop direction,
display system

CLEARCUT The tragedy of Industrial Forestry
Book design | Publisher: Sierra Club Books
Earth Island Press

12冊のアートブックから取り出したページナンバーを複写機で20倍以上に拡大しカレンダーの数字として使用。
This bound calendar book for Obrero was created using the typefaces of the page numbers from 12 different art books. The numbers were photocopied and enlarged to about 20 times the original size.

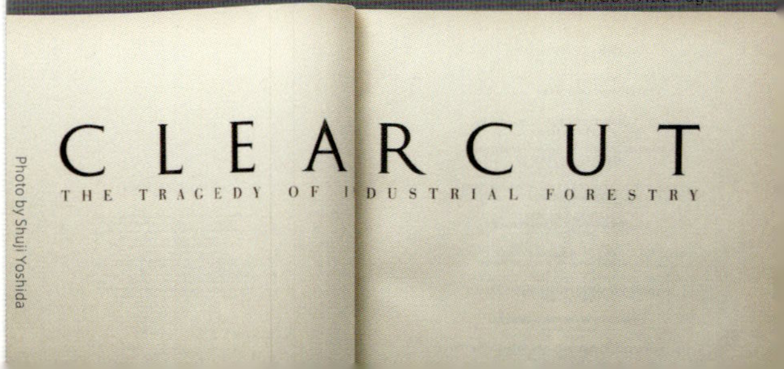

1995

Tamotsu Yagi's Exhibition for the SF MoMA Opening

Photo by Ben Blackwell

TAMOTSU YAGI EXHIBIT san francisco, california
Exhibition at: San Francisco Museum of Modern Art
Curator: Paolo Polledri January - July, 1995

SF MoMA TAMOTSU YAGI EXHIBITION The San Francisco Museum of Modern Art designed by Mario Botta opened January 27, 1995, at its current location in the SoMA district. The SF MoMA is the second largest U.S. museum devoted to Modern Art that includes architectural and graphic design exhibition spaces. Selected works from Tamotsu Yagi's collection were featured in a special exhibit at the grand opening. Tamotsu Yagi was also honored by the induction of over 100 examples of his work to the permanent collection of the SF MoMA. For this exhibition, works from business cards to

SF MOMAでのバ木保展 1995年1月18日にリニューアルオープンした同美術館は、建築家マリオ・ボッタによって設計され、名実ともにニューヨーク近代美術館に次ぐ存在となりました。その斬新な建築デザインは、ダウンタウンの新しいランドマークに。この美術館には、建築とグラフィックのパーマネント展示スペースがあり、オープニング特別展として、半年間、建築では、チャールス＆レイ・イームズ、フランク・ゲーリー、倉俣史朗が、グラフィックでは、すでにパーマネントコレクションされているいくつかの私の作品が披露されました。

Timeline | 220

three-dimensional conceptual objects were displayed in a dynamic and playful fashion. Some works for example were mounted at a slight angle or positioned close to ground level.

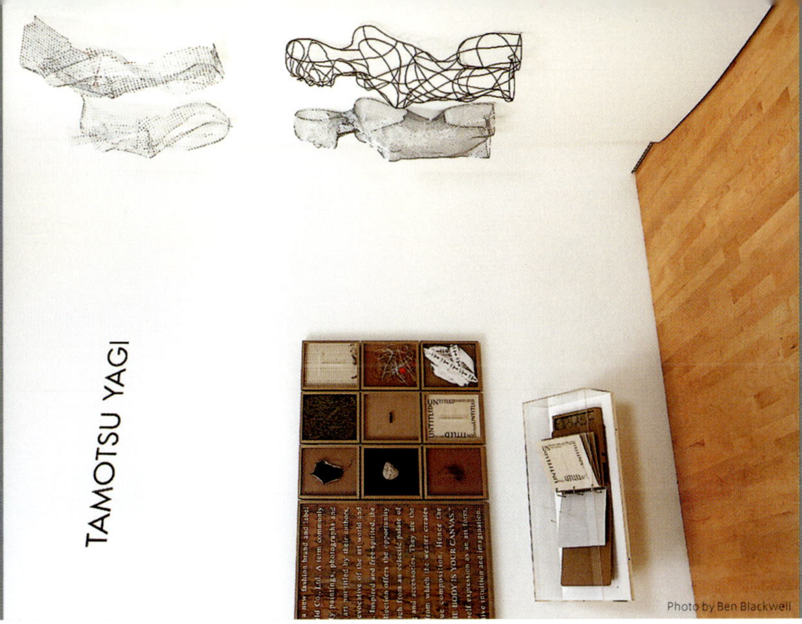

TAMOTSU YAGI

Photo by Ben Blackwell

SF MoMA TAMOTSU YAGI EXHIBITION Entrance

DAVINCI This is an example of the brand identity for a workshop held in Europe for Davinci Virtual Corporation, a subsidiary of Anderson Consulting Inc. Leonardo Davinci's 'mirror writing' inspired the design.

DAVINCI

IKKO TANAKA design studio

A.Y. BLDG., 3-2-2, KITA-AOYAMA,
MINATO-KU, TOKYO, 107 JAPAN
TEL : 3470-2611 FAX : 3403-6873

A Letter From Ikko Tanaka

SF MoMAの展覧会の一部をギンザグラフィックギャラリーで巡回するために、田中一光氏がサンフランシスコに来られた。帰国後、お礼の手紙をいただいた。

After his visit to the *Tamotsu Yagi exhibition* at the opening of the SF MoMA, Tanaka Ikko wrote this letter. Later a similar exhibit of Tamotsu Yagi's collection opened at the Ginza Graphic Gallery, Tokyo. The ggg is the only space specializing in graphic design in the Ginza District of Tokyo.

DAVINCI
by Anderson Consulting Inc. palo alto, california
Graphic identity design

「ダヴィンチ」のためのブランドアイデンティティとバーチャルコーポレーション・エキシビションのデザイン。ヨーロッパで開催される「ダリウエイ」のブランド。レオナルド・ダ・ヴィンチにインスパイアされ、ミラーライティング（鏡文字）という手法で、ロゴタイプを制作した。

原寸 | Actual Size

八木　保　様

サンフランシスコでは、何かとお世話になり、ありがとうございました。
休日のところ、空港まで迎え下さり、また、市内の案内や、ご自宅に
お招き下さるなど、本当にありがとうございました。
ＳＦ.MOMAでの「八木保展」は、期待した通りその洗練を極めたデザイン
に触れ、９月の東京展がいよいよ楽しみになってきました。
また、夜には Chez Panisse での美味しいカリフォルニアキュージーヌの

Center for Ecoliteracy

59

CENTER FOR ECOLITERACY berkeley, california
Corporate identity, Stationery design

センター・フォー・エコリテラシー エスプリ退社後、ダグから同団体を主催する物理学者、哲学者フリチョフ・カプラ氏を紹介されたことではじまったプロジェクトでした。NPOの自然保護団体で資金難だったので、ボランティアで仕事をすることを教えてはいけないと言ったのでテンスだがヤるべきだと教え出ました。それには、ダグからデザインをボランティア活動に活かすべきだと教えれたことにも起因しています。ステーショナリーをデザインする際には、子どもたちが見つけてきた4種の木の葉や枝をモチーフにして、季節の移り変わりを4色のリサイクルペーパーで表現しました。

4色のリサイクルペーパーを使用したレターヘッドの右上の角を折り曲げると、裏面には鳥の巣が印刷されている。名刺に印刷された鳥の巣と組み合わせると、一つのイメージが完成する。
The stationery was designed using four different types of recycled papers. In a playful manner, the images were designed to connect within the entire stationery line. For example, the image of the bird's nest on the back of the letterhead connects to the same image on the business card.

IZUMI MASATOSHI STONE WORKS 1 san francisco, california
Graphic design

ARNE NAESS san francisco, california
Book design | Publisher: Kluwer Academic Pub

INTEL santa clara, california
Graphic design: Intel Pentium Pro logo design

インテルは、世界最大の多国籍半導体メーカー。現在はアップル製品にもインテルのプロセッサが搭載されている。インテル製品はコンピュータの中のパーツであるためにブランドイメージをつくることが難しい。そこでチップにブランドネームをつけることにないたのロゴタイプをデザインしました。

Intel is known for their computer motherboards and chips used by many different computer manufacturers. I was asked to design the Pentium Pro logo that was used alongside the Intel logo.

center for ecoliteracy

2522 SAN PABLO AVENUE
BERKELEY, CALIFORNIA 94702
TELEPHONE 510.845.4595
FACSIMILE 510.845.1439

THE CENTER FOR ECOLITERACY was co-founded by Fritjof Capra, physicist and systems thinker; Peter Buckley, an environmental philanthropist and Zenobia Barlow, now its executive director. The Center is best known for its pioneering work with school garden school lunches, and integrating ecological principles and sustainability into school curricula.

Presentation Board

Envelope Design

IZUMI MASATOSHI STONE WORKS 2 san francisco, california
Graphic design

リサイクルペーパーの上に、子どもたちが見つけてきた自然の素材を円形にレイアウトしたプレゼンボード。左/手前に合わせた4色のリサイクルペーパーを使って封筒に印刷した、実際のサンプル。

This is a presentation board, designed for the Center for Ecoliteracy using four different types of recycled papers and leaves my children gathered from the neighbourhood. The collage of the circular leaves were later applied to the stationery representing the four seasons and the concept of repeated education.

Photo by Stephen Rahn

CENTER FOR ECOLITERACY Letterhead

原寸 | Actual Size

LUMINOUS — Shiro Kuramata tokyo, japan
Exhibition poster design | Exhibition at: Axis Gallery | July 15 – August 7, 1996

六本木アクシスギャラリーで開催された倉俣史朗の展覧会。同時期に原美術館でも倉俣展は開催されていた。アクシスギャラリーではとくに素材、サンプル、プロトタイプなどが展示された。私はポスターをデザインした。

This is a poster I designed for the Luminous: Shiro Kuramata exhibition which took place in three galleries across Tokyo. One of the galleries the exhibition took place in was the Roppongi, Axis gallery, which showcased the materials and prototypes of his works.

Luminous: Shiro Kuramata

To Be Dosa
CHRISTINA KIM / Dosa

CK：何よりボトルの底部分の形が好きです。クラゲのように見えませんか？

TY：なるほど、言われてみればたしかにそう見えますね。この本のタイトルもそうなのですが、人の選択眼、感性の多様性にはいつも驚かされます。いつも視点や興味がぜんぜん違うのですから……。

CK：育った環境、土地や風土によっても、人の感性やモノの見方は違いますね。

ロサンゼルスという場所

TY：クリスティーナさんは、もともとニューヨークを拠点にしていたのに、ここロサンゼルスにスタジオを移したのは、なぜですか？

CK：母もロサンゼルスのダウンタウンに住んでいたということ、それと自然光に恵まれ、ニューヨークよりはるかに安い家賃でこの広いスタジオを借りていられることが大きな理由です。同じ屋根の下で、製品の企画開発から倉庫まで一貫してマネージすることは、ニューヨークでは難しいことですから。そういった意味でもリンドン・ジョンズ氏と制作した環境をとても気に入っています。建築家であるリンドン・ジョンズ氏とコラボレーションして1999年に完成したこのスタジオは、ニューヨークよりも集中してファッションに向き合えますし、1999年に……

TY：クリスティーナさんは韓国語で巧みな職人、匠人という意味です。響きも、どんなに困難な状況や環境に対しても適応できる知識と柔軟性を備えている登山家……というほど、それに母のブランドネームがDOSAとてもぴったりとくる器用な職人なので、母は今も80歳なのですが、今もトーサで働いてくれています。

TY：ドーサと日本との関係について聞かせてください。3月11日の東日本大震災から3カ月後に、ボランティア活動のために福島に行かれましたよね？震災後の日本に向き合ったときの気持ちはどんなものでしたか？

CK：私が福島に赴いた理由は、ドーサというブランドが日本のサポートなくしては存在していないからです。16年前、母とブランドを分けてビジネスを再スタートした当時、私は資金も乏しく厳しい状況になりました。そんななか、日本のクライアントはコレクション発表前にもかかわらず、私たちの力を信じて資金を融資してくれました。その恩に感じている気持ちはけっして忘れられることはありません。コレクションは大好評でしたが、その数年後に阪神淡路大震災が起こったとき、私は日本への納品の準備をしていたところで、地震時に私とスタッフはキッチンにいました。被害の大きさを知って、とにかく私たちができることをしなくてはと、美しい神戸の被災者のみなさんにあたたかい飲み物と服をとれるように、スタッフ一同、2日間でスタジオにあったフリース素材で500枚のブランケットをつくって送りました。その後、すばらしい感謝状をたくさんいただき、ニュースとしてもそれを大きく取り上げられました。少しでも力になりたいという気持ちが、これほどまでに反響を呼んだことに驚き、以来、少しでも困った人々の助けになるよう努力しています。

TY：それから今回の震災での活動につながったのですね。

CK：募金という支援もそうですが、私は実際に被災地に行き、現場と向き合うことに意味があると思います。被害にあった人々の気持ちを受け入れ、共感することが、私たちができる一番のサポートだと……。その経験から何か新たな寿命の延長にできるモノには新たな意味を与えることに、環境問題を意識し、無意味に捨てられてしまうだけのモノに新しいデザインする、当たり前に捨てられてしまうプラスチックボトルですが、これもデザインの一つであることには違いありません。そんなボトルの底部分を再利用してリデザインする、環境問題を意識し、無意味に捨てられてしまうだけのモノに新たな意味を与えることに、寿命の延長にできたらと考えました。

TY：すてきなお話をありがとうございました。ドーサの姿勢から感じることができ、すばらしいですね。

TY：それでも、マテリアルへの着眼点が、ユニークです。

ドーサ

TY：クリスティーナさんを知ったのは、今から10年程前に、レストラン・シェ・パニーズから、あなたがデザインなさったイベント告知のポスターが送られたときです。当時は、ご自身の衣類ブランドドーサ（DOSA）は存じ上げていませんでしたが、月のイメージが大きくプリントされたポスターの印象は圧倒的でTYDのスタジオのインスピレーションボードに大切に飾っていました。そこで今日は、そんなクリスティーナさんの創造の原点に迫りたいと思います。

CK：お声をかけてくださって、ありがとうございます。そんな昔のポスターを覚えていらっしゃるのですね。あれは「月の位相（phases of the moon）」と題したコレクションを発表した際に制作したポスターです。

TY：本当に美しいポスターで、印象的な月のイメージが目に焼き付きました。クリスティーナさんのイメージを印刷物に定着させる手腕には感心していますよ。それ以上に驚かされることは、「ドーサ」におけるブランディングデザインやロゴなどのグラフィック的なデザインエレメントからブランドアイデンティティを確立するというフローチャートではなく、まるで物語を伝えるようにブランドが目指しているイメージを表現し、そのことによってドーサのコンセプトを伝えようとしているようです。

CK：私は、イメージやメッセージから伝わる何かから能力を考えているので、そのデザイン以外の要素は、そぎ落としすぎるように心がけています。過去に絵を描いたことが好きです。ビジュアルに最低限、言葉で語るよりも絵を足すように、複数的に説明することがとても好きです。ビジュアルに最低限の情報を伝える方が、より核心を伝達できるように感じています。

TY：ちなみに、月のポスターのインスピレーション源は何だったのですか？

CK：しいて言えば、生まれ育った家庭環境でしょうか。私は学者や科学者の多い家庭で育ちましたが、なかでも陶磁や中流圏体の研究者である叔父の影響を大きく受けました。さまざまな研究機材、クリスタルや陶器の一部に囲まれた。そう、パネルのスタジオのようにマテリアルに囲まれた環境で育ったんです。私自身も科学のある道を進む気持ちはなかったけれど、ニューヨークタイムズ紙の「NLのロゴタイプに、自身の作品として提供されていましたよ？プラスチックボトルの底を使ったデザインは印象的でしたが、なぜプラスチックボトルを？

CK：既存の再利用可能なマテリアルに新たな価値を与える実験をしてみたかったのです。当たり前に捨てられてしまうプラスチックボトルですが、これもデザインの一つであることには違いありません。そんなボトルの底部分を再利用して新たにリデザインする、環境問題を意識し、無意味に捨てられてしまうだけのモノに新たな意味を与えることに、寿命の延長にできたらと考えました。

TY: Christina, I was first introduced to your women's clothing line, Dosa, through our mutual friend Alice Waters of the Chez Panisse restaurant in Berkeley, California. I later became aware of your numerous collaborations with Chez Panisse, including tableware designs for Heath Ceramics, and of your commitment to working with artisans from around the world. However, I was particularly impressed by a Dosa poster design with striking images of a solar eclipse, which was printed on very thin paper. I remember pinning the poster on the image board at my studio.

CK: That's so wonderful, and a nice place to start our conversation. That poster was from our 'phases of the moon' collection.

TY: I really like your use of imagery in the printed materials that announce each season's projects and collections. The 'phases of the moon' series had a very strong visual message, and a sensibility that is now recognize as distinctly Dosa. I know that creating printed matter can be challenging for brands, especially if the imagery lacks the direct identity of a logo. You have mastered this process, and your series of images are a form of story-telling that speaks to your brand concept and vision.

TY: Where did the inspiration for the moon image come from?

CK: You know Tamotsu, I grew up in a family of scholars and scientists. I was brought up around an uncle who was a meteorite specialist. I was surrounded by his equipment and finds; crystals, rocks and stones, like the ones I saw at your office. So, I came from a family of scientists but I just did not have the mind for science. Interestingly, the subject still found its way into my work.

TY: Speaking of 'finds' and materials, can you tell me a bit about your recent artwork for the NY Times 'T' magazine? Why did you incorporate plastic bottles?

CK: I tried to give a new sense of value to an everyday object that has become an environmental concern. The plastic bottle is ubiquitous and as a result of its widespread use, almost invisible. But just because it's ordinary does not mean that it has no value in its design—someone designed this object. Once I recognized the design value, I found beauty in the repetitions within the perimeters of each bottle. By reassembling diverse multiples into an interesting visual, I wanted to lengthen the original life of the plastic bottle and give it a new meaning.

TY: What specifically drew you to this material?

CK: I love the translucence and lightness of the material, and the shapes and different patterns of the bottles. The bottom of the bottle looks like jellyfish to me. Like moon glow. Don't you think?

TY: Oh yes, I see it now and I love what you see as a jellyfish! I am fascinated by what people really interpret from their observations. Everyone sees things differently.

TY: Christina, what made you move from New York to base your studio in downtown Los Angeles?

CK: My mother was located in downtown Los Angeles, and I realized that I could create a more conscientious design and production space here than in New York. I would be able to maximize local resources like the sunlight, comfortable climate and abundance of space to create a more pleasant work environment. The affordable rent in downtown L.A. has allowed me to design a space that defies the sweatshop image associated with the garment industry. In 1999 dosa moved to a 12,000 square foot space to explore the possibilities of what a workshop could be. Architect Lindon Schultz and I worked together to make a deliberately democratic space; the sewing factory and the showroom share one generous space complete with a communal kitchen. There is also enough extra space for Dosa to recycle ad store fabric scraps until they can be repurposed.

TY: What does Dosa mean?

CK: Dosa is my mom's nickname. My mother is a master craftswoman and her friends gave her that nickname. Pu-won, my mother's closest friend, is 84 years old and still works with me here at Dosa. Dosa in Korean means someone who is skilled, an expert or master teacher–someone who can go into the mountains, adapt and survive. Funnily enough, the word 'dosa' has very different meaning in two cultures. I am closely connected to. In Korea, I think the understanding of dosa as a traditional food helps people there connect with me in a very light and humorous way.

TY: Let's talk about your relationship with Japan. You recently went to Fukushima 3 months after the earthquake. What made you go visit the area after the devastation?

CK: A mutual reverence for the handmade creates a beautiful synergy. This shared understanding I have with the Japanese runs deep for me. Because the ideas of shinagi and wabi sabi are also present in Korean aesthetics, they have long inspired me. In many ways my work at Dosa is a hands-on exploration of these ideals. Not surprisingly, in Japan, my work is received by the consumer with a respect for the hand, curiosity for the process and an inherent understanding of the ideals that is unusual in the world of 'fashion.' Why did I go to Fukushima...because Dosa would not be here today if I did not have Japanese support. About 16 years ago, my mother and I were splitting the company and I really had no money. My Japanese clients believed in my work so much, they supported me by funding money in advance to produce the collection. I was so overwhelmed with gratitude for their kindness.

TY: Wow, that's incredible. What a touching story.

CK: When the big Kobe earthquake struck, we had a customer there. We were in the kitchen at Dosa when we heard the news, and I just said 'we have to do something.' I had this idea of reusing fleece fabric to make blankets because I had heard how cold it was in Kobe. In two days we made 500 blankets. It's amazing how much you can accomplish in just a little time during a disaster. We received so many positive letters, and what we did became world news for a day. Ever since, I try to help people in need in any small way I can.

TY: I understand why you felt a need to support Japan during a difficult time. While most were fleeing the area, you went into the hard hit city of Soma to visit the community you raised money for. That is really incredible.

CK: For me, donating money is one thing, but I believe the best gift you can truly give is to connect directly with the community. Often what you get back is even greater.

TY: Thank you for an inspiring conversation about your work and vision. Christina, you are truly by definition 'Dosa.'

TY: Tamotsu Yagi
CK: Christina Kim

9 DERING STREET
HANDEMBROIDERED
100% COTTON

Photo by Noelle Hoeppe

Tamotsu Yagi's Exhibitions in Japan

TAMOTSU YAGI A View of Nature tokyo, japan
Exhibition at: Ginza Graphic Gallery
Curator: Tanaka Ikko November 1 - 26, 1995

TAMOTSU YAGI Inspire tokyo, japan
Exhibition at: Matsuya Ginza
Curator: Masayuki Kurokawa
October 25 - November 13, 1995

MIKKA BOZU by Rock Field kobe, japan
Graphic identity design | Package design
Illustrator: Patricia Curtain

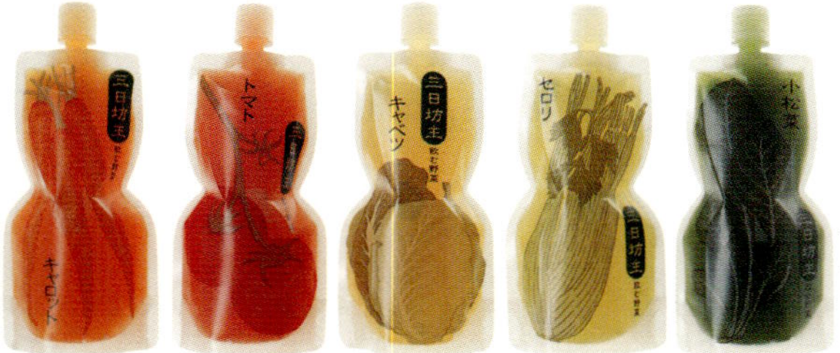

C3 by Henri Charpentier ashiya, japan
Corporate identity design | Graphic identity design
Package design

Photo by Mitsumasa Fujitsuka

TAMOTSU YAGI - A VIEW OF NATURE The Tamotsu Yagi exhibition at the Ginza Graphic Gallery was named *A View of Nature*, a collection of my designs that were inspired by nature. The selected works that were displayed at the ggg were hand picked by curator Tanaka Ikko and where also once exhibited at the San Francisco Museum of Modern Art.

TAMOTSU YAGI - INSPIRE The *Inspire* exhibition was similar to the one held at the Ginza Graphic Gallery, however what differentiated this exhibit from the previous was it paired the object of inspiration for the design alongside the design itself. For example, the inspiration for the PETA logo came from an old 1950s streamline kettle that I had bought at the Sausalito Flea Market therefore the two were displayed together.

MIKKA BOZU is a juice brand of Rock Field. The concept behind this brand was for the juice to be consumed within three days therefore no preservatives were added. This allowed the product to be consumed in its freshest state, with maximum health benefits.

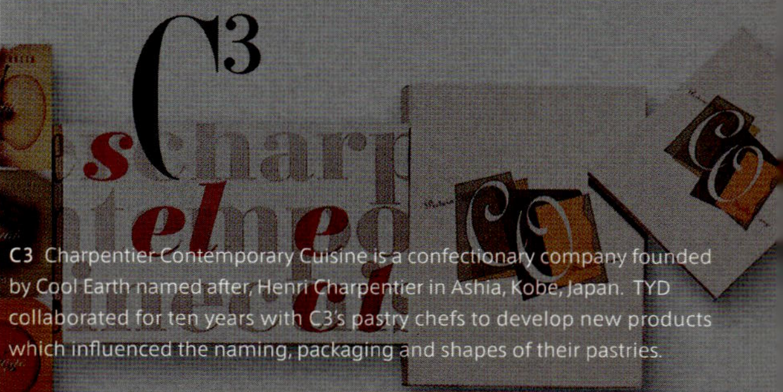

This container was designed so when full, it was three dimensional, however when empty, the container was flat taking up minimal space when discarded. The container was made from natural materials making it environmentally safe

自然観 SF MOMAで行なったオープニングエキシビジョンの一部の展示を中心に、私が興味をもって取り組んできた自然のモティーフとエコロジーをテーマにした作品を立体的な表現で展示しました。特にボランティアを中心に参加したデザインワークを展示し、自然環境の大切さをビジュアルで伝えました。

インスパイア 展覧会の主題は、私のデザインがいかに自然からインスピレーションを得ているかを提示し論証すること。集められたオブジェからインスパイアされるマークやロゴタイプ、カラーシステムを立体で表現しました。

TAMOTSU YAGI'S EXHIBITION at Matsuya Ginza 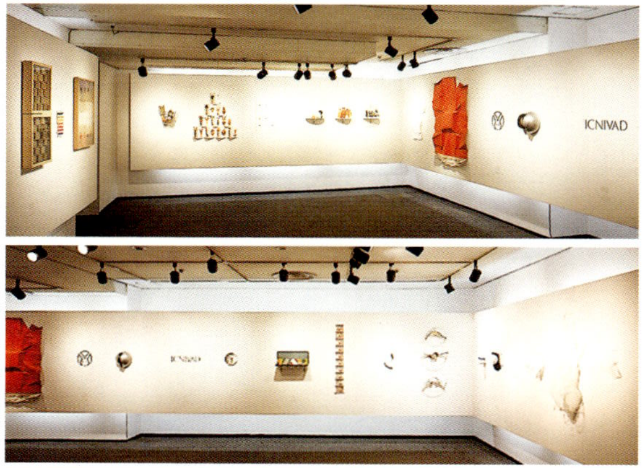
Photo by Mitsumasa Fujitsuka

シーキューブ 洋菓子ブランドのアンリ・シャルパンティエの新感覚ブランドとして、TYDとシーキューブとのコラボレーションでスタートしたプロジェクトです。シーキューブという ネーミングは、フランスのシェフ、アンリ・シャルパンティエ（Charpentier）、食の店舗スタイル（Cuisine）、現代的な感覚（Contemporary）のそれぞれの頭文字をとって「C3」と名付けました。

三日坊主 食品メーカー、ロックフィールドのブランドとしてスタートしたプロジェクト。三日以内に飲むというフレッシュな飲み物、人の健康を真剣に考えた商品づくりとは、時代にあった商品とは何か、プロジェクトを通じて岩田弘三氏の商品開発への真摯な姿勢がとてもよく伝わってきました。

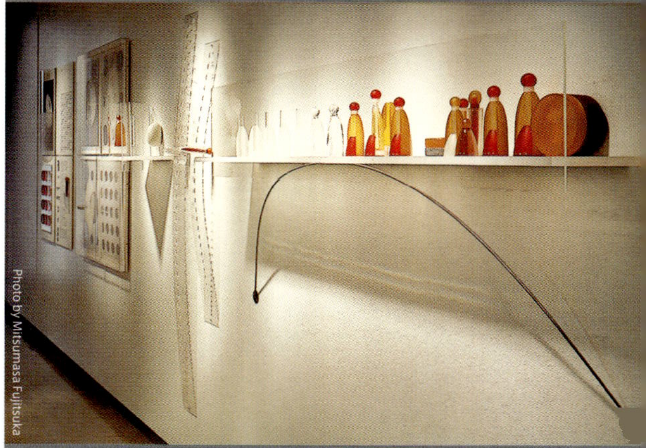

Photo by Stephen Rahn

C3 Logomark Concept

C3 Charpentier Contemporary Cuisine is a confectionary company founded by Cool Earth named after Henri Charpentier in Ashia, Kobe, Japan. TYD collaborated for ten years with C3's pastry chefs to develop new products which influenced the naming, packaging and shapes of their pastries.

Graphic Design for Retail and Public Spaces

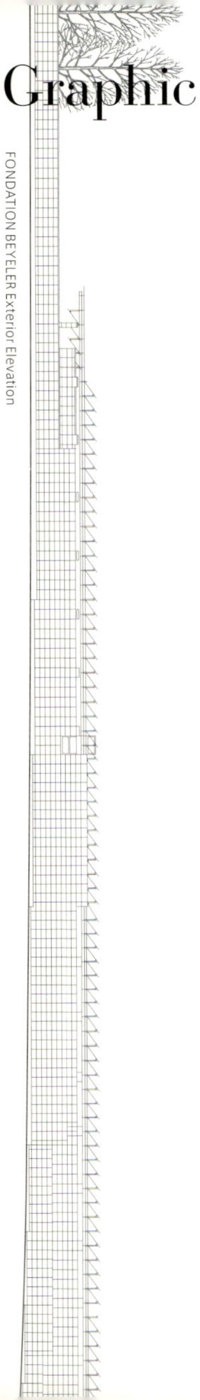

FONDATION BEYELER basel, switzerland
Graphic identity design | Signage system design
Architect: Renzo Piano

URASENKE FOUNDATION san francisco, california
Graphic identity design

OPAQUE tokyo, japan
Graphic identity design | Signage system design
Facade design: SANAA Interior designer: Kanji Ueki

TANTO TANTO at Opaque tokyo, japan
Graphic design: menu | Interior designer: Kanji Ueki

TAMOTSU YAGI Inspiration to Insight
Book design | Publisher: Rikuyosha

08 09

FONDATION BEYELER This project was referred to me by an old friend and gallery owner from Basel, Switzerland. Long time art dealer Ernst Beyeler launched this foundation with a vision of combining groups of works by major artists from the last hundred years that includes Monet's Water Lilies, in a museum setting. Renzo Piano designed the building to radiate simplicity while maintaining harmony with its setting. I was commissioned to complement Renzo Piano's considerable attention to the design of the museum and create the logo and signage design system.

FONDATION **BEYELER**

OPAQUE GINZA is a select shop that involved a collaboration of many designers including architect Kazuyo Sejima + Ryue Nishizawa of SANAA, interior designer Kanji Ueki of Cassapo & Associates and TYD. To augment the uniqueness and innovation of the store, a restaurant was strategically placed in the basement. Taking into consideration the conspicuous nature of the glass facade, I thought best to understate the sign by using acrylic.

OPAQUE Facade with the Acrylic Opaque Logo

ファウンデーション・バイエラー レンゾ・ピアノの設計による建築の完成を機に、ファウンデーションのロゴタイプをデザインしてほしいと、アートディーラーのツース氏から依頼がありました。もとバイエラーのキューレーターであった彼がコーディネイトしてくれたサンフランシスコでの打ち合わせで、できる限りシンプルでなおかつ印象に残るロゴタイプにしたいとクライアントの要望を受けて、2種類のタイプフェイスを組み合わせてのロゴタイプをデザインしました。

オペーク「オペーク・ギンザ」はワールドの核となるセレクトショップ。ファサードデザインは妹島和世氏、インテリアは植木莞爾氏に依頼しました。私は、一連のグラフィックデザインを担当。「OPAQUE」のロゴのネーミングも開発しました。オペークのコンセプトは現在も健在です。併設のイタリアンレストラン「タントタント」のロゴデザインとアートワークもデザインしました。

Photo by Nacasa & Partners

Photo by Shuji Yoshida

私が常にコンセプトにしている「観る」「聴く」「嗅ぐ」「触れる」「味わう」という五感をテーマに、プロジェクトにビデザインプロセスから紹介した、この仕事と周辺のシリーズはデザイナーの仕事を取り扱った書籍。

Most of my designs involve the five senses as a source of inspiration, so the book was titled *Tamotsu Yagi–Inspiration to Insight*. This book traced the design process behind a few projects I was working on at the time.

FONDATION BEYELER Exterior Elevation

20 00

ANDERSEN

ANDERSEN hiroshima, japan
Corporate identity design | Brand identity design
Package design

ROCK FIELD kobe, japan
Corporate identity design

FAMILIAR kobe, japan
Corporate identity design | Catalogue design
Seasonal concept creation

Photo by Shuji Yoshida

ANDERSEN was founded in 1948 and opened its first retail store in Hiroshima in 1967. Andersen bakery introduces 'life with bread' by offering authentic European bread throughout Japan. They also operate high quality chocolate shops through a collaboration with famed French chocolatier Jean-Paul Hevin. This Andersen logo was designed for the store renewal for the Isetan department store's food court in Shinjuku, Japan.

株式会社アンデルセン 1948年創業、1967年広島に第1号店をオープン。現在全国で小売直営店舗「アンデルセン」を展開。アンデルセンの現在のロゴは、1999年アンデルセン伊勢丹新宿店のニューアルオープンに合わせて新しくデザインし、店舗のサインやパッケージに採用しています。その後、2002年に本店である広島アンデルセンのリニューアルにあわせて、再度このロゴをベースに全デザインのリニューアルをし、全国の店へと展開されました。

株式会社ファミリア 1950年、神戸・元町で創業した日本初の子ども服のアパレルメーカー。その品質の高さには定評があります。2000年、銀座にあるファミリア東京店のリニューアル時に、植木莞爾氏のインテリア、TYDによるコーポレイトアイディのデザインによってイメージを一新。「One Smile Fits All」をスローガンに、神戸元町本店も植木氏のデザインによって2003年にオープンしました。

FAMILIAR Ginza Interior

familiar

FAMILIAR was founded in 1950 in the popular area of Motomachi in Kobe, as the first children's clothing company in Japan. Committed to producing quality children's clothing, they refreshed the Tokyo, Ginza store in 2000 by remodeling the store. It helped update the corporate identity, at the same time the company slogan, 'One smile fits all' was also created.

Photo by Nacasa & Partners

Confetti of Color
2001 Fall & Winter Collection

ファミリア コンセプトアートセンターションを年に2回、春夏、秋冬のテーマ、シーズンのオリジナルカラーの開発、2001年にスタートし、今も継続中。

Starting in 2001, we began to develop concept presentations for Familiar as a guide for them to be inspired for the spring and summer, fall and winter collection. The themed concept included, a name of the concept, seasonal color palettes and types of materials to be used.

FAMILIAR Illustration

From chapter 6: Apple Retail Store

Pg. 128-147
02

APPLE cupertino, california
Creative consulting: Apple retail store design
Designers: Tim Kobe, IDSA, and Wilhelm Oehl, IDSA, of Eight Inc.; Charlie Kridler of Gensler; Kanji Ueki of Casappo & Associates; Peter Bohlin of Bohlin Cywinski Jackson; Tamotsu Yagi of TYD; Sylvia Bistrong of ISP Design; Andy Dreyfus of Apple Computer, Inc.; Tommaso Latini of Fisher Development.

GRAND HYATT TOKYO tokyo, japan
Corporate identity design | Graphic design: brochures, restaurants | Amenity design | Signage system design
Architect: Don Siembieda
Interior designers: Tony Chi and Associates, Super Potato

GRAND HYATT TOKYO opened in the popular area of Roppongi Hills as the premier luxury hotel in the area. It took three years to complete the project, which during that time, the comprehensive graphic identity was developed including: restaurant logos, menus, take away packages, printed brochures, amenity and signage designs.

グランドハイアット東京 「今までホテルのプロジェクトを経験したことのないデザイナーに依頼したい」とTYDに依頼がありました。約3年の歳月をかけたプロジェクトでグラフィックアイデンティティを中心に、アメニティからサイン計画まで、広範なデザイン開発に関わることになりました。なかでも、ホテル内のウェディングとレストランアスレチックのデザインにも力を注ぎました。写真撮影とビジュアルは、グランドハイアット香港の協力で完成することができました。

コンテンポラリーな和。「グランドハイアット東京」のオープニングのために用意されたブロシュア。表紙に使用された樹果のお盆が印象的だった。

This is a brochure for the grand opening of the Grand Hyatt Tokyo which we wanted to convey a contemporary japanese feel so we used a bold image of a traditional japanese tray in red lacquer, cropped at an angle.

GRAND HYATT TOKYO Keycard

Photo by Shuji Yoshida

FIORENTINA PacLage
GRAND HYATT TOKYO Wedding Kit

GRAND HYATT TOKYO
THE FRENCH KITCHEN
fiorentina

GRAND HYATT TOKYO Amenity Design

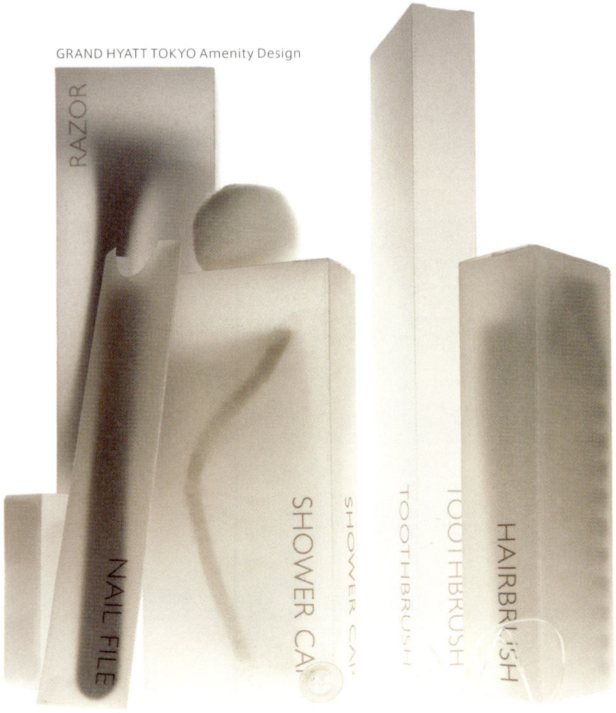

宿泊するお客様にとって何かの印象に残る、思い出になるアイテムとして、一部が透明のカードキーをデザイン。右／必要なアメニティアイテムだけを使ってもらえるように、中身が見える半透明のパッケージをデザインした。

The room keycard was designed to leave a memorable impression therefore a clear strip was incorporated down the center of the card. The amenities package was designed with a transparent material so guests could peek inside the package before opening, which was both a thoughtful and economical solution.

03

Culinary Delights

DELICA rf-1
A Japanese Delicatessen

DELICA rf-1 opened in San Francisco's historical Ferry Building Marketplace, a food market for residents and tourist alike, offering specialty food purveyors, restaurants and cafes serving cuisines and foods that celebrate the cultural diversity of the Bay Area. The idea of Delica rf-1 was to enrich this diversity by introducing sozai, freshly prepared Japanese dishes, inspired by local ingredients. During the buildout, the shop window was tastefully covered with still life photographs by Charles Jones.

バークレーにあるレストランシェ・パニーズのオーナー、アリス・ウォータース氏の協力を得て、彼女の食に対する考えを元に、メッセージが店の入口の壁にシルクスクリーンでプリントされた。デリカ・アール・エフ・ワンは、資源確保持を意識した食生活を目指している。

"Delica rf-1 comes to California both eager to learn from and contribute to the bay Area's thriving food community. Drawing inspiration from Alice Water's delicious revolution", we look forward to an ongoing exchange of ideas between America and Japan that will stimulate the best cuisine and the most sustainable food practices in both countries." – Delica rf-1

DELICA RF-1 Temporary Construction Store Window

Delica RF - 1 san francisco, california
Graphic identity design | Signage design

SAKURANO DEPARTMENT STORE sendai, japan
Corporate identity design

MOC CORPORATION tokyo, japan
Graphic identity design

DOUBLES EDITION tokyo, japan
Graphic identity design

CITRUS NOTES tokyo, japan
Graphic identity design | Interior designer: Masaru Ito

Fashion

CITRUS NOTES

CITRUS NOTES is a women's fashion brand which opened its flagship store in the exciting urban development of Tokyo's Roppongi Hills. The graphic identity was developed to capture the essence of the brand which aimed to target young customers seeking to refine their wardrobe with fashionable and polished silhouettes.

デリカ・アール・エフ・ワン サンフランシスコのランドマークとして有名であり、かつ食を中心とした店舗が多く入っているエリー ビルディングにオープンした。日本の「惣菜」を扱うアメリカでの一号店。上の写真はオープン前の数ヶ月間、食をアピールするために、人通りの多いウインドウに貼られたチャールズ・ジョーンズ氏が1966年に撮った写真。彼の本の前書きはアリス・ウォーターズ氏が書いています。

シトラス・ノーツ。「仕事を着る個性を高く感度な現代女性をテーマになりたい」大人っぽくありたいというテーマにしたブランド。六本木ヒルズ、表参道ヒルズにオープンした後も都心のメージャーなファッションビルにブランドを展開していきました。

This image is a computer rendering of the Citrus Notes exhibition at the Tokyo Forum Convention Center, which debuted the brand to the public and the press. The exhibition space and the striking shop interior was designed by Masaru Ito

東京デザインフォーラムビルの展示会。友人のインテリアデザイナーの伊藤勝がデザインした、スペースとビルのコントラクチャーと商品のバランスがとても話題になった。

Ito Masaru Design Project / Sei

Timeline | 230

04

Pg. 108-123

From chapter 5: **Hiroshima City Naka Incineration Plant**

HIROSHIMA CITY NAKA INCINERATION PLANT hiroshima, japan
Graphic identity design | Signage system design
Naming: Ecorium | Architect: Yoshio Taniguchi

FELISSIMODE interior
Photo by Nacasa & Partners

foNTANA feliciti

C3- BLOCCO BALOCCO During the development of Blocco Balocco, a new product by the confectionery company C3, I decided to introduce a new packaging material. After sourcing new materials, I saw the potential in using tin containers, which I used for Blocco Balocco. Tin allowed for new graphic expressions like embossing and coloring similar to the process of anodized-aluminum, which we maximized in the design. *Blocco*, which means brick in Italian, inspired the design of this product.

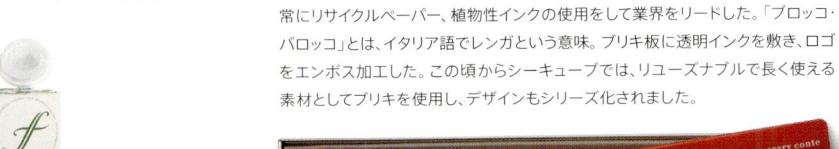

ブロッコ・バロッコ 2004年からスタートしたシーキューブのパッケージデザイン。常にリサイクルペーパー、植物性インクの使用などして業界をリードした。「ブロッコ・バロッコとは、イタリア語でレンガの意味。ブリキ板に透明インクを吹き、ロゴをエンボス加工しました。この頃からシーキューブでは、リユースナブルで長く使えるような素材としてブリキを使用し、デザインモジュール化されました。

Photo by Stefano Massei

BLOCCO BALOCCO by C3 ashiya, japan
Package design

Photo by Stefano Massei

FONTANA tokyo, japan
Graphic identity design

FELICITI kobe, japan
Graphic identity design | Water bottle design

FELICIMODE nagoya, japan
Graphic identity design

EARTH AT PLAY tokyo, japan
Book design | Photographer: Ayumi Nakanishi

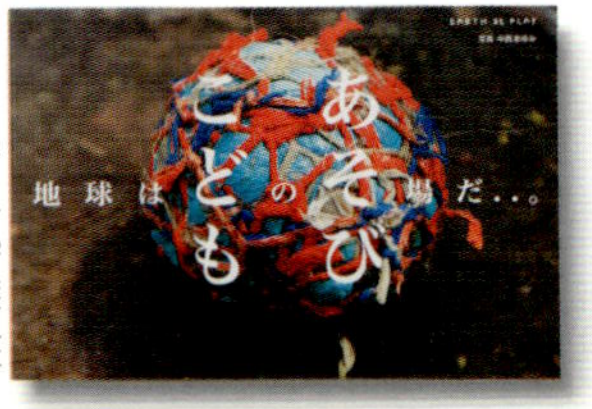

Photo by Shuji Yoshida

シーキューブのパッケージを通して、リサイクルのアイデアを顧客に提案。使用したパッケージを再利用してすてきたちにアピールしたショップイベントでのディスプレイなどに展開。Through playful construction, we wanted to inspire playful ideas for reusing the C3 paper packaging. We recreated fun figures like this bear out of C3 packaging and utilized them as store displays.

カタログをそのまま開いたような店、フェリシモード、フェリシモ初の店舗、名古屋高島屋にオープン。ショップ用のパッケージはすべて再利用可能なプラスティックを使用した。Felicimode was Felicti's first flagship store which opened at the Takashimaya department store in Nagoya, Japan after years of solely selling products online. The shopping bags for the store was designed from recycled plastic.

20 05

Synergy

SYNERGY We were asked to redesign Bridgestone Sports professional golf line, Synergy. During the development process, I came up with material palettes for two color directions. With light and dark green being the concept, the dark British Green was chosen for the head of the golf clubs.

Synergy Material Palette

Photo by Stefano Massei

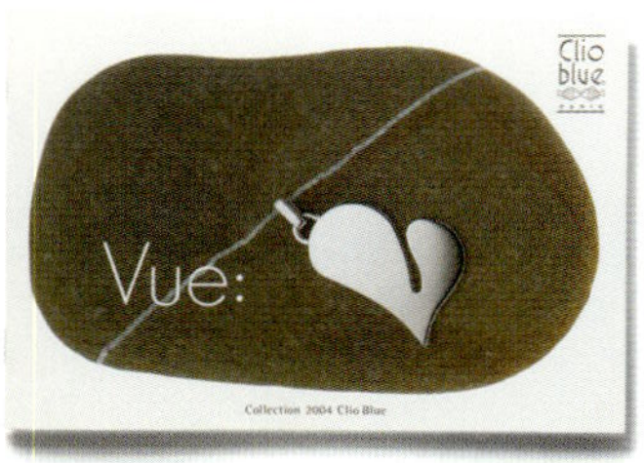

THE TOKYO CLUB

THE TOKYO CLUB was founded in 1884 and is the oldest private British style member's clubs in Japan. This was the second project working with the architect, Yoshio Taniguchi and I developed the signage system. Since only members were allowed in the club, the signage for the building was kept to a minimum. I chose Rotis for the base typeface for the signage.

シナジー ブリヂストンスポーツの新しいゴルフクラブの開発プロジェクト。TYDはマテリアルパレット2案をプレゼンテーションしました。2案ともグリーンがコンセプトカラーだったので、新芽を彷彿とさせる明るい緑とブリティッシュグリーンという黒に近い深みのある系縁のパレットで表現しました。実際のゴルフのヘッドはこのブリティッシュグリーンが採用されました。

東京倶楽部 1884年（明治17年）創設され、122年の歴史のある会員制ジェントルマンズクラブ。英国のジェントルマンズクラブを範として「東京倶楽部」の設立は発案されました。建築家・谷口吉生氏とのプロジェクト。タイプフェイスには「ロティス」を基本にサイネージを展開しました。

Timeline | 232

Jewelry

CLIO BLUE kobe, japan
Graphic identity design

Photo by Shuji Yoshida

「クリオ・ブルー」は1981年にパリで設立されたジュエリーブランド。日本支店のためにカタログを中心とした、販売促進のためのグラフィックデザインをしました。撮影はステファノ・マセイが担当しました。Clio Blue is a jewelry company that was founded 1981 in Paris, France. This catalog was designed for the Japanese market and the still life images were photographed by Stefano Massei.

Private Club

SYNERGY tokyo, japan
Logo design | Product development consulting

FOUR SEASONS HOTEL TOKYO AT MARUNOUCHI tokyo, japan
Graphic design: restaurant Ekki
Hotel artwork brochure design

NEXTMARUNI 12 CHAIRS milan, italy
Chair design | Graphic identity design: invitation, brochure
Exhibition at: Galleria Antonia Jannone
Curator: Masayuki Kurokawa April 13 - May 11, 2005

THE TOKYO CLUB tokyo, japan
Signage system design | Architect: Yoshio Taniguchi

THE TOKYO CLUB Entrance

道路に面したソロ。一度訪れたメンバーにとって、記憶に残る建築であるため、ロゴはまじに行かなければ見えないほど小さく、切り抜きのステンレスで表現。Since the club is a member's only establishment, the entrance sign was designed to be indistinct from a distance. The logo was visible from up close, and the detail finish of the sign was beautifully made of stainless steel.

Awareness and Wellness

DAVID BROWER CENTER

DAVID BROWER CENTER in Berkeley, California is a center for environmental and social action, combining both environmental, non-profit offices and program facilities in a 50,000 square-foot space. The David Brower Center provides a central place of congregation for the non-profit community and also houses a retail space, theater, public art gallery and an organic restaurant. The David Brower center is one of Northern California's most advanced green buildings with the highest LEED platinum rating. The building was designed by Daniel Solomon, principal architect of Solomon E.T.C.-WRT, and is 40% more energy efficient than other comparable buildings. TYD proudly provided the graphic identity and signage design for the center.

DAVID BROWER CENTER Building

デビット・ブラワー・センター ノーベル平和賞に3度もノミネートされたデビット・ブラワー氏。このプロジェクトは、元エスプリ・ニューヨーク社のピーター・バックリー氏の紹介でスタートしました。内容はロゴタイプとグラフィックエレメントのリデザイン、使用されていたロゴタイプのイメージを、風格のあるアカデミックな表現にリデザインしました。ダニエル・ソロモン氏の設計によるビルは、LEED（Leadership in Energy & Environmental Design）でも、プラチナランクに認定されています。このプロジェクトもボランティアとして参加しました。

VINYASA Compact Powder

DAVID BROWER CENTER berkeley, california
Graphic identity design | Signage design

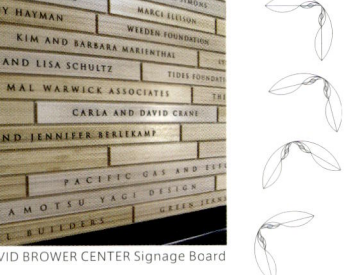

DAVID BROWER CENTER Signage Board

デビット・ブラワー・センターのオーニング用にデザインした長さ約10mのバナー。ビルの顔になるので、1日中インパクトが持続するようにグラデーションを用いてデザインしました。This banner for The David Brower Center was designed for the grand opening of the establishment. Taking into consideration that the movement of shadow from the building that would be casted throughout the day, bright gradient colors were used.

VINYASA is Felissimo's cosmetic line with the concept of happiness and sharing wellness from person to person. Vinyasa is a Sanskrit word for "sequential movement" that interlinks postures to form a continuous flow. The Vinyasa brand captures the essence of wellness and personal care.

ヴィニアーサ フェリシモ発のカラー化粧品で「から人へ贈る幸せ」がブランドのテーマ。「VINYASA」とは、サンスクリットのヨガ用語で「動作の連続」という意味。私たちはブランドのネーミングからスタート、メインの商品であったコンパクトパウダーのデザインを中心に一連の化粧品のプロダクトデザインと、ブランドアイデンティティを手がけました。

VINYASA Compact Powder

VINYASA hong kong
Graphic identity design
Package design | Naming

ヴィニアーサのカラー、自然の素材を活かし、基本色12色をどんな組み合わせにしても、健康的でコンテンポラリーに見えるように選んだ。The twelve colors for the Vinyasa line was inspired from natural colors of fruits and flowers, representing a healthy new lifestyle.

Photo by Stefano Massei

06 nextmaruni

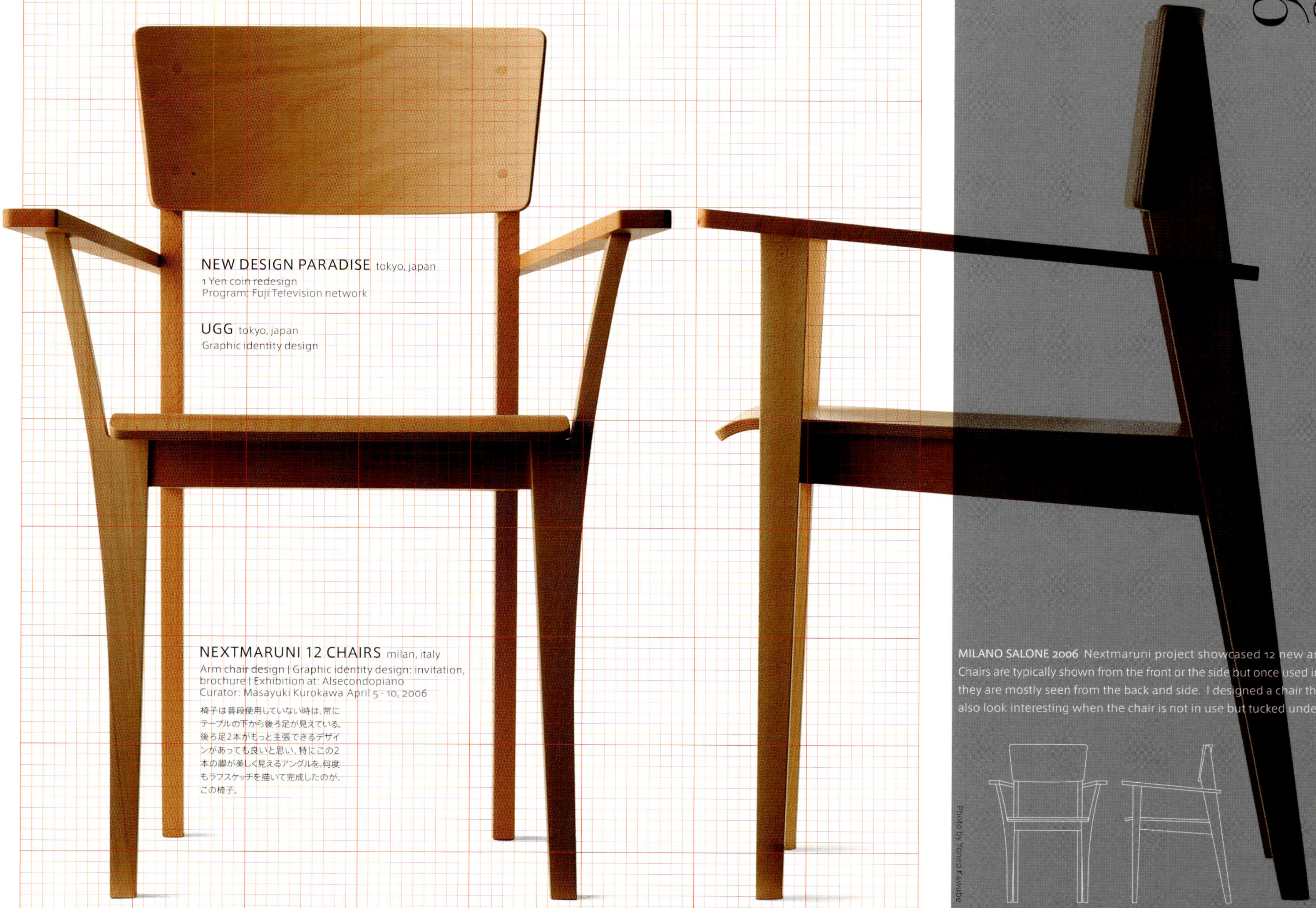

MILANO SALONE 2006 Nextmaruni project showcased 12 new armchairs. Chairs are typically shown from the front or the side but once used in context, they are mostly seen from the back and side. I designed a chair that would also look interesting when the chair is not in use but tucked under a table.

Photo by Yoneo Kawabe

NEW DESIGN PARADISE tokyo, japan
1 Yen coin redesign
Program: Fuji Television network

UGG tokyo, japan
Graphic identity design

NEXTMARUNI 12 CHAIRS milan, italy
Arm chair design | Graphic identity design: invitation, brochure | Exhibition at: Alsecondopiano
Curator: Masayuki Kurokawa April 5 - 10, 2006

椅子は普段使用していない時に、テーブルの下から後ろ足が見えている。後ろ足2本がもっと主張できるデザインがあっても良いと思い、特にこの2本の脚が美しく見えるアングルを、何度もラフスケッチを描いて完成したのが、この椅子。

Designing with the aesthetic of traditional Japanese *wa* style was a topic that never really interested me until the nextmaruni chair project lead me to an opportunity to really research and revisit its history of craft discipline. No doubt, Japanese craft has always had a huge influence on me but to design in this style was a new concept for me. However, once I started, the topic fascinated me further and I began to take on many *wa* projects

HATA MUSEUM kyoto, japan
Graphic identity design

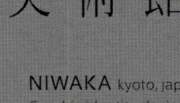

羽田美術館

NIWAKA kyoto, japan
Graphic identity design
Architect: Tadao Ando

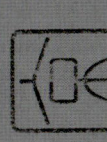

俄

KYO kyoto, japan
Graphic identity design | Catalog design
Interior design: Super Potato

京

EN ARTS kyoto, japan
Graphic identity design
Interior designer: Hiroshi Yoshikawa

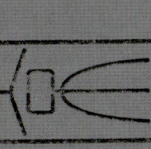

ITOCHU kyoto, japan
Graphic identity design | Package design

伊と忠

GAKUSOU Frame

Photo by Yoneo Kawabe

Japanese *Wa* Projects

KIMONO DE LA FAMILLIE HATA
Book design | Publisher: Musee de la Chambre de Commerce et d'Industrie de Lyon

KIMONOS DE LA FAMILLE HATA
Photo by Shuji Yoshida

羽田登喜男氏は、京友禅に加賀友禅を融合させて独自の境地を開いた人物。1988年、友禅の重要無形文化財保持者（人間国宝）に認定される。1996年、リヨン染織美術館にて、「羽田家のキモノ展」が開催されるにあたって、作品集をデザインした。

In 1988, Hata Tokio was recognized as a Japanese living treasure for his excellence in *Yuzen*, a traditional paste-resist method of dyeing textiles. In 1996, *Musee Des Tissus et Des Arts Decoratifs* in Lyon, France exhibited the Hata family collection of examples of their dye works on kimonos

MY 100 FAVORITE JAPANESE GOODS
Book design | Publisher: Rutles

Photo by Shuji Yoshida

TYDが「本の装丁・デザインを手がけた「わたし好みのデザイン和もの100選」の著者である裏地桂子氏は、「手のひらの和もの」をテーマに、ハイブリー・ジュエリー・京都内のセレクトショップ「泉」の商品カタログを手がけた。TYDは、商品カタログをデザインした。Keiko Uraji, a writer and creative coordinator produced a book based on 100 of her favorite Japanese goods ranging from foods to tableware.

KAISHI by kisara nara, japan
Kaishi design

懐紙の柄には、お茶を点てる時の手の動きの勢いと動きを曲線で表現した。Kaishi are traditional Japanese papers that *wagashi* (Japanese sweets) are placed on during tea ceremonies. The design for this Kaishi was inspired by the swirling movement of whisking Japanese Matcha green tea.

和の仕事 日本の美意識をテーマにしたマルニ木工の椅子のプロジェクトを境に、2005年頃から和のプロジェクトを手がけることが多くなりました。それまでは日本の四季を思い浮かべるような、自然をモチーフにして古い使い込まれた菓子型を選んでフレームにしました。

俄 京都を発信地に、国内外で展開するジュエリーブランド。とくに結婚指輪に定評があります。デザインは既存の和文ロゴの原型を残してリファインしました。2008年、安藤忠雄氏による本社ビルが下鴨に完成し、ビルの入り口に新しいロゴを設置されました。

伊と忠 明治28年創業の「伊と忠」は、銀座に長襦袢と別誂草履の「伊と忠GINZA」をオープン。新しいブランドアイデンティティの開発では、広くから使用されていたマークのエレメントを現代風のモノグラムのパターンへと発展させました。

エン・アーツ ギャラリー「eN arts」は、アートと人との素敵な縁(eN)を提案したいという直美・ロウ氏の、古都・京都から現代アートを発信したいという強い想いから、円山公園にある古い和風建築の外装を一切壊さず、内装をモダンにリノヴェーションオープンしました。私たちはロゴマークをデザインしました。

07
Pg. 69-84
From chapter 3: Kenzo Estate

AKIE ABE the wife of the former Prime Minister of Japan came to me to discuss a gift packaging project. As the wife of a Prime Minister, she frequently traveled to other countries meeting important dignitaries and naturally brought gifts from Japan. She began wrapping her own gifts and eventually realized that she wanted her own personalized packaging system, which I was asked to design. I referenced traditional Japanese elements in a contemporary context: Japanese *sakura* (cherry blossom), which I felt represented Mrs. Abe's personality was used for her monogram. Crisp *mizuhiki* (celebratory strings made of paper) was used to secure the bright blue wrapping tissue. I was honored that Mrs. Abe had asked me to represent my country through design for dignitaries all over the world.

Hirano Shrine in Kyoto is notable for their gardens and has been a popular annual cherry blossom viewing site since the year 985.

Photo by Ko Kado

安倍昭恵
Akie Abe

Photo by Shuji Yoshida

AKIE ABE Gift Packaging

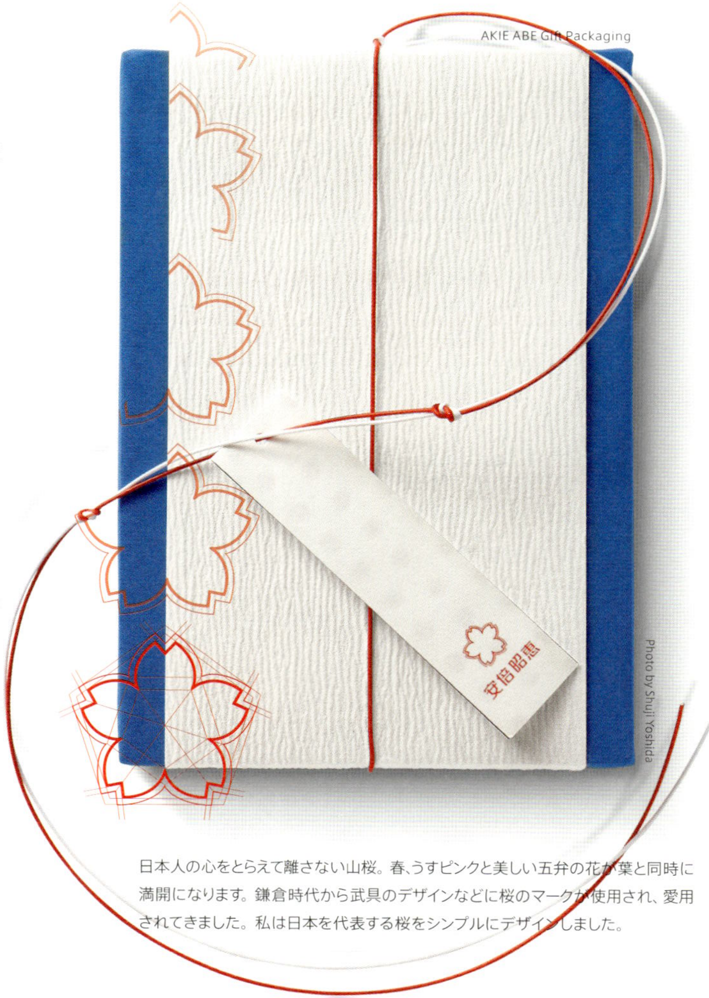

日本人の心をとらえて離さない八重桜。春うすピンクと美しい五弁の花びら葉と同時に満開になります。鎌倉時代から武具などのデザインに桜に使用され、愛用されてきました。私は日本を代表する桜をシンプルにデザインしました。

KENZO ESTATE napa valley, california
Corporate identity design | Graphic identity design
Package design | Architect: Howard Backen
Consulting Winemaker: Heidi Barrett
Vineyard Manager: David Abreu

AKIE ABE tokyo, japan
Graphic identity design | Package design

JEN'S KITCHEN - BE ORGANIC
Book design | Publisher: Rock Field

Photo by Shuji Yoshida

THE SILVER ROAD
Book design | Publisher: Kodansha

Photo by Shuji Yoshida

KENZO ESTATE YUI Bottle

元内閣総理大臣夫人である安倍昭恵氏からの依頼では海外の要人へのギフトは既製品を贈答できないという事情があり、日本の象徴である桜の花をデザインに和を表現した。

レストランジェパニーズのオーナー、アリスウォーターズ氏の片腕で、ジェニファー・シャーマン女史を迎えて、ロックフィールドが名古屋ミッドランドスクエアに出店したビー・オーガニック一号店。日本であまり知られていないジェニファーの知名度を上げるため、彼女のパワフルでキレのある生活スタイルを紹介がしたい雑誌。

Rock Field Company opened a deli called Be Organic in Nagoya, Japan's Midland Square. Jennifer Sherman, former head chef at Chez Panisse restaurant in Berkeley, California and a close friend of Alice Waters was named the executive chef. To inform the Japanese public of Jen's cooking style and her commitment to using organic ingredients, a book titled Jen's Kitchen was published containing recipes and her sources of inspirations.

「食卓を彩るシルバー」の著者、佐藤よし子氏は、1988年「ザ・クイーンズ・フィニッシングスクール」を神戸に開校。校長として教鞭をとる。アンティークシルバーウェアを中心に、銀器の歴史や様式などについての基本知識、テーブルセッティング方法を通じて、美しいシルバーの魅力を紹介した書籍。

The Silver Road is a book on Sato Yoshiko's antique silver ware collection. Sato Yoshiko is a writer and founder of The Queen's Finishing School, founded, 1988 in Kobe, Japan.

Pg. 85-100

From chapter 4: Rohto: Episteme

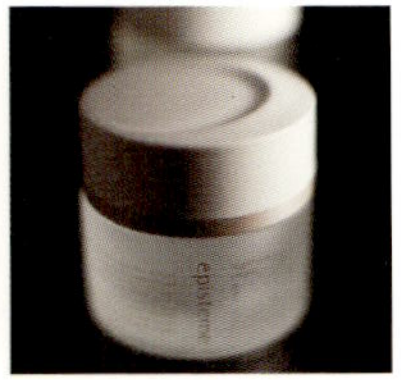

EPISTEME tokyo, japan
Brand identity design | Package design
Shop and Showroom design | Creative consulting 2008

イヤックスのカタログ 顧客が自分たちのライフスタイルにあった家具をどのように選び、新しい生活空間に取り込めばいいか、イヤックス以外の商品や椅子、ランプ、インテリアの小物も紹介も合めて、今までにないカタログを試みた。

The concept behind the Inax catalog was to incorporate its furniture selections as part of a lifestyle. Interior scenes were staged and built inside photo studios and photographed for the catalog.

BARDESSONO yountville, california
Graphic identity design | Signage system design

モンチェックインの際に手渡されるバル夜ごとめたバインダーの中には、ナパバレーのワイナリーの地図やレストランストラなどの観光情報を差し込み、また手前の黒いエンヴェロープには部屋の鍵が入る、チェックアウト時にはバインダーごと持ち帰ることができる。

The compendium kit that TYD developed included items such as information about local wineries, activities list, and the room keycards. Since the hotel is a green building, we only used natural and recycled materials for example, the spine of the compendium is made from branches from the area.

INAX tokyo, japan
Graphic identity design | Catalog design

BARDESSONO The compendium kit for the Bardessono hotel in Napa Valley's Yountville, was designed to be carried and used by the guest as a memory keepsake. The compendium was handed to the guest upon check-in, which included room keys, a welcome note and basic information about the hotel services and amenities. In addition, the compendium included detailed maps and activities list of nearby wineries and culinary points of interest. In keeping with the LEED certification (one of only 2 platinum certified hotels in the U.S), the compendium design is a part of the luxury experience at the Bardessono and its commitment to green design.

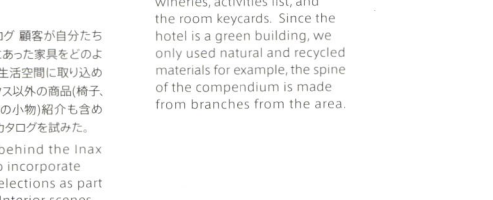

バーデソノ ナパバレーの近郊ヤントビルにあるブティックホテル。環境を意識したホテルにふさわしいビジュアルとサイネージを提案。印刷物にはリサイクルペーパーを使用。印刷とサイネージの製作は地元の業者を使いました。オーナーテルはLEED(Leadership in Energy & Environmental Design)で、一番評価の高いプラチナを取得しています。

BARDESSONO Compendium Kit

Photo by Shuji Yoshida

INAX Catalog

Pg. 157-176 | 09/10

OPPOSITE HOUSE a View From the Guest Floor
Photo by Katsuki Miyoshino

OPPOSITE HOUSE Penthouse Signage
Photo by Katsuki Miyoshino

THE OPPOSITE HOUSE is a 100 room boutique Hotel in Beijing, China that was designed by renowned architect, Kengo Kuma. The theme of the traditional courtyard style home in China is enhanced with an extraordinary mix of old and new elements. We collaborated with Kuma throughout the project and developed the signage system design.

OPPOSITE HOUSE Signage

OPPOSITE HOUSE Signage Study Model

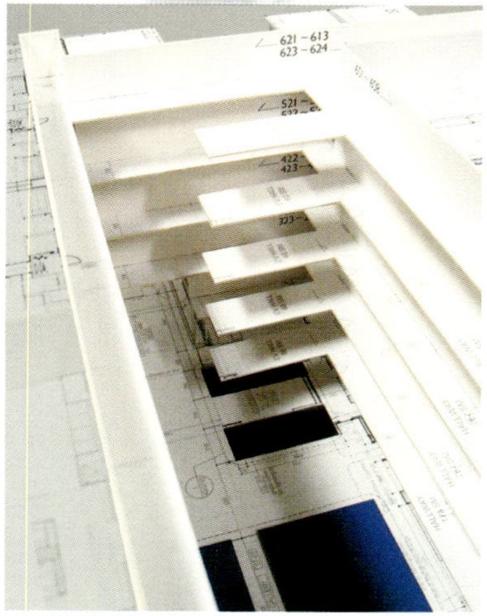

From chapter 7: Palm

PALM sunnyvale, california
Graphic identity design | Corporate logo redesign
Package design

OPPOSITE HOUSE beijing, china
Signage system design | Architect: Kengo Kuma

To contrast the uneven and natural surface of the wooden walls, I designed an elegant signage system. Each letter was made from a single piece of laser-cut stainless steel strip. The pins integrated into the stainless steel strip made it easy to mount onto the uneven surface of the wood walls

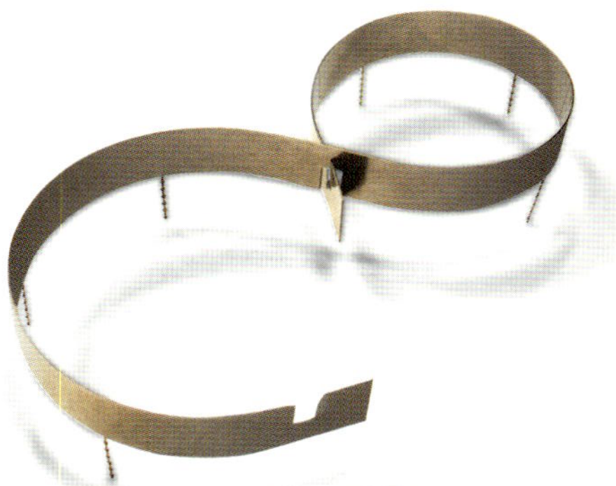

We made this model to study the placements of the signage throughout the hotel from the perspective of the guests. Final adjustments were made during a site visit.

オポジット・ハウス 2008年北京で開催されるオリンピックの大規模ホテルの建設ラッシュのなか、外資系のオフィスとブティックが並ぶエリアで知られる三里屯に、隈研吾氏が設計した100室規模のブティックホテルです。ホテル名の「オポジット（反対）」は、中国古来の住居形式四合院をヒントに、居住部の反対側にゲスト用の部屋を設けたことから、名付けられました。新感覚のサインデザインを提案しました。その「Timelessなもの」というクライアントからの要望で、3種類のマテリアルとデザインが決まりました。サインを取り付ける壁面は荒削りのリサイクルの木。ラフな木の表面とステンレスを曲げたタイプフェイスがホテルのイメージとあったので、この方向で進めました。0〜9までの数字型を安定させて壁に差し込むために、何度もステンレスのピンと凹み位置を調整し、一度にレーザーカットでつくられるようデザイン的な配慮を行ないました。

ルームナンバーの8は、ステンレスの板金を曲げて中心に重ね合わせ、表現した。レーザーカッターを使って、壁に入るピンも同じ素材でカットすることができた。

ルームナンバーのスタディー模型図面をもとに各フロアの模型をつくって、ゲストなどのように部屋をたどるかをスタディでルームナンバーの位置を仮決めした。さらに現場でのプリントで再確認して取り付けた。

Timeline | 238

KEPLINGER WINES Label Design

Photo by Kazuya Enomoto

KEPLINGER WINES Label Design Process

Photo by Shuji Yoshida

KEPLINGER WINES napa valley, california
Graphic identity design | Label design

This label design artwork for Keplinger Wines was inspired by the golden rectangle as wine making is an art form grounded in science. For the artwork, we made a template as a guide to form an actual grapevine into the shape of the golden rectangle.

In order to incorporate both the scientific and natural aspects of wine making, we used the golden rectangle and the tendril of the grapevine as design elements for the label. For a sophisticated look, we embossed the tendril and all other elements were engraved.

黄金分割の円状に紙のフェンスをつくり、そのジルエットに紙のフェンスをつくって葡萄の蔓を添わせて葡萄の成長のプロセスを視覚的にプレゼンテーションした。

ワインラベルでは成長していく葡萄の蔓にエンボス加工を施し、黄金分割と文字はエングレービングによって繊細な線で表現し、高級感のある仕上がりとなった。ステーショナリーもすべてエングレービングで印刷された。

KEPLINGER WINES Helen Keplinger earned her wine degree from UC Davis, and has worked for Paradigm, Fiddlehead and Kenzo Estate in addition to a winery in Priorat, Spain. Helen and husband/business partner, Douglas Warner managed to find the perfect soil, altitude, and weather conditions required to grow the finest Grenache and Syrah grapes in Knights Valley for Keplinger wines. Having worked with Helen on previous project at Kenzo Estate, she enlisted us to design the brand identity including the wine labels for Keplinger Winery.

JEAN PROUVÉ EXHIBITION was shown on September 12-23, 2009 at the Hotel Flex in Hiroshima, Japan. The exhibition was coordinated by three Jean Prouve enthusiasts; Kazumi Sadahiro, the owner of the Flex Hotel restaurant; Kengo Nakamura, the owner of Reflexion, a boutique store, in Hiroshima and Yoshiyuki Mizoguchi, the owner of furniture gallery SIGN, Tokyo.

ケプリンガーワイン 著名なワインメーカーであるヘイジー・パレット氏のもとで経験を積んだヘレンケプリンガー氏が、新たにプロデュースするワインレーベルのプロジェクト。広島出身の3人によって、地方から何か文化的なことを発信しようと計画されました。

「ジャン・プルーヴェ」展 広島出身の3人によって、地方から何か文化的なことを発信しようと計画されました。展覧会場は広島の川辺に佇むデザイナーズホテル「Flex43・キャラントトロア」のオーナー貞廣一鑑さんが提供。イベント期間中のコーディネイトは地元広島の若者に支持されているセレクトショップ「REFLEXION」のオーナー中本健吾さんが担当。そして東京広尾のインテリアショップ「SIGN」の溝口至亮さんがジャン・プルーヴェ、シャルロット・ペリアンなどの作品約30点を集め、TYDは会場構成とグラフィックデザインをしました。

Photo by Yasuyuki Takaki

JEAN PROUVÉ Exhibition

JEAN PROUVÉ EXHIBITION hiroshima, japan
Graphic design: Printed matter | Exhibition design
Exhibition at: Hotel Flex / Casafeliz Confeito
September 12 - 23, 2009

JEAN PROUVÉ EXHIBITION Poster

Photo by Stefano Massei

Pictured is Jean Prouvé's iconic porthole panel taken from one of his prefab homes he designed. It was placed at the entrance of the exhibition and was a piece that left a lasting impression on me.

入り口のジャン・プルーヴェのアイコンであるにで穴が空いたドアパネルが訪れる人に強い印象を与えた。

An Architectural Eye

KULAPAT YANTRASAST / wHY Architecture

建築に対する文化の違い

TY: I've known the architect Tadao Ando for many years, and first met you when you worked for his firm. You helped locate my current office space in Los Angeles, and we've since become good friends. Kulapat, you have a very unique and multicultural background. A native of Thailand, you travelled extensively as a child. You later received your Master's Degree and Ph.D in Architecture from the University of Tokyo, under Japanese Government Scholarship. This range of experiences must have been advantageous while working on projects around the globe, both in Ando's office and now on your own.

KY: Yes, I learned many things in Ando's office besides architecture such as how to communicate with clients and even the need to be gregarious. One important lesson that related to your motto "no detail is small" was the significance of etiquette and details, in social environments. I continued to practice this with my clients, which helped me mature and develop a successful business.

TY: You now host Design Salon lecture events at your office to connect clients, colleagues, and friends socially over food and wine. This forum allows people to get to know one another beyond their professional interactions. Design Salon offers a great creative platform to exchange and debate design concepts, and connect people with similar interests.

KY: It's important to have this kind of social event to bring people together, especially in LA. The city is so spread out, it can be difficult for people to stay in touch with one another. There are plenty of creative minds here, and it would be a shame if they couldn't meet and collaborate. Besides, socializing is fun and we get to know more about each other while sharing our common interests in design, art and architecture.

TY: Historically, many foreigners came to Japan to learn about architecture. Now, numerous people also travel to Japan to learn about the culinary arts. When I first began studying design, American influences were the trend. I find it fascinating to see how this has evolved.

KY: I believe the Internet has had a marked influence on this shift. Foreigners have always viewed the Japanese way of life as unique, and very different "in a good way." The quality and stature of architecture has also risen substantially from twenty years ago, when I lived in Japan.

TY: Do you attribute this to a higher level of standards practiced by Japanese architects?

KY: That has something to do with it, but the Japanese perception of architecture also contributes to this greater expectation. In Japan, most people live in apartments, especially those who live in a city. The concept

L & M Gallery Photo by Kelly Barrie

に住宅に対する考え方の違いがあるかと思います。私は大阪で個人住宅の設計に関わることがあります が、日本の大都市では、マンションなどの集合住宅に住む人がほとんどです。そのため、戸建て住宅を建てるということの重みが著名国、とくにアメリカとは大きく違っていて、自分たちが一生楽しむ家をつくるような思い入れで、我々建築家に仕事を依頼してくるのです。そのせいか、細かいディテールにもこだわる建築家の持ち味を十二分に発揮してもらいたいという気持ちの強いクライアントが多い。だからこそ、日本には名作の誉れ高い住宅作品がたくさんあります。アメリカのクライアントは、自分が住む家なのだから自分のアイデアを形にすることを望み、建築家にゆだねるようなことはしません。こんなところも、日本とアメリカの根本的な違う建築文化の違いを感じます。

KY: こちらこそ、どうぞよろしくお願いします。

TY: 私は建築家の安藤忠雄さんに感銘を受けて渡米したくちなんですが。クラパットさんはタイで生まれ、建築を学んだ後、東京大学で修士課程、博士号を取得されたというユニークな経歴の持ち主でいらっしゃいます。wHY大学のロスの事務所を設立されてからは私たちもたちまち親しく、たちまちに移転して以来、頻繁に物件を紹介していただき、私たちの多文化を理解しているクラパットさんだからこそ、さまざまなクライアントとのコミュニケーションもスムーズな気がします。世界を舞台に活動されているうえで、大きな強みの一つなのではないでしょうか？

KY: 安藤事務所では多くを学びました。建築はもちろん、クライアントとのコミュニケーションや社交の大切さ、気配りの大切さ、クライアントと"No Detail is Small"と同じように考えてきましたが、日本では、多くの経験を積むなか・・・。

建築とグラフィック

TY: 最近のデザイン書籍を見ていると、建築家とのコラボレーションによる建築物のグラフィックデザインに新しさを感じます。二次元のグラフィックが建築を表装するによって、三次元的、空間的な広がりをもつこのかな一番前はファッションのなかのグラフィックデザインが面白かったのですが、近年は建築グラフィックに興味を覚えます。

KY: 建築デザインのトレンドが比較的シンプルなものになってきてることは、理由の一つではないでしょうか？ 建築がシンプルだからこそ、グラフィックデザインを受け入れやすく、調和がとれやすくなっていると思うようにデザインされたグラフィックデザイナーとのコラボレーションを通して、空間が生きてくる。グラフィックデザインは、建築家にとっても非常に重要なことですから。

TY: 建築家の合田さんとのプロジェクトでは、合田さんは建築デザインだけを依頼されていたのにもかかわらず、元からあるグラフィックデザインへの興味という理由から、独断でTYDにデザインを頼んできたというケースがあり、が悪いという良い建築には良いグラフィックが不可欠だと、良いという彼は言っていました。グラフィックも妥協するには違いないし。

KY: グラフィックもそうですが、家具やアートなどすべての調和から選ぶなどのですよね。たとえば、TYDとクラパットさんの事務所で進めているポモナ・カレッジの芸術学部校舎のデザインもそうですが、トータルに考えるとしば日本重要に思えます。環境とグラフィックがその土地、使用者のライフスタイルにいかに溶け込むかが大切です。ボモナ・カレッジは、LEED(Leadership in Energy and Environmental Design)という建築物の環境配慮基準に基づいて、設計され、ライフスタイルと調和する建築デザインや未来のデザインを見るとき、クライアントさんの葉っぱの形に切り抜いた外壁のデザインを見るとき、大学の環境への配慮姿勢はもちろんですが、グラフィックが建築家というだけでなく一人の人間として、ものの見方や考え方が上手い建築に落とし込んでいるのだなと感じました。

KY: 環境に優しい建築は世界でもトップレベルです。それが日本にとっては20年も前から、日本の考え方やライフスタイルは良いい意味で異国でしたが、私の関わり方には興味がないのですかね？

TY: 日本人建築家のレベルが高いからですかね？

KY: もちろん、巨匠といわれる建築家の影響も大きいですが、日本人の建築、と

of someone building their own home is very different than it is in the States ...it's a huge step for someone to have a house built from the ground up in Japan. So Japanese people treat architecture like a special work of art. Therefore, they give complete trust to the architect and request little input regarding their personal preferences. The outcome of this trust is an architectural piece that is pure in a sense, a masterpiece of the architect without any influence from the client. In the States, the client usually has an idea of what they want and approaches the architect with a specific program or vision. This is one major difference between architecture in Japan and in the States.

TY: I recently read an architecture book and noticed how much the graphic design illustrating the architectural process has improved. Flat drawings were represented in three dimensional space, which offered a more comprehensive perspective and made them more interesting. While fashion and graphic design imagery used to be more intriguing than architectural renderings, the opposite now seems to be true.

KY: The trend in architecture is that the design is becoming more simple. This is largely due to what you say about the influence of graphic design within architecture, simple architecture coalesces with great graphic design. Everything you see in architectural space needs to be well designed and balanced.

TY: Yoshio Taniguchi was commissioned to redesign and construct an entire commercial building, but the client insisted on using old graphic design elements. Taniguchi knew that this was inconsistent, and was resistant to work on the project. He decided to hire us to design the graphics without telling the client, confident that when the client saw the new graphics harmonize with the architecture they would agree. Quite simply, good graphic design can complete good architecture.

KY: Yes, the graphic design can enhance a building...but color, furniture and art are also critical to the overall structure.

TY: I can't stress enough the importance of viewing design comprehensively. Our collaboration on the new Art Center at Pomona College is an excellent example. This building will be LEED (Leadership in Energy and Environmental Design) certified, which carries through to all aspects of the design. Your concept for the roof as an outline of a leaf expresses a deep connection between the building's message and architecture. It's important for the graphic design and architecture to merge just as subtly, and to support the overall theme.

KY: Using the shape of a leaf in an environmentally sound building may be a little cliche, but the message is still clear. I have to say, it was challenging to incorporate this natural shape into the design. From a distance, you won't be able to recognize that the roof is cut out in the shape of a leaf. But once you stand inside and look up, you will actually see a leaf with the sky behind it. It's easy to say that the building will be LEED certified, but to convey the feel of a LEED certified building is one of the biggest challenges for an architect.

TY: Kulapat, I look forward to working with you and wHY Architecture on the signage for the Pomona Arts Center, and to the building's future completion.

TY: Tamotsu Yagi
KY: Kulapat Yantrasast

クラパット・ヤントラサー タイバンコク生まれ、東京大学建築学部にて修士課程、および博士号を取得後、1996-2003年、安藤忠雄建築研究所にてさまざまな建築プロジェクトに関わる。2003年にwHY建築事務所を設立し、美術館の設計など、国境を問わず各国でプロジェクトを進行している。

KULAPAT YANTRASAST was born in Bangkok, Thailand. He graduated with a Masters Degree and a Ph.D. in Architecture from the University of Tokyo. Yantrasast worked in Japan as a close associate to Tadao Ando from 1996-2003. He co-founded wHY Architecture and Design in 2003. His firm's worldwide architectural projects include residential, retail, museum and gallery designs.

Photo by Kelly Barrie

L & M Gallery www.lmgallery.com

Architectural Graphics

09

THE FORUM BUILDING is located on Aoyama Street near the Harajuku District of Tokyo designed by Architect, Yoshio Taniguchi. This small office building has a pilotis design, which is unconventional for a building its size. TYD was commissioned to design the signage system for the building and since the architecture was simple, I kept the signage to a minimum to compliment its minimal and elegant design.

FORUM BUILDING

THE 500 COLOR PENCIL PROJECT by Felissimo was the ultimate project involving the process of "creative organization." I was asked to sort 500 colored pencils into 20 sets containing 25 pencils and design its packaging. Colored pencils were sorted and packaged by color group organized by tonal gradations.

HAL-CHAN MEMO Kuramata Shiro, in his inspirational and dream-like manner drew sketches inspired by his daughter, Halko. In memory of Shiro, Mrs. Kuramata wanted a personal book to give to his closest friends. The result was 50 handmade books, Hal-chan Memo. Most of the pages were printed in-house at TYD and assembled by hand. To incorporate one distinct feature of Shiro's designs into the book, the same purple color as the legs of Shiro's iconic *Miss Blanche* chair was used for the metal binding.

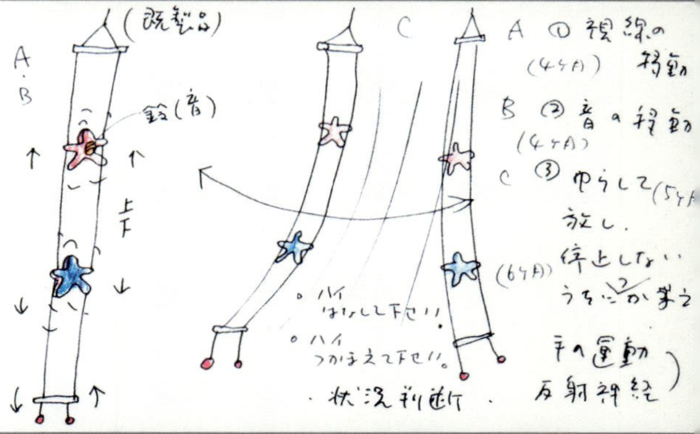

HAL-CHAN MEMO Shiro Kuramata's Sketch

FORUM BUILDING Entrance

FORUM BUILDING tokyo, japan
Signage system design | Architect: Yoshio Taniguchi

外装に使われた美しいステンレス素材を、ロゴタイプを投影するように カットして、サインに仕上げた。

To compliment the stainless steel panels used for the exterior of the building, I used the same material for the signage to maintain congruency. I chose the Gill Sans typeface which best suited the overall concept of the architecture.

NITTO tokyo, japan
Graphic identity design

500 COLORED PENCILS kobe, japan
Package design
Photo by Shuji Yoshida

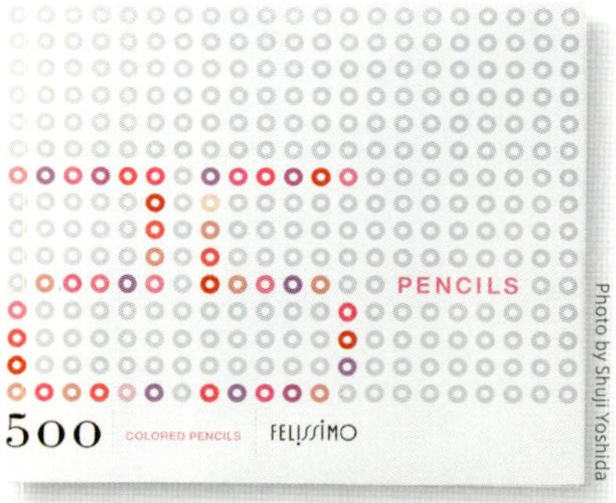

HAL-CHAN MEMO tokyo, japan
Book design

101 YEAR ANNIVERSARY WORKS - IN - PROGRESS FOR MIHOYA GLASS tokyo, japan
Chair design | Exhibition at: Axis Gallery
Curator: Masahiro Mihoya October 27 - November 8, 2009

FORUM BUILDING Exterior

フォーラム・ビルディング 青山通りに面した角地に、谷口吉生氏によって設計されました。青山通りを背にして、左側には吉村順三氏設計の青山タワービルがあり、右側には隈研吾氏設計の梅窓院へ続く竹林の参道の入り口があります。ビルは青山通りから歩道へと視線が抜けて、周辺の環境と一体となるように設計されており、1階のピロティ部分にエントランスがあります。TYDでは、今まで使用されたロゴタイプをバランス良く再調整。エントランス入口はステンレスの切り文字で、各プロセスモダングレーをベースカラーとし、サインはシンプルなデザインにしました。

500色の色鉛筆 今まで、多くかけてきたフェリシモのプロジェクトのなかで、一番気に入っている商品です。500色の色鉛筆には一本ずつに名前がついていて、明るい色から鮮やかな色、それと今までの色鉛筆では見たことのない色のバリエーションがあります。まるでパステルの色を使っているような感じがし、今まで黒い紙の上に描くことのなかったのですが、500色の色鉛筆を使うようになって黒い紙の上にもラフスケッチを描くことが多くなりました。

晴ちゃんメモ 躍るように描かれたスケッチ、故倉俣史朗氏が愛娘、晴子ちゃんに話しかけているかのように書かれた言葉。スケッチブックをめくっていくと、今までの倉俣氏の作品アイデアがここに生まれたのか、と思わせるようなスケッチの数々が、50冊限定でバインディングされすべて手作業で作成された本は、TYDのコピー機でオリジナルスケッチブックをコピーし、一つひとつ丁寧に折ってつくられました。代表作品である『ミスブランチ』の脚部分と同じ色のスパイラルワイヤーを特注し、倉俣さん、そして妻の美恵子さんの想いを閉じ込めました。

HAL-CHAN MEMO Detail
Photo by Shuji Yoshida

20 10

SHIRO KURAMATA and ETTORE SOTTSASS Exhibition Book Cover Shown in the Cropped Area

KURAMATA SHIRO ETTORE SOTTSASS

EXHIBITION "SHIRO KURAMATA and ETTORE SOTTSASS" tokyo, japan
Graphic design: Exhibition printed matter | Book design
Publisher: ADP 2010
Exhibition Director: Yasuko Seki
Exhibition at: 21_21 DESIGN SIGHT | Directors: Issey Miyake, Naoto Fukasawa, Taku Satoh | Architect: Tadao Ando

Photo by Shuji Yoshida

Exhibition

The Hal-chan Memo Book has a playful construction to bind the loose, french folded pages of the book. The outer cover was made from an ordinary envelope that we modified. For fun, we bound a paper bag into the book to store Hal-Chan's folded paper cranes.

表紙は、天地を切った厚紙の封筒でつくられたカバーに覆われている。最後のページにバッグを挟み込み、カバーを開かないためのハンドルがカバーから出てくるので、手持ちできる。The Hal-chan Memo Bookには、フレンチ製本されたページを束ねるための遊び心ある構造が施されている。外側のカバーは、通常の封筒を加工して作られた。楽しみのために、Hal-chanの折り紙の鶴を収納するためのペーパーバッグを本に綴じ込んだ。

MISS BLANCHE The *Miss Blanche* chair designed by Shiro Kuramata was inspired by the corsage worn by the character Blanche DuBois, in Tennessee Williams' play *'A Streetcar Named Desire.'* The chair embodies the poetic and dream-like nature of Kuramata's designs. *Miss Blanche* chair went into limited production and only 56 were made. Originally designed for Kagu Tokyo Designer's Week in 1988, the *Miss Blanche* chair is considered Kuramata's most iconic masterpiece.

「ミス・ブランチ」は倉俣史朗氏の代表作のひとつで、コンテンポラリーで洗練されたデザインで、12ヶ月間、スタジオ内の自然光の入る所に置いて、最高の光が差し込むのを待った。オフィスで何カットも撮影し、そのなかで一番気に入ったこのカットを部分拡大して、ポスターと本の表紙に展開した。Shiro Kuramata's iconic *Miss Blanche* chair was chosen for the cover image of the *Shiro Kuramata Ettore Sottsass* exhibition book. Using a digital camera, I took photographs and chose this image which was also used for the exhibition poster.

Recent Projects

SHIRO KURAMATA and ETTORE SOTTSASS EXHIBITION

I was fortunate to have met and worked with Shiro Kuramata, who later became a good friend of mine. We collaborated on numerous projects such as the Esprit Hong Kong Store, Esprit House Tokyo as well as many other interior design projects in Asia. I then met Ettore Sottsass during the Esprit collaborative eyewear project and remember having to frequently travel to Milan. The Shiro Kuramata and Ettore Sottsass exhibition at the 21_21 DESIGN SIGHT brought back old memories and reconnected friends. I received an email from Yasuko Seki, the exhibition director, which started this exciting project and shortly after, I was sitting with Issey Miyake, the exhibition planner at the first meeting with Mieko Kuramata, the wife of Shiro.

TOMORROWLAND

is a Japanese fashion company and brand founded by Hiroyuki Sasaki in 1978, with many locations throughout Japan. I met Mr. Sasaki 35 years ago through a friend of mine and was amazed that the company and brand were under the same name, which is something very rare in Japan. Mr. Sasaki wanted an understated and timeless logo, one that could be used in harmony with the image of the other fashion brands.

Photo by Masaya Yoshimura

TOMORROWLAND
SUPER A MARKET

「倉俣史朗とエットレ・ソットサス」展　私は、エスプリのダグと通じて倉俣史朗氏とずいぶん多くのプロジェクトに協働することができました。エスプリ香港店をはじめ、アジア地区のインテリアデザインやエスプリハウス東京など、数えただけでもいくつもあります。ソットサス氏とは、彼がエスプリのアイウェアの開発したことをきっかけに、ヨーロッパ各地のエスプリストアのインテリアデザインを担当することになり、ミラノとサンフランシスコを何度も往復しました。今回の21_21 DESIGN SIGHTでのプロジェクトは、本展も参加することになった関康子さんの一通のメールから、幸運にも参加することができました。東京のキックオフミーティングでは、久しぶりに三宅一生氏をはじめ懐かしい友人と会いすることができ、また倉俣美恵子夫人や晴子さん、本展プロジェクトに関わる大勢の方と再会できました。会期中の3月11日には東日本大震災があり、影響もありましたが7月18日、無事終了しました。株式会社トゥモローランド　創業者である佐々木啓之氏との出会いは約35年前になります。友人からの紹介でした。この時からすでに佐々木さんは株式会社名もトゥモローランドのCIと各ブランドのアイデンティティについて考えておられました。トゥモローランドが自身の会社名と同じ、「Tomorrowland」でブランド名を統一したこととはとても新でした。ロゴ制作を打合せの際に、佐々木さんがよく言われていた「ロゴはできる限りシンプルに。なぜなら優美で気品あるものの本質は、いつも純真で単純なものであるから」ということを、私はラフも覚えています。

Photo by Kozo Takayama

SUPER A MARKET Interior

ETTORE SOTTSASS Poster

SHIRO KURAMATA and ETTORE SOTTSASS Exhibition Book

Photo by Shuji Yoshida

1981年、アクシスのオープニングで行われたエットレ・ソットサス展で、このときはじめてソットサスと出会い、B1のポスターをデザインした。

The Axis building opening in 1980 was celebrated with the Ettore Sottsass exhibition, which took place on the top floor gallery space. This is the poster I designed in 1981 for the exhibition.

SUPER A MARKET BY TOMORROWLAND
tokyo, japan
Graphic identity design

SUPER A MARKET Packaging Tape

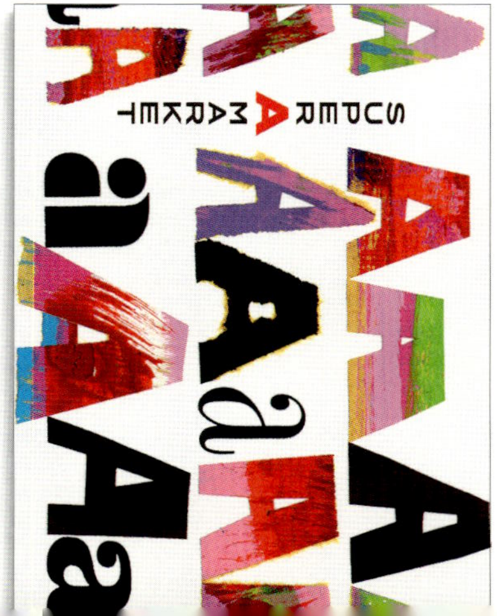

SUPER A MARKET Store Sign

SUPER A MARKET is a select shop, bar and restaurant owned by Tomorrowland, located in Aoyama, Japan. Having designed the Tomorrowland logo 30 years ago, Mr. Sasaki, the owner of the company came to me to develop the graphic identity for the new store, designed by Wonderwall. During the time of the opening, the disastrous Earthquake struck Japan. To contribute to the relief effort, Tomorrowland's designers made pins to raise money for this cause.

スーパー・A・マーケット 佐々木啓之氏の依頼でスタートしたこのプロジェクトは、既存の青山の店内を改装し、衣・食・住すべてを楽しめる新空間へと生まれ変わらせる、そんなショップのグラフィックデザインをしました。ネーミングは佐々木さんとのディナーの際に、グリエイティブな会話のやり取りから決定。インテリアデザインはワンダーウォールの片山正通氏が担当。東日本大震災の発生後、募金したカスタマーに、トゥモローランドと縁のある人たちがデザインしたバッジをプレゼントするなど、コミュニティを大切にする姿勢は佐々木さんの意志そのものだといいます。

wHY Architecture

POMONA COLLEGE The signage design project for the Pomona College Studio Art Hall, in Pomona, California was commissioned to us by wHY Architecture located in Culver City, California. The building's design represents an integrated vision of the arts and the environment at Pomona College, providing the campus with an inspiring indoor and outdoor space for the teaching and expression of art, while serving as an example of environmentally conscious design. The building design maximizes natural light and ventilation while it minimizes energy usage, utilizing both photovoltaic and solar hot water panels to create energy on site, all of which contributes to its LEED Gold standing.

ESTEROS DEL IBERA is a collaborative book project that Doug Tompkins and I are currently working on. Doug and I have collaborated on many nature conservation books in the past and this one is about the Ibera Wetlands (in Spanish: *Eteros del Ibera*) a stunning natural reserve with an immense array of wildlife in the Northeast region of Argentina. The Ibera Wetlands are the second largest wetlands in the world and is also one of the most important fresh water reservoirs in the continent. Doug is currently dedicated to turning this beautiful natural reserve into a protected National park.

Photo Credit:
Roberto Carra P202 P203 P204 P205 P206 P207 P208 P211 P212 P214 P215
Stephen Rahn P218 P222 P223
Shuji Yoshida P236 P237
Stefano Massei P229

ポモナ・カレッジ ロサンゼルス郊外のクレアモントにキャンパスを置く、小規模校ポモナ・カレッジのサイネージ計画。wHYアーキテクトより推薦を受け、コラボレーションというかたちで現在進行中のプロジェクトです。建築に使用されている材料や、システムすべてを環境問題に対応させ、現段階でLEEDのゴールドを得ています。アルゼンチンに位置するイベラ湿地帯は世界で2番目に広大な湿地帯であり、書籍プロジェクト。

イベラ湿地帯 ダグラス・トンプキンス氏と共同で現在製作しているイベラ湿地帯についての書籍プロジェクト。アルゼンチンに位置するイベラ湿地帯は世界で2番目に広大な湿地帯であり、さらなる自然環境保護のために保護区と認定されています。ダグが発起人となり、この一帯を国立公園として認定させるべく、このプロジェクトがスタートしました。

Photo by Juan Ramon Diaz Colodrero

タイムラインの年号は改正の都合で、多少前後している場合もあります。
Few entries in the timeline are placed out of sequence as they are grouped by content.

When we were working on the Super A Market project, we received many illustrations of the letter 'A' by Fabrice Moreau to incorporate into our graphic designs. Every "A" had so much character that we chose to use them all. The collage was applied to the multipurpose paper tape. The tape was designed to be ripped and used to seal the package systems and also functioned as a decorative element.

スーパー・A・マーケットのグラフィックデザインを進めるとき、トゥモローランドからたくさんのファブリス・モーロー氏の「A」のイラストが届いたことに。どの「A」をみてもキャラクターがあるため、パッケージをとめるための紙ステッカーとして使うことに。紙ステッカーは手で切ってちぎれるようにして、使用するようにデザインしました。

TAMOTSU YAGI BIOGRAPHY

Tamotsu Yagi was born in 1949 in Kobe, Japan. He worked for a multidisciplinary design firm in Tokyo for eighteen years, and moved to California in 1984 when he was named Art Director for the San Francisco-based clothing company Esprit. Here, Yagi was in charge of all aspects of visual presentation and image design, from advertising and catalogues, to packaging, product identification and store graphics. He soon created the iconic and internationally recognized "Esprit Graphic Look," which led the company to win the AIGA's (American Institute of Graphic Arts) Design Leadership Award in 1986. In 1990, Yagi was chosen to be a member of the prestigious AGI (Alliance Graphique International), and was one of the youngest inductees in its history. The following year he ventured out on his own to establish Tamotsu Yagi Design, an independent multidisciplinary studio based in San Francisco. Within three years, Yagi received the Clio Award for the Tribù perfume bottle he designed for Benetton. One year later, Yagi was honored by the induction of over 100 examples of his work into the permanent collection of the San Francisco Museum of Modern Art. Select works from this collection were also featured in a special exhibit at the grand opening of the SF MoMA building in 1995.

Yagi's achievements and awards stem from his unique approach to design, and his love and respect for nature. His special skills, values and cultural sensitivity create the foundation for his acclaimed career. Yagi's design work is a singular fusion of East and West, an uncommon blend of Japanese sensibilities and California vitality that is both studied and spontaneous. Yagi makes extensive use of visual symbols which have traditionally had a greater importance in the East, and intuitively applies this cultural understanding to create designs that transcend language in their ability to communicate ideas. He also extends the borders of media in search of new possibilities by relying on his considerable knowledge of historically significant precedents in all areas of design. Through his lens, colors, shapes and textures derived from nature are synthesized to create new forms. By his hand, new applications of old techniques create extraordinary objects from ordinary materials.

Tamotsu Yagi Design is currently based in Venice, California. The studio continues to work on an eclectic array of design projects worldwide. The firm's underlying inspiration and commitment to creating ecologically responsible products is reflected in their motto, "Good design is in the nature of things."

TYD Client List
Art Design Publishing
Akebono
Andersen Bakery
Andersen Consultant
Anderson
Angel Spine
Apple
AT Company
Axis
Bardessono Hotel
Be Organic
Benetton Cosmetic
Bikosha
Bornelund
Bridgestone Sports
C3
Callaway Editions
Casa Brutus
Casappo and Associates
Center for Ecoliteracy
Chaya
Citrus Notes
Clio Blue Japan
Commercial Arts Institute
Cool Earth
Coup De Chance
Cross Plus
Daihatsu
Danskin
Dentsu
Delica r-f-1
Delitate
Descente
Doubles Edition
Dressterior
en Arts
Episteme
Esprit
Eugene & Associates
Fabrica
Familiar
Feliciti
Felissimo
Fila
Fish Dance
Flaart
Fontanta
Forum Building
Foundation Beyeler
Foundation For Deep Ecology
Four Seasons Hotel Tokyo at Marunouchi
Grand Hyatt Tokyo
Hakuhodo
Hata Museum
Hamano Institute
Heibonsha Publishing
Henri Charpentier
Hiroshima City Naka Incineration Plant
Hollywood Ranch Market
Hype Associates
Inax
Index
Indivi
Indivi By A/T
Indivi Home/Life
Intel
Ira-Hiti
Itochu
Its' Demo
Ja-Unep
Japonesque
Kengo Kuma & Associates
Kenzo Estate

Photo by Stefano Massei

Keplinger Wines
Kirin Beer
Kisara
Kluwer Academic Publishing
Kurakawa Masayuki Architect
Kuramata Design Office
Kyo
Kyoto Art Council
Kyuryudo Art Publishing
Laune
Lawson
Lecien
Libroport
Magazine House
Mandarina Duck Japan
Marcal
Maruni Mokko
Mazda
Mihoya Glass
Moc
Nakagawa Shoten
Nara Sports
NeXT
Next Door
Nissha Printing Company
Nitto
Niwaka
Nokia
Obrero
Onward
Opaque
Opaque Ginza
Pacific Art & Design Consultants
Palm
Pen Magazine
Pixar
Pomona College
Renihue
Rikuyo-Sha Publishing
Robundo Publishing Company
Rockfield
Rohto
Sakurano Department Store
San Francisco Museum of Modern Art
Shiseido
Shogakukan
Showa-Sangyo
Sign
Space & Device Technology
Super A Market
Swire Properties
Synergy
Takaki Bakery
Takeo Kikuchi
The Cuisine Magazine Publishing
The David Brower Center
The Ecoforestry Institute
The Elmwood institute
The Opposite House
The Prime Minister Of Japan
The Tokyo Club
Tokio Hata
Tomorrowland
Tres Demure
United Colors of Benetton
Untitled
Urasenke Foundation
Vinyasa
Voicemail
Waraku
wHY Architecture
World
Yoshio Taniguchi and Associates
21_21 Design Sight
40 Degrees South

INDEX

Photo by Stefano Massei

Anodizing is an electrolytic process most commonly applied to aluminum to create a layer of aluminum oxide. This layer is integrated with the aluminum making the surface very durable and resistant to corrosion. A secondary process can be performed where dyes can be used to add color.

アナダイズ加工 アルミに陽極処理を加えて酸化皮膜を生じさせ、銀色のアルミ質に色を付ける加工技術で、日本の理研が開発した手法。塗料を使わず化学反応による彩色方法のため、最大限の軽量化を求められるアウトドア製品や自動車のパーツなどの彩色に用いられる。
P40

Roberto Carra Born Parma, Italy. Carra is an internationally renowned photographer, graphic designer and art director. He began his career as a graphic designer for *L'Uomo Vogue* magazine and later became an art director. His interest then turned to still life photography and later freelanced for top fashion companies and fashion magazines in Europe. Then in 1982, he became the in-house still life photographer for Esprit, an apparel company based in San Francisco. He now works on environmental related works, lifestyle documentation and the possibilities of digital imaging.

ロベルト・カーラ イタリア、パルマ生まれのフォトグラファー、グラフィックデザイナー、アートディレクター。イタリアの『ルオモヴォーグ』マガジンのグラフィックデザイナーを経て、アートディレクターに就任。その後、フリーランスのファッションフォトグラファーとして、ヨーロッパを中心に雑誌やファッションブランドの世界で活躍。1982年には、エスプリのインハウスフォトグラファーに就任し、スチルライフ写真を中心に撮影、エスプリ本社のあるサンフランシスコに移住。現在、環境問題に着目し、ドキュメンタリー写真などを制作中。
P41

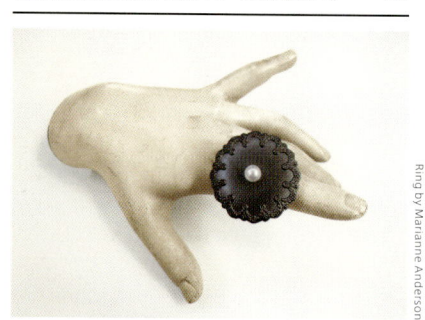

Ring by Marianne Anderson

Chariots on Fire Created in 2006 by two friends Ritz Yagi and Oriana Reich who met as graphic design students at Central Saint Martins in London in 2000. They reconnected after graduating with a shared passion for collecting and sharing special finds from travels. Chariots on Fire's collection of vintage and contemporary jewelry focuses on design and craftsmanship, many of which are handmade edition pieces.

チャリオッツ・オン・ファイアー 2006年創立。ヴィンテージやコンテンポラリージュエリーを扱うオンラインショップ。オーナーである八木理都子とオリアナ・レイチは、ロンドン芸術大学セントラル・セントマーチンズ・カレッジ・オブ・アート・アンド・デザインで出会い、ともに2000年に卒業。ハンドメイドのモノ、作家による少量生産の作品を取り扱う。サンフランシスコに、ジャン・プルーヴェなどの家具を什器として使用した、予約制のショップを創立。最近では、香港のセレクトショップ「カポック」、2011年8月にはアボット・キニーにある和のコンテンポラリーギャラリー「トータス」でもポップアップショップを開催する。
www.chariotsonfire.com
P22-23

Chez Panisse Founded in 1971 by Alice Waters and a group of friends in Berkeley, California. The restaurant was named after a character (Honoré Panisse) in Marcel Pagnol's 1930s movie, as an homage to the sentiment, informality and comedy of the film. Alice and Chez Panisse believe that the best tasting food comes from ingredients that are grown locally, organically and harvested in methods that are ecologically sound. The search for the freshest seasonal ingredients determine the restaurant's cuisine. In doing so, the restaurant and local suppliers have developed a close networking relationship. Through this philosophy, Chez Panisse is known to be a pioneer of the "California Cuisine" movement and has inspired many chefs worldwide. They will be celebrating their 40th anniversary in 2011.

シェ・パニース 1971年創立し、40周年を迎えたカリフォルニア・バークレーにあるレストラン。カリフォルニア料理の発祥の地ともいわれ、生態学的に健全に育てられた食材、オーガニック食材のみを使った料理を出すことで、その名前を全米に知られる。マルセル・パニョル監督が1930年代に製作した三部作「マリウス」「ファニー」「セザー」に出てくる初老の紳士「パニース」が店名の由来。「シェ・パニース」が独特なレストランである要因の一つは、アラカルト・メニューが存在しないということ。毎夜、出されるものはフィックスされたコース一つのみで、店を訪れる顧客全員が、同じコースを食す。創設者であり、カリフォルニア・キュイジーヌの母としても知られるアリス・ウォーターズは、30年以上前からオーガニック料理をつくり続け、スローフード、地産地消の価値を訴えてきた女性で、アメリカでは盤石の信頼を確立している。
www.chezpanisse.com
P224

Engraving is the art and technique of incising grooves or designs into a usually hard, flat surface for printing. Modern day engraving dates back to the 1430s and was discovered by old German master printers, however engraving for decorative purposes dates back to the first century AD.

エングレービング 銅版を写真製版やグレーバーで彫刻し、インクを詰めて紙に転写する1430年代にドイツで生まれた印刷技法で、熟練した高度な技が必要とされる。細かい線や文字などの再現性がよく、最高級印刷の分類に属する。世界の王室が愛用し、企業でも信頼の証としても採用され、最近では偽造防止の観点からも注目を浴び、ブランドのタグなど、用途はさまざま。印字部分が盛り上がるという特徴もある。
P79

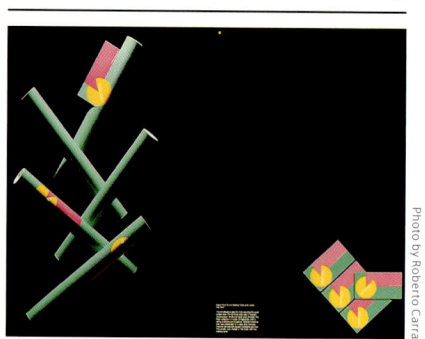

Photo by Roberto Carra

Esprit: The Comprehensive Design Principle was published in 1989. When the *Esprit's Graphic Work 1984-1986* debuted as a promotional book, it was very well received by the public and multiple publishers showed interest in having it published. Douglas R. Tompkins, the owner of Esprit, decided to create a new and improved book to publish with additional fashion and architectural information as well as photographs taken by in-house still life photographer, Roberto Carra. This book revealed Esprit's design principle and the products that reflect Esprit's visual communication and corporate image. The 300 page book was later published in Japan by Robundo and printed by Nissha Printing Co.

『エスプリ：コンプリヘンシブ・デザイン・プリンシブル』1984年〜1986年のファッションブランド、エスプリのビジュアルコミュニケーションやブランディングにかかせないデザイン思想と実践をまとめたもの。本書の発行目的はプロモーションだけでなく、ミュージアムやデザイン学校のライブラリーに入れて、デザインの可能性を伝えるため。ある日、この本を見た3つの出版社から再編集して出版したいという依頼を受けた。世界中のエスプリのインテリアと建築を加えて出版したものが『Esprit : The Comprehensive Design Principle』。300ページオールカラーのこの本は、1989年、当時￥15,000で、日本で出版販売され、完売した。
P132-13

Lucio Fontana Born Rosario, Argentina, 1899-1968. Fontana was an Italian-Argentinian painter and sculptor. He was best known as the founder of *Spatialism* and his involvement with the *Arte Povera* movement. He is well known for this work involving cutting the surface of monochromatic canvasses.

ルーチョ・フォンタナ 1899年〜1968年 20世紀のイタリアの美術家、彫刻家、画家。フォンタナの代表作品は、キャンバスをペイントするのではなく、ナイフで切り裂くという手法によるもの。
P34

Mauro Giaconi Born Buenos Aires, Argentina, 1977. Giaconi studied Fine Arts at the National School of Fine Arts *Prilidiano Pueyrredon* beginning in 1998. After his studies, he dedicated his career to the arts as well as restoring murals and buildings

マルオ・ジアコーニ 1977年 アルゼンチンのブエノスアイレス生まれのアーティスト。1996年にブエノスアイレス大学にて建築を学んだ後、1998年にP・プエレドン芸術大学に進学、2007年にはロンドン芸術大学セントラル・セントマーチンズ・カレッジ・オブ・アート・アンド・デザインを卒業。
www.maurogiaconi.com.ar
P188-189

International Klein Blue Discovered in 1957 by French Aritisit Yves Klein 1928-1962. Klein was a leading member of the French artistic movement of *Nouveau Réalisme* and a pioneer in the development of performance, minimal and pop art. The Klein blue's visual impact comes from the heavy use of Ultramarine, a blue pigment. He created this color to best represent the concepts he wished to convey as an artist. An interesting fact about the International Klein Blue is that it is outside the range of the colors shown on computer monitors.

インターナショナル・クライン・ブルー フランスのアーティスト、イヴ・クライン（1934年〜1991年）が好んで用いた青い顔料。クラインは単品の作品を制作するモノクロニズムを代表するフランスの画家。青色を宇宙の神秘的なエネルギーに通ずるもっとも非物質的かつ抽象的な色として重用し、1957年に自らの理想的な染料を開発、特許を取得。ミラノで「イヴ・クライン・モノクロームの提案、ブルーの時代」のタイトルで行なわれた個展で、この染料をキャンバス一面に塗布した青色の絵画の作品群を発表した。また海綿でつくったレリーフや彫刻にこの色を染み込ませ青色にした作品も発表している。
www.international-klein-blue.com
P110

Photo by Hiroo Namiki

Anodizing: Corona Kogyo Corporation コロナ工業株式会社 www.coronakogyo.co.jp　Engraving: Digital Engraving デジタルエングレービング www.digitalengraving.com　Chez Panisse: Edible Schoolyard www.edibleschoolyard.org　*Menus for Chez Panisse*: ISBN 978-1-61689-029-2　Esprit: The Comprehensive Design Principle Tamotsu Yagi Design 八木保デザイン www.yagidesign.com　International Klein Blue: NADiff ナディッフギャラリー www.nadiff.com

Masatoshi Izumi Born in Kagawa, Japan, 1938. Masatoshi was born into a family of stone sculptors. The Masatoshi family have been crafting traditional stone sculptures and have passed on the technique from generation to generation. In 1964, he co-founded the Stone Atelier in the small town of Mure, Kanagawa Prefecture. He later met Isamu Noguchi, an artist who also on occasion worked with stone and they have collaborated together. Their collaboration was instrumental in popularizing stone art worldwide.

和泉 正敏 1938年 香川県生まれ。代々続く石工の家に生まれた和泉正敏は、彫刻家イサム・ノグチのパートナーとして彼の作品制作に協力してきた。庵治石の産地として知られている牟礼にアトリエを構え、世界中から集められたさまざまな石材を使って数多くの作品を制作。
www.izumi-stoneworks.com P30-31

Steve Jobs Born, San Francisco, California, USA, 1955. Jobs is the co-founder and former CEO of Apple Inc. He is a business magnate, inventor and electronics guru. Jobs left Apple in 1985 and started NeXT, a computer platform development company. He later returned to Apple in 1996 with immense success. Thoughout his career, he served as chief executive of Pixar Animation Studios and also became a member of the board of directors of The Walt Disney Company.

スティーブ・ジョブズ 1955年生まれ。スティーブ・ウォズニアック、ロン・ウェイン、マイク・マークラらともに、商用パーソナルコンピュータで成功を収めたアップルの共同設立者の一人。その圧倒的なカリスマ性から、発言や行動が常に注目を集め続ける。1985年退職後、1996年にはアップルへの復帰を果たした。
www.apple.com/pr/bios/steve-jobs.html P130-147

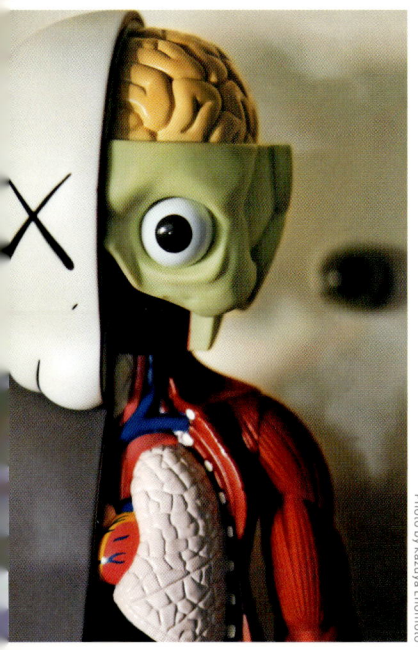

KAWS Born New Jersey, USA, 1974. KAWS grew up under the name Brian Donnelly in New Jersey and graduated from the school of Visual Arts in New York. Growing up in New Jersey, he was known for his graffiti art and later moved to New York in the 1990. Today he is known for his limited edition vinyl toys and collaboration with a variety of companies such as Comme des Garçons, BAPE and Dos Equis Beer. He has also worked on Walt Disney's *101 Dalmatians* as an animator.

カウス (本名、ブライアン・ドネリー) 1974年ニュージャージー生まれのアーティスト。ニューヨークのビジュアルアーツでファインアートを専攻し、90年代にはグラフィティアーティストとしてニューヨークで活動。96年に大学を卒業後、ディズニーで背景を描くフリーランスアニメイターとして『101匹ワンちゃんシリーズ』などを担当。コム・デ・ギャルソン、ア・ベイシング・エイプなどのファッションブランドとのコラボレーションも積極的に行ない、上記写真のようなフィギュアも、自身のブランド『オリジナル・フェイク』として発表している。
www.kawsone.com P151

Artwork by Linda Connor & courtesy of Lick Observatory Plate Archive

the school lunch initiative
+ dosa
fundraiser
winter 2005

Christina Kim Born Seoul, South Korea. Christina moved to Los Angeles with her family when she was 15 years old. With a background in fine arts, her clothing company, Dosa is in itself an ongoing, personal project driven by her life philosophies. With Dosa, Christina has created a platform to recognize global artisans for their craft and connect with them on a human level. Her long lasting garments are colorful and considered. Christina has also been involved in numerous special projects including installations in Bologna, Italy and fundraising projects with the Chez Panisse foundation.

クリスティーナ・キム ソウル生まれ。「ドーサ」は、15歳で渡米したキムが、母親と1984年にロサンゼルスで開業したファッションブランド。半年以上を旅に出、各土地の文化から得たインスピレーションを取り入れ、その土地の人とともに洋服や小物をつくり出す。ファッション以外にも興味のあることには果敢に取り組んでおり、インスタレーションの展示をメキシコのオアハカやイタリアのボローニャで行なっている。ベルリン映画祭のために現地に赴き、古い映画のポスターを加工してつくった大きな緞帳を制作した。現代の消費社会に対しても、ライフスタイルやアパレル業界の新しい取り組み方法を提言している。
www.dosainc.com P224-225

Photo by Kazuya Enomoto

Photo by Stefano Massei

Shiro Kuramata Born Tokyo, Japan 1934-1991. Kuramata was most recognized as a member of Memphis, the Italian design group that was based in Milan and founded by Ettore Sottsass in 1981. During the 70s and 80s, he experimented with the possibilities of new technologies of acrylic, glass, aluminum and steel mesh. One of the most famous pieces he designed was the *Miss Blanche* chair. Its acrylic body was embedded with red artificial roses and the legs were constructed of purple anodized aluminum tubes.

倉俣 史朗 1934年～1991年 東京生まれ。インテリアデザイナー。1981年、エットレ・ソットサスがはじめたミラノ発デザインプロジェクト「メンフィス」に参加。代表作品は、バラの造花が透明なアクリル樹脂に埋め込まれ、紫色にアナダイズ加工されたアルミ脚のついた椅子「ミス・ブランチ」などがある。欧米の追随に陥らず日本的な形態に頼らずでもない日本固有の美意識を感じるデザインによって、フランス文化省文化勲章を受章するなど、国際的に評価を得した。写真は、1989年にデザインされ、2008年に数量限定でイッセイ・ミヤケから発売された香水瓶、L'Eau D'Issey。 P178

Masayuki Kurokawa Born Kanagawa, Japan, 1937. Kurokawa is an architect and product designer. He completed doctoral courses at Waseda University's Graduate School of Architecture. In 1967, he established Kurokawa Masayuki Architect Studio and received many major awards in his field. Many of his works are a part of the permanent collection at The Denver Art Museum and the Metropolitan Museum of Art. His most popular GOM series is a part of the collection at the Museum of Modern Art in New York. He is also the director of nextmaruni, a Japanese wood furniture manufacturer.

黒川 雅之 1937年 愛知県名古屋市生まれの建築家・プロダクトデザイナー。株式会社黒川雅之建築設計事務所、物学研究会、デザイントープなどを主宰。1979年、インダストリアルデザインの代表作「GOMシリーズ」がニューヨーク近代美術館の永久コレクションに選ばれる。
www.k-system.net P33

LEED Stands for, Leadership in Energy and Environmental Design and is a green building certification system. It was developed by the USGB and provides building owners guidelines for a green building design and its construction.

LEED (Leadership in Energy and Environmental Design) : USGBC (米国グリーンビルディング協議会)からなる組織で、建築物が環境改善にどのように貢献しているかの指標を明確にし、それに基づいて対象建築物の点数をつけて評価を行なう。各建築物の環境面でのマイナス要因を縮小する取り組みを、評価・公表することで、省エネ対策の普及を目指し、かつ評価されたビルの経済的効果や、ビルで働く人々や地域住民の利益にも貢献することを狙い、認定制度を開始した。認定建築物のなかにはレンゾ・ピアノによるアカデミー・オブ・サイエンスなどがある。
www.usgbc.org/LEED P65

Artwork by Alan Kitching

Letterpress is a process of relief printing where raised letters or surfaces pick up ink from a roller and is impressed onto paper. This method was used by Johannes Gutenburg in the mid-15th century making it the oldest form of printing. This style of printing was considered the standard form of printing from the mid-15th century until the 19th century.

レタープレス 欧州、米国での活版印刷の呼び名。ハンコのような出っぱりのある凸版が使用され、そこにインクを付け、紙をのせ上から圧力をかけて紙にインクを転写する印刷方式。活版印刷は文字の一つひとつが個別の活字でできており、文字を差し換えたり、印刷が終わった後にバラバラに戻して新たに別の版を組むことができるので、英語では「movabletype」と呼ばれている。写真の木版で刷られたポスターはアラン・キッチングによるもの。 P213

Masatoshi Izumi: The Isamu Noguchi Garden Museum Japan イサムノグチ庭園美術館 www.isamunoguchi.or.jp KAWS: Original Fake オリジナルフェイク www.original-fake.com Masayuki Kurokawa: K-System 黒川 雅之 www.k-system.net Letter Press: Julie Holcomb ジュリー・ホルカム www.julieholcombprinters.com

Artwork by Bunya Enomoto

Richard Long Born Bristol, England, 1945. Long is a sculptor, photographer, painter and land artist. From 1962-1965, he studied at the West of England College of Art and from 1966-1968, he studied at St. Martin's School of Art. Shortly after his studies, he became associated with the emergence of land art. He compiles large and small pieces of stone, drift wood and sand, found in nature to create shapes and forms. The above logo is his name in Japanese, designed by Fumiya Enomoto for the Richard Long exhibition at the Century Cultural Foundation in 1983. He continues to live and work in Bristol, England.

リチャード・ロング 1945年生まれ。イギリスの彫刻家・美術家。ランドアートに分類される作品を数多く発表。1960年代から、画廊や美術館など場所に束縛されない、自然を舞台とした作品を発表する。作品は自然を探索中に石を並べて写真を撮ったり、そのときの歩行記録を基に制作される。採集した石をギャラリーに幾何学的に配置する作品も多い。採集した石は切ったり削ったりはせず、そのままの状態で用いる。歩行場所は、当初はイギリス国内であったが、やがて世界各地の辺境にまで広がる。作品は、自然への干渉を最小限に抑えている点で際立っており、作品をつくるきっかけは、美術学校にあるような粘土や石膏といった素材ではなく、ありのままの自然に着目したことにある。
www.richardlong.org P183

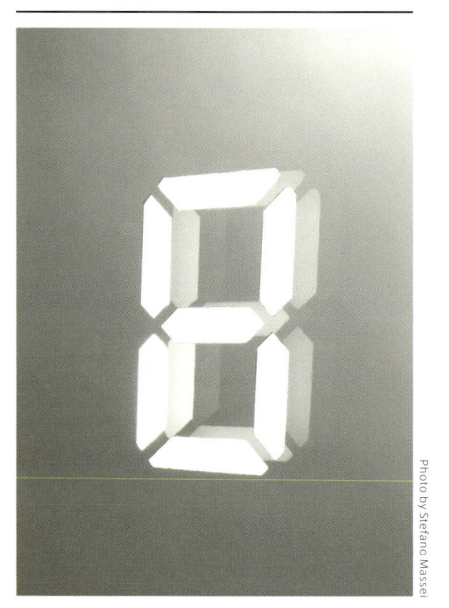

Miyajima Tatsuo Born Tokyo, Japan, 1957. Tatsuo is an installation artist. Although much of his works consist of perpetual digital counters, his works of art reflect humanist ideas and Buddhist philiosophies. Pictured is a close up detail of a digital counter of a larger art piece called Changing Time with Changing Self No.27-W.

宮島 達男 1957年 東京生まれ。デジタルテクノロジーを駆使し、デジタル表示による時計を連想させるインスタレーションの作品などが多く、発光ダイオード(LED)を使用したデジタルカウンターなどLEDの作品を特徴とし、仏教的思想に基づいて作品を制作する。また、コンピュータグラフィックス、ビデオなどを使用した作品も手がけている。作品「Changing Time with Changing Self No.27–W」は、94 x 94 x 4.8cmの鏡に、40のデジタルカウンターが止まることなくカウントダウンを繰り返していく数字を刻んでいる作品。 P191

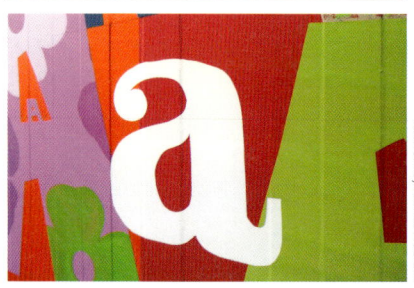

Artwork by Fabrice Moureau

Fabrice Moureau Born Vallée de la Loire, France, 1962. Moureau studied graphic design, exhibition display design and water color painting at École de l'Union Centrale des Arts Décoratifs from 1981-1984. He also traveled around the world documenting folk culture of various countries including Japan. In his paintings, he captures the scenes of historic architecture, castles, gardens, plants and city streets as light shines upon them. He has been commissioned to create illustrations for Hermés and most recently created artwork (pictured above), for the fashion brand, Tomorrowland's new boutique shop, Super A Market in Aoyama, Japan.

ファブリス・モアロー 1962年フランス・ロワール地方ブロワ生まれのアーティスト。1981年~84年、国立美術専門学校(Ecole National Superienne)で、グラフィックデザイン、エキジビジョンディスプレイ、水彩画を学ぶ。日本をはじめ世界各地を旅し、民族文化の記録をスケッチブックに残した。ファブリスは、造形が深い建築遺産や城や庭園、植物や街の路地など、その風景のなかで光が織りなす繊細な表情を水彩画によって表現する。日本初のエキジビションではパリのさまざまな屋根を描いた。トタンや石づくり、瓦屋根など、それぞれの素材が混じり合う風景をグレーとベージュの優しいコントラストで表現。パリの意外な色彩と印象、これも真のパリの姿でもある。今回一緒にトゥモローランドのスーパーAマーケットのプロジェクトに参加した。 P245

Charlotte Perriand Born Paris, France, 1903 - 1999. Perriand studied at the École de l'Union Centrale des Arts Décoratifs. She was recognized by critics at the early age of 24 for her Bar Under the Roof furniture designs. Throughout her career, Perriand collaborated with many renowned designers such as Pierre Jeanneret, Jean Prouvé and Le Corbusier.

シャルロット・ペリアン 1903年~1999年 フランス、パリ生まれのデザイナー。パリの装飾美術連学校を卒業後、自らアトリエを構える。24歳のときにサロン・トートヌンヌに出品した「屋根裏のバー」が認められ、ル・コルビュジエのアトリエに入る。独立後もル・コルビュジエ、ピエール・ジャンヌレ、ジャン・プルーヴェらと良好な関係を維持。1940年には、日本の商工省が輸出工芸指導の装飾美術顧問として招聘されて来日。日本の家具にも多大な影響を受けると同時に日本家具インダストリアルデザインにも影響を与える。 P152-153

Renzo Piano Born Genoa, Italy, 1937. Piano was the 1998 laureate of The Pritzker Architecture Prize, the most honorable award an architect can receive. It's known to be the Nobel Prize of architecture. His grandfather, father, four uncles and brother were all contractors but Renzo decided to become an architect. He graduated from the Politecnico di Milano and later taught there. In 1981, he founded the Renzo Piano Building Workshop, employing hundreds of people. Some of his works include the Kansai International Airport in Osaka, The California Academy of Sciences in San Francisco and he also designed the Centre Pompidou in Paris with fellow architect Richard Rogers.

レンゾ・ピアノ 1937年生まれ。イタリアを代表する建築家。インテリアから公共建築まで幅広く手がけている。ミラノ工科大学卒業、フランコ・アルビーニの下で働いた後、1965年、スタジオ・ピアノを設立。代表作に、国際舞台に衝撃を与えたパリのポンピドゥー・センター、20世紀の建築におけるエンジニアリング・構造設計の最大の成果である関西国際空港旅客ターミナル、バーゼル近郊に位置するバイラー財団美術館などがある。彼の設計による超高層ビルがベルリン以外ではシドニーなどに設計されたほか、現在ロンドンのテムズ川南岸において「シャード・ロンドン・ブリッジ」という87階建て高さ310mのピラミッド型超高層ビル計画が進み、2012年ごろの完成が予定されている。1998年には建築界のノーベル賞と言われるプリツカー賞を受賞。
www.rpbw.com P65, 227

PKZ stands for Paul Kehl of Zurich, who in 1881 founded the first large scale men's clothing firm in Switzerland. The PKZ advertisement posters were remarkably fashionable since they were designed by reputable graphic designers of the time. The poster on P186 was designed by Heini Fischer.

PKZ 「ポール・キール・チューリッヒ」の頭文字であり、1881年、スイス発のメンズファッションの百貨店である。作品は、百貨店の宣伝ポスターとして著名なグラフィックデザイナー数名にデザインを依頼した際に、そのなかの一人ヘイニー・フィッシャーによる1952年の作品。 P186

Photo by Stefano Massei

Photo by Stefano Massei

Photo by Kazuya Enomoto

Jean Prouvé Born Paris, France, 1901-1984. Prouvé's career consisted of a metal artisan, industrial designer and self taught architect. He never considered himself a modern designer but rather more of an engineer and constructor. He focused on techniques where the construction and materials used were efficient; thereby insuring it could be mass-produced. His attention to efficiency, helped to build offices, hospitals, schools and many public buildings including residential buildings. In his career, he collaborated on furniture designs with French designer, Charlotte Perriand and many others. As chairman of the jury for the Centre Pompidou architectural competition in 1971, Prouvé played a pivotal role in selecting the design of Renzo Piano and Richard Rogers.

Richard Long & Tatsuo Miyajima: Benesse Art Site Naoshima ベネッセアートサイト直島 www.benesse-artsite.jp   Fabrice Moureau: Super A Market www.superamarket.jp   Charlotte Perriand & Jean Prouvé: SIGN www.sign-tokyo.net

Yasuko Seki Born Tokyo, Japan. Seki co-founded Tri-plus Inc., in 2001 and is the editor and marketing director. She was the chief editor of Axis magazine from 1991-1996. She has been involved with exhibitions, publishing, planning, and editing projects throughout her career. In 2011, Seki directed the *Shiro Kuramata and Ettore Sottsass* exhibition at the 21_21 DESIGN SIGHT museum in Tokyo, which was designed by Tadao Ando.

関 康子 東京生まれ、デザインエディター。有限会社トライプラス代表 1991〜96年デザイン誌『AXIS』編集長。96年「ルミナス:倉俣史朗」展の企画と倉俣史朗特集号をもってアクシス退社。その後フリーランスのエディターとして活動すると同時に、2001年にはトライプラス(Tri+)を共同設立する。「good design for children」をスローガンに掲げ、子どもの「遊び、学び、デザイン」のための商品開発、展覧会・出版企画・編集ワークショップの企画運営などにある。2011年、「倉俣史朗とエットレ・ソットサス」展 (21_21 DESIGN SIGHT)でディレクターを務める。著書に『世界のおもちゃ100選』(中央公論新社)、AERA DESIGN『ニッポンのデザイナー100人』『ニッポンをデザインした巨匠たち』(共著、朝日新聞社)、『倉俣史朗とエットレ・ソットサス』展覧会ブック(編著、ADP)など。
www.tri-plus.com　　　　　　　　　　　　　　　　　　　P4-9

Ettore Sottsass Born Innsbruck, Austria, 1917-2007. Sottsass was an Italian architect and designer. He once served as a design consultant for Olivetti, a company that produced typewriters, computers and other products. The *Valentine* typewriter is one of Sottsass' most recognized designs. In 1981, he founded the Memphis Group, which consisted of numerous talented international architects and designers. From 1981-1987, the Memphis group designed post modern furniture, fabrics, ceramics, glass and metal objects. In the 1980s, Esprit, hired Sottsass to design the interiors for the European retail stores. He also designed the fixtures and sculptures at the Esprit store in Los Angeles, California.

エットレ・ソットサス 1917年〜2007年、オーストリア、インスブルック生まれ。イタリアの建築家、インダストリアルデザイナー。戦後のイタリアデザインの評価を高めた一人。そのデザインや思想は大きな影響力をもち、派手で独創的に優れたその作品とデザインのスタンスは、称賛と同時に批判も受けるというユニークな存在だった。1960年代にはオリベッティの事務機「テクネ3」、ポータブルタイプライター「バレンタイン」など、数多くのデザイン開発を行なった。1981年にはソットサスアソシエイツのメンバーや世界中の若手デザイナー・建築家らで「メンフィス」を結成。メンフィスという名の由来は、彼らがボブ・ディランの「Stuck Inside of Mobile With the Memphis Blues Again」を聴きながら飲んでいたときに決まったと言われている。
www.sottsass.it　　　　　　　　　　　　　　　　　　　P244

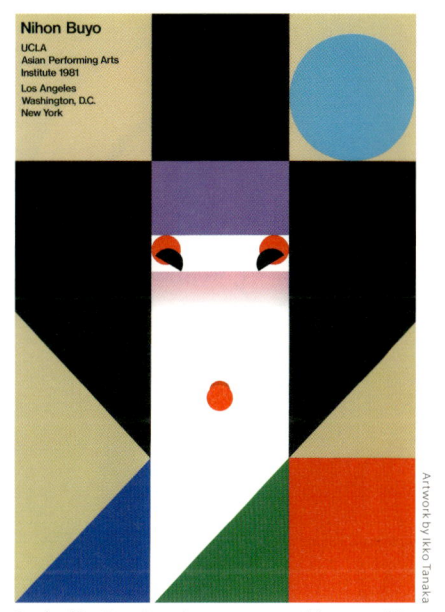

Tanaka Ikko Born Nara, Japan, 1930-2002. Ikko opened his design office in 1963. His list of accomplishments since 1959 is as impressive as it is extensive. He is also an AGI member. Many of his works are included in the permanent collection of the Museum of Modern Art in New York and the Stedelijk Museum in Amsterdam. This poster was designed for performances of various arts at UCLA and to promote *Nihon Buyou*, (literal translation is "Japanese dance.")

田中一光 1930年〜2002年、奈良生まれ。グラフィックデザイナー、AGIのメンバー。昭和期を代表するグラフィックデザイナーとして活躍した。1963年に自身のデザインオフィスを設立。数多くの賞を受賞し、作品の多くはニューヨーク近代美術館などに所蔵されている。作風は琳派に大きな影響を受けている。上記作品は田中一光デザインの、カリフォルニア大学ロサンゼルス校で開催された日本舞踊公演のためのポスター。
P221

Yoshio Taniguchi Born Tokyo, Japan,1937. Taniguchi is the son of Yoshiro Taniguchi who was also a famous architect. He graduated from Keio University where he studied engineering and then later graduated with a Master's degree in architecture from Harvard University. His recent work includes the redesign of the New York Museum of Modern Art.

谷口吉生 1937年生まれ、建築家、日本芸術院会員。東京藝術大学客員教授。1967年、ハーバード大学建築学科(建築学修士)修了、1964〜72年東京大学都市工学科丹下研究室および丹下健三・都市・建築設計研究所勤務を経て、1979年谷口建築設計研究所を設立。2004年にニューヨーク近代美術館を手がける。代表作品に、東京国立博物館法隆寺宝物館、丸亀市猪熊弦一郎現代美術館、豊田市美術館、土門拳記念館などがある。
P111

Douglas R. Tompkins Born Ohio, USA, 1943. Tompkins founded The North Face in 1963, then co-founded Esprit, an international clothing company with his former wife Susie Tompkins (now Buell) in 1970. He was a documentary filmmaker for a short period of time and is also a ski racer, white water kayaker, rock climber, mountaineer, bush pilot, art collector, foil fencer, organic farmer, art director, environmentalist and long time conservationist. In 1989, Tompkins sold his shares in the various international companies that comprised the Esprit company and married Kris McDivitt Tompkins, one of the world's foremost female conservationists. Today, they live and work in Chile and Argentina, where they purchased and conserved over 2 million acres of wilderness which they plan to dedicate back to the people & the earth.

ダグラス・トンプキンス 1943年 オハイオ州で生まれ、ニューヨークで幼少時を過ごし、高校を中退。1963年にノースフェイス社を創業。その後、さまざまなドキュメンタリー映画の制作にも携わり、1970年には前妻であるスージー・トンプキンスとエスプリを共同創立した。スキーレーサー、カヤック競技者、ロッククライマー、登山家、パイロット、アートコレクター、フェンシングプレイヤー、無農薬農園主、アートディレクター、環境保護者、自然保護論者など、多様な顔を持つ。1989年には、エスプリの創業者としての地位を離れ、自然保護論者でもあるクリス・マックデビット・トンプキンスと再婚し、チリとアルゼンチンに広大な土地を購入。自ら自然保護の土地信託団体を創設、ファッションというバックグラウンドがあるなかで、南米パタゴニア地方に私立自然保護公園を設立し、自然が人間の乱開発によって破壊されないように自然保護活動を進めており、現在はアルゼンチン、イベラ湿地帯の環境プロジェクトを進行中。　　P12-15

Oliviero Toscani Born Milan, Italy. Tosacni is an Italian photographer who studied photography and design at the *Hochschule für Gestaltung* in Zurich. He is internationally renowned as the creative force behind many advertisements for companies such as Esprit, Valentino, Chanel, Elle, Vogue, GQ, Harper's Bazaar, Esquire etc. From 1982 - 2000, he was the creative director for the Italian fashion company United Colors of Benetton known for their controversial ads.

オリビエロ・トスカーニ 1942年イタリア、ミラノ生まれ。ファッションフォトグラファーの先駆者の一人、『ELLE』で独自で躍動感溢れる写真を撮り、一躍有名に。1984年、エスプリのファッション写真を手がけ、以後のファッションブランド、ベネトンの一連の広告キャンペーンはデザイン界を圧倒した。『COLORS』マガジンのクリエイティブディレクターを担当した。
www.olivierotoscanistudio.com　　　　　　　　　　　　P46

Akira Yagi Born in Gojyozaka, Kyoto in 1955. Yagi's father Kazuo was a ceramic artist and a famous pioneer of Japanese contemporary ceramics. Akira was inspired by and learned directly from his father but has since established his own style. He mostly works on the wheel using porcelain and is especially known for *seihakuji* (blueish-white glaze) and black glaze. He has received many prizes and his work is represented in many permanent collections in Japan and abroad, including The National Museum of Modern Art in Kyoto, Smithsonian Institution and The British Museum. He is also a professor at Kyoto University of Art and Design.

八木 明 1955年京都五条坂に祖父八木一艸、父八木一夫の長男として生まれる。磁器土を素材に青白磁・黒釉及び漆を使った器や造形作品を制作。1979年より個展・グループ展で作品発表。1997年文化庁在外研修派遣にて渡米。1999年日本陶磁協会賞、2009年京都美術文化賞等多数受賞。所蔵:京都国立近代美術館・スミソニアン協会・大英博物館他国内外の美術館にコレクションされている。現在、京都造形芸術大学教授、IAC会員、日本陶磁協会会員、東洋陶磁学会会員。
P101

Ettore Sottsass: Somewhere www.somewhere.com　　谷口吉生: Hiroshima City Naka Incineration Plant 広島市環境局中工場 To visit email: ka-na-kojo@city.hiroshima.jp TEL: 082-249-8517 FAX: 082-248-9468
Douglas R. Tompkins: Conservation Land Trust www.theconservationlandtrust.org

BEHIND THE SCENES

From top left: Fellini, our new & youngest TYD staff, chopsticks maintenance, Sanshiyo via Kyoto, New years feast by Hide, TYD's favorite SF snacks: Pastrami sandwich, Pakwan Lamb Biryani, Hon's Wun-Tun House curry, Scream sorbets, Blue Bottle Coffee via Kelly Lasser, Stefano Massei, TYD staff Ritz Yagi, photo magic, book contents, Hiroshi Fujiwara, Kazuya Enomoto, The Hotel California at TYD: a nice place to stay, including free breakfast, lunch & dinner, unusual flower from TYD botanical collection, TYD staff Takumi Yagi, Fedex boxes recycled as moving materials, Seki Yasuko, Kulapat Yantrasast, objects waiting to be photographed, Water lily, TYD gourmet cabinet, TYD staff Yosei Shibata & Shinsuke Ito hard at work, Peter Skillman, Douglas R. Tompkins, thank you Neil Trama & for being the in house chef, Chris Tompkins, bird flies into TYD, mango plant, book contents, Gimmicks team, Christina Kim, color study, making of the vertical garden, Masaki Morisaki, Fellini.

左上：ニュースタッフ、フェリーニ。とり箸のメンテナンス。京都からの山椒。ヒデさんによるおせち。TYDのおすすめサンフランシスコメニュー：パストラミサンドウィッチ、パクアンのラムブリアーニ、ハンズワンタンハウスのカレー、スクリームのシャーベット、ブルーボトルコーヒー（スペシャルサンクス：2年間にわたりコーヒーを送り続けてくれているケリー・ラッサーさんへ）。カメラマン、ステファーノ・マセーさんの撮影風景。TYDスタッフ、八木理都子、ステファーノとの撮影風景。当初予定していた目次レイアウト。藤原ヒロシさんのカメラ。書籍制作に貢献してくれた榎本一弥さん。ホテルカリフォルニアのロゴマーク（TYDオフィスのゲストルーム）。オフィス内の植物。TYDスタッフ、八木巧。Fedexボックスをリサイクルした梱包。本書エディターの関康子さん。和訳や対談ページなどで関わってくれたクラバット・ヤントラサーさん。撮影されるのを待つオブジェ達。アンティークに改造した食器棚のロッカー。TYDスタッフ、伊藤心介と柴田陽生。パムページで貢献してくれたピーター・スキルマンさん。エスプリ時代から懇意にしているダグラス・トンプキンスさん。英文エディターとして活躍してくれたニール・トラマさん。ダグラス・トンプキンスさん同様、古くから懇意にしているクリス・トンプキンスさん。オフィス内に突然訪れたハト。オフィスパティオで栽培しているマンゴー。本書台割。本書イメージ撮影を担当してくれたギミックチーム。対談ページで関わってくれたクリスティーナ・キムさん。カラースタディー。バーティカルガーデン制作。レイアウト調整などで貢献してくれた森崎真紀さん。オフィスの忠犬フェリーニ。

AFTERWORD

CREDIT

The Graphic Eye

出版が決まったとき、私の頭の中には、本のタイトル案がすでにありました。2005年、サンフランシスコのペーパーシティーの記事で、私のライフスタイルの特集が組まれ、そのときのタイトルが、「The Graphic Eye」でした。私がグラフィックデザイナーだということ、そして私の仕事内容とライフスタイルを理解してくれたうえで、そのときライターだったダイアン・セークさんが、タイトルとして使ったのが「The Graphic Eye」だったのです。いつか書籍が出せればタイトルで使いたいとずっと思っていました。今回、「The Graphic Eye of Tamotsu Yagi」という、一冊の本にまとめることができ、ご協力くださった皆様に感謝しております。

When I was asked to publish a retrospective of my graphic work, I knew what the title of the book would be. In 2005, Diane Dorrans Saeks approached me about writing an article about my design work for *Paper City* magazine. As I am the art director of my own graphic design company, Diane cleverly titled the article The Graphic Eye. I was intrigued by her clever choice of words and it left a lasting impression on me. With great appreciation, I named this book *The Graphic Eye of Tamotsu Yagi*.

Kazuya Enomoto

八木 保の選択眼
The Graphic Eye of Tamotsu Yagi

発行日：第一刷　2011年11月15日
著者：八木 保
アートディレクション：八木 保
デザイン：
伊藤 心介　Tamotsu Yagi Design
柴田 陽生　Tamotsu Yagi Design
八木 理都子　Tamotsu Yagi Design
森崎 真紀
編集 協力：関 康子　TRI+
コーディネーション：
榎本 一弥　Commercial Arts Institute
八木 章画　有限会社1956
八木 宏嗣　株式会社インデス
八木 巧　Tamotsu Yagi Design
フォトグラファー：
ステファーノ・マセー　Studio Massei
吉田 秀司　ギミックスプロダクション
文章監修(和文)：関 康子　TRI+
翻訳：
クラパット・ヤントラサー　wHY Architecture and Design
ケリー・ラサー　Shelter Design
ニール・トラマ　Blunt Force Trama
森崎 紀子　Volcano Design
柴田 陽生　Tamotsu Yagi Design
ナタリー・クラッグ　Tamotsu Yagi Design
八木 巧　Tamotsu Yagi Design
八木 理都子　Tamotsu Yagi Design
プリンティングディレクション・制作管理：
榎本 一弥　Commercial Arts Institute

発行者：久保田 啓子
発行所：株式会社ADP (Art Design Publishing)
〒165-0024 東京都中野区松が丘2-14-12
Tel 03-5942-6011 / Fax 03-5942-6015
http://www.ad-publish.com
振替：00160-2-355359
印刷・製本：凸版印刷株式会社

ⓒ Tamotsu Yagi Design 2011
Printed in Japan
ISBN978-4-903348-22-3 C0072

定価はカバーに表示してあります。落丁本・乱丁本はご購入書店名を明記の上、株式会社ADP宛にお送り下さい。

送料小社負担にてお取り替え致します。本書の無断複写(コピー)は著作権法上での例外を除き、禁じられています。
掲載作品につきましては、多くの皆様にご協力いただき、誠にありがとうございました。なお一部の作品につきましては、最終的に連絡がつかなかったものもあります。ご諒承下さいますようお願い致します。The Publishers would like to thank all those who have kindly contributed their work for this book. For those who we could not reach, we are deeply grateful for allowing us to use your work in this book.

長さの単位について：本書に置く単位については、センチメートルを採用して表記しています。
Note: The dimensions in this book are noted in centimeters

本書の無断コピー、複製、引用を禁止します。

GRAPHIC EYE CREW

Ritz Yagi

Tamotsu Yagi

Takumi Yagi

Shinsuke Ito

Yosei Shibata

Stefano Massei

Kelly Lasser

Neil Trama

Kulapat Yantrasast

Shuji Yoshida

Natalie Klug

Noriko Morisaki

Masaki Morisaki

Photo by Stefano Massei

THE GRAPHIC EYE NO DETAIL IS SMALL

of TAMOTSU YAGI

yagidesign.com